W9-ARA-626

To Kimberly

never again would birds' song be the same

For information about permission to reproduce selections from
this book, write to Permissions, Houghton Mifflin Harcourt,
215 Park Avenue South, New York, New York 10003.

www.hmhbooks.com

Library of Congress Cataloging-in-Publication Data is available

Typefaces: Minion, Univers Condensed

Printed in China

SCP 10 9 8 7 6 5 4 3 2

CONTENTS

Acknowledgments 4

Editor's Note: Learning from the Birds 5

1. An Integrated Approach to Field Identification of Birds 6
2. Principles and Pitfalls of Field Identification 18
3. How Birds Are Built: Terminology and Bird Topography 44
4. Plumages, Molt, and Wear: Understanding What You See 74
5. Behavior and Voice: Understanding and Using Them in Identification 92
6. Identification Beyond the Species Level 106
7. Techniques and Resources for Learning Bird Identification 130
8. Learning to Identify Waterfowl 141
9. The Scaup 160
10. The Winter Loons 168
11. Learning to Identify Seabirds 182
12. Learning to Identify Herons and Egrets 186
13. Learning to Identify the Diurnal Raptors 188
14. The Accipiters 198
15. Learning to Identify Shorebirds 210
16. The Small *Calidris* Sandpipers 226
17. Learning to Identify Gulls 242
18. Learning to Identify Terns 272
19. The Medium-sized Terns 285
20. The Jaegers 300
21. Learning to Identify Owls 316
22. Learning to Identify Hummingbirds 318
23. The Challenging Small Hummingbirds 330
24. Learning to Identify Woodpeckers 342
25. Learning to Identify Tyrant Flycatchers 344
26. The *Empidonax* Flycatchers 347
27. Learning to Identify Swallows 388
28. Learning to Identify Warblers 390
29. The Blackpoll Trio 412
30. Learning to Identify Sparrows 419
31. The *Spizella* Sparrows 434

Photo Credits 441

Index 442

ACKNOWLEDGMENTS

In the first edition of this guide I offered thanks to scores of individuals who helped me in gathering the detailed information that formed the basis of that book. This new edition takes a new approach, more conceptual and less detail-oriented, but once again I am indebted to so many people that I cannot hope to thank them all.

During the last six years I have benefited immensely from my association with Black Swamp Bird Observatory (BSBO) in Oak Harbor, Ohio, where my wife, Kimberly, is now executive director. In writing this guide I was constantly drawing on BSBO's resources and research.

In researching the first edition of this guide I spent thousands of hours studying bird specimens at nine major museums and universities. With the different focus of this edition I still had to spend many hours at the University of Michigan Museum of Zoology, and I'm grateful to Janet Hinshaw for access to that fine collection.

Describing how to learn ID is different from describing field marks, and it took time to make that shift. A critical step involved the intensive ID workshops that I organized through Victor Emanuel Nature Tours. In these workshops I learned much from my co-leaders, particularly David Wolf, Victor Emanuel, Kim Eckert, Jeff Gordon, and Steve Hilty — and I learned even more from the participants in the classes.

While I was actively compiling this book I received invaluable specific information and help from many individuals, including Tom Bartlett, Richard J. Cannings, Delores Coles, Ted Eubanks, Ted Floyd, Chuck Hagner, Tom Kashmer, Cin-Ty Lee, Tony Leukering, Michael Retter, Julie Shieldcastle, and Mark Shieldcastle.

More than half the photos used in this guide were taken by others. People who went out of their way to provide images include Rick Bowers, Brian E. Small, Doug Wechsler, Tony Leukering, Ian Davies, and Mark Shieldcastle. Many thanks to them and to all the others listed on page 441. Preliminary work on photos was done by Barb Myers, Julie Shieldcastle, and Theresa Domanski.

My agent, Wendy Strothman, provided guidance throughout the project. At Houghton Mifflin Harcourt my editor, Lisa White, one of the world's finest young editors of natural history books, furnished just the right balance of patience and prodding. Others at HMH who helped in various ways include Beth Burleigh Fuller, Brian Moore, Jill Lazer, Tim Mudie, and Michaela Sullivan.

Finally, there are no words to thank Kimberly Kaufman. As an educator and writer, as a sharp birder who can pick out that distant rarity, as an experienced bander who can gauge a bird's primary coverts at a glance, as a photographer who took many of the best images used in this guide, as a friend who quietly helps me on everything, as a source of inspiration, Kim touched every page of this book (and of my life) and made it better.

LEARNING FROM THE BIRDS
A Note from Kenn Kaufman

Twenty years have passed since I finished the
first edition of *A Field Guide to Advanced Birding*.
Often the person who learns the most from a book is
its author, and certainly that was true for me; the effort
of writing and illustrating *Advanced Birding* taught me how
little I had known when I had so blithely launched into the project.
But in completing the book I did, in fact, learn some things about field
identification of birds. After it was done I went on to other projects, including a series of field guides aimed more at beginners than at experts.
But having done *Advanced Birding*, I was asked to teach workshops on
bird identification, so I've continued to do several annually ever since.

Just as the author learns the most from a book, so the instructor can
be the one who learns the most from a class. In teaching bird identification, I learned a tremendous amount from my students. It might not
have worked that way if I had simply lectured. But we took the courses
outdoors, where I endeavored to teach by asking questions and leading
the group to discover answers for themselves. During these sessions of
discovery, I came to some realizations about the learning process. One
revelation was the importance of *understanding*. It was clear that birders could memorize dozens of field marks and song descriptions and
still misidentify birds, simply because they didn't really understand
what they were seeing and hearing.

Eventually, too, I came to realize that my programs on bird identification were different from those taught by others. I had observed
many ID classes in which the instructor would simply go through all
the sparrows, for example, or all the hawks, one species at a time, talking about the field marks of each. My instinct in teaching was to try to
give the overview, to focus on those principles that would apply to the
whole group of birds. Only after we had discussed the common patterns and pitfalls would we get around to specific field marks.

This book takes the same approach. The focus is on *understanding*
what we see and hear. Some chapters cover concepts that should apply
to all birds, while others discuss the special challenges of various bird
families. I also include chapters on tough species groups, to serve as
"samples" of how overall principles can be put into practice.

If you study this book, it should enhance your ability to identify all
birds, not just the ones actually discussed here. I predict that as you
gain a greater understanding of what you are seeing and hearing, you
will enjoy all birds even more.

1. AN INTEGRATED APPROACH TO FIELD IDENTIFICATION OF BIRDS

In the two decades since the first edition of *Advanced Birding* was published, the amount of information available has increased by staggering amounts. In the late 1980s, a serious birder's reference library on ID would have included *Gulls: A Guide to Identification* by P. J. Grant, *Shorebirds: An Identification Guide* by Peter Hayman *et al.,* and a handful of detailed articles from British and American birding magazines. Today there are multiple fine books specifically treating the identification of gulls, shorebirds, hawks, hummingbirds, and any other group you can think of, and so many fine articles have been published that it is impossible to keep track of them all. In the late 1980s, Peter Pyle had just produced a first slim guide to the molts and plumages of songbirds. Today that guide has been superseded by two fat volumes by Pyle, totalling over 1,500 pages, detailing molt, plumage sequences, and geographic variation of every North American bird. In the late 1980s an expert birder asked me, in all seriousness, whether the Pomarine Jaeger even has a distinct plumage as a juvenile. Today it takes a few clicks on the Internet to find dozens of photos of this plumage, and many of these actually are identified correctly! What had been a trickle of published material has become a torrent. While the challenge formerly had been to find basic information on identifying most birds, the challenge now is to sift through the blizzards of information to find those points that are relevant, significant, and reliable.

As times change, reference books and field guides must change also. The first edition of *Advanced Birding* included detailed chapters on identification of 34 species pairs or groups, providing information that was not readily available to most birders. Simply updating that book now without changing its focus would hardly serve a useful purpose, because virtually all birders have access to vastly more information today than they did in 1990.

If I were to simply list more and more field marks for more species, this guide would take on the dimensions of an encyclopedia before it added materially to what is already available. So in this edition I have taken a different approach altogether, and the focus here is on how to identify birds, or how to *learn to* identify birds. In other words, it's not about memorizing field marks, it's about truly understanding what you see and hear.

Most of this book, then, consists of a thorough exploration of how to look at birds and how to listen to them, how to come to grips with the special challenges of each group of birds. Unlike many field guides, this one is not designed for quick reference in the field. The best time to study it is before going out to look at birds. The first seven chapters will help orient you to universal aspects of bird recognition. Then, if you're heading to the tidal flats or the sewage ponds, read the chapter on learning to identify shorebirds. If you're heading to a hawkwatch site, read the chapter on learning to identify birds of prey. And so on.

In addition to all these introductory chapters, I have included ten "sample" chapters treating specific groups in depth. These should be useful in their own right, but they also illustrate various principles: the challenges involved in identifying jaegers, for example, are very different from those we encounter with Empidonax flycatchers. As you master the identification of more groups of birds, you will develop the kind of background knowledge that makes it easier to learn even more.

SCHOOLS OF THOUGHT: IMPRESSIONS VS. FEATHER-EDGES

Since the 1980s, the birding world has put a lot of discussion into two distinct approaches to identification. One involves what is often called "giss" (for "general impressions of size and shape"), or "birding by impression." The other involves a careful study of fine details, down to the pattern of individual feathers (this may be referred to, sometimes with a hint of sarcasm, as the "feather-edges" approach).

Both of these styles seem to be at least partly a reaction against the system of simplistic field marks. Under that system, everything was reduced to simple on-off characters: the bird has wing bars or doesn't, it has streaks below or doesn't, and so on. That approach, ignoring both the obvious aspects of shape and the subtle nuances of fine detail, led to a lot of superficial identifications and a lot of potential for error. Simple field marks hold many traps and pitfalls for the unwary. Both of these other approaches, impressions and feather-edges, have their drawbacks and their strengths, and a serious birder will work on developing both.

Identifying birds by impression has been called "the new Cape May school of birding," which would be a surprise to the experts who were practicing this approach in California in the 1960s or in Massachusetts

An American Pipit in early May. Birding by impression, we could note that this is a buffy bird with a horizontal stance, walking on the ground in a wide-open field, wagging its tail up and down, and thus identify it without looking at a single field mark. Birding by detail, we might look at fine points of face pattern to rule out possible vagrant pipits from Asia and note the patterns of individual covert feathers to determine that the bird is more than a year old. Both approaches are valuable, and a skilled birder uses them in combination.

in the 1940s. Still, this style of ID has been raised to a higher level and well publicized by several experts associated with Cape May, New Jersey, especially Pete Dunne, Michael O'Brien, and Kevin Karlson.

Most people, even if they have not considered it, are already subconsciously capable of using this approach. We may use it frequently in other contexts. If we know a person well, we may recognize her from half a mile away by subtle clues of posture or the way she walks. Likewise, if we know a bird well, we may recognize it at a great distance by almost subliminal hints of its shape and actions. An experienced birder seeing a speck soaring slowly over a faraway ridge might identify it as a Turkey Vulture without being able to discern a single detail. An experienced birder seeing a flock of birds wheeling tightly in the air over a distant mudflat might identify the birds as Dunlins, even without being able to see anything of color or markings. In these cases, factors of place, season, habitat, and probability are added to clues provided by shape and actions to create an identification that seems almost intuitive but in fact is based on real evidence.

Identifying birds by looking at fine detail is an approach that goes back even further — to the days when most birds were identified in the hand. Until the latter part of the 20th century, of course, such fine points usually couldn't be seen in the field, but optics today are so good that we often can see details of individual feathers — either in the field, or in digital photos later. This has allowed birders to rediscover some of the same technical details that were familiar to museum ornithologists a century ago and to employ in the field some of the same fine points that are used by banders examining birds in the hand. This kind of detailed study opens up many avenues for identifying the age and sex and subspecies of a bird, not just its species, in ways that simply would not be possible in birding by general impression.

Both of these approaches — impressions and fine details — have their advantages and drawbacks. An experienced birder may identify many birds by quick impression and may be highly accurate with this approach, but occasional birds give very misleading first impressions. As described on pp. 32 – 40 under Common Pitfalls of Field Identification, individual birds can be aberrant in small ways that utterly change their superficial appearance. External factors such as lighting can also change the way a bird looks, and weather can have a major impact — for example, birds fly differently and even perch in different postures in strong winds. For reasons like these, our first impression of a bird may be seriously off base. If we merely mistake one common species for another one that would be equally common, there's no harm done. But any time we identify a rare bird by general impressions, we need to follow up by checking on more specific points.

It might seem that the other approach — the close-up, detailed approach — would be less prone to error, but there is such a thing as looking at the feathers and missing the bird. British humorist Bill Oddie once pointed out that a detailed description of a Sky Lark could be passed off as a detailed description of a Pectoral Sandpiper, so long as it didn't say too much about the bird's size or shape! In actual practice this kind of thing doesn't happen too often, but there have been a number of cases in which birders got rather far along in identifying an odd bird to age or subspecies even though they had the species (or even the family) wrong. So any detailed study of feather-edges might be on more solid ground if birders were to start by stepping back and looking at the whole bird and its relation to its surroundings.

These two approaches might be compared to two methods of learning to read. Popular at one time was the "look-say" method, in which children were taught to recognize the appearance of whole words, with less attention to individual letters. The early results of this were impressive, with two-year-olds proudly recognizing and pronouncing words such as "cat" and "horse." However, this approach left the young readers ill-equipped to figure out words that they didn't recognize. At the other extreme, the phonics method focused on the sounds of individual letters (as confusing as those may be in written English), teaching children to sound out letters, syllables, and words. This approach was slower at the start but it was shown to produce readers who ultimately would know more words.

In practice, of course, once we learn to read, we readily recognize whole words. We see a word like "incredible" and we don't have to sound out the letters or stop to think whether the "c" is hard or soft; the word registers in a flash and we're on to the next word. Only when we hit an unfamiliar word does our grasp of phonics come into play, as we pause to try to pronounce the word and consider what it means.

Similarly, our first identification of a bird may involve careful consideration of details, but once we know it well we may name it at a glance by impressions alone. Only when we see an odd individual or unfamiliar species, or see a bird under misleading conditions, or want to determine more than just the species involved, might we go back to the careful analysis of fine details.

This book will focus mainly on details and concrete field marks, because that is the necessary approach for someone dealing with a new or unfamiliar bird. I could go on for pages describing the flight behavior of a Pomarine Jaeger, for example, but until you have seen that bird for yourself and watched it flying, such a description would be almost meaningless. Once you have spent a lot of time watching Pomarine Jaegers, you may be able to name them instantly by their bulky shape, broad inner part of the wing, powerful wingbeats, etc., but first you have to see those things on birds of known identity, and to know their identity you have to see the kinds of details that this book describes and illustrates.

I know that some beginners are tempted to try to recognize birds by impressions right off the bat. It is tempting to take this shortcut, to bypass the details and go straight to an instinctive mastery of the bird. But how does this work in real life? Suppose an eager new birder sees a distant hawk flying, decides that its wingbeats look only moderate in speed, and calls it a Cooper's Hawk. The next distant hawk seems to have faster wingbeats, so he calls it a Sharp-shinned Hawk. If the first bird was actually a Red-shouldered Hawk and the second was a Cooper's, our birder has started to build a mental reference library that is flawed from the outset. Of course there's nothing wrong with watching the actions of distant unknown hawks, but we shouldn't use our impressions of them as a basis for comparison. That should be reserved for birds that we have definitely identified by specific details.

Therefore, this book's focus on detail is not meant to deny the importance of impressions; it merely acknowledges that details can be learned from a book while impressions must be learned through actual experience.

To be truly effective and accurate at field identification, we need to develop and cultivate both of these skill sets, combining them into an integrated approach that considers the whole bird in its surroundings as well as all of its details.

TWO KINDS OF CERTAINTY IN NAMING BIRDS

Years ago, as an avid beginner, I had to leave many birds unidentified. Back then I used to imagine a day when I would be able to name every bird with complete confidence. It took a long time to realize that that day would never come. Some birds would always be too distant, seen or heard too briefly, to be named with certainty. But beyond that, there was a more fundamental issue: some birds simply would not fit in any of the categories that we might construct for them.

For most birders, the basic unit of identification is the species. Seeing a Grasshopper Sparrow, few birders would be satisfied merely to call it "sparrow, sp." But on the other hand, relatively few birders will look closely enough to see anything that would indicate the subspecies involved. Naming it to species as "Grasshopper Sparrow" is enough for practically everyone. Most of the time, in most places, the species makes sense as a basic category. Grasshopper Sparrows, Henslow's Sparrows, and Field Sparrows may all be nesting in the same general area, without there ever being any question which is which. Likewise, we may have several local species of warblers or woodpeckers or hawks, all clearly separable with no intermediates between them, and it can seem as if "the species" is the solid building block of bird communities. Under this scenario, identifying every individual to species seems a reasonable goal.

When we look over a wider area, however, this tidy picture breaks down. We find situations in which it is almost impossible to say what is a species and what isn't. On the western Great Plains there is much interbreeding between Lazuli and Indigo buntings, and between Black-headed and Rose-breasted grosbeaks, yet each is still considered a full species. Western "Red-shafted" and eastern "Yellow-shafted" flickers also interbreed there, and these have been lumped into one species for decades now.

adult male
Baltimore Oriole

Bullock's and Baltimore orioles also interbreed there, and they were lumped into one species (Northern Oriole) for several years before being re-split again. Blue-winged Warblers and Golden-winged Warblers interbreed wherever their ranges come in contact in the East, and the same is true for Townsend's and Hermit warblers in the West. (In both of these species pairs of warblers, there are many that look like "pure" individuals of one species or the other but which have genes of both.)

There are places in the Pacific Northwest where Glaucous-winged and Western gulls interbreed so much that hybrids outnumber either of the "pure" parental forms, and traces of hybrid influence can be seen far north and south of the hybrid zone. And there are other cases in which two populations meet, with a certain amount of mixing: Black-capped and Carolina chickadees, Tufted and Black-crested titmice, Golden-fronted and Red-bellied woodpeckers, Red-naped and Yellow-bellied sapsuckers, and many more.

These cases of contact and interbreeding are not the only situations in which it's hard to define what is a species. Ornithologists have been stymied recently by questions about Red Crossbills, which have nine or more "types" in North America that defy easy classification. Each of these crossbill types tends to specialize on a certain species of coniferous tree, they have different callnotes, and they seem to overlap broadly in range without interbreeding — much. But they are all so similar that many scientists are leery of wholesale splitting of the crossbills. Another kind of problem involves Common and Hoary redpolls, widespread in far northern regions around the world. The very pale populations of Hoaries from the high Arctic and the browner populations of Commons from the subarctic seem clearly different, but some birds from intermediate latitudes seem to blur the line between them. Birders may think they are being "conservative" by identifying only the palest birds as Hoaries, but that leaves the intermediate birds as question marks. Scientists disagree as to whether the redpolls are good species or examples of some other kind of variation.

These are all cases of reality not fitting neatly into the biological species concept, the set of definitions that has been used by most ornithologists in recent decades. It's worth noting that many other species concepts have been proposed and that not one of them fits perfectly with reality. The diversity of life confounds our every attempt to define and categorize it. This uncertainty

As this book goes to press, there is discussion of splitting the Western Scrub-Jay into two or three species, including California Scrub-Jay (shown here) and Woodhouse's Scrub-Jay (of the interior West). Where these two come in contact, there is at least one population that has been shown to belong to the Woodhouse's group genetically, but which looks more like the California group. How would such birds be classified?

shouldn't spoil our enjoyment of birding; if we see a White-breasted Nuthatch or a Pine Siskin at the bird feeder, we can virtually always be confident about using those names for what we are seeing. But we need to remember that some birds simply won't fit into any species category that we might use.

So there are cases in which we can't put a definite name on a bird no matter how closely we study it. A more frequent challenge to our sense of certainty comes from all those occasions when we don't see or hear the bird quite so well.

Once we have had a lot of field experience, we may be able to recognize an amazing number of birds from just a glimpse or a brief call-note, but it's easy to slip into a sense of overconfidence in these quick identifications. There are many pitfalls that can hijack the ID process — pitfalls of our perceptions, pitfalls furnished by variations in the birds themselves. I discuss many of these potential problems in the next chapter.

One of the basic issues involves the way our minds work when we perceive a fragment of information. When we glimpse a bird, our minds may instantly compare the glimpse to a mental list of possible species, may instantly pick one as the most likely, and may quickly start to fill in more of the details of what that species would look like. Within moments, we may genuinely believe that we saw markings that the bird in front of us doesn't even have. This all occurs so rapidly in the subconscious mind that it takes a strong conscious effort to overcome the effect. It leads to situations in which observers honestly believe that they have seen confirming details on a bird that wasn't there.

In my own birding history, after several years of active fieldwork, I went through a stage in which I think I misidentified a lot of birds. By that time I knew a lot, but my confidence had surpassed my abilities, and I can remember making many snap calls that were probably in error. Probably not every birder goes through this stage, but it may happen to many of us. In my case I was lucky: I caught myself in several awful mistakes, situations in which I had completely miscalled birds with no good excuse, and gradually I learned to put on the brakes and exercise more caution in these quick calls. But even today I still have to remind myself not to put absolute faith in the accuracy of my snap judgments.

An unfortunate type of pressure operates on us when we achieve a moderate level of expertise. When we interact with less-experienced birders in the field, they may gauge our competence by our air of confidence — and we know it. When a bird pops up in front of us, and a group of eager beginners turns to ask us what it is, it's very hard to admit that we're not sure. It is very tempting in that case to pick the most likely ID and announce it in an authoritative tone, keeping our uncertainty to ourselves. This scenario probably plays out a thousand times every weekend on bird club field trips. It can take a lot of self-confidence for an experienced birder to admit to uncertainty about naming a bird. But if we're willing to make that leap, to admit that some birds defy easy identification, we can teach other birders one of the most valuable lessons of all: the idea that sometimes the correct answer is "I don't know."

PERILS OF PICTURE-MATCHING

If we look at the history of books on bird identification, and trace the development of such books from the late 1800s to the present day, we'll see many changes. The most striking change involves two simultaneous and opposite trends: as the amount of illustrative material has increased, the amount of text has decreased. There are some exceptions, of course. But early works on identification included some heavy tomes that were virtually all text with almost no pictures, while by contrast, some popular (and valuable) identification books today are mostly pictures, with very little text.

The shift away from text and toward pictures has made bird identification much easier in many ways. It has also, in some subtle ways, made bird identification less accurate. Even with excellent and accurate illustrations, the trend toward ID by picture-matching has led to more misidentifications, and it is useful for a birder to understand why.

Early volumes such as those by Robert Ridgway were valuable to scientists identifying birds in the hand, and they included very detailed descriptions, generally based on examination of multiple specimens: "Pileum [crown] warm brown, sometimes paler at the center, with fine black shaft streaks, the feathers having gray edges when fresh. Throat white with fine gray streaks, sometimes washed with yellow, or, rarely, unmarked white." It made for tedious reading, but anyone who slogged through comparing their specimens to descriptions, or reading descriptions in order to identify birds in the field, would certainly come away with the idea that a bird's appearance could vary in many ways.

Some popular books early in the 20th century included simple text and pictures that were only marginally helpful in identification. By contrast, Roger Peterson's first *Field Guide to the Birds* in 1934 did focus on field identification, with extensive text (including much information about behavior and habitat) and with simple illustrations that emphasized only key marks. Because the illustrations were so diagrammatic, no one expected the birds to look exactly like the pictures, and the variation in actual birds was not seen as a conflict with what was shown in the books. But from the 1950s on, illustrations in field guides (including Peterson's own) became much more detailed and lifelike, while the text tended to be reduced. With the improvement and increase in illustrations, it became easier for birders to expect that a bird would look "just like the picture in the book."

Active birders today are likely to own several field guides, with a cumulative total of many thousands of highly detailed bird pictures, but all of this illustrative material doesn't necessarily lead to more accurate identifications. Birders today are likely to spend less time carefully analyzing what they have seen and more time looking through pictures to try to find one that matches. This same approach reaches its extreme with new birders who don't own any field guides at all, but who see something intriguing — a bright yellow bird in the back yard, for example — and start searching the Internet for a photo that matches. Within a few clicks, their memory of what they actually saw will be compromised by the influence of the online images. In either case, in books or online, there is a serious possibility of choosing a picture based on some superficial resemblance and not on the most important identifying characteristics.

Experienced birders are less likely to fall into this trap when identifying birds to species, but it may trip them up when they start to consider the subspecies, age, or sex of a particular bird. Even birders who are cautious about naming a bird to species may turn overly casual at the next step. After carefully identifying a bird as, say, a Mourning Warbler, they may immediately say, "and it's a first-year male," with little evidence to back this up.

This problem stems partly from a dilemma in producing field guides. Such books have to show some variations within species, and those variations have to be labeled somehow, and it's tempting to put too much importance on the label. When an illustration is labeled as showing an adult female, our subconscious response may be: "If I see an adult female it will look just like this picture, and if I see a bird that looks like this picture, it will be an adult female." But it's possible that neither of these assumptions is correct. Some adult females may look different from the picture, and some other age/sex classes of the species may look just like the picture (for example, young males in some species are quite similar to adult females). The same thing happens with illustrations labeled as to subspecies; just because a bird looks like a particular picture, that doesn't necessarily mean that the bird belongs to that subspecies. Field guide format simply doesn't allow room to discuss the amount of variation within each age, sex, and subspecies, or the amount of overlap among these classes, and without that information we can't interpret what it really means if a bird seems to match a certain picture.

That interpretation is a key element that is sometimes lacking in field guides. Because of individual variation (as I'll point out again later in this book), no two birds look exactly the same, and no bird ever looks exactly like its illustration. No matter how closely a bird resembles a given picture, it will always differ in some ways. What do the differences mean? In some cases, a major difference in markings or color or shape may just reflect seasonal or individual variation. In other cases, a very slight difference may mean that the bird belongs to a different species. No amount of picture-matching will tell us which kind of situation applies to a given bird; to make accurate identifications, we have to go back to the basic theme of this book, that is, *understanding* what we are seeing.

These four gulls show obvious similarities — and obvious differences. Most large gull species are quite variable in plumage, and many of them are quite similar to each other, so we could have serious problems if we tried to identify these birds simply by matching them to pictures. Depending on what pictures we had for comparison, and how much faith we placed in superficial similarity, we might match up any of these birds to any of five or six different species. What we need is not just a collection of pictures, but serious interpretation of those pictures. We need to know which of the visible characters are actually important in identifying the species involved. Without knowing those criteria, we may wind up putting names on these birds, based on the closest resemblance we can find, but we'll never be certain of our identifications. In challenging ID situations, the best pictures in the world won't help us unless we understand what we're seeing.

EXPERT BIRDERS AND THEIR RESPONSIBILITY TO BEGINNERS

In the twenty years since the first edition of this book was published, a stunning amount of new information has come to light. With many more serious birders adding to our collective knowledge, the kind of information and understanding that represented "advanced birding" in 1990 has been far surpassed by now. One result of this information explosion is that the gap between what an expert knows and what a beginner knows is now wider than ever.

With increasing numbers of birders gathering at popular spots, and with the explosive growth of online communication and networking, there are also far more contacts between experts and beginners than at any time in the past. I believe that experts have a responsibility to handle these contacts with care and diplomacy, to avoid dampening the enthusiasm of the beginning bird watchers. The fact is that there are literally tens of millions of people in North America who enjoy birds at a casual level and who will never become highly skilled birders — *and there is no reason why they should.* Their approach is just as legitimate as the interest of the most ardent field ornithologist, and their casual enjoyment deserves our respect.

Unfortunately, some expert birders lose sight of this. They insist that every newcomer to birding should move in the direction of increasing their skill level, that every beginner should start off with advanced references and learn to use them. This attitude — of teaching people to swim by throwing everyone into the deep end of the pool — has predictably bad results. I've met many people who were tempted to give up birding altogether after run-ins with well-intentioned but foolish "experts." If you insist on trying to turn all beginners into "real birders," you might as well be shooting hawks or chopping down old-growth forest, because you are hurting the cause of bird conservation. We need those millions of people who simply like birds. We need millions of perpetual beginners who value our wildlife and who support conservation efforts. In the larger perspective, broad support for conservation is far more important than accurate field identification, and a truly advanced birder will never do anything to discourage the casual bird enthusiasts.

2. PRINCIPLES AND PITFALLS OF FIELD IDENTIFICATION

Given this book's focus on advanced birding, chapters covering the basics might seem out of place. Aren't the basics for beginners, not advanced birders?

Actually, beginning birders rarely learn the basics when they are getting started. Most people learn to identify birds in about the same way that most human infants learn language. Think about it: a baby doesn't start by learning about nouns and verbs and adjectives. The baby learns a few words that bring immediate reactions, then goes on to learn more words, and gradually begins to put sentences together. The actual rules or principles of language are learned much later, if at all. Likewise, in most cases, a beginning birder learns a few obvious birds at first, then gradually starts to figure out the more challenging ones. Basic principles come later.

In my case, learning on my own, there were some basics about identification that I didn't learn until I'd been actively birding for more than ten years. Once I learned these basic points, however, things became easier to understand, and some things about birds that had mystified me for years suddenly fell into place.

In this chapter I cover some basic rules that apply to the identification of all birds. I also treat some common pitfalls that may trip us up, no matter how much we know about what the bird is *supposed* to look and sound like. The arrangement of the chapter features 13 basic principles, then 11 pitfalls, then one final principle to wrap things up.

PRINCIPLES OF FIELD IDENTIFICATION

Principle 1. Learn the Common Birds

Much of the excitement in the modern game of birding involves looking for rare species. For many birders, the search for rarities becomes the main focus of time afield, and even brand-new beginners may be drawn into this mindset. But ironically, the truly skilled birders are able to find rarities mostly because they are so familiar with the common species. They may not have the quickest reflexes or the biggest lists, but they have all spent a lot of time in careful observation of the common birds.

Time and again I've seen that we need to know the common species to be sure we're identifying the rare ones correctly. When I started birding in the eastern U.S., I never looked closely at female Ruby-throated Hummingbirds, because I thought I didn't have to: the Ruby-throat was supposed to be the only hummingbird species there. But because I hadn't looked closely, I was ill-prepared for picking out any stray hummingbird that might have appeared. When Black-capped Gnatcatchers were still known from only a handful of records in Arizona, our big problem in identifying the females was that we didn't know the common Blue-gray Gnatcatcher well enough. For picking out young Lesser Black-backed Gulls out of range, an absolute prerequisite is a thorough familiarity with young Herring Gulls. And so on. Time spent studying the common species is always time well invested.

In the field, many birders spend 95 percent of their time looking *for* birds and only 5 percent of their time, or less, actually looking *at* birds. Just spending an extra minute watching each bird after we've identified it can go a long way toward improving our identification skills.

Great Blue Heron is such a common bird that we identify it in an instant, without a second glance. But how do we rule out a vagrant Gray Heron, an Old World species that is very similar to the Great Blue and that could show up as a stray practically anywhere in North America? The key to picking out a Gray Heron would be to know the Great Blue Heron extremely well.

A female Red-winged Blackbird may seem obvious when seen in the marsh in summer, with male Red-wings all around. But a lone female that arrives at a bird feeder in the woods in winter may cause some consternation at first. Taking time to study the "obvious" birds will help us to recognize them when they show up in unexpected surroundings.

Principle 2. Consider Shapes

Bird shapes are extremely important in field identification. Throughout this book, you will find this point emphasized again and again. Both for quick impressions and for detailed analysis, the shape and structure of a bird will be among its most significant characteristics. At times — when the light is bad, when size is deceptive, when the bird itself is an aberrant individual with odd markings — the shape will be the key point that keeps us from going astray in our identification.

Unfortunately, shape is a difficult thing to learn from pictures. Even for the best illustrators, it's a major struggle to get the shapes of birds exactly right. Single photographs, too, are often misleading. You may build up an accurate impression by studying large series of photos, but for the most part, shapes of birds must be learned through observation in the field.

Some aspects of birds' shapes are obvious. For example, if the bill, legs, or tail happen to be exceptionally long, we'll notice that immediately. But other points can be much more subtle. Look at the head: is the crown relatively flat, rounded, peaked, double-peaked? Does the forehead look steep relative to the base of the upper mandible? Does the head seem large, small, or "normal" for the size of the body, and is the neck notably long or short? And the body itself: is it elongated, slender, chunky? Do not think only in terms of the straight profile view common in field guides. What is the shape of the head when viewed from directly in front or behind? What shape is the body when seen from below? Look at the wings: where do the wingtips fall, relative to the base of the tail? Look at the legs: their length and thickness are worth noting, not only on large wading birds, but on songbirds as well. These are just examples; there are many other aspects of shape worth studying.

Mourning Dove (left) is so widespread and common over most of North America that birders may ignore it — so when they get to the range of White-tipped Dove (right), they might overlook it at first. Both are plain birds without a lot of obvious markings, and their major difference in shape is the first thing that an alert birder might notice. The White-tipped Dove's very heavy body, shorter wingtips, shorter tail, and stronger legs and feet add up to a very different overall impression.

Adding to overall impressions of shape are a bird's typical posture. Many tyrant flycatchers tend to perch very upright, giving them a different overall look from vireos, which tend to perch more horizontally. Behavioral mannerisms also come into play. Looking at the short tail of a Winter Wren, for example, we also note that it is often held up vertically above the bird's back; looking at the long tail of a Bewick's Wren, we also note that it is often flipped about expressively.

Keep in mind that the arrangement of a bird's feathers may change the appearance of its shape from moment to moment. The body feathers may be sleeked down when the bird is afraid, puffed out when the bird is cold; the head feathers may be raised when the bird is excited. This is part of the reason why single photographs can be misleading. But despite these momentary variations, every bird has a characteristic shape that will become evident after we watch it for a while.

Developing a sensitivity to the specific shapes of particular birds will be very helpful when we encounter what may be an aberrant individual. If, for example, we're looking at a flock of common birds and notice an individual that looks exceptionally pale or dark, naturally we'll wonder if it might be some other species. A key point here is that if it really is a different species, it's almost certain to show differences in shape, size, or behavior. If it's exactly the same shape as the birds around it, chances are it's just an oddly marked individual of the same species.

Shape is even more important in recognizing birds in flight, when it may be even harder to see colors and markings. An experienced birder can recognize a high percentage of birds just by their shape and flight action. But of course, the appearance of the shape of the wings and tail may be changing constantly in flight, so it takes more time to learn the silhouettes of flying birds.

These three images of a Common Raven in flight were taken just moments apart. The shapes of the wings and tail appear utterly different in these three shots — as expected. The key is to watch birds in flight until all the characteristic silhouettes of a species fit together into a composite picture of its typical structure.

Principle 3. Learn Natural Groupings of Birds

Identification is a process of classification. Sometimes the first thing that we glimpse or hear is so obvious that we know instantly what species of bird we're seeing, or even its species, age, and sex, as when an adult male Bullock's Oriole suddenly lands in front of us. But many times we may go through a process of narrowing down the identification. For example, we may glimpse a movement and not even be sure it's a bird at first; then as we get better views, we may decide progressively that it's a bird, that it looks like a small songbird, that it appears to be a wren, that it's either a Winter Wren or a House Wren, and finally that it's a House Wren. This process of classification gets us steadily closer to the correct identifica-  tion through a series of steps. Obviously it's easier to choose among a few species of wrens than it is to choose among the more than 700 possible species in North America. So narrowing down the choices is a worthwhile part of identification.

We can apply this concept when a mystery bird pops up — looking for clues as to whether it's a vireo or flycatcher, for example. But we can also apply it when studying reference materials, by paying attention to natural groupings of birds. Often it's useful to look at the *genus* to which a bird belongs. For example, look at these three bird names:

Pectoral Sandpiper
Solitary Sandpiper
Lesser Yellowlegs

On the basis of their English names, we might expect Solitary and Pectoral sandpipers to be similar and the yellowlegs to be different. But their scientific names tell a different story:

Pectoral Sandpiper   *Calidris melanotos*
Solitary Sandpiper   *Tringa solitaria*
Lesser Yellowlegs   *Tringa flavipes*

Solitary Sandpiper and Lesser Yellowlegs both belong to the genus *Tringa,* and they are in fact more similar to each other in shape, behavior, and flight action than either is to the Pectoral Sandpiper, a member of a different genus.

Breaking bird families down by genus is more useful in some families than others, but it's worth trying any time we're studying field guides or other reference works. With some groups it provides a major advantage. Saying that a bird looks like "a flycatcher" means very little, since the flycatchers make up such a huge and diverse family. To be able to say that a particular flycatcher looks like a *Myiarchus,* or a *Contopus,* or an *Empidonax,* takes us most of the way to an identification.

Their English names don't suggest this relationship, but Lesser Yellowlegs (right) and Solitary Sandpiper (center) are both in the genus *Tringa,* while Pectoral Sandpiper (left) is in a different genus, *Calidris.* In the field, the two species on the right seem much more similar in their overall slender build, slim bills, delicate feeding behavior, and head-bobbing action. In studying a group such as sandpipers, it is always worthwhile to look at the scientific names to see which birds belong to the same genus, as this will help us to place them in natural groups and to see similarities and differences among species.

Principle 4. Always Use Multiple Field Characteristics

For a while I was telling birders, "You should never identify a bird by just one field mark." This was sound advice, but I encountered some resistance to the idea, and finally someone pointed out to me that I was couching this principle in negative terms. Of course, a suggestion is more likely to be remembered and acted upon if it is presented in a positive way. So to put it in positive terms, my new version is that you should positively never identify a bird by just one field mark!

The field mark most often quoted for Swainson's Thrush is its prominent eye-ring. However, Hermit Thrushes like this one also usually have strong eye-rings and are often misidentified as Swainson's.

Beginning birders, struggling to come to grips with difficult groups of birds, may settle on "one diagnostic mark" to pick out a species. But reliance on any one single mark may lead to error part of the time. Individual and seasonal variation in the appearance of birds — and variation in their voices, behavior, habitat, etc. — means that no single characteristic is ever 100 percent reliable. It's fine to start by checking just one easy-to-see mark, but to be certain, we should always follow up by looking for confirming evidence.

Principle 5. Expect to See Variation

No bird ever looks "just like the picture in the book." That may sound like an illustrator's cop-out, but it's just a fact. No two individual birds look *exactly* alike, if we look closely enough.

In Chapter 7 I describe some specific exercises for learning about variation. But as a basic principle of identification, it's important just to realize that this variation exists. In fact, one of the hallmarks of a highly skilled birder is the ability to interpret variation: how different does a bird have to look or sound before we recognize it as a different species? A strikingly pale bird among a flock of starlings may turn out to be just an aberrant starling, while a subtly different bird among a flock of Least Sandpipers, barely noticeable as anything distinct, could prove to be a vagrant Long-toed Stint. (In the vast majority of cases, of course, a subtly different bird among Least Sandpipers will turn out to be another Least Sandpiper. This is another case of needing to study the common birds to become familiar with the normal range of variation in this species.)

There is no magic shortcut to being able to interpret variation. The only key is to expect to see some variation in every bird species, train ourselves to look for it, and try to get a sense for the limits of normal variation in the birds that we get to study.

Principle 6. Consider the Condition of the Bird's Plumage

Just as all individual birds look different, even the same individual will look different over time, changing in subtle ways from day to day throughout the year. Birds are almost completely covered with feathers, of course; and although feathers are marvelous structures, they do wear out and have to be replaced. These processes of wear and replacement (molt) result in changes to a bird's appearance that can be obvious with a close look. I will discuss these subjects in some detail in Chapter 4, as well as under several species groups later in the book. But this is such an important point that it should be a basic part of looking at *any* bird.

The difference between fresh and worn plumage, and the appearance of molt in progress, are best learned by looking at a lot of birds (or a lot of very good bird photos). The timing of the molt varies among species, but many go through a complete replacement of feathers in

Two views of a Ring-billed Gull in its first year of life. The left image is from October. The bird has already molted many feathers: fresh juveniles in midsummer are heavily marked with brown on the back, scapulars, head, and underparts, and most of those feathers have been replaced by gray or white ones. Its wing coverts, marked with brown, are already showing some wear, but its wingtips still look fresh and black, with white edges on the inner primaries. The right image is from seven months later, in May. This bird appears not to have molted any of its wing feathers yet; all the coverts are now worn and faded to white, the wingtips are faded to brown and are ragged and frayed. If we saw this merely as a bird with whitish coverts and brown primaries, without noting that these areas were extremely worn, we might be at a loss to identify it.

late summer or fall; so we can see many birds in fresh plumage in fall or early winter, while many adult birds will be in worn plumage by midsummer. Feathers in fresh condition have a crisp look, and this is especially apparent on the large feathers of the wings, tail, and scapulars. Feathers in worn condition often look ragged or frayed along the edges, and their colors often fade somewhat. Wear can affect the bird's appearance both by wearing away markings on the edges or tips of feathers (especially pale areas) and by making the overall color of the feathers paler or duller.

Determining the condition of the plumage has a direct bearing on how we view many standard field marks. A hawk that has a broad white tip on the tail in fresh plumage will have a narrow white tip, or perhaps none at all, when the plumage is very worn. A gull that has big white spots in the wingtips in fresh plumage will have smaller spots when the plumage is worn. A flycatcher or warbler that has broad pale wing bars in fresh plumage will have steadily narrower wing bars as the plumage becomes worn; Eastern Wood-Pewees, for example, arrive in North America in spring with obvious wing bars, but these become narrower during the summer, and the birds may look essentially plain-winged by the time they leave in fall (because they won't molt until they reach the wintering grounds).

Many other examples are more subtle. On birds with streaked upperparts, the pattern may be formed by individual feathers with dark central stripes and pale edges; as the feathers become worn, the pale edges become partially worn away while the dark centers fade slightly, and the overall effect of streaking becomes much less obvious. Fine barring or vermiculations on feathers may become less visible in worn condition. For example, adult Northern Shrikes in fresh plumage (fall and early winter) usually show fairly obvious fine barring on the chest, but by the following summer, when the plumage is worn, the barring may be faint or invisible, increasing the chance of confusion with Loggerhead Shrike.

This Broad-winged Hawk, photographed in early July, is a one-year-old bird. Its wing shape, wing pattern, and tail shape don't match typical field guide illustrations, and for that reason it could be confusing to birders. Two generations of feathers are evident in its wings, with older, paler, browner feathers (some secondaries and the outer three primaries) contrasting with the darker ones that have been replaced (including the primary next to the outer three, which is still growing in). The visible tail feathers all show the adult pattern, so they must have been recently replaced, with the outer feathers still growing and giving the tail an odd shape. A bird like this, which otherwise could be mystifying, is easy to decipher if we understand the basics of molt.

When birds are in the active process of molt, it changes their appearance in other ways. The mix of old and new feathers among the body plumage can make the bird look patchy, even if it has no definite seasonal color change. And the shape of the wings and tail, as well as their apparent patterns, can be strongly affected when some feathers are missing or only partially grown. Of course, birds can lose feathers to accidents at any time of year, but normal molt is recognized by the fact that it is symmetrical: feathers in the same positions will be missing or growing on both wings at once.

Principle 7. Learn to See Details

In using this book, or in consulting any work on serious field identification, you will find many references to very fine details. The treatment may come down to looking at the shapes or patterns of individual feathers, the spacing between the tips of individual primaries on the wingtips, or the position of the nostril on the bill. Can such details be seen in the field? Yes, they can. But in addition to requiring good optics, they require a certain level of concentration and a fair amount of practice. You can train your eyes to see the fine points.

You can, and should, practice on common birds. Look at the Mourning Dove: it has many subtle shadings of color. Look at the European Starling in winter plumage: it has a very complex pattern. In order to describe such patterns accurately, we have to know the names of the different feather groups on the bird, as described in the following chapter on bird topography. But if you will practice looking closely at fine details on common birds, you'll have the skills needed to see the essential details when a rare or unknown bird shows up.

Birders in Europe tend to carry spotting scopes more often than those in North America, and this may contribute to the general sense that the average

A starling at the bird feeder in winter offers brilliant opportunities for learning to see details and for learning to recognize different feather groups. On this individual, for example, we can see dark subterminal edgings on the inner primaries, iridescence on the greater coverts, and white and buff tips on the scapulars, if we know where and how to look. Sure, we can tell it's a European Starling without noting those details, but we're honing our perceptions so we'll be ready to identify more challenging birds.

European birder has more skill at identification. Carrying a scope and trying to aim it at fast-moving small birds can be aggravating, but it can also yield views of fine points that we would seldom get to see through binoculars. If you become seriously interested in improving your knowledge of field identification, you should consider getting a good telescope and using it for close observation of all types of birds.

Principle 8. Understand the Difference Between Absolute Field Marks and Relative Field Marks

When we're trying to separate similar species, a high percentage of the clues that we'll have to use are only relative or comparative field marks.

For example, Piping Plover is paler above than Semipalmated Plover; Orchard Oriole tends to have a shorter bill than Hooded Oriole. In the case of these species pairs there are other differences as well, and enough of these relative field marks will add up to a distinctive overall appearance for birders with enough experience. But if we are seeing one of these birds for the first time, and if there's no other bird nearby for comparison, we're not in a position to say whether its bill is "longer" or "shorter," or whether its back is "paler" or "darker." In these cases we have to proceed with caution and not rely too heavily on our impressions of how the bird fits into these relative differences.

When we refer to a field mark as "absolute," we don't mean that it's foolproof or 100 percent reliable. No field mark is ever fail-safe by

Compared to Brown Thrasher, Long-billed Thrasher is supposed to have blacker streaks below, a more whitish ground color below, a darker stripe in the malar area, a grayer face, a longer bill, and often a more orange-yellow tinge to the eye. So could the bird shown on the left here be a Long-billed Thrasher? No, not if we can compare it directly to the genuine Long-billed on the right. But direct comparisons between these two are seldom possible in the field. Usually we are viewing one species in isolation, judging such comparative marks against memory.

itself. What we mean is that it's an on-off, yes-no kind of difference rather than a comparative one. For example, a Laughing Gull in its first winter has a dark band that extends across all the tail feathers, while a Franklin's Gull of the same age has this dark band more restricted, not extending to the outermost tail feathers. This isn't completely diagnostic by itself, because a Laughing Gull *might* have an abnormality that results in a lack of pigment only in the outermost tail feathers, or it might have accidentally lost these feathers and had white ones grow in their place. But barring that kind of bizarre coincidence, this is an on-off characteristic, easier to judge than the question of whether the bill is longer (like that of a Laughing Gull) or shorter (like that of a Franklin's). Whenever possible, we should look for such absolute field marks to back up our impressions of the relative ones.

Principle 9. Consider Context, but Don't Rely on It Completely

Skilled birders always carry an active awareness of their location, habitat, and season. These factors work constantly as filters to narrow down the likely choices in bird identification. There may be ten thousand kinds of birds in the world, but only a handful of them are predictably likely to be right here, right now. That small short-tailed bird overhead, with a high, bounding, undulating flight: could it be a Common Redpoll? In upstate New York in January, yes. In the same place in July, no. In southern Texas at any season, no.

Beyond location and date, there are strong clues in the habitat and in the bird's place in the habitat. A small bird with a brownish back and with dark streaks on a white chest could be an Ovenbird if it's on the ground inside the forest, a Purple Finch if it's in a treetop in the same forest, or a Savannah Sparrow in an open grassy field. Obviously there are plenty of other differences among these three birds, but their place in their surroundings will be one of the points that a skilled birder takes into account instantly at first glance.

These "filters" of place, habitat, and date take some time to learn, and once learned, they are among the main advantages of experience. But of course they are not completely reliable. Birds do show up at unexpected places and times, so we always have to take our own assumptions with a grain of salt and follow up on our own snap judgments. For example, an orange-and-black songbird seen flying into a tall elm in Kentucky is almost certainly going to be a Baltimore Oriole. But it might be some exotic bird, like a minivet or a troupial, escaped from a zoo; or it *might* be a Bullock's Oriole, even though that would be an extremely rare find in this eastern state. If our assumptions make us pass up some rare bird, thinking it to be a common one, there's no harm done, but we'll miss out on some excitement that way. The point is that nothing is impossible, and the helpful clues of place, habitat, and date will take us only so far.

Principle 10. Consider Behavior, but Don't Rely on It Completely

With experience, we often can recognize birds on the basis of their behavior, without reference to their colors or markings. Part of their distinctive behavior involves where they are in a particular habitat (as noted in the previous point) and part of it involves their actions.

There are some particularly good examples among the shorebirds, in which many species in drab winter plumages can be quite similar in superficial pattern. At a pond with some mudflats next to water, there's a good chance that the Least Sandpipers will be walking on the mud while the Western Sandpipers will be wading in very shallow water. The Lesser Yellowlegs will be walking about daintily in the shallows, the Greater Yellowlegs will be dashing about more actively in the water, while Long-billed Dowitchers will be standing huddled in one spot in shallow water, probing straight down into the submerged mud with their bills. If we squint until we see only vague shapes, we could still almost identify all these shorebirds just by their behavior.

Almost — but not quite. There is always the chance for exceptions. These behavioral clues work most of the time, but occasionally a yellowlegs will probe deep into the mud, a Least Sandpiper will wade in water up to its belly, a dowitcher will walk about on the flats and pick at things. If we are more locked in to a behavior than the bird is, our reliance on behavior as a field mark could lead us astray.

Principle 11. Look at Flying Birds

Most birders seem to have an aversion to looking at birds in flight. I suspect this is partly because we are so conditioned to looking at birds through binoculars, and the challenge of finding a bird through the bins is much harder when the bird is in rapid motion. If we make re-

peated attempts to pick up a flying swift (for example) through the binoculars and keep coming up with nothing but empty sky, we may start subconsciously avoiding the attempt in order to avoid the frustration. But looking at birds in flight is so important that it's worth going through the frustration, practicing until we can find the bird quickly, and then taking the time to watch birds in flight and study what we can see.

Cave Swallow. This species often strays out of range, and it is much more likely to be found by birders who actively look at birds in flight.

This is obviously important for birds like swallows or swifts that we may see only in flight, and for seabirds, hawks, and other largely aerial types. But it's also important for other birds. Even for a small bird flying across a clearing, it's helpful if we can get a sense of whether the bird looks like a thrush, a warbler, or something else. Here's a way to learn to recognize a species in flight: if we're using binoculars to watch a perched bird and it flies, rather than looking away immediately, we can try to follow it in the binoculars as it flies, noting as much as we can on this bird of known identity. Of course, it's also good to practice on any flying bird: if we can see enough pattern to identify it, then we can study its shape and flight action as well.

Principle 12. Listen!

The importance of sound to birding is a basic point that every birder should understand. Sound is more important with some bird groups than others (almost essential for flycatchers, only mildly helpful for gulls), and more important in some habitats than others (essential in tropical rain forest, seldom useful far out at sea). And people with very poor hearing can still become expert birders with a focus on less vocal groups. But to the extent that it's possible, birders should always be listening for any sounds from

We might have to call this "meadowlark sp." unless it sings or calls, revealing its identity as an Eastern.

birds, as an aid to locating them, identifying them, and understanding what they are doing. In Chapter 5, I go into some detail on how to recognize, learn, and remember bird voices.

Principle 13. Learn to Leave Some Birds Unidentified

If you spend enough time in the field with serious birders, eventually you'll see a situation in which a hawk flies past and opinions are divided on its identity, with some experienced observers calling it a Cooper's and other observers, also experienced, calling it a Sharp-shinned. Or you'll be present when a distant jaeger is identified, with great confidence, as a Parasitic by some and as a Pomarine by others. In such situations it's possible that some of the birders really do know what it is and the others are just mistaken, but it's also possible that no one has offered up the correct answer. Am I suggesting that the bird in question could be some third species that no one has called? No, I'm just saying that it might be a situation in which the correct answer is "I don't know."

Sometimes we just don't see the bird well enough to tell what it is. Sometimes, even if we see it very well, it won't be readily identifiable. There are many factors (including some of the pitfalls discussed in the next section) that could make the identity of a given bird obscure. When faced with a bird that doesn't seem to add up, there's no reason why we have to put a name on it. We can take notes, take photos, record its voice, and resolve to research it after the fact, but we should never feel pressured to name the bird on the spot. Indeed, one of the marks of a genuine expert is the fact that he or she has learned, possibly through painful experience, when to say, "I don't know."

COMMON PITFALLS OF FIELD IDENTIFICATION

No matter how well we have studied the field marks of birds, we still can be thrown off by a variety of common pitfalls. I discuss a few of them here. The first one is psychological; the next two are perceptual things, subject to the way we are seeing the bird. The last seven involve ways that a particular individual bird might be misleading.

Pitfall 1. Expectations and Desire

When we are birding, it takes a conscious effort for us to see what is really in front of us. Without this effort, the images that reach our brains are likely to be altered by the unconscious filters of what we expect to see and what we want to see.

I cannot begin to count all the times that I have almost passed up some interesting or unusual bird, just because I didn't expect it to be there. The examples are legion: the flock of "House Sparrows" in a vacant lot in a southwestern city that turned out to be Lark Buntings when I took a second look; the "mockingbird" on a roadside wire that turned out to be a Scissor-tailed Flycatcher. And there's no telling how many genuine rarities I've missed because I passed them off as some expected species. Roger Tory Peterson used to tell of a busload of birders who saw a white bird on a rooftop in Massachusetts, assumed it was a pigeon, and kept going. A second busload came along later and stopped to study the bird, which turned out to be an Ivory Gull.

In practice, of course, it's useful to have expectations about what we're likely to see. Without them, we'd be back to square one on every bird, and we would never get anywhere. The trick is to check every bird against our expectations, quickly, in a way that's a compromise between efficiency and accuracy. For example, driving through an area where Red-tailed Hawks are abundant, we may see a hawk perched on a distant pole. A quick check shows that it is about the right shape and size for a Red-tail and it has a white blaze in the right general area of the scapulars. We haven't ruled out every other bird of prey in the world, we haven't seen many actual field marks, but what we see is consistent with the expected species, and our off-the-cuff identification is probably correct. Unless we are raptor buffs who don't care about other birds, we'll probably leave it at that. Only if something about the bird looks distinctly wrong for a Red-tail are we likely to haul out the telescope and take a closer look.

This approach works well for general birding. It goes awry when something about that bird really is wrong for Red-tailed Hawk, but we fail to notice because we are so focused on what is expected.

The opposite kind of problem occurs when our desire to find a rare bird alters our perceptions of the common bird in front of us. Everyone who has been birding for more than a few weeks has probably had that experience. When we're really primed to see a Northern

We're hurrying to a birding site when we see this distant hawk. Is it a Red-tail? Probably. Will we stop to check? Probably not.

Goshawk, those Cooper's Hawks look huge. When we're hoping for a Yellow-billed Loon, all the Common Loons suddenly have pale bills. And it goes on from there.

Our subconscious drive to find a rarity can genuinely alter our perceptions, so that our minds put more emphasis on some visual marks than others and ignore things that don't fit with what we want the bird to be. Years ago I reviewed a report of a Swainson's Hawk found in January in the American southwest, where it would have represented an amazing record. The man had written a very detailed description of the bird, and it was a perfect description of Swainson's, down to the last detail. He also submitted photographs, and the photos proved beyond all doubt that the bird was a Red-tailed Hawk. But I believe that the man's description was an honest account of what he had "seen," with his subconscious filling in all the details that would support his initial identification. This was a case of desire and expectation working together to thwart a correct diagnosis: he wanted it to be a Swainson's Hawk, and if it were indeed a Swainson's, he expected it to have all of these shape characteristics and field marks.

We're all subject to these subconscious influences. When I am looking at a potential rarity, I try to ask myself: What do I want most here? Do I want this bird to be that particular species? Or do I genuinely want to know what it really is? Consciously applying the latter approach can help us to discern what the bird actually looks like and sounds like and reach a correct identification without too many embarrassing detours.

Pitfall 2. Impressions of Size

Size is one of those basic things that is cited in almost every treatment of how to recognize birds. But size is also devilishly difficult to judge

in the field. One of the pitfalls that confounds the identification process most often is when birders misjudge a bird's size. Frequently we'll hear a birder say, "It looked like a ———— , but it was too large" (or too small). Ask how the birder knew its size, and often he won't have a good answer.

Here, a lone Black Guillemot swims on open water. Is it the size of a Mallard, or much larger, like a Common Loon? Actually, it's much smaller than either. But there's no way that we could be sure of that from this photo, or from this kind of view in the field.

I used to think that I could accurately judge the sizes of most birds that I saw. That now seems unlikely to me. I think that what was happening was that I immediately recognized each bird by its shape, behavior, or other marks, and my subconscious then filled in what I knew to be the size of that species. On my first trip to Australia, where entire families of birds were profoundly unfamiliar, my first impressions of size were often grossly incorrect. These days, I'm sure I still make unconscious assumptions about the size of every bird I see, but I try to consciously temper those assumptions with a grain of salt until I get confirmation.

When dealing with an unknown bird, size is important, of course, but the best way to judge it is by direct comparison to another bird. If no others are close by, we may get a sense of its size by comparison to other nearby objects, such as leaves or fence posts. Indeed, our subconscious

Consider this illustration of four sparrows. If your eyes work like most people's eyes, in the upper panel, the dark bird will look larger, while in the lower panel, the pale bird will look larger. In fact, all are the same size, and the illusion of a size difference is caused by the differences in contrast.

mind will usually make such comparisons for us. The toughest situations are those in which the bird is completely isolated, with nothing nearby for size reference. A lone bird in the sky, on the water, or on barren open ground may be much larger or smaller than we first imagine it to be.

Even in situations when the bird may be seen in comparison to others, there are a couple of optical illusions that can alter our perceptions. One is that contrast can make a bird appear larger. Against a light background such as a white sand beach, a dark bird may seem larger than a pale one, even if they are the same size. On the other hand, against a dark background, a white bird may stand out as looking larger.

A trickier illusion, first pointed out by the late P. J. Grant, comes into play when we look at birds through telescopes at high magnification. If we zero in on a group of birds that are all of the same size, the ones that are farther away may seem larger. This optical illusion seems to be caused by the way that our eyes compensate for the compressed field of view through the scope. You can test this for yourself in a small way by putting two identical objects (two quarters, for example) on the floor, one directly behind the other, and looking at them through a scope from a moderate distance away. In this situation, the farther one may look larger. Different people seem to be more affected than others by this illusion, but in some cases it could be critically important if we are trying to determine the size of a mystery bird within a flock.

Pitfall 3. Impressions of Color

Color is an elusive and tricky thing, shifting with every change in light conditions. Artists painting field guide illustrations generally do them as if lighting were neutral, shining evenly on the bird from all sides. In the field, birds seldom look like that, and everything about their colors can appear to change from moment to moment in ways that can be very misleading for birders.

The quality of the light changes at different times of day. In the low-angled light of early morning or late afternoon sun, colors all look warmer: brown birds take on orange or red tones, white birds can look yellow or pink. Under the glare of midday sun, brightly colored birds can look dull. In deep shadow, gray birds may look bluish. Even under normal light, the smooth surface of a bird's eye or bill can catch the light and momentarily look pale or white.

Reflected light can alter a bird's appearance as much as direct light, and the effects can be more potentially confusing. Small birds hopping among foliage often look tinged with green or yellow. Terns and other white birds flying over tropical waters may appear tinged with green or blue below. Snow on the ground can affect the appearance of birds overhead, even those that are flying quite high: a stunningly white bird against the sky on a sunny day may turn out to be a normal Mallard, or Common Loon, or Red-tailed Hawk, lit up from below with light reflected from snow-covered fields. In all of these cases, a closer look should clarify what is going on. But in situations like these, if we get only a brief look, we may be left with a very misleading impression of the bird's color.

On a sunny day in winter, we might see a strikingly pale bird against the blue sky. Is the bird really so white? No, it's a normal Red-tailed Hawk, lit up from below with light reflecting from the snow.

The surroundings also can affect our perceptions of color. Birds sitting on snow, ice, or white sand may seem much darker than they really are. This is especially relevant for gulls, which are often seen in such situations, and in which the darkness of the gray on the back may be an important field mark. Even if we're fully aware of the effects of this illusion, it can still throw us off, at least temporarily.

Pitfall 4. Abnormal Pigmentation

Beyond the realm of normal variations in birds, there are various kinds of abnormal conditions, including odd quirks of pigmentation. An active birder occasionally will run across a bird with strikingly unusual colors or markings for its species.

It may look like a "baby Bald Eagle," but it's a White-throated Sparrow that lacks almost all the melanin on its head feathers and on two of its tertials. When a birder sees something like this, it's a natural first instinct to try to find this white-headed bird in a field guide.

The most common such abnormality involves patches of white in the plumage, or even a bird that looks mostly or entirely white. This condition often has been called albinism, although that term is not correct in most cases, and amelanism or leucism would be preferred terms. Whatever it is called, it often trips up inexperienced birders. Every year I hear reports of Snow Buntings, or even McKay's Buntings, consorting with flocks of House Sparrows in summer, and of course these birds invariably turn out to be House Sparrows with white feathers. But not all birds with abnormal white are so easily diagnosed. Any time we're tempted to identify a rare bird solely on the basis of some white marking, we should consider the possibility that the white may be abnormal. Usually such aberrant markings are asymmetrical, not expressed equally on both sides of the bird, but that doesn't always hold true.

Several other kinds of abnormal pigmentation are possible. They can result in birds with a very pale or washed-out appearance, birds that have red replaced by yellow, or birds that are exceptionally dark. These abnormalities usually affect the plumage, but in some cases they can affect the bill, legs, or other areas. In Chapter 4 (with the discussion of plumages and molts), I give a somewhat more detailed description of these abnormalities of plumage color. But as a first step, it is important to recognize simply that such odd colorations are possible and to consider such things when we try to identify an odd-looking bird.

Pitfall 5. Accidental Discoloration

Abnormal color as described above may last for a bird's lifetime, or at least for the period from one molt to the next, but it tends to be fairly rare. On the other hand, a bird's plumage, bill, or legs may be temporarily stained, and this kind of discoloration is very common. Wild birds get messy in a variety of ways that may change their appearance and cause confusion for birders.

Zonotrichia sparrows wintering in suburban areas in the Southwest may feed on fallen olives, staining their faces partly black in the process. This Golden-crowned Sparrow could pose an identification challenge if we were unaware of this potential for staining.

It's impossible to list all the ways that a bird may be discolored, but some are especially common. Birds that feed on soft fruit may have dark stains around the base of the bill; birds that feed at blossoms may have the forehead, face, or throat dusted with yellow or red pollen. Waterbirds may have the legs or underparts discolored temporarily by mud (or permanently by oil or chemicals in the water). Swans and geese often have their white heads stained orange by the iron con-

Orange staining on the head and neck of this Trumpeter Swan results from iron content in the mud where it feeds.

tent in the soil where they have been grubbing for food; the same kind of staining is often seen on Sandhill Cranes and some other birds. On a bird such as a swan, this color is not likely to affect our identification. But it can be confusing if we see a duck that normally has limited white on its neck or face pattern, such as a male Northern Pintail or Blue-winged Teal, and the white has been replaced by orange staining.

Pitfall 6. Effects of Missing or Disarranged Feathers

In the chapter following this one, I include a lot of detail about the arrangement of feathers on a bird's body and, especially, the complicated feather structure of the wings and tail. This amount of detail might seem unnecessary, and in fact it usually isn't needed for identifying most birds in normal plumage. It can be essential background, however, for identifying some challenging species. And even birds that are normally no problem at all can have a confusing appearance if some of their feathers are missing or in disarray. In that situation, it helps to know the normal arrangement of feathers so that we can figure out what's wrong.

Body feathers are often differently colored at the base, often a dull dark gray, and we usually don't see this because the bases are covered by the overlapping tips of other feathers. If some feathers are missing or scuffed out of place, however, the darker underlying area may be exposed, looking like a dark spot or patch. This can create, for example, the impression that a bird has a dark spot on the underparts where none is supposed to exist.

Missing feathers in the wings or tail also can create some odd impressions. The appearance of a "forked tail" can result when the central tail feathers are missing. When larger flight feathers of the wings are missing, either through the normal process of molt or through accidental loss, this can change the appearance of wing shape and pattern. Missing covert feathers in the wings can reveal underlying colors and change the appearance of wing pattern. In all of these cases, knowing the normal arrangement of the feathers will help us to understand what we're seeing.

Pitfall 7. Variations in Voice

Vocalizations are usually useful in identifying birds, and often they're absolutely critical. But they're not always reliable. Voices of most species vary to some extent. In some cases, the variation is extreme.

In many of the more primitive groups of birds, the voice is innate, not learned; the bird apparently is born with the instinct to make the right sounds. This is true even for some with very distinctive songs, such as doves and at least some of the flycatchers. Among most of the true songbirds, however, there is a major element of learning in the song. In these species, the young bird apparently has a mental "template" and an instinctive ability to recognize the song of its own kind. However, males have to hear that song during a critical learning period while they are still young, or they will never learn to sing it correctly.

Studies of some tyrant flycatchers have shown that they inherit their songs. We may have to rely on voice to identify this Yellow-bellied Flycatcher, but at least its song will have a reliable genetic basis. True songbirds, on the other hand, have an element of learning in their songs, which opens up the chance for error and for more variations.

This element of learning is probably part of the reason why we occasionally run across a bird singing the "wrong" song: a Field Sparrow that sings like a Chipping Sparrow, for example, or a Chestnut-sided Warbler that sings like an Indigo Bunting. It's likely that something went awry in the learning process for these birds. Interestingly, at least in some species, the song is learned but the callnotes are instinctive, so the calls may be more reliably definitive. At times the callnotes vary in odd ways also, however. Friends and I once kept tabs on a wintering Yellow-rumped Warbler that consistently gave a soft *whit* callnote, quite unlike the typical *chek*.

The most reliable way to tell this Fish Crow from the American Crow is by its voice. Unfortunately, crows make a lot of different sounds, so we may have to hear more than a few notes to be sure that we've identified the species correctly.

When we encounter a bird that seems to be giving the wrong song or calls, it is not necessarily doing something abnormal. Many birds have a wide variety of different songs and calls, and we may spend a lot of time with a species before we hear some of them. And birds in some groups are exceptionally variable in voice. After years of paying close attention to American Crows and Blue Jays, I still sometimes hear them doing things I've never heard before. There are regional variations in voice in many species, including well-established local "dialects" that can trip up traveling birders. And a number of species from different families are accomplished mimics, able to copy sounds from their environment and incorporate them into their own songs. In Chapter 5, in the discussion of learning to recognize birds by sound, I will discuss some of these variations in more detail. The main point is that we can be led astray in a variety of ways when birding by ear, and if a rare or unexpected bird is identified only by sound, we may need additional evidence to back it up.

Pitfall 8. Bill Deformities

The precise shape of the bill is sometimes a critical field mark for separating similar species. Indeed, bill shape comes into play as an important field mark in one challenging group after another, from loons and egrets to sandpipers and terns, from hummingbirds and flycatchers to finches. Because of this, it's important to note that the occasional bird develops a malformed bill. If the deformity is not serious enough to prevent feeding, the bird may live a normal life and may look mostly normal aside from its bill shape. The mandibles may be crossed, or one or both mandibles may be abnormally long; other kinds of deformities are also possible.

In most cases, a bird with a deformed bill is still readily identifiable. A Red-headed Woodpecker with an exceptionally long bill, for example, is still obviously a Red-headed Woodpecker. But in cases in which bill length is a key field

Bill shape is usually a field mark for separating the two species of water-thrushes. It wouldn't be helpful, however, on this Northern Waterthrush, with its oddly crossed mandible tips.

mark, even a slight deformity could throw off the identification process. This is something to keep in mind if we find a bird for which the bill shape and the plumage don't seem to add up to the same species — it could be a problem with either the plumage or the bill.

Pitfall 9. Hybrids

In the wild, as a general rule, distinct species of birds seldom interbreed. But that's only the general situation, and there are enough exceptions to that rule that an active birder can expect to run into hybrids eventually. In some areas, and in some groups of birds, they are actually quite common. Mallard × American Black Duck hybrids are quite numerous in the northeast, for example, and Glaucous-winged × Western Gulls are very common along much of our Pacific Coast — even outnumbering the two parental species in some areas. Golden-winged × Blue-winged Warblers, Hermit × Townsend's Warblers, and Baltimore × Bullock's Orioles are all combinations that are seen regularly in some areas. Hundreds of other hybrid combinations have been found at least once.

In most cases, hybrids combine some characteristics of both parental species. (See the section on hybrids in Chapter 6.) Sometimes, this combination may result in a pattern that suggests another species entirely. For example, I once saw a White-throated Sparrow × Dark-eyed Junco hybrid that was very suggestive of a Black-chinned Sparrow, and I've seen photos of Northern Pintail × Green-winged Teal hybrids that looked very much like male Baikal Teal.

Hybrids between Golden-winged and Blue-winged warblers are now widely recognized, but when they were first noticed, they were thought to represent new species. This one, the most frequently seen hybrid type, is still informally referred to as "Brewster's Warbler." Several other hybrid warbler combinations have been found, but most only very rarely.

Pitfall 10. Escapees

Exotic birds from all over the world are kept in North America as zoo exhibits or as pets. Sometimes they escape, and some may live for weeks, or even years, in the wild. Although some such fugitives are truly exotic in appearance (think parrots and toucans), many are not. Exotic waterfowl are often seen free-flying in North America, and they may look only moderately different from our usual ducks. Females or young of various bishops, canaries, and finches could be confused with

The African weavers known as bishops (genus *Euplectes*) are often kept as zoo birds or pets. Males in breeding plumage have spectacular colors, but females, nonbreeding males, and young can be obscure and sparrowlike, and they can cause serious consternation for birders.

North American sparrows or buntings, for example. There isn't much we can do to prepare for this specific problem, short of learning all the birds of the world or studying all the birds in the local zoo, but it's something to keep in mind if we see a bird that doesn't add up.

Pitfall 11. Cosmic Mind-Benders

This may not happen even once in an average birding lifetime, but it's possible every time we go out: a bird that looks unfamiliar might be a vagrant that has strayed far outside its normal range. Strong-flying migratory birds sometimes go off course and may wind up literally thousands of miles away from where they are "supposed" to be.

Several years ago, birders in Maine found an odd streaky flycatcher. Looking through their North American field guides, they decided that — even though it didn't look exactly right — it had to be a Sulphur-bellied Flycatcher, a remarkable stray from the American southwest. However, photographs proved that it was actually a far more remarkable bird, a Variegated Flycatcher from South America, the first one ever for this continent! In subsequent years there have been more records elsewhere in North America, but birders have been tripped up yet again, because a couple of supposed Variegated Flycatchers have turned out to represent another tropical stray, Piratic Flycatcher. The moral of this story is not that birders in the U.S. and Canada should memorize every South American bird. No, this merely demonstrates that we must keep an open mind when we find a bird that doesn't quite add up. We don't have to match it to something in our field guides, because it could be something else entirely.

What do you do if you find a bird that matches nothing in any of your field guides? You keep an open mind. It's probably just an odd plumage of a familiar bird, but it could turn out to be a mega-rarity, like this Piratic Flycatcher from the American tropics.

And now, after this review of possible pitfalls, I'd like to present one final basic principle to keep in mind.

Principle 14. Don't Let It Get You Down

One obvious message of this book is that, if you want to, you can make progress on learning to identify any of the most difficult North American birds. But I hope that everyone will see the other side of the coin:

you don't *have* to take on all of these challenges.

If any group of birds leaves you confused, irritated, or uninterested, it's okay to simply ignore that group. You can enter "gull, sp." or "sparrows, unidentified" in your notes, if you like, and that will be a perfectly accurate and acceptable identification. If a drab *Empidonax* flycatcher pops up in front of you, and you don't feel like trying to work it out, you can ignore it and go on looking for tanagers or orioles. As long as you're not causing serious disturbance to the birds, their habitat, or other people, there is no "wrong way" to go birding.

I've often said that birding is something that we do for enjoyment — so, if you enjoy it, you're a good birder. If you enjoy it a lot, you're a great birder. If, as a great birder, you decide to learn more about identifying difficult species, I hope this book will help you. But if you decide not to tackle these challenges, please continue to pursue your birding in whatever way brings you the most satisfaction.

3. HOW BIRDS ARE BUILT: TERMINOLOGY AND BIRD TOPOGRAPHY

Birding and field ornithology are relatively free of technical jargon, and that's a good thing. But advanced field identification may depend on fine details of specific parts of a bird. To be able to describe what we are seeing, and even to be able to understand what we are seeing, we need to learn some basic terminology for bird parts, or "bird topography."

If a field mark involves the greater coverts, for example, it's best if we're all calling them "greater coverts." The alternative would be something like "that group of medium-sized feathers near the center of the wing, in front of the flight feathers, where the second wing bar would be if this bird happened to have wing bars" — or something much more imprecise, like "the middle of the wing," which doesn't tell us what group of feathers is meant. So I recommend that you take the time to learn the standard terminology. Not only will it make communication easier, it will also do a lot to sharpen your awareness of the patterns of birds.

This chapter goes through the parts of a bird in detail, illustrating and describing the different groups of feathers and other structural characteristics, and discussing how these points contribute to the overall appearance of the bird in the field. I would encourage you to read the entire chapter more than once, studying the illustrations to see how the different pieces fit together and how the visible impressions of birds are created. In the long run, understanding the visible structure of the bird may do more than anything else to enhance your skill at identification.

FEATHER STRUCTURE AND FEATHER TYPES

Birds are essentially covered with feathers, so to understand what we're seeing when we look at a bird, we have to understand some things about them. Feathers are among the most remarkable structures in nature, lightweight but strong, with various types providing insulation, decoration, flat surfaces for flight, and many other benefits.

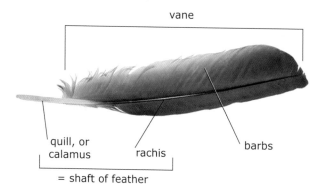

vane

quill, or
calamus

rachis

barbs

= shaft of feather

The basic structure of a typical feather involves a central **shaft,** with stiff but flexible **vanes** attached to either side. (The hollow basal part of the shaft is also called the **quill,** or **calamus,** while the distal part with the vanes attached is also called the **rachis.** But it is clear enough to refer to the whole thing as the shaft of the feather.) The vane of the feather is a remarkable structure, with a series of thin filaments, called **barbs,** that are normally locked together by tiny hooks called **barbules.** If you pick up a large feather, you'll find that you can easily separate the barbs and then "zip" them back together. A bird, when it's preening, can do the same thing.

Two extreme closeups of a vane of a large feather, showing how the barbs are arranged. At right, the vane is separated, and the tiny barbules are visible along the barb at the right edge of the break. By preening, the bird can zip the barbs back together.

By far the most numerous feathers on the typical bird are the **contour feathers,** which cover the head and body. Contour feathers tend to be very small and very numerous on the head and neck, larger on the body. The body feathers usually are well formed at the tips but loose and fluffy at the base; the basal parts of these body feathers are usually hidden by the tips of other feathers overlapping them, so we don't notice this in the field. These fluffy basal parts of the contour feathers help to provide insulation. On many birds there is a smaller structure, called an **aftershaft,** on the underside of the contour feathers, and this is usually soft and fluffy also, adding to the insulating qualities of the plumage. Only rarely, when a bird's feathers are strongly disarranged, will we glimpse this underlying layer.

A body feather of the American Woodcock. At left, the feather as seen from above. In viewing the bird we would see only the tip of this feather, and the fluffy base would be hidden by another feather overlapping this one. The entire feather is less than two inches long, but barely half an inch of its tip would be visible on the bird. At right, the same feather viewed from the side, showing the fluffy aftershaft that lies below the feather's base.

The contour feathers of the body vary considerably in size and shape. Those of the underparts are often somewhat looser and more fluffy than those of the upperparts. The scapular feathers, which cover the bases of the wings, are often larger, and this is especially true on larger, strong-flying birds such as gulls, shorebirds, and raptors. Protecting the base of the tail from above and below are large strong feathers, known as upper-tail coverts and undertail coverts.

Some of these feathers differ in structure or even in size between different age groups of the same species (as I discuss in some detail in Chapter 6). The body feathers of juveniles, especially on the nape, back, and undertail coverts, are often looser in

An undertail covert feather from a Bald Eagle. This single feather is more than six inches long and two inches wide. These are among the largest of the contour feathers on the bird's body, although the flight feathers of the wings and tail are many times larger as well as being incredibly stiff and strong.

structure than those of adults. In some species, such as Ruddy Turnstones and some other shorebirds, the scapulars of juveniles are much smaller than those of adults, and this difference can be readily seen in the field.

The smaller feathers that cover the inner and leading areas of the wing are similar in structure to the contour feathers of the body. However, the larger feathers of the wing — the **flight feathers,** or **remiges** (singular: remex) — are quite different. Strong and stiff, they provide the broad flat surfaces of the wing necessary for flight. While contour feathers have the shaft close to the center, the flight feathers of the wings are asymmetrical, with a narrow outer vane and broad inner vane; this uneven distribution of the vanes is usually more pronounced on the primaries than on the secondaries.

Primary from a "Yellow-shafted" Northern Flicker (showing the yellow shaft)

Secondary from a Blue Jay

Primaries and secondaries usually have very strong shafts, with little or no loose structure of the vanes toward the bases. A modification of the primaries on many birds is an **emargination,** which is an indented distal part of the vane on the leading edge. In some groups of birds, the number of emarginated outer primaries is a characteristic that may be used for in-hand identification. The trailing edge of some outer primaries may show a **notch,** mainly on large soaring birds such as many raptors. The combination of the emargination on the leading edge and the notch on the trailing edge creates the look of separated or "fingered" outer primaries on such birds in flight.

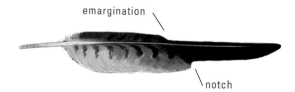

emargination

notch

A closeup view of the outer primaries of a male Northern Cardinal, as seen from above. There is obvious emargination on three of these feathers and slight emargination on another two. Notice that the outer edges of the primaries (the edges that would still be visible when the wing was folded) are brightly colored, but the inner vanes are not. Notice also that the inner vanes are translucent, and we can easily see through one feather to the outline of the next feather below it.

Tail feathers, or **rectrices** (singular: rectrix), are not as asymmetrical as primaries. The central tail feathers usually have the shaft positioned in the center, while the outer ones usually have the shaft offset toward the outer edge, so that the outer vane is narrower than the inner vane. Like the flight feathers of the wings, the tail feathers are very strong and stiff. The tail serves for steering and maneuvering in flight and as some additional sail area in some kinds of soaring. For some climbing birds such as woodpeckers, the tail feathers also serve as props when the bird is clinging to a vertical surface.

Tail feathers from a Steller's Jay. Left: one of the outer rectrices. Right: one of the central rectrices.

In most birds, flight feathers of the wings and tail (primaries, secondaries, and rectrices) differ in shape between juveniles and older birds, with these feathers on juveniles being narrower and more tapered toward the tips. There are exceptions; for example, many hummingbirds show just the opposite tendency, with juveniles having the primaries and tail feathers broader and more rounded or blunt-tipped than those of adults (and these feathers are often broader in females than in males of the same age). In many large strong-flying birds, the flight feathers of the wings and tail are also longer in juveniles than in adults.

Contour feathers and flight feathers are responsible for most of what we see on birds, but a few other types of specialized feathers are worth mentioning.

Beneath the contour feathers on the bodies of most birds are **down** feathers in varying amounts. These are soft and fluffy, usually lack a central shaft, and serve mostly for insulation. Also lying beneath the contour feathers are other feathers called **semiplumes,** which have central shafts and which usually look intermediate between down and contour feathers. They are usually located along the edges of the feather tracts (see below) and are usually hidden, but it may be these semiplumes that are modified to become the long ornamental plumes of egrets and herons.

Ornamental plume from a Great Egret, probably a modified semiplume.

Specialized feathers called **filoplumes,** important to the birds but seldom noticed by birders, are found on most birds. Filoplumes are thin, hairlike feathers, each ending in a tuft of short barbs, located near the bases of certain body feathers and many flight feathers. They seem to have a sensory function, allowing the birds to make appropriate adjustments to the positions of the nearby contour feathers and flight feathers. The hairlike feathers extending past the nape feathers on some songbirds are filoplumes.

Bristles are also specialized feathers. They consist of a bare, tapered shaft, with a few extra barbs at the base. Semibristles are similar but they have a few barbs or branches along the sides. Bristles and semibristles

The rictal bristles around the base of the bill of this Acadian Flycatcher are specialized feathers often found on birds that catch insects in midair.

are found mostly on birds' heads, especially around the eyes and bill, where they may serve both as sensory organs and for protection. Bristles make up the tufts that cover the base of the upper mandible on birds like woodpeckers and ravens. Many birds that catch insects in midair, such as most nightjars and most North American flycatchers, have long bristles called **rictal bristles** around the base of the bill. In a few cases, the prominence or shape of rictal bristles may play a part in identification; for example, the rictal bristles of Chuck-will's-widow have filaments branching off their sides, while those of Whip-poor-will are simple, lacking the side branches.

ARRANGEMENT OF FEATHERS: FEATHER TRACTS

Although a bird's body will appear to be completely covered with feathers, the feathers are not uniformly distributed in the way they are attached to the body. Instead, on most birds (including all of those native to North America), feathers are attached to the skin in dense concentrations in **feather tracts,** also called **pterylae.** Between these tracts are areas of skin with few feathers or no feathers attached, called **apteria.** In the field, we rarely even glimpse these areas of bare skin, because feathers from the adjacent tracts usually spread out neatly to cover them.

A basic but important point is that the base of each feather is inserted so that the tip of the feather points back, toward the tail end of the bird. This arrangement means that the feathers naturally lie smooth with a minimum of friction when the bird is flying. It is also part of the reason why birds at rest habitually face directly into the wind; when they turn to face away from the wind, their feathers are blown up or ruffled up from behind, which looks as if it would be uncomfortable at the very least.

Within the tracts, feathers generally line up in neat rows, the tip of one covering the base of the next one, like shingles on a roof. Often we can see this arrangement of feathers reflected in the pattern of the bird. For example, a long continuous stripe, such as one running down the bird's back or along its side below the wing, is likely to be created by a long row of feathers with the same pattern. Of course, this arrangement means that the stripe can appear broken or jagged any time the feathers are disarranged, and this may change from moment to moment as the bird moves around.

Another consequence of the arrangement of feather tracts is that any bird, even one that is completely uniform in color, can appear to have the indication of a "pattern" created by the shape of its feather coat. A bird with plain underparts will appear, in some lights, to have blurry stripes below, because of the play of light and shadow across these rows of feathers.

This female Summer Tanager has no real head pattern, being simply shades of yellow all over. However, in a close view like this, we can see many varied textures and subtle patterns created by the different sizes of feathers and their arrangement in different feather tracts.

BIRD PARTS AND THEIR PATTERNS

Head feathers and head patterns. Some of the smallest feathers are those around and in front of a bird's eye, and the feathers of the forehead and the base of the throat also tend to be very small. The feathers of the crown tend to be longer, and when they are notably long they form a crest. Many birds, however, have somewhat elongated feathers on the crown, and they may raise these when they are excited, giving the appearance of a short crest. The feathers of the nape also tend to be long and somewhat loose on many groups of birds, and the lower throat feathers are often densely packed and fluffy. Many of the groups of longer feathers on the head can be puffed out or sleeked down, changing the appearance of head shape substantially.

Partly following the edges of the feather tracts on the head, certain elements of head pattern occur over and over on different groups of birds, and it is very useful to have standard terms for these features.

The terms **median crown stripe** and **lateral crown stripe** are self-explanatory. However, they cannot be applied to all birds with patterned crowns. If the crown is uniformly covered with fine streaks, for example, it would be wrong to designate one streak as "median" and another as "lateral."

When the **supercilium,** or **eyebrow,** is distinctively colored, it is almost always paler than the areas immediately above and below it (the crown or the lateral crown stripe above, the eyestripe below). The extent of the supercilium varies a lot among species, so it's important for observers to note the shape of this mark — wide or narrow, extending far behind the eye or not. Sometimes it contrasts sharply with the crown, and sometimes it blends smoothly into a darker area above, and this can make a big difference in the appearance of the face. The part of the supercilium lying forward of the eye is sometimes referred to, incorrectly, as the lores, but it should be called the **supraloral area.**

The term **eyestripe** indicates a horizontal stripe at the level of the eye. When it exists only behind the eye, it is sometimes called the **post-ocular stripe;** when it exists only between the eye and the bill, it is sometimes called the **loral stripe.** But referring to these simply as sections of the eyestripe would be equally clear.

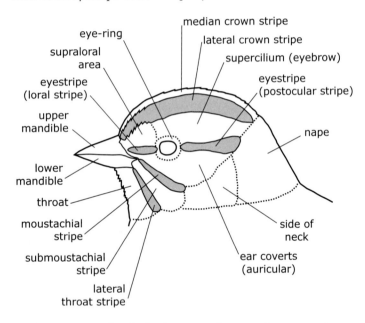

The **ear coverts** (auriculars) cover and protect the ear openings, and this group of feathers is obvious on the faces of most birds. Usually the long feathers of the ear coverts are somewhat simplified, with a lacy or spiny texture, while the short feathers at the back of the ear coverts are stiff and probably help to funnel sound into the ear.

Between the ear coverts and the center of the throat there can be up to three stripes, and these are most easily defined by their points of origin at the base of the bill. The **moustachial stripe** originates at the point of the gape and follows closely along the lower forward edge of the ear coverts; when present, this is almost invariably a dark stripe. The broader (and usually pale) stripe that often appears just below this is called the **submoustachial stripe.** The lowest of the three possible stripes, originating from the lower angle of the base of the lower mandible, is called the "malar stripe" in many older books, but this is anatomically misleading; a preferred term is **lateral throat stripe.** Of course, many birds show only one or two of these possible stripes, and on some birds you may need a close look to be sure just where the stripe falls. If you can't be certain, saying that a stripe exists in the **malar region** is better than guessing at its precise location.

When there is no contrasting lateral throat stripe and no different color in the malar region, the term **throat** can be applied to these areas in addition to the center of the throat. The term **chin** is sometimes useful for describing limited areas of the upper throat, just below the bill. The lower edge of the throat is usually easy to determine (except on long-necked birds) by the change in texture of the feathers where the throat meets the upper breast.

The **nape** is the back of the head, and the division between the **crown** and the nape is somewhat arbitrary. On long-necked birds, this term would apply only to the back of the head, while the area below the nape would be called the **hindneck.** The area below the ear coverts, between the throat and the nape, can be referred to as the **side of the neck.**

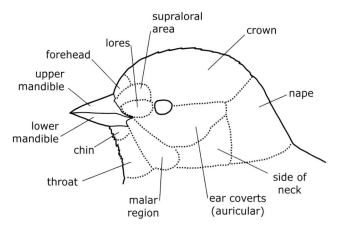

An **eye-ring** (or lack of an eye-ring) is often cited as a field mark in some groups of birds, but in reality, noting simple presence or absence doesn't cover the amount of variation in this feature. Most birds have very small feathers arranged in narrow rows encircling or partly encircling the eye. Even if these tiny feathers are the same color as the rest of the face, their very presence can give a hint of an eye-ring. A true eye-ring pattern results when these feathers are sharply paler than the surrounding areas. If the color is strikingly contrasted, or if the pale area extends over a wider circle involving more feathers, the eye-ring will be more conspicuous. In describing an eye-ring, we need to note whether it is narrow or wide, or wider at some points than others; we need to note whether it is broken or complete, whether it contrasts sharply or fades smoothly into the surrounding area, and whether it is connected to a pale area on the lores (the latter creates the "spectacled" pattern seen on some birds).

The bold eye-ring of Swainson's Thrush (right) is often mentioned as a major field mark for the species. The Gray-cheeked Thrush (left) is not so marked, but considering the pale area above and behind the eye, it would be misleading to say it lacks an eye-ring altogether. Descriptions must allow for more than simple presence or absence of this mark.

The noticeable yellow orbital ring on this Semipalmated Plover is one point that helps to separate the species from Common Ringed Plover.

A true eye-ring involves a pattern on feathers, but in addition, almost all birds have a very narrow ring of bare skin immediately surrounding the eye. This is called the **orbital ring.** It is seldom obvious on songbirds, but it may be contrastingly colored and quite conspicuous on some larger birds such as gulls, plovers, and doves. Color of the orbital ring may be a significant factor in identifying some gulls and other birds.

Body-plumage terms. The edges of different feather groups on the body are sometimes difficult to see, especially on the underparts. The **breast** is the area that extends all the way across the underparts, just below the throat; these feathers are attached to the front of the lower neck, and especially toward the center they are distinctly different from the **belly** feathers just below them. The feathers of the **sides** and **flanks**

are all attached to the same feather tract, with the terms applying to the forward and rearward parts of the same feather group. The feathers of the sides often cover the leading edge of the wing, especially on some birds such as ducks. Feathers from the flanks also spread out to cover the belly.

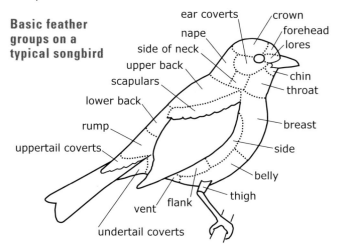

Basic feather groups on a typical songbird

ear coverts
crown
nape
forehead
side of neck
lores
upper back
scapulars
chin
lower back
throat
rump
breast
uppertail coverts
side
belly
vent
flank
thigh
undertail coverts

Behind the flanks, along the bird's side before the base of the tail, the **femoral tract** is rarely noticeable on small birds but may be obvious on some large waterbirds. The area between the belly and the undertail coverts is called the **vent.** The **undertail coverts** are relatively large well-developed feathers that protect the base of the tail from below.

The difference between the **upper back** and the **scapulars** can be hard to see on many small birds, although it can be very obvious on large birds. The upper back (or interscapular region) has been called the "mantle" in some references (a poor choice of terms, since "mantle" also has been used to describe the entire upper surface of the back, scapulars, and wings in gulls). The scapulars grow from the humeral tract of feathers, located where the wing meets the body, and they play an important role in protecting the base of the wing. Large birds such as shorebirds and gulls may appear to have their scapular feathers arranged in four neat rows, but in reality these feathers are all attached close together near the shoulder, and the ones that appear to be positioned toward the rear are just longer than the feathers lying above them. The long scapular feathers thus can appear to change position in an extreme way on large birds, sometimes covering most of the wing, sometimes leaving most of the wing exposed.

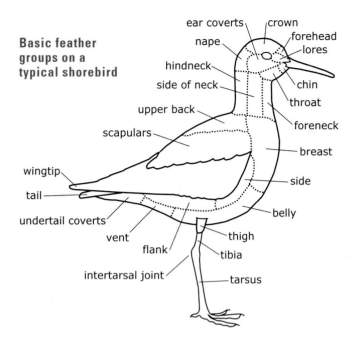

Basic feather groups on a typical shorebird

ear coverts
crown
forehead
lores
nape
hindneck
side of neck
upper back
scapulars
wingtip
tail
undertail coverts
vent
flank
intertarsal joint
chin
throat
foreneck
breast
side
belly
thigh
tibia
tarsus

Moving down toward the tail, it can be useful to distinguish between the **lower back** and the **rump,** and it is important to note the distinction between the rump and the **uppertail coverts.** The latter are relatively long well-formed feathers that protect the base of the tail from above. They may be colored or patterned differently from the rump, or from the tail, or both.

Tail structure terms. The number of **tail feathers,** or **rectrices** (singular: rectrix), varies. Many birds have twelve, but there are many exceptions; for example, most hummingbirds, nightjars, and cuckoos have ten, while most waterfowl, grouse, and snipes have more than twelve. Even within species, there can be variation in the number. In specifying a particular tail feather, they are numbered from the central pair outward. Thus, on a typical bird, each of the two central rectrices would be designated r1, with the numbers going out to r6 on either side.

A basic but essential point is that a bird's tail folds up with the central pair of tail feathers on top and the outermost pair on the bottom. Looking at the upperside of the folded tail, we can see one feather of the central pair in its entirety, plus the outer edges of most of the others. Looking at the underside, often we can see only the outermost pair.

A bird with white outer tail feathers may look white-tailed from below, dark-tailed from above. So in describing a bird's tail color or pattern, we need to determine which surface we are seeing.

On most birds the bases of the tail feathers are never visible, being hidden by the tail coverts. Recognizing the uppertail coverts as such may take some concentration: what looks at first glance like the "base of the tail" on flying gulls, shorebirds, hawks, and other birds may actually be the uppertail coverts. When these are contrastingly colored, they may be a significant part of the bird's pattern in flight.

The shape of a bird's tail is determined by the length and shape of the individual feathers, and of course by the way the feathers are being held at a given moment. The same tail may appear broadly rounded when it is fanned widely, square-tipped when it is tightly closed. Even when the tail is folded, a slight sideways shift in position of individual feathers can change the apparent shape from square-tipped to notched at the tip. When the tail is strongly graduated — that is, when the outer pairs of rectrices are progressively much shorter than the central pairs — this will be obvious when the tail is fanned, and it may be apparent when the tail is viewed from below, especially if the tips of the outer tail feathers have a contrasting pattern.

On this Black-billed Cuckoo, contrasting pattern on the tips of the tail feathers makes it obvious that the outer ones are much shorter.

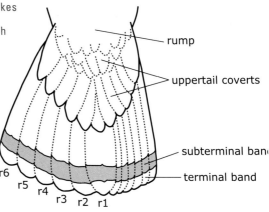

Structure of tail and adjacent feathers, as seen from above

- rump
- uppertail coverts
- subterminal band
- terminal band

r6 r5 r4 r3 r2 r1

Wing-structure terms. Wing structure is the most important aspect of bird topography to learn. We can bluff our way through describing a bird's body pattern if necessary, but we can't begin to describe its wing pattern until we know how the wing is built. Learning the wing's structure and its terminology can have an added payoff, however, in increasing our sense of wonder. The architecture of a bird's wing is extraordinary — far more complex than any aircraft wing ever designed by humans, even if we confine our gaze to the feather covering and ignore the bones and the system of muscles driving the bird's flight.

Most of the surface area of the wing is composed only of long, strong feathers, and the part containing bone and muscle is only a fraction of it. This is worth remembering, because when feathers are missing, the shape of the wing will be changed.

The long flight feathers of the outer part of the wing, including those that make up the wingtip, are the **primaries.** The primaries attach to the bones of the bird's "hand" (metacarpus), while the **secondaries** are attached to the ulna, which is analogous to our lower arm between the hand and the elbow. On small birds it may be difficult to see the difference between the innermost primary and the outermost secondary, but they are clearly different in where they attach to the wing.

Most North American birds have ten primaries, although some water birds have eleven and members of several songbird families show only nine. In cases when identification involves the pattern or shape of specific primaries, such as some hummingbirds and gulls, they are numbered from the innermost (p1) to the outermost (p10). The number of secondaries is more variable; hummingbirds have only six, while some albatrosses may have up to forty. Field identification seldom involves reference to individual secondaries, but when it is necessary to identify them, they are numbered from the outermost inward toward the body.

The innermost secondaries are called the **tertials.** I show these on the diagram of the upperside of the spread wing, but on flying birds these are routinely hidden by the scapulars, which fan out over the base of the wing in flight. The primaries, secondaries, and tertials collectively are referred to as the flight feathers of the wing.

The bases of the flight feathers are protected by rows of feathers called coverts. These in turn have their own protection: the bases of the **greater coverts** lie beneath the **median coverts,** and above those are multiple rows of **lesser coverts.** All of these are more developed on the secondaries. The terms "greater coverts," "median coverts," and "lesser coverts" refer to those over the secondaries on the upperside of the wing. These groups of feathers can be readily distinguished on some large birds, such as gulls, when seen from above in flight.

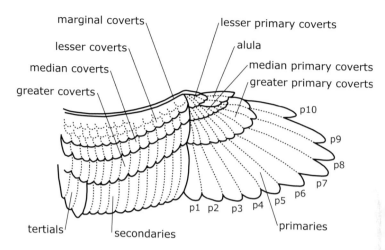

marginal coverts

lesser primary coverts

lesser coverts

alula

median coverts

median primary coverts

greater coverts

greater primary coverts

p10

p9

p8

p7

p6

p5

p1 p2 p3 p4

primaries

tertials

secondaries

Spread wing, as seen from above

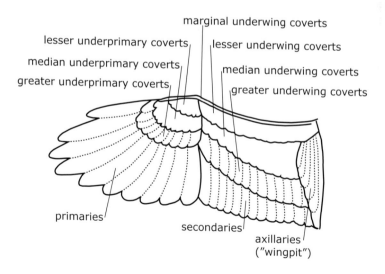

marginal underwing coverts

lesser underprimary coverts

lesser underwing coverts

median underprimary coverts

median underwing coverts

greater underprimary coverts

greater underwing coverts

primaries

secondaries

axillaries
("wingpit")

Spread wing, as seen from below

On large birds we may be able to distinguish multiple rows of primary coverts, but more typically (especially on small birds) we notice only the **greater primary coverts.** The median and lesser primary coverts are seldom visible on small birds and only occasionally noticeable on large birds. More conspicuous in this area is the **alula.** This group of feathers attaches to the bird's "thumb" and can be moved independently; it is put to use in some aerial maneuvers, such as landing. Occasionally the alula contrasts in color with the rest of the wing, but more often it is similar in color to the primary coverts.

The same groups of coverts are found on the underside of the wing as well, although they are not usually so well defined there. In referring to these coverts we specify that they are on the underwing. All of the underwing coverts and underprimary coverts taken together can be called the **wing-linings.**

The folded wing has an utterly different aspect from the open wing. On pp. 62–63 is a series of illustrations showing a wing gradually moving from completely closed to fully spread, and studying this sequence should make it easier to understand how the wing works. Basically the wing closes up so that the longest feathers, most important for control in flight, are folded underneath, against the body, and they are protected by other feathers that lie on top of them.

On the folded wing, the coverts of the secondaries are prominent. The coverts of the primaries are far less conspicuous, being largely folded out of sight. Therefore, primary coverts are labeled as such, while the term "coverts" (unmodified) is understood to mean the secondary coverts. Similarly, references to coverts and primary coverts indicate those on the upperside of the wing unless indicated otherwise. In this way, the most cumbersome terms (such as "median underprimary coverts") are reserved for the parts of the wing that we need to describe least often; and even these unwieldy terms are perfectly clear in meaning.

The greater coverts are conspicuous on the folded wings of most birds and the median coverts a little less so. The two wing bars conspicuous on each wing of many songbirds are formed by contrasting pale tips to these two sets of coverts. The lesser coverts are usually much less noticeable, partly because they are often covered by the scapulars and/or by feathers from the side of the breast. The red on a male Redwinged Blackbird is limited to the lesser coverts, and it can be very obvious (when the bird is displaying with its wings held slightly out to the sides) or completely hidden (when the wing is tucked up among the body feathers).

Distinguishing among the tertials, secondaries, and primaries on the folded wing takes some practice. The tertials may be conspicuous, and on many birds they have dark centers and sharply defined pale edges, making a prominent part of the pattern of the upperparts. On some birds, such as many sandpipers, pipits, and grassland sparrows, the tertials are very long, reaching practically to the ends of the longest primaries (and perhaps helping to protect the long flight feathers from abrasion against the grass). The rest of the flight feathers are mostly hidden on the folded wing, except for the outer edges of the secondaries and the outer edges and tips of the primaries. On many birds, these outer edges are contrastingly paler than the rest of the feather; but these pale edgings, being exposed to abrasion, are likely to be reduced as the plumage becomes older and more worn.

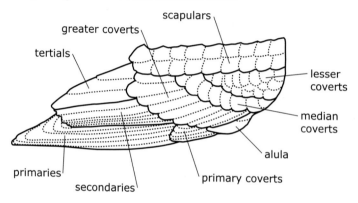

Folded wing (plus scapulars) of a typical songbird

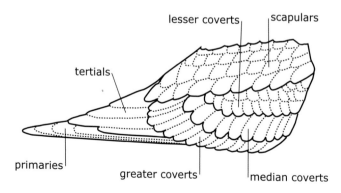

Folded wing (plus scapulars) of a typical sandpiper

MOVEMENT OF FEATHERS ON AN OPENING WING

This is the wing of a male House Finch as it appears when completely folded. At this stage, the most obvious feather groups are the greater coverts, tertials, and the tips of the primaries. Study each illustration to see how each feather group is gradually revealed as the wing spreads open.

As the wing starts to open, the secondaries begin to emerge from underneath the tertials and the primaries are appearing from underneath the secondaries. The coverts and the tertials show little change in position so far.

The basic structure of the open wing starts to be apparent here, and the primary coverts are now more clearly identifiable.

As the wing continues to open, the extent of the outer part of the wing (the primaries and the primary coverts) starts to become more obvious.

The wing is now mostly spread, and the greater coverts have only begun to spread out from their original position on the folded wing.

Here the wing is spread essentially all the way. We can see all nine primaries, all nine secondaries (six "regular" secondaries and three tertials), and corresponding sets of coverts. Even with the wing completely spread, the tertials have barely shifted from their original position; they function to protect the wing at rest, not to aid substantially in flight.

We should not expect to see all the feather groups of the upperside of the folded wing on every bird. Parts of the wing are frequently obscured by overlapping breast and scapular feathers. This overlapping tendency reaches its extreme in ducks and some other swimming birds, in which practically the entire wing may be hidden among the body plumage. Also, the relative position and prominence of various feather groups on the folded wing will vary among different bird families. The coverts make up a larger percentage of the visible wing on sandpipers than on warblers, for example, but the sandpipers in turn are more likely to have more of the coverts hidden by the large scapulars. Studying diagrams and photos of a number of different bird groups is a good way to learn the variation in wing structure.

Bill terms. Bill shapes of birds reflect their adaptations to a tremendous variety of food sources and feeding behaviors, and they are also very important in field identification. It's worthwhile to take a close look at bills, in order to be able to see their distinctive shapes and to describe their shapes and colors.

The upper mandible is also called the maxilla, the lower mandible is also simply called the mandible. For clarity and to be sure of being understood, I use the terms "upper mandible" and "lower mandible" in this book. The upper mandible is attached directly (but with slight flexibility) to the front of the skull, while the lower mandible is attached to the quadrate, a complicated lower jaw bone with a considerable range of motion. The angle between a bird's upper mandible and its forehead remains essentially constant, while the lower mandible is the one that changes angle; this can be important to know if we have a brief view of a bird with its bill open.

The top ridge of the upper mandible is called the **culmen,** and it is sometimes referred to specifically in detailed descriptions of bill shape

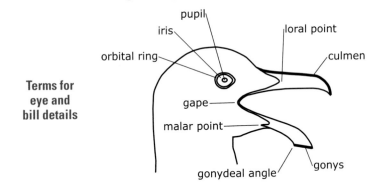

Terms for eye and bill details

or color. On the underside of the lower mandible, the ridge near the tip is called the **gonys.** It is usually not noticeable on most birds, but is obvious on a few such as gulls and terns, in which the **gonydeal angle** is an important element in bill shape.

The arrangement of feathering around the base of the bill is worth noticing and provides a significant field mark in some groups of birds, such as some waterfowl. To be able to describe the shape of this feathering, we may note how far forward the feathering extends at the **loral point** on the upper mandible or how far back the unfeathered area of the lower mandible extends at the **malar point.**

Some groups of birds have special features of the bill that are important in identification. Ducks, for example, have a nail at the tip of the upper mandible, and its shape and color can be significant. Some seabirds have a complex bill structure, and fine details of the bill may be critical for identification.

There are often slight differences in bill shape between the sexes. In many shorebirds, females on average are longer-billed than males, often noticeably so. In woodpeckers, males are often longer-billed than females. There are also age differences at times, as it may take up to a few months for the bill to reach full adult size in some birds.

Bill color often varies with season. Sometimes the difference is striking, as when the bill of Forster's Tern changes from mostly black in winter to mostly orange in summer. Often it is more subtle; many warblers, for example, have the bill slightly darker in spring than in fall.

Leg and foot terms. We commonly refer to the tarsus (also called tarsometatarsus) as the bird's "leg," but in reality this is the base of the foot. The joint labeled as the intertarsal joint on the accompanying diagram could be compared to the human ankle joint, while the tibia above that (also called tibiotarsus) is analogous to our lower leg. The bird's knee joint and upper leg (femur) are inside its body. The feathered area where the leg meets the body is labeled as the thigh, but the part of the bird analogous to the human thigh is not visible.

For purposes of field identification, there is nothing wrong with referring to the toes as the foot, and the tarsus as the leg; these terms will be easily understood by other birders. At times, though, we may have to refer specifically to the **tibia, tarsus,** and **intertarsal joint,** mainly on long-legged birds.

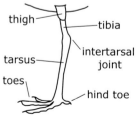

SAMPLE ILLUSTRATIONS OF BIRD TOPOGRAPHY

Illustrators' diagrams of bird topography (including my own diagrams) typically show an idealized bird in an impossibly perfect pose, showing all the feather groups and other parts to best advantage. In real life, we don't see birds that way. The following photographs and their accompanying labeled diagrams are intended to give a practical idea of how these feather groups might look in the field.

Purple Finch, adult male. Birds at the feeder offer fine opportunities for close-up studies of bird topography.

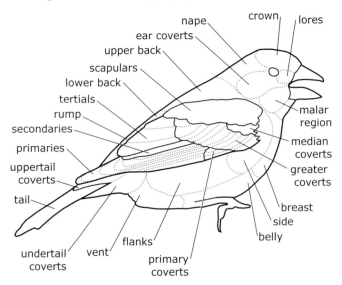

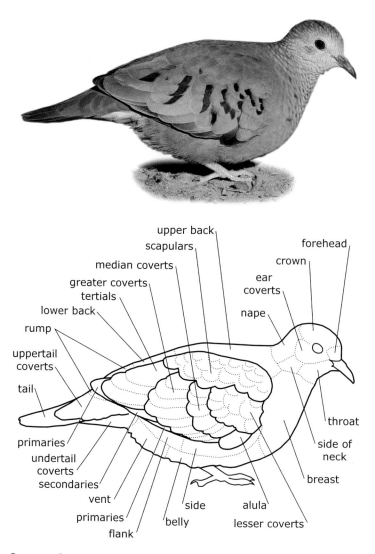

Common Ground-Dove, male. This species lacks the black marks on the scapulars shown by the Ruddy Ground-Dove, but this is useful only if we can distinguish scapulars from coverts. Common Ground-Dove has bright rufous on the primaries, but that is completely hidden here, as we can see just the tips and a bit of the edges of the primaries.

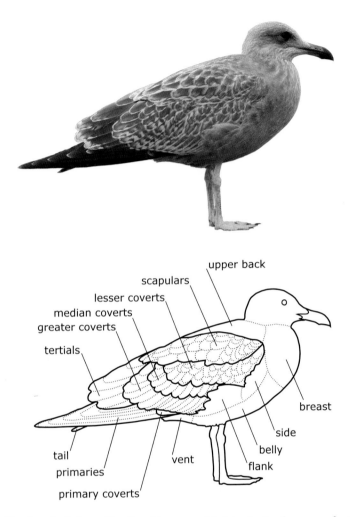

Herring Gull, juvenile. On this young bird in fresh plumage, photographed in August, the feathers of the wing and scapulars all have pale fringes, making it relatively easy to pick out the different groups of feathers. Note that the scapulars, coverts, and tertials make up a major percentage of the visible area of the bird. Note also that the feathers of the sides and flanks are covering the front of the wing and hiding many of the coverts.

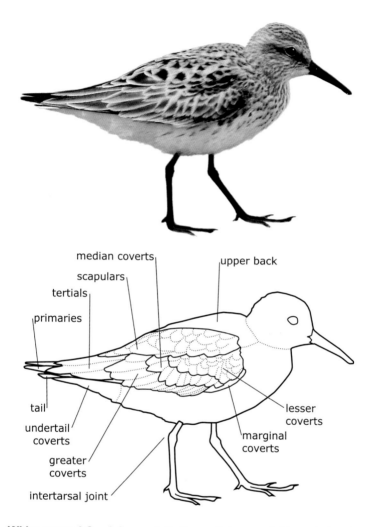

White-rumped Sandpiper, adult. One well-known field mark for this species is the fact that the tips of the primaries extend beyond the tip of the tail, but this has limited value for the observer unless we can recognize the primaries and tail. On this bird we can actually see the tips of the primaries of both wings, with the tail barely visible below them. As with most shorebirds, the tertials and coverts make up a major part of the visible part of the wing when the wing is folded, and here the secondaries are not visible at all.

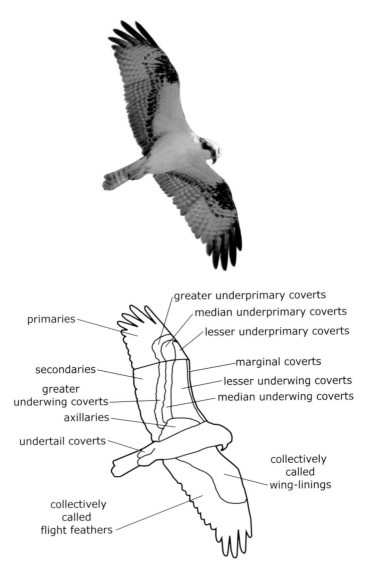

Osprey. Looking at the bird in flight overhead, we can make out some groups of feathers on its wings; however, the division between median and lesser underwing coverts is somewhat vague, and the division between greater, median, and lesser underprimary coverts is more so.

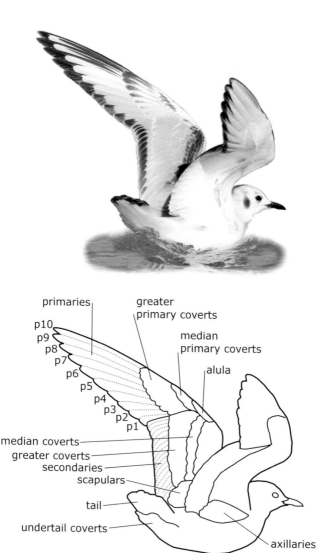

Bonaparte's Gull, first-cycle immature. The various groups of coverts can be discerned on the upperside of the wing, but the distinctions are obscure on the underside. As this bird pauses on the water with its wings raised, the markings of individual primaries (numbered here) could be determined by a practiced observer.

American Wigeon, male. This duck has a huge white patch on the secondary coverts on the upperside of the wing, but only a sliver of the white shows here between the scapulars and the feathers of the underparts (and with a slight shift of position, this white could be hidden). The only obvious parts of the wing are the ornate tertials, plus the wingtips (primary tips) of both wings. On the underparts, the division between the side and the flank is arbitrary. Behind the flank, feathers of the femoral tract are evident here (and on many ducks) but seldom noticed on most birds. With the head and neck hunched down into the body plumage, the breast feathers appear to practically encircle the neck; this tract of feathers would be shifted forward if the bird were alert, with head raised.

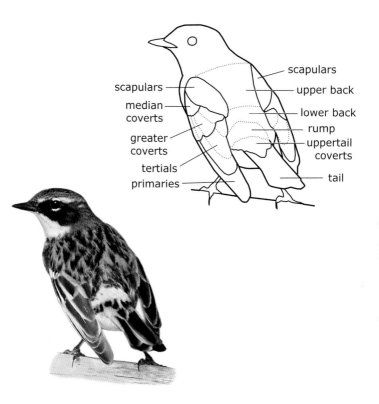

scapulars

scapulars — upper back

median coverts — lower back

greater coverts — rump

— uppertail coverts

tertials

primaries

tail

Yellow-rumped Warbler, adult male in spring. Seen from this angle, the bird demonstrates that it is well named: the yellow really is on the rump, while the uppertail coverts are gray with black centers. Looking at the bird from the back like this, with its wings drooped at the moment, we don't notice much about the wings except for the prominent tertials and primary tips. If the wings were folded neatly, with the wingtips crossed just above the base of the tail, the yellow rump patch would be mostly or completely hidden.

4. PLUMAGES, MOLT, AND WEAR: UNDERSTANDING WHAT YOU SEE

Feathers, as noted in the previous chapter, are marvels of flexible, lightweight strength, providing birds with insulation, decoration, and extended surfaces for flight. But they do wear out eventually and have to be replaced. These processes — the gradual wear on the feathers, and their replacement, or molt — have major effects on what a bird looks like at any given time. As a result, they also have a major effect on our attempts to identify birds.

Molt and plumage sequences are complex subjects, worthy of entire books of their own, but in this chapter I will just discuss them from the standpoint of a field observer.

MOLT STRATEGIES AND THE TERMINOLOGIES WE USE FOR THEM

It's important to begin by understanding that there is nothing random about molt in wild birds. Growing new feathers is a physical process that burns up energy, and shedding old feathers can cause a temporary reduction, however slight, in the bird's protective covering or its ability to fly. These slight disadvantages have to be balanced against the advantages of having new feathers. Of course, none of this involves any conscious decision on the part of the individual bird. But it's safe to assume that the frequency, timing, and extent of molt for each species (or even different populations of the same species) have been shaped by natural selection operating on them in the past. What we could refer to as their "strategies" of molt must have somehow increased their chance of survival and their chance of breeding successfully.

Since birds have so many different lifestyles, there are many different molt strategies. As a general rule, since molt burns up energy, most birds are not in active molt at the same time that they are actively migrating or caring for young (but there are exceptions). Most birds molt the flight feathers of the wings and tail a few at a time, maintaining their ability to fly, but in some groups the flight feathers are molted simultaneously and the birds are flightless for a few weeks until the feathers grow back. Most smaller birds replace each of their feathers at least once per year, but there are exceptions; and some very large birds may retain some of the largest flight feathers of the wings for two or three years or even longer, replacing just a few of them each year.

Trying to fit all of these diverse molt strategies into a cohesive system of definitions has been an absorbing challenge for some ornithologists. Recent breakthroughs in understanding of molt have given us a set of terms and definitions that should be applicable to all birds. In this book I provide only a simplified overview of molt and plumage sequences, focusing on the ways that these can affect field identification.

One thing to keep in mind is that it is harder to learn the terminology than it is to understand the outline of what is actually going on with the plumage. For example, it can be confusing to consider that an individual Red-tailed Hawk may be exhibiting either a Simple Basic Strategy or a Complex Basic Strategy in molt, depending on whether or not it molts some body feathers during its first winter. But for purposes of field identification, it is more important to understand that a Red-tailed Hawk will wear essentially all the same feathers from the time it leaves the nest until sometime the following spring, and then begin a major but gradual molt that will be completed sometime in early fall, so that we can expect to see young Red-taileds with all-brown tails throughout the winter season and into spring.

In order to communicate about molt and plumages at all, however, we have to have a few terms defined and understood.

A century ago, discussions of plumages gave them names tied to times of year (such as summer plumage and winter plumage) or to the breeding cyle (such as breeding and nonbreeding plumages). Seasonal names worked well for limited areas of study in the north temperate zone. But when applied to birds in more tropical areas, or to birds that migrated across the equator, that system broke down; some birds were molting into "summer plumages" in late fall, or wearing "winter plumage" during the southern hemisphere summer. Names associated with breeding cycle also raised problems: some birds remained in the same plumage all year, whether breeding or not; and many female ducks were actively nesting and caring for young after molting into a so-called "nonbreeding plumage."

Under some systems, this female Ring-necked Duck would be said to be in "breeding plumage" in midwinter, molting into "nonbreeding plumage" before the start of nesting season in spring.

Bird banders in North America have long used a system based on calendar years, identifying a young bird as Hatching Year (HY) and

After Hatching Year (AHY), or invoking Second Year, Third Year, etc., where these plumages could be separated. Again, this system runs into trouble in warm climates, where a bird hatched December 31 might be classified in a different age cohort from one hatched the next day.

Today, most serious students of field ID in North America use a set of terms and definitions based on the Humphrey-Parkes system. Introduced by Philip Humphrey and Ken Parkes in 1959, this system (often abbreviated as H-P) ignores external factors such as seasons, breeding status, and calendar years, and focuses on the plumages and molts themselves, finding common patterns that apply across all bird groups. Recent refinements of the system by Steve N. G. Howell, Peter Pyle, Chris Corben, and others have given us a terminology that seems to encompass every variation in molt strategies.

Many field guides, including some aimed at experienced birders, avoid the use of the Humphrey-Parkes terminology, and with good reason. The terminology is somewhat confusing and becomes more so when it is misused, which often happens when birders try to apply it without fully understanding it. Even if we understand the system completely, often we can't apply it to what we see in the field — we can't necessarily tell what plumage a bird is in just by looking at it.

In practice, then, I recommend learning the modified Humphrey-Parkes system, because it's the best way to understand what is going on, but I don't necessarily recommend trying to apply that terminology in the field. In many cases there are more general terms that are just as informative and safer to use. Without knowing whether a particular bird has molted certain feathers, we may not be able to say whether it is in first basic plumage or formative plumage, but a more general term like "first-winter" or "first-cycle" may be perfectly appropriate.

This Western Gull seen in January is in its second annual cycle. To say whether it is in second basic or second alternate plumage would be tricky and not very helpful. It probably completed the prebasic molt around October, but prealternate molt may have begun even before the prebasic was completed. Calling this bird "second-cycle" might seem less precise but it is more accurate.

PLUMAGES AND THE MOLTS THAT PRODUCE THEM

In this section I will discuss the plumages and their associated molts first, and then give examples of species with different molt strategies in order to illustrate how these plumages fit into the annual cycles of birds.

Basic plumage is well named. This is the one plumage shared by all bird species. A bird that goes through only one molt per year will always be in basic plumage. This plumage is produced by the **prebasic molt.** Prebasic molt typically is complete — that is, it involves replacement of all the feathers — but may be incomplete in many large birds that do not replace all of the large flight feathers of the wings every year. Timing of prebasic molt varies among species, but for many in North America it occurs in late summer or fall, after the nesting season and either before or after fall migration.

The Green Jay has only one molt cycle per year as an adult, so it is always in basic plumage. Brightness of color is no criterion for basic vs. alternate.

Alternate plumage is also logically named. Many birds have a second plumage during each annual cycle, alternating with the basic plumage. This alternate plumage is acquired during the **prealternate molt.** Unlike the prebasic molt, prealternate is seldom complete — only a very few species are known to go through a complete molt twice a year. Typically the prealternate molt replaces a certain percentage of the head and body feathers, and may also involve coverts on the wing, but it rarely includes the large flight feathers of the wings and tail.

Sometimes the effects of the prealternate molt are obvious, as when the male Indigo Bunting molts from the mostly brown basic plumage of winter to the bright blue alternate plumage of summer; but in other cases the basic and alternate plumages are colored and patterned essentially the same, so the change is not noticeable. In many species that show seasonal change, the alternate plumage is the more brightly colored "breeding" or "summer" plumage, but this is not always the case. In most ducks, the basic plumage, acquired in fall, is the more brightly colored "breeding" plumage, and the ducks are pairing up on the wintering grounds while in this plumage. They molt into a duller alternate plumage in spring (females) or early summer (males), and the females are actively caring for young while in this plumage.

Many bird species take more than one year to reach their definitive basic plumage and definitive alternate plumage, the technical terms for "adult" plumage. Before they reach that stage, they may go through stages such as first alternate plumage, second basic plumage, and so on. The molts in which they acquire these have names to match, such as first prealternate molt or second prebasic molt. When there are no longer changes with age, we can call their molts the definitive prebasic molt and definitive prealternate molt.

Juvenile plumage is often very distinctive and easily recognized in the field, although the terminology for it has been quite confusing! This is the first coat of feathers that a bird wears, generally the plumage in which it fledges. For the last century, ornithologists in North America have mostly spelled this term "juvenal," applied only to the plumage and not the bird itself, so that a juvenile bird was said to be in juvenal plumage. European ornithologists, meanwhile, have simply used the spelling "juvenile" for both meanings, and this has not hampered their understanding of the subject. Some American experts insist that the separate spelling for the plumage is necessary, pointing out that the term "juvenile" is often misused for any bird that is not an adult. This is true, but I think that a better response is to insist on correct use of the word. "Juvenile" does not mean the same thing as "immature" or "subadult," and it should be used only for birds that are still wearing their first coat of feathers. In this book I drop the "-al" ending and refer to both the bird and its plumage with the spelling "juvenile."

Putting aside the spelling issue, this first plumage often looks quite different from any later plumage of the species. Examples are legion: Juvenile shorebirds often have crisp pale edges on the scapulars and coverts, even if adults are plain and unmarked there. Songbirds that are plain-breasted as adults are often streaked or spotted below in juvenile plumage; many that have plain wings as adults will show narrow wing bars in juvenile plumage. Even when the juvenile is colored and patterned like the adult, the juvenile body plumage is often somewhat

juvenile American Robin

looser and softer, especially in some areas such as the undertail coverts. In small birds, the juvenile plumage may be held only very briefly before it begins to be replaced in the next partial molt, while some larger birds are in juvenile plumage for nearly a full year. But because the pattern is so often different, birders need to be aware of the existence of juvenile plumage to avoid being mystified by these young birds.

What happens after juvenile plumage? This is where things get tricky. Because this plumage is so distinctive in many birds, it was long considered to be a unique plumage stage of young birds. Many small birds, after wearing juvenile plumage for a few weeks, molt into a "first-winter" plumage that looks very much like basic plumage of adults. It was long considered that these birds were undergoing a prebasic molt and molting into first basic plumage. However, work by Steve Howell and others has demonstrated otherwise. Despite appearances, the juvenile plumage is itself the first basic plumage — after all, it is acquired by a complete molt, or the growing of a complete set of feathers, like the prebasic molts of older birds. If the young bird then has a partial molt into a different plumage for its first winter, it is this inserted first-winter plumage, not the different-looking juvenile plumage, that is the unique part of the first annual cycle.

Formative plumage is the term now used for this unique "first-winter" plumage that follows juvenile plumage in many birds. As you might expect, the molt that produces it is called the **preformative molt,** and it is usually an incomplete molt. Its extent varies by species and often by individual as well, with the bird replacing a variable percentage of the head and body feathers but usually not the flight feathers of the wings or tail. Of course, many birds do not have a formative plumage; they remain in juvenile plumage until they begin their first prealternate molt into their first alternate plumage, or they hold the plumage for close to a year and then have a complete prebasic molt. There are also cases in which it's hard to say whether the bird has a formative plumage or not. When the bird remains in juvenile plumage into late fall or early winter and then begins a partial molt, it may be a matter of opinion whether this molt should be considered preformative or prealternate. Cases like this help to indicate why birders shouldn't get too hung up on trying to assign plumage classes to birds that we see in the field. It's more important to understand the essentials of what's going on than it is to put labels on things.

A **supplemental plumage** may occur in the annual cycles of some birds, acquired through an extra **presupplemental molt**, so that some body feathers may be replaced three times in the course of a year. When these occur at all, their timing varies among species. An extra molt during a bird's first annual cycle, before the preformative molt, might be considered another presupplemental molt producing another supplemental plumage, although the term auxiliary preformative molt has also been used. In most cases these extra plumages are not well understood, and they usually do not create enough difference to be noticeable in the field, so for the most part, birders can ignore them. One exception involves the ptarmigan, which may show three distinct appearances (and intermediate stages between them) during the annual cycle because of the inserted supplemental plumage.

The terms defined above should cover all the plumages and all the molts possible for every bird. In the next section I'll illustrate how these plumages and molts fit into the lifestyles of various species.

It's important to note that a bird's appearance can change without it having acquired a new plumage. We might think of the European Starling as showing a "winter plumage" heavily speckled with white and buff, and a "breeding plumage" that is mostly glossy black with colorful iridescence, but in fact there is no molt separating these stages. What happens is that the head and body feathers in basic plumage have extensive white or buff tips, and as these wear away in late winter and early spring, more of the underlying glossy black is revealed. We might say that this "strategy" gives the bird the advantages of a slightly more camouflaged appearance in winter and a more flashy appearance for the breeding season, without the energy drain of a prealternate molt. Something similar happens with some other birds; for example, the male Snow Bunting acquires its snappy white and black pattern of summer without a molt, by the wearing away of the brown and buff and gray feather edgings that make the pattern look more muted in winter.

MOLT STRATEGIES IN THE LIVES OF BIRDS

Simple Basic Strategy: This is the molt strategy in which the bird has only one molt per year, a more or less complete prebasic molt, and in which there is no formative plumage during the first annual cycle. This strategy occurs only in a few groups of large birds. For the bird to successfully skip the formative plumage and wear its juvenile (= first basic) plumage for essentially its first year of life, that juvenile plumage has to be strong and well developed, not soft and loose like the briefly held juvenile plumage of some songbirds.

Simple Basic Strategy describes the molt of the Barn Owl. It may go through two generations of natal down before it leaves the nest, but once it fledges, it wears essentially the same feathers until the next prebasic molt. As an older bird it may molt some head and body feathers at any season, but its main molt is usually in summer and early fall, on the nesting grounds. Like many large birds, it generally does not molt all the primaries in every annual cycle, so the wings may have flight feathers grown in different years.

Complex Basic Strategy: This is a common pattern in which the adults have only one molt per annual cycle and are always in basic plumage, and it is called "complex" because there is a formative plumage inserted in the first cycle. A wide variety of birds, from geese to House Sparrows, exhibit this molt strategy.

juvenile   formative   adult male
                                      basic

Complex Basic Strategy, as illustrated by Cedar Waxwing. Its juvenile plumage is distinctly different from later plumages, but it does not last long; by late fall the bird has molted into a formative plumage that is quite similar to the basic plumage of adults. In molting from juvenile to formative plumage, it does not replace the feathers of the wings or tail, so those may become fairly worn before the time of the next molt. Thereafter it has just one prebasic molt per annual cycle. This prebasic molt occurs in fall, and it generally takes place after the birds leave the breeding grounds (because of their nomadic nature, it may be hard to say that waxwings ever settle in on wintering grounds).

Simple Alternate Strategy: In this strategy, adults have basic and alternate plumages in every annual cycle. It is called "simple" because only one plumage is inserted into the first cycle, between the time of fledging and the next prebasic molt. This inserted plumage may be either formative or alternate, or it may be difficult to tell which it represents, but the point is that the bird does not have both a preformative and a prealternate molt before the time of the next prebasic molt. This strategy is uncommon and is found mostly in some large waterbirds.

juvenile

first
alternate
plumage

adult
alternate
plumage

Simple Alternate Strategy in the molt of White-faced Ibis. The bird is in full juvenile plumage for only a month or two before beginning a protracted molt that seems to combine elements of a preformative and prealternate molt; this results in gradual replacement of many body feathers from fall to spring. The first-cycle bird shown here (center), photographed in May, could be considered to be in formative or first alternate plumage; the dull sheen on the upperparts and the streaked neck in late spring indicate that it is not an adult. In its second cycle (not shown), it goes through prebasic molt in summer and early fall and a prealternate molt in early spring, producing basic and alternate plumages that are variably duller than those of full adults. In adults, the prebasic molt occurs mainly in early fall, and it is complete or nearly complete; their prealternate molt in early spring involves most of the head and body plumage and some lesser coverts.

Complex Alternate Strategy: This is the system in which the adults have basic and alternate plumages in each annual cycle and in which there is an additional plumage, generally the formative plumage, added in to the first cycle. Despite what the name might suggest, this is much more common than the Simple Alternate Strategy, and the "simple" probably evolved from the "complex" through loss of one of the molts in the first plumage cycle. Complex Alternate Strategy applies to most species that have distinctly different "breeding" and "winter" plumages, as well as to many in which basic and alternate plumages are not obviously different. The majority of these, especially among the songbirds, have an extra (formative) plumage inserted in the first annual cycle, hence the name "Complex."

adult male in basic plumage (December)

adult male in prealternate molt (March)

adult male in alternate plumage (June)

juvenile (September)

Complex Alternate Strategy in the molt of American Goldfinch. Adults have basic and alternate plumages in every annual cycle, and in this species the difference between basic and alternate is strikingly obvious, especially in males. The prebasic molt occurs in fall, with all the feathers replaced, so birds are in very fresh basic plumage in early winter. The adult male has rather plain-colored body plumage in basic, but its wings have broad wing bars, and the bright yellow on the lesser coverts separates the adult male from females and young males at this season. The prealternate molt begins in early spring, and this molt involves mostly the head and body feathers, not the tail or wing feathers (although occasionally a couple of the innermost greater coverts are replaced). In full alternate plumage in early summer, the male's head and body feathers are brightly colored, but the wings show the effects of wear, with the wing bars and other white feather edges much reduced. By late summer and early fall, the adults will be looking quite worn; at that season the juveniles stand out because their plumage is so fresh, with very broad buff wing bars and tertial edges. During the fall, the juveniles will go through a preformative molt, replacing much of the body plumage and some of the coverts in the wing, and in their formative plumage they will look similar to adults in basic plumage. The addition of this formative plumage in the first annual cycle is the reason why this molt strategy is called "complex" rather than "simple." This is a common molt pattern, occurring in many species, although it does not result in such dramatic color changes in most.

As mentioned earlier, some birds exhibiting Complex Alternate Strategy have an additional plumage inserted in the annual cycle. This phenomenon of the supplemental plumage and presupplemental molt seems to be relatively rare. When it does occur, the timing varies among species. With the notable exception of male ptarmigan, it usually does not create a difference that would be obvious in the field.

male Willow
Ptarmigan in May

Willow Ptarmigan is among the few bird species to have three plumages and three molts per annual cycle as an adult. Furthermore, the molts of males and females are significantly different in timing. In basic plumage (winter), both sexes have all-white feathering except for the black tail. Starting in early spring, the male has a presupplemental molt involving mainly the head, neck, and upperparts, producing the white-bodied, rufous-headed supplemental plumage shown here. The male wears this supplemental plumage until midsummer, then has a prealternate molt of head and body feathers, producing a mostly mottled brown alternate plumage worn in late summer and early fall, until the time of the prebasic molt in fall. Meanwhile, the female molts from white basic plumage to mottled brown alternate plumage in late spring, making her much less conspicuous than the male in early summer. The female's presupplemental molt of a few head and body feathers occurs in late summer, and then her prebasic molt into the white basic plumage of winter occurs in fall.

MOLT OF FLIGHT FEATHERS

The molt of head and body feathers is often hard to notice except when the incoming feathers are a distinctly different color from the old ones. Even when we can see its effects, it often looks somewhat patchy and irregular. But the molt of the flight feathers can be much more obvious, especially on large birds, since it will change the apparent shape of the wings and tail when some feathers are missing. Furthermore, any such gaps in the wings or tail can affect the birds' ability to fly, so they cannot afford to have an irregular or patchy molt of these flight feathers. Normal molt of the primaries, secondaries, tertials, and tail feathers will usually follow a fairly precise sequence in each species and generally will be symmetrical, so that gaps on one side are matched to gaps on the other side.

One simple but extreme approach is synchronous molt, in which all the large flight feathers are dropped at about the same time and they all grow back in together over a period of a few weeks. Among North American birds, the best-known examples include the ducks, geese, and swans, which drop all of their primaries and secondaries, and the associated coverts, in late summer. After those replacement feathers have mostly grown in, the birds molt the tertials and tail feathers, along with the body plumage. Other North American birds with synchronous molt of the flight feathers include loons, grebes, coots, gallinules, rails, many alcids, and the Anhinga. These are all water birds (or marsh birds) that can survive a flightless period of several weeks as long as they are in a habitat with enough food and enough space to evade predators. Most of them go through this flightless stage in late summer, when food is abundant.

This adult Bonaparte's Gull in September shows the normal progression of molt. The primaries molt from the inner-most outward, and all of its inner primaries already have been replaced, looking fresh and smooth-edged. The outermost primary (p10) is still the old one from the previous year's molt. Next to that, p9 is just begin-ning to grow, and its rounded black tip can be seen through the translucent white inner vane of p10. The next primary inward, p8, is almost full-grown, and the rest appear to be full-grown. Probably within a week or two, when p9 is mostly grown, that outermost primary on each wing will drop out and its replacement will begin to grow. Most of the outer secondaries are missing on this bird; the remaining ones are probably old feathers that will be replaced also.

Most birds maintain the ability to fly during molt by replacing the flight feathers one at a time. Although there are exceptions, in the majority of species the primaries molt from the innermost outward. The innermost (p1) is dropped from both wings at about the same time, and when its replacement is partly grown, p2 is dropped, and so on. It is easy to see this process on the wings of gulls in flight, with some one-year-old birds starting to molt the innermost primaries as early as late spring, adults mostly starting in mid- to late summer. For a gull, replacement of all the primaries, one by one, can take two to four months or even longer, with the larger species taking more time.

In addition to this "standard" pattern of molting primaries from the innermost outward, there are other patterns shown by certain species. These include some in which the molt begins in the middle of the primaries and proceeds in both directions, and some in which the molt begins at two different points among the primaries at the same time.

Molt of the secondaries usually starts later than primary molt. The typical pattern among most small and medium-sized birds is that the tertials molt first, starting about the same time as the innermost primaries. After the new tertials are grown (and the primary molt is well along in its process), the secondaries begin to molt, starting with the outermost and proceeding inward toward the body, the opposite direction from the primaries. The process can be more variable in large birds: their secondary molt can start at two points at once and can proceed in either direction, and they may drop multiple secondaries at the same time. Looking at a molting large bird in flight, the gaps in its secondaries may look more irregular than those in the primaries.

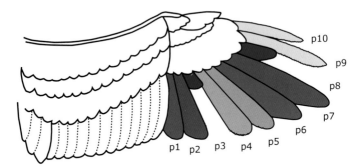

A simplified diagram of *Staffelmauser,* or staggered molt, in the primaries of a large bird. Darkest shades of blue represent the newest and freshest feathers, while the paler blues represent older generations of feathers. See the text for more details.

In some very large or long-winged birds, each primary grows so slowly that the bird replaces only a few of them in each annual cycle. In these cases, after two or three years, the bird may start a second "wave" of molt in the primaries. To give an example, when p6 is being replaced for the first time, the bird might also replace p1 for a second time, and the molt might proceed outward from there. A few months later, the bird might have p1, p2, p6, and p7 quite fresh, and gaps where the replacements for p3 and p8 are just beginning to grow. Meanwhile, p4 and p5 may look moderately worn since they are still retained from the previous year, and p9 and p10 may look very worn since they are retained from two years earlier. This kind of molt can produce three or four or even five generations of feathers among the primaries of a very large bird, and the difference in freshness of the feathers might be noticeable, especially if the oldest retained primaries are from juvenile plumage and have a different pattern. This "stepwise" or "staggered" molt is often known by the German term "*Staffelmauser*." (German ornithologists have given us some great words, like *Staffelmauser* and *Zugunruhe,* that we can use to impress our nonbirding friends.)

Molt of the tail feathers is more variable among species. In many small birds the central tail feathers are molted first and then the replacement of feathers proceeds outward, but there are some in which the molt begins with the outermost feathers and moves inward. In others, the molt is staggered, with pairs of rectrices between the innermost and outermost being replaced in an irregular sequence.

EFFECTS OF WEAR ON THE PLUMAGE

If we put a feather in a protected spot, away from sunlight and any source of abrasion, it might look unchanged for decades, or even centuries. But a feather attached to a live bird in the wild will be subject to many kinds of wear and tear, and its appearance will gradually change over time. Most such change will be slight and subtle, but ultimately the wear on the individual feathers can change the overall appearance of the bird.

Various effects of wear are discussed in Chapter 2, Principles and Pitfalls of Identification, under Consider the Condition of the Bird's Plumage (p. 24). Some of the most obvious effects involve white or pale markings on the edges or tips of dark feathers. These pale areas often are not as structurally strong as the parts of the feather that contain more melanin, so they may wear away faster. For this reason, markings like white wing bars and white outer edges to tail feathers will be broadest and most obvious when the plumage is fresh, becoming obscure or even absent when the plumage is very worn.

Fading or "bleaching" of the plumage is also a big factor for some birds, especially gulls in their first plumage cycle. Some gulls that are mostly mottled brown in their first winter may have the coverts on the wing bleached to white by the time of their first summer. This may be more pronounced and may proceed more rapidly in climates where there is more winter sunshine.

Many gulls have black on the wingtips, and the melanin apparently helps to strengthen the feathers. On these examples of fresh and worn outer primaries of gulls, notice how the white areas of the feathers tend to wear away much faster than the black areas.

The effects of fading are not the same on all feather colors. Many birds show no obvious color change after many months wearing the same plumage. Some birds even get brighter. For example, the red areas on the male House Finch may be a relatively soft rose-red when the plumage is fresh, but after many months in the sun, the same feathers may turn a brighter scarlet.

Vesper Sparrow has only one molt per year as an adult, a prebasic molt in late summer or early fall. Birds seen in late fall, like the one at left, have a clean look, with distinct wing bars and pale edges on the feathers of the upperparts. Six or seven months later, in early summer, when they are still wearing the same feathers, Vesper Sparrows like the one at right do not look so crisp. This bird's wing bars are mostly worn away and its overall pattern is more muted. By midsummer, just before the molt begins, it may look even more drab than this. With experience, the difference between fresh and worn plumage becomes obvious at a glance.

Finally, as mentioned above for European Starling and Snow Bunting, plumage wear does not always make birds look bad. In some species, the bright "breeding plumage" is achieved without molt, by the wearing away of dull feather tips to unveil the brighter pattern below.

NORMAL MOLT VS. ACCIDENTAL FEATHER LOSS

Every feather grows from a specialized pocket of skin cells called a follicle. In the process of normal molt, the new feather begins to develop in the follicle, and as it grows, it pushes out the old feather; so by the time the old feather is lost, its replacement is ready to emerge.

At times, however, a feather will be lost through some accident. If the follicle has not been damaged, ordinarily a new feather will soon start to grow. However, the new feather may not look like the one it is replacing, or like the feathers around it. Depending on the bird's hormonal state, it may grow a brightly colored "breeding plumage" feather even if the rest of the bird is in dull plumage. If the feather is being grown at a season when food is scarce, or if the bird is under some other kind of stress, the feather may be oddly colored, pale, or dull.

MOLT AS IT RELATES TO MIGRATION

For birds that are nonmigratory, and that live where food is always abundant, timing of the molt may not be critical. But migratory birds have to fit the energy demands of molting in among the other major events in their lives, including migration, raising young, and surviving periods when resources are scarce. Birds have developed a variety of different approaches to fitting the molt(s) into the annual cycle.

For the majority of North American birds, the prebasic molt occurs in late summer or fall, after the breeding season. Some migratory species undergo this molt before their fall migration, before they leave the vicinity of the breeding grounds; some others go through this molt after fall migration, on the wintering grounds. Different approaches may apply even to closely related species. For example, among some very similar small flycatchers, Hammond's goes through the prebasic molt before it leaves the breeding grounds, while Dusky and Gray flycatchers molt mainly on the wintering grounds; Acadian Flycatcher molts on the breeding grounds, while Willow and Alder flycatchers molt on the wintering grounds. These differences in timing create some differences in the relative condition of the plumage, fresh vs. worn, that can have an impact on identification in some cases.

However, molting before or after fall migration are not the only two possibilities. There are some migratory birds that begin the molt on the breeding grounds, then suspend molt while they migrate, resuming and completing the process after they arrive on the wintering grounds. There are also some birds, mainly large ones with a long slow process of molt, that continue the molt of the large flight feathers even as they migrate. Some Cooper's Hawks molting the flight feathers are seen during fall migration. Swainson's Hawks and Broad-winged Hawks, long-distance migrants among the raptors, rarely molt during fall migration, but one-year-old birds in spring may begin their prebasic molt of some inner primaries while they are still migrating north. Some raptors also continue the slow process of replacing their flight feathers during the time that they are actively raising young.

One of the most intriguing approaches, at least for birders who are interested in distribution, involves a "molt migration." Some birds will travel to a region removed from both the breeding grounds and the wintering grounds in order to go through their prebasic molt. The best-known examples involve many waterfowl that will become flightless for a period of weeks during wing molt. Male Canvasbacks, for example, leave the immediate nesting area about the time that females begin to incubate, and after a few days they may fly a long distance to large shallow lakes where they will remain for up to three months or more while they go through their molt. These staging areas may be hundreds of miles north of the breeding areas in some cases.

Photographed in southeast Arizona in August, this Western Kingbird is in active molt. Contrast is obvious in the wings, where the median coverts are old but the greater coverts (and the inner primary coverts) look fresh. The inner three primaries are new, and the fourth is just growing, while the remaining outer primaries are old and worn. Molt also appears to be in process on the tail, where the central tail feathers look fresher than the others. The patchy appearance of the head and back suggest that these areas are molting as well. Flocks of Western Kingbirds are common in the southern Arizona lowlands during late summer, probably taking advantage of the abundant insect life after the onset of the summer rains.

Another kind of molt migration involves many adult songbirds in the West that leave their breeding areas in July, shortly after their young become independent, and fly to the region of southeastern Arizona and northern Sonora. While many areas of the western U.S. dry out in late summer, southeastern Arizona has a summer rainy season commencing in July, and the lowlands there are actually at their greenest in August. Insect life and other wild bird food becomes abundant at that season. Various species, including Lazuli Bunting, Bullock's Oriole, Western Tanager, and Black-headed Grosbeak, appear in large numbers in areas where they had not nested, and many of these birds apparently are staging in this area while they go through at least part of their prebasic molt (adults) or preformative molt (young birds).

When we see a bird with a patchy mix of colors, like this young male Summer Tanager, we may be tempted to say that "it's molting." But in this case, it almost certainly isn't. The wing shows a mix of yellow-green feathers and slightly fresher red feathers, but there are no gaps and no partially grown feathers. Photographed during migration in late April, this bird probably had gone through a partial prealternate molt in late winter or early spring. Now in its first alternate plumage, it probably will look like this until late summer, when it begins its prebasic molt.

5. BEHAVIOR AND VOICE: UNDERSTANDING AND USING THEM IN IDENTIFICATION

Picture this scene. We are out on the high plains of west Texas on a cold winter day. Crossing the grasslands, we come to a stretch that looks heavily grazed, with short grass and much bare soil, and it is here that we see a flock of small birds flush from the ground ahead of us. A couple of dozen compact, chunky birds, looking pale overall, fly up high and circle widely over the flats, sticking fairly close together. When they circle near us, we can hear soft rasping and metallic notes coming from the flock. Without hesitation, we identify these birds: McCown's Longspurs.

In this case we have not seen a single thing that could be regarded as a traditional field mark, yet our identification is undoubtedly correct. It is based on solid criteria of season, habitat, behavior, and voice. Field guides and other identification books seldom put much emphasis on these points — they are more likely to focus on shape, color, and markings, and they do so with good reason: the latter points are much easier to describe and illustrate. This book, likewise, is mostly devoted to things that can be communicated effectively in book form. But in this chapter I want to talk about those ID criteria that could be grouped loosely under the heading of "things that can't be shown in a picture of the bird."

A fascinating reference work on this subject is *Pete Dunne's Essential Field Guide Companion.* That boldly conceived book has almost no pictures at all — except for Dunne's evocative word pictures of the behavior of every North American bird. It could serve admirably as a supplement to any other field guide, filling in the other half of the story, the half that can't be conveyed in pictures. I know of no other reference that gives such species-by-species information in such accessible form. In this chapter I am giving only a brief overview of these kinds of ID features that can't be illustrated.

HABITAT AND MICROHABITAT

When an experienced birder glimpses a bird and names it instantly, it's probable that the bird's habitat (and its location within the habitat) contributed to the speedy identification. Often this happens at a completely subconscious level, and if asked, the birder might have to think about it for a minute to be able to describe what she or he noticed about habitat clues. But especially when we're in familiar territory, clues of this type provide a major part of our initial impressions of birds.

It can be hard to tease out the habitat aspect because it is so intertwined with other clues. For example, if we're out in midwinter in the midwest, going past a hedgerow through open weedy fields, and a little flock of small slim birds flushes from low in the bushes and flies low along the hedgerow, we might quickly call them American Tree Sparrows. In this case, the time of year, the size and shape of the birds, and the fact that they're in a small flock are all contributing to our impression of what they are. But we would not name them so quickly if we encountered the same flock in the middle of a dense forest, because Tree Sparrows, despite their name, tend to be in more open areas. So the habitat is among several puzzle pieces that fall into place at the same instant.

We may be more clearly reminded of habitat's importance when we're confronted with a bird that's not in its expected surroundings. Some friends and I once saw a Pied-billed Grebe flying over the desert, and we were in utter consternation for a minute until we figured out what it was. We all agreed that it was the unfamiliar setting that had us confused; we had seen grebes flying earlier that week — in a place where we expected them, over a marshy lake — and we had recognized them right away.

We can learn to use habitat more effectively as a clue for identifying birds, and even for finding specific birds. Part of this involves making a conscious effort to look at the surroundings of birds after we've identified them. If we've found a Bell's Vireo, for example, and have seen it and heard its distinctive song, our next move should be to step back and see what's around it. What habitat is the bird using? This is a species that occurs in various settings, including streamside groves of willows and mesquites in the southwest, thickets of sand plum on the southern Great Plains, and the edges of second-growth woods in the upper midwest. Even though the plant species are different, these places are similar in having dense low cover. The birds evidently key in on the structure of the habitat, and we can learn to do the same.

It can be a major advantage in birding if you can recognize the dominant plants in a region. I know some birders who refer to every evergreen tree as a "pine," but there are differences between pines, spruces, junipers, etc., and these different trees tend to attract different kinds of birds. But even if you don't memorize the names of many plant species, it's important to cultivate an awareness of what different habitats look like. Marsh Wren and Sedge Wren are both found in marshes, sometimes in the same ones; but Marsh Wren favors the areas with standing water and tall plants such as cattails and bulrushes, while Sedge Wren is likely to be in stands of shorter sedges on wet soil — or even in fields where the ground is barely moist. Even without knowing a single plant species, we can recognize that these places look different.

In addition to recognizing habitat, it's important to think about a bird's place within it. Especially in a complex habitat like a forest, bird species occupy many different niches, with some walking on the forest floor, some living in undergrowth or at midlevels in the trees, some sticking to the treetops, some foraging along the edge. This has practical applications for identification. For example, Red-eyed Vireo and Swainson's Warbler are very superficially similar, whitish below and with a dark eyeline, and they occur in some of the same eastern woodlands. But if we glimpse such a bird foraging methodically in the treetops, it won't be a Swainson's Warbler. If we glimpse such a bird foraging on the ground under dense low thickets, it almost certainly won't be a Red-eyed Vireo. Their foraging niches are so different that they might as well be on different planets.

Red-eyed Vireos spend most of their time high in trees, and this usual niche could be considered one of the field marks for the species.

FORAGING BEHAVIOR

Most birds, at most seasons, spend a major part of their waking hours searching for food, so foraging behavior is a big part of their overall behavior. It also ties in with their use of habitat and specifically where in the habitat they are likely to be.

Many tyrant flycatchers typically forage by sitting upright on a perch, flying out to catch insects in midair, and then returning to a perch, often to the same place where they began. This behavior is so well known, and so associated with this family, that when it is practiced by other birds — as it is by waxwings, some warblers, even starlings and some woodpeckers — it is referred to as "flycatching." Although this foraging style is common to most tyrant flycatchers in North America, there are many tropical flycatchers that forage differently. North of Mexico, the Northern Beardless-Tyrannulet, a representative of this tropical group, rather seldom flies out to catch insects in midair; more often it hovers briefly to pick insects from foliage, or it searches for them along branches in the manner of a vireo. The same is true for the various species of tropical flycatchers known as elaenias that have been recorded as rare strays in North America.

Even among our flycatchers that typically "flycatch," there are differences in where and how they do it. Kingbirds and Scissor-tailed Flycatchers usually perch in the open and may make long swooping flights after distant insects. Wood-pewees and crested flycatchers are more likely to be inside the forest, flycatching in openings at midlevels in the trees, while Yellow-bellied Flycatcher may flycatch from low perches in the deep shadows. Olive-sided Flycatcher typically chooses a perch on a high dead snag above the treetops, and birders who know this may spot it and identify it from far away.

Similar kinds of comparisons could be made about the foraging behavior of birds in most groups. Some of these things are mentioned in later chapters of this book, but differences in foraging behavior could be found in almost any family of birds.

Not necessarily related to foraging, but distinctive in the behavior of many birds, are characteristic actions. The tail-bobbing of certain warblers would fall into this category. The action is obvious and easily noticed in some, such as Palm and Prairie warblers and the two waterthrushes, but a number of others have tail-bobbing actions that are less conspicuous. Some hummingbirds bob and fan their tails vigorously while hovering, while others hold their tails relatively still. Wing-flicking behavior is common in some birds — kinglets

As if it were not flashy enough in pattern, the Painted Redstart draws attention by its behavior, flitting about and posturing with its wings drooped and tail partly spread.

are famous for their habit of abruptly flicking the wings partly open and then snapping them folded again. (Hutton's Vireo, which looks very much like a wannabe Ruby-crowned Kinglet, has the same wing-flicking behavior.)

The foraging behavior of Sanderlings on the beach — running back and forth as they pursue the retreating waves — often makes them recognizable from half a mile away, regardless of what plumage they are wearing.

These aspects of foraging behavior and typical actions are best learned through experience, but we can speed up the learning process by actively thinking about it and by spending a little more time watching the birds that we've already identified. Having spotted a bird such as a Yellow-throated Vireo, for example, we might name it instantly, but it would be worthwhile to watch it for a minute to see what it is doing. How is it foraging? How do its actions compare to those of other vireos we've seen? This extra observation will pay off in a deeper familiarity with the birds beyond their field marks.

SOCIAL BEHAVIOR

Some birds are highly social. Some are solitary. Some are in between, and some vary their behavior under different conditions. There are temporary variations, of course, and at times we'll see a lone individual of even the most gregarious species. But most of the time, the degree of social behavior (flocking vs. solitary) and the behavior of flocks can be a significant aid in identifying birds.

This is a seasonal thing, of course. Many birds that gather in flocks for most of the year will break up into isolated pairs on territories during the breeding season. But some birds are highly social in their nesting, and this can be a factor in identification. If we're looking at a high dirt bank hundreds of yards away and we see numerous holes in the bank, with small birds fluttering in and out, we can confidently call them Bank Swallows. If we see swarms of small birds flying to and from hidden spots under a bridge, they are almost certainly Cliff or Cave swallows, perhaps with a few Barn Swallows thrown in. They won't be Northern Rough-winged Swallows, because Rough-wings don't nest in colonies. And it goes without saying that they won't be vireos, warblers, native sparrows, flycatchers, wrens, etc., because none of those birds nest in tight colonies either.

During migration and winter, however, many birds can be found in flocks. It's useful to make the distinction between mixed-species flocks and single-species flocks. A classic sight in North American woodlands in winter is a mixed flock of chickadees, titmice, nuthatches, creepers, woodpeckers, kinglets, and others, all moving through the woods in loose association. As varied as these flocks may be, there are certain things we can predict about most of them. The chickadees, if they are present, are likely to be the core of the flock, with half a dozen to a dozen or more birds that travel together and interact mainly with each other. The flock may include a pair of White-breasted Nuthatches, but only as long as the flock is traveling through the nuthatches' winter territory; if the flock moves on, the pair of nuthatches drops behind, and another pair may join the flock. The same thing may happen with single Brown Creepers or Ruby-crowned Kinglets. As the flock moves about during the course of a day, its species composition may remain roughly the same, but the individuals present may change, with only the nucleus of chickadees remaining the same.

In this case we will never see the roles reversed: we won't see a winter flock of Ruby-crowned Kinglets with one or two chickadees around the edge. The birds don't behave that way. Even where they are common, Ruby-crowned Kinglets don't form winter flocks; they maintain individual territories, driving away others of their own species but sometimes associating with flocks of other small songbirds. During migration the territorial behavior largely disappears, and we may see loose flocks of kinglets, or a number of kinglets as part of a mixed flock of other songbirds.

While many birds may join foraging flocks in an opportunistic way, especially during migration, there are fewer that regularly form single-species flocks. With experience, we learn to recognize this kind of behavior as one of the identifying characters of the bird. In eastern North America, medium-sized birds with longish tails, seen flying in a straggling flock overhead, may well turn out to be Common Grackles. They won't be Brown Thrashers, because thrashers don't do that. A flock of smaller, compact birds, swooping in together to land in a treetop, may well be Cedar Waxwings. They also might be European Starlings, or Bohemian Waxwings, but they won't be Hermit Thrushes, because Hermit Thrushes don't do that. The behavior of the flock immediately narrows down the likely choices.

In earlier chapters I drummed on the importance of looking at the shapes of birds, and this is an area where it pays off. Often we can recognize a single-species flock as such almost at a glance, without laboriously going through and identifying every individual, by the fact that the birds are all the same shape and size. There are some variations that affect this: for example, many species of blackbirds are noted for forming flocks, and male blackbirds are larger than females — more noticeably so in the larger species. In a flock of Great-tailed Grackles, for example, the adult males will be very obviously larger and longer-tailed than the females, and if we didn't know that, we might think we were seeing a mixed flock of two kinds of birds. But despite such exceptions, it's useful to develop the skill of quickly assessing a flock to see if it contains more than one species. A sensitivity to this can help the birder discover unusual species, such as a Dickcissel associating with a flock of House Sparrows.

A flock of Short-billed Dowitchers (with one Lesser Yellowlegs) circles over a flooded field in the upper midwest, seen here both at a distance and (in the inset) up close. Individual Wilson's Snipes might be similar in shape to dowitchers, but they would never form a flock like this.

Flocks differ in how cohesive they are, or how tightly the birds are associating with each other, and this is worth noticing. There are many differences even within bird families. Among shorebirds, for example, Greater Yellowlegs seem to travel in very loose aggregations at best, Lesser Yellowlegs may be in larger and somewhat tighter flocks, and dowitchers may stick together in tight groups. Among ducks, teal often form tight clusters, and flocks of wigeon may stick tightly together, but Wood Duck flocks tend to be loose aggregations of pairs.

Flocks also have their characteristic behavior. A flock of blackbirds may "roll" across an open field, with birds from the back constantly lifting off and flying up to the leading edge. In higher flight, flocks of

Red-winged Blackbirds, Brewer's Blackbirds, or Common Grackles may have a strongly undulating or wavy look, and a chorus of callnotes may descend from the flock. By comparison, flocks of Brown-headed or Bronzed cowbirds have a more direct look in flight, and cowbirds and European Starlings tend to be silent in flight (although the starlings will make rasping notes if alarmed).

FLIGHT BEHAVIOR

Flocks are often noticed most easily when they are flying, so the subject of social behavior leads naturally to flight behavior. In the course of a normal day's birding, many birds will be seen only in flight, and their behavior in the air will be an important factor in identifying them.

Beginning birders often have a mental block about looking at birds in flight. Part of this may be owing to the challenge of finding a flying bird in binoculars. When we're first learning to use the bins, and having enough trouble getting them on a bird that's sitting still, it can be frustrating to try to aim them at a fast-moving bird in the air. The ability to lock onto flying birds is a skill worth developing; but especially with smaller birds at a moderate distance, a naked-eye view may be the best way to identify them. For many birds in flight, things like colors and markings are much less important than size, shape, and especially flight action.

There are many variations in the ways that birds fly. You can, and should, practice seeing these flight styles with common birds. Some typically fly in a straight line, with steady wingbeats, as with most ducks. Some flap several times rapidly and then glide; accipiters are famous for doing this. Some birds, such as many woodpeckers and finches, have an undulating flight because they will flap several times and then fold the wings against the body, rising as they flap, falling as they coast with the wings closed.

Shape, flight action, and color pattern all come into play in identifying birds in the air. Over most of North America, Belted Kingfisher can be identified out to the limit of vision simply by its jerky, "gear-shifting" wingbeats. Its shape and pattern are distinctive also, but once we know the bird, we don't have to see those things; its wing action is enough.

The depth of the wingbeats also provides many clues. Blue Jays and Steller's Jays fly with deep downstrokes, the wings practically seeming to meet below the body, then raising the wings only about to the horizontal. Spotted Sandpiper usually flies with very shallow, fast wingbeats, while the wingbeats of Solitary Sandpiper are much deeper. Of course, wingbeat speed is also important, and it usually has a structural basis. Northern Mockingbird has larger wings for its size than its relatives, the thrashers and Gray Catbird, and its wingbeats are much slower. Diving ducks have smaller wings for their body size than dabbling ducks, and their wingbeats are faster; the whirring wings of a Ruddy Duck in flight are a far cry from the elegant wingbeats of a Northern Pintail. Soaring or gliding birds adopt many different postures, but some are characteristic, like the flat-winged soaring of Golden Eagle or the dihedral (shallow V) wing position of Northern Harrier.

The best way to learn these aspects is to watch birds in the field and to watch birds of known identity rather than puzzling over the flight of distant mystery birds. With birds spotted flying at close range in good light, we may be able to see many of the same field marks that would be obvious on the perched bird. Here's another very worthwhile approach: if we're watching a perched bird that we've already identified, and it flies, most birders will look away, but this is precisely the time that we should focus and watch how it flies. Trying to describe the flight style in words will help to fix it in memory.

An awareness of flight styles becomes essential when we start looking at seabirds. In many cases, their flight behavior provides the best means of separating species, especially at a distance. It also provides a quick separation of unrelated birds. In pictures, Northern Fulmar might look much like a gull, but its rapid wingbeats and stiff-winged glides are utterly unlike any gull's flight.

One potential pitfall to identifying birds by flight action is that this behavior can vary with conditions. Birds may fly differently in strong winds, and their wingbeats may be faster when they are in molt and missing some wing feathers. Many species also have territorial or courtship flight displays that may be very different from their usual flight behavior. American Golden-Plovers in display will fly with very slow, deep, exaggerated wingbeats. Cooper's Hawks have a flight display that involves very deep, slow wingbeats, punctuated with glides with the wings held up in a steep dihedral, utterly different from the normal flight. They often flare the white undertail coverts out to the side while performing this display, making even their shape and pattern look odd. Pairs of Brown Noddies in courtship may fly much faster than usual, with fast, flicking wingbeats.

VOCAL BEHAVIOR

Birds, as a class, are extremely vocal creatures. That's a lucky thing for birders, obviously, because the voices of birds help us so much in both finding and identifying them. In Chapter 7 I'll discuss techniques for learning to recognize bird voices, but a few basics about vocal behavior are worth mentioning here.

Learning. It's useful to know something about the learning process — not ours, but theirs. In most orders of birds, all of the vocalizations apparently are innate. That is, the bird seems to be born knowing all the calls of its species, even if it doesn't start to make those calls until later. In other groups, there is an element of learning in at least some of the vocalizations.

The order Passeriformes, the passerines or perching birds, includes many families and more than half the bird species in the world. The order is broadly divided into two suborders, the oscines and suboscines, distinguished mainly by the structure of the syrinx, the voice-producing organ in birds. Suboscines are represented in North America mainly by the tyrant flycatchers. Oscines include everything after the flycatchers on our checklists, from shrikes and vireos to finches: these are the true "songbirds," even though some are far less musical than others. Most of the oscines are thought to learn their songs. So are most parrots and, surprisingly, at least some of the hummingbirds, but for birders in North America, the important thing to know about is the learning process in typical songbirds.

Most songbirds seem to have a critical learning period when they are very young — generally within their first year, and often mainly within the first couple of months. If they do not hear the song of their own species during that time, they will never learn to sing it properly. They seem to have some kind of inner "template," so that they can pick out their own species' song from all the other sounds in their surroundings, but they have to hear it to learn it. These birds do not start to sing right away, and in fact they often wait many months before they enter a period of "subsong." This is a sort of "practice" period in which they may utter long disorganized series of sounds, often at soft volume, like a human baby quietly babbling. Within a relatively short time after subsong begins, usually within a few weeks, the bird has put the pieces together and can deliver the song of its species.

It's useful for birders to know this because the learning process sometimes goes awry, and the occasional bird learns the song of a different species. Usually such "wrong" songs sound a little off, as if there were a clash between the inner template and what was learned, but such birds can be genuinely confusing. Also potentially confusing are young male birds doing subsongs, which may be heard especially in fall and in early spring; they may sound like slightly odd versions of the normal song, or they may sound totally unrecognizable.

Not directly relevant to identification, but fascinating nonetheless, is the fact that brood parasites such as the Brown-headed Cowbird have the song innate, not learned. Since they are raised by foster parents, they might not necessarily even hear the song of their own species during the critical learning period, so it is fortunate for them that they have the song hard-wired.

Song dialects. A number of species have well-defined local dialects of song, maintained by birds learning the songs in their own "neighborhoods." One of the most striking examples in North America, and one that has been studied extensively, involves White-crowned Sparrow. By traveling from one valley to another in the northern Rockies, or by moving a few miles along the Pacific Coast, we can move from the range of one dialect into another that sounds clearly different. The tone quality and certain shared elements should make all of these birds recognizable as White-crowneds, but the change in song pattern could be confusing to birders who were accustomed to hearing just one local dialect.

Local dialects of White-crowned Sparrow songs may be maintained through local learning over many generations. On the central California coast, some local dialects are known to have remained essentially unchanged for decades.

Individual variation. Even bird vocalizations that sound identical to us may not be. Field experiments have shown that many birds can recognize each other as individuals by subtle differences in even relatively simple call notes. The implication for field birders is that the more carefully we listen, the more likely we are to hear variations. So just as no bird ever looks exactly like the picture in the book, we might say that no bird ever sounds exactly like the published recordings, either.

Song repertoires. There are many species of birds in which individual males typically have more than one song. A few remarkable cases involve some wrens that may have more than a hundred different songs, and some mockingbirds and thrashers that may have several hundred.

Most birds are not so extreme. But anyone who has listened to the varied songs of common backyard birds such as Song Sparrows and Northern Cardinals should be prepared for the fact that less familiar birds may also have a number of distinctly different songs.

In many cases, male birds will use the songs from their repertoire seemingly at random, but there are also cases in which certain songs are used for particular situations. Many of the North American warblers have two distinct song types used for different purposes, as described in Chapter 28. Among the tyrant flycatchers, a number of species have very distinctive "dawn songs," as described in Chapter 25; these may sound very different from any vocalization uttered later in the day, and since the birds can be hard to see in the half-light of dawn, they are potentially very confusing for birders.

Mimicry. Some birds with large repertoires add to them by copying or imitating sounds that they hear, in a behavior called mimicry or "vocal appropriation." They usually copy other birds, but adept mimics such as mockingbirds may also take on the sounds of machinery, doorbells, cell phone ringtones, or other things in their surroundings. Unlike most songbirds, which have a critical learning period only during an early stage of their lives, some mimics apparently learn new vocalizations throughout their lives, continuing to add to their repertoires. In addition to Northern Mockingbirds and their relatives, other accomplished mimics in North America include several jays and other corvids, several species of finches (such as Lesser and Lawrence's goldfinches and Cassin's Finch), and the European Starling, which has fooled generations of birders with its imitations of meadowlarks and other birds.

Hooded Orioles will often work imitations of other birds into their phrases, but it's easy to miss these sounds unless you know the local bird voices well and listen for them in the oriole's rapid delivery.

Callnotes. In general, bird songs are complex vocalizations that are given mainly in territorial or pair-bond situations. Calls are generally simpler and are given in a very wide variety of situations. Many birds (especially among non-passerines) do not have any vocalization that would be considered a song, but most birds have calls, and most birds have a considerable variety of calls. These may include simple contact calls, alarm calls, the begging calls of the young, and others.

Contact calls are the ones heard most often and the ones of most interest to birders. These would include familiar sounds like the low *tchuck* of a Common Yellowthroat or the *pick* of a Downy Woodpecker. There is evidence that even when the song is learned, as in most true songbirds, the calls are almost certainly instinctive or innate, so they may display less individual variation than songs. The term "contact call" reflects the belief that many birds use these short notes to stay in contact with others of their species, but in practice, these are often used in situations of mild alarm as well.

Flight calls. Many birds have short notes, given in flight, that are different from their usual contact calls given when perched. These have been well studied in the warblers, and there is more discussion of them in Chapter 28.

Many birds that migrate at night are very vocal as they fly. One of the fascinating experiences for birders in spring and fall, especially in the eastern two-thirds of North America, is to stand outside on a calm night and listen for the calls of these migrants passing overhead. In Chapter 7, I'll discuss some techniques for learning to identify these nocturnal flight calls.

TIMING AND EXPECTATIONS

One of the keys to identification is knowing what to expect at a given place and time, so one of the most useful resources that you can get is a local checklist with seasonal annotations. The best ones include bar graphs to show occurrence through the year, with a bar of varying thickness to show when each species is abundant, common, uncommon, rare, or absent. Simple seasonal codes might tell us that the Golden-crowned Kinglet, for example, occurs locally in fall, winter, and spring. A bar graph, by contrast, can give far more information in the same amount of space. Such a graph might show that Golden-crowned Kinglet first shows up in late September, becomes common for the latter two-thirds of October and early November, then remains uncommon through the winter until it has another spike in numbers from late March to late April, with numbers then rapidly trailing off into early May and the last few going through in about the third week of May — and it will tell us that far more efficiently than we can describe it in words!

Knowing what is expected can help to steer us away from serious error. Orange-crowned Warbler is a subtle bird, easily confused with other species. In the northeastern U.S. it almost never arrives as a fall migrant earlier than mid-September, so an August bird that looks like an Orange-crowned is probably something else. In a similar vein, Common Nighthawk is a late spring migrant in the southwest, rare before the end of May and not showing up in numbers until June, so a nighthawk seen in April is almost certainly a Lesser Nighthawk. Of course, birds have wings, and they do occur out of season at times. But if we know we've found a bird at the "wrong" season, we'll look at it more closely and try to document it.

Hermit Thrush is widespread during the winter in North America. Similar species of brown thrushes are generally deep in the tropics at that season. Finding one of the others in midwinter is not impossible, but it is at least very unlikely; and if we're aware of that, we'll look very critically at any brown thrush that appears to be anything other than a Hermit.

6. IDENTIFICATION BEYOND THE SPECIES LEVEL

Most birders, most of the time, are satisfied if we can identify a bird to species. We see a lone American Crow at the edge of a field or a lone Canada Goose winging overhead, and it may not occur to us even to wonder whether it is a male or a female, an adult or a first-winter bird.

But when we start to delve into challenging bird identifications, we are forced to consider questions like this. In some cases involving shorebirds, for example, it is easier to determine the age of a bird than to determine its species. During August, looking at small sandpipers, we can instantly tell the fresh-plumaged juveniles from the worn or molting adults, but it may take a much closer look to tell the species apart. Looking at *Selasphorus* hummingbirds in summer, we may be able to distinguish among adult females, young males, and young females, without being able to tell which species they are. Similar situations abound in many groups of birds. And then there are cases in which the geographic variation within a species will have a major impact on its identification: for example, Song Sparrow and Fox Sparrow look utterly different from each other in eastern North America, but in the Pacific northwest they might more easily be confused. A birder who pursues a serious interest in identifying birds to species will almost inevitably start to think about identifying them beyond the species level.

VARIATION AND ITS MEANINGS

Beginners studying field guides soon notice that adult male birds tend to be the most brightly colored members of their species — in an obvious way, as with Northern Cardinals and Wood Ducks, or more subtly, with American Robins. After a while, subconsciously, we may start to regard this as a universal trait. Early in my birding, whenever I saw a bird that looked exceptionally bright, I would say, "It must be an adult male" — even if it were something like a Blue Jay or Red-headed Woodpecker, in which the sexes are alike. It took some time before I managed to break that habit, and it took even longer before I began to develop some understanding of the variation within species.

In fact, the relative brightness or dullness of plumage often does signal something about the age and sex of a bird. There is a general tendency across many species for adult males to have the brightest colors and most distinct markings, and for young females to have the most muted colors and markings. But every species has its own degree of variation within each age and sex group, so general impressions don't mean much unless we know the specifics. If one bird in a flock looks particularly dull, it might be a young female, but it also could be an adult male in worn plumage, or it could be a stray of some drab subspecies, or it could just reflect an extreme of individual variation. We won't be able to say unless we look at how the details apply to the species in question.

In recent decades, much of the progress in identifying birds beyond the species level has been driven by bird banding projects. Banders have good reason to try to determine as much as possible about each bird that they handle, since knowing the age and sex of each bird adds greatly to the value of the data collected. With the bird up close, banders don't have to rely on impressions of color; they can quickly assess fine details such as the shapes and patterns of specific feathers or the exact stage of molt. They can achieve a remarkable level of precision, if they have enough information available on the species at hand.

The best source of that information — the "bible" for banders — is a two-volume work by Peter Pyle, *Identification Guide to North American Birds,* Part 1 (1997) and Part 2 (2008). At more than 1,550 pages, dense with text and with simple black-and-white diagrams, these volumes are not for the faint-hearted. But this is currently the most important reference work on identification of North American birds. Nothing else published in the last 50 years even comes close. True, much of the material can be applied only in the hand, but a patient and careful observer can see many of these points in the field as well; and even if we can't see these points, it's good to know what they are and why we can't see them. If you get really serious about identifying birds beyond the species level, eventually you'll get Pyle 1 and Pyle 2, as we call these books, and you'll use them.

In this chapter I give an overview of identifying birds to sex, age, and subspecies, and the approaches for doing so that are most useful and effective in the field. The characteristics for identifying age and sex of a bird are often intertwined, and often we may need to know one to determine the other, so the separation of these under two separate headings is somewhat artificial.

IDENTIFYING FEMALES VS. MALES

These notes apply mainly to adult birds, since the criteria for younger birds are often different, as discussed in the next section. There are many species in which females and males are, to all obvious appearances, basically identical. Those species in which the sexes differ in visible ways are said to be sexually dimorphic, a useful term to know.

Size. Among North American birds, there is typically a slight average difference in size between females and males. Those species in which the sexes average exactly the same size might be considered the exceptions. Generally the size differences are much too slight to be noticed in the field, but in some cases they can be detected when members of a pair are seen together, and in a few species they are striking.

The typical pattern is for males to be slightly larger than females, but there are a number of groups in which the opposite is true. Females average larger than males in most of the birds of prey, and sometimes the difference is obvious, as in the accipiters and in Peregrine Falcon. Females average larger than males in most of the sandpipers, although there are a couple of striking exceptions: males of Ruff and Pectoral Sandpiper are much larger than females (probably a reflection of their mating systems, in which no pair bond is formed and the males put their energy into courtship displays to attract females).

In cases in which one sex is noticeably larger than the other, this is worth knowing for a couple of reasons. One is that it can help us to tell the sexes apart when we see a mated pair together. The other is that it can affect our attempts to identify the birds to species in some cases, as when a medium-small accipiter might be either a large female Sharp-shinned or a small male Cooper's Hawk.

Bill shape. Some groups of birds show average differences in bill size and shape between females and males. These can reflect slight differences in foraging behavior; if the sexes are not foraging in exactly the same way, then members of a mated pair are not competing directly for the same food. In woodpeckers, males average slightly larger overall than females, but they also have proportionately longer bills in a number of species, and the sexes may tend to focus on different areas of trees. In the sandpiper family, differences in average bill length between the sexes may be very noticeable, especially since bill shape is often an important field mark. Sometimes the differences are extreme: in Long-billed Dowitcher, for example, females average only slightly larger than males, but their bills average more than 15 percent longer, and there is practically no overlap in bill length between the sexes.

As with overall size, one of the main reasons to be aware of sex differences in bill shape is that in some cases, as with certain sandpipers, it can have a major impact on our attempts to identify these birds to species.

Color pattern. Among North American birds, sexual dimorphism in color runs the gamut from some species in which females and males look utterly different, such as most warblers and ducks, to others in which they are essentially identical, such as chickadees and geese. Even within the same family there are examples of both extremes. Most woodpeckers show only minor differences in head pattern between females and males; but in some, like Red-headed Woodpecker, the sexes are virtually identical, while in others they look very different in a number of respects.

Sexual dimorphism isn't always obvious; in some cases it is very slight, or only an average difference, not likely to be noticed unless members of a pair are together. Male Mourning Doves are slightly more colorful than females, but this can be hard to judge unless they are seen together, and some field guides do not even attempt to illustrate it. Female Cedar Waxwings have slightly less black on

This female Williamson's Sapsucker looks utterly different from the male, which is mostly black with white and yellow trim. In most members of the woodpecker family, the sexes are more similar than this. Female and male Williamson's were originally described as two different species and were sometimes even put in different genera until they were found nesting together.

the throat and average fewer red secondary tips than males, but most field guides do not indicate that there is any difference in the sexes. This kind of subtle detail is best learned from more exhaustive references, such as Pyle's identification guide.

Shapes of individual feathers. In many species, the shapes of individual flight feathers can be an important age characteristic, with the tips being shaped differently in juveniles and adults. There are fewer sex-specific differences in feather shapes, but a few are worth noting. In many adult hummingbirds, the tail feathers differ between females and males more obviously in their color patterns than in their shapes. In some hummingbirds, such as Broad-tailed, the outer primaries are also uniquely shaped in males, and it is this shape that produces the metallic trilling in flight. Sound production in flight is also the function for the distinct shape of the outer primaries in the male American Woodcock and for the longer, narrower outer tail feathers of the male Wilson's Snipe, because it is air passing over these feathers that produces the "twittering" of the male woodcock and the "winnowing" of the male snipe in their aerial displays above the breeding grounds.

Of course, the precise shape of the outer tail feathers on a snipe could not be considered a field mark, but some such feather shape details are certainly visible in the field. In flycatchers of the genus *Tyrannus*, such as kingbirds and Scissor-tailed Flycatcher, the outer primaries are sharply narrowed at the tip in adult males, much more so than in adult females or younger birds. The degree of attenuation varies among species, but with knowledge of the species involved, it is often possible to separate males and females by this point even though their plumage patterns are otherwise identical.

Perching with its wings drooped, this Eastern Kingbird shows off the sharply narrowed tips of its outer primaries, revealing that it is an adult male. Since kingbirds often perch conspicuously in the open, this point often can be seen in the field.

Voice. Vocal differences between males and females are fairly common, but this varies among species. In most passerines, of course, males are much more vocal than females during the nesting season, singing to defend a territory and to attract a mate; some female birds do sing, and in a few species they are almost as vocal as the males, but these are exceptions. In most cases, a songbird doing the full song of its species will be a male. For example, a bird that appears to be a female Varied Bunting, perched atop a mesquite and singing, is certain to be a one-year-old male instead.

In most passerines, the main call notes of females and males are the same. There are slight differences in pitch in some birds: in Dusky and Gray flycatchers, for example, the short *whit* note of the female is slightly lower than the male's. In non-passerines, the sex differences in voice can be much more pronounced. For example, in most of the true ducks, calls of females and males are utterly different, while the vocalizations of the sexes are much more similar in geese, swans, and whistling-ducks.

Bill colors and eye colors. Many birds have bill colors that change with the seasons, but in most cases bill colors are not useful for distinguishing the sexes. Notable exceptions include many of the true ducks. For some ducks in which the females and males are similar in plumage, such as American Black Duck, bill color is among the easiest ways to tell the sexes apart. Another notable exception that can be found in most back yards is the European Starling: at least in the breeding season, when the bill is bright yellow, the base of the lower mandible is pink in females, blue in males.

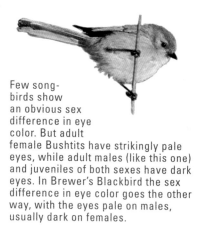

Few songbirds show an obvious sex difference in eye color. But adult female Bushtits have strikingly pale eyes, while adult males (like this one) and juveniles of both sexes have dark eyes. In Brewer's Blackbird the sex difference in eye color goes the other way, with the eyes pale on males, usually dark on females.

European Starling is also noted for showing a sex difference in eye color in adults. In both sexes the iris is dark brown, but on the female the outer edge of the iris usually is contrastingly yellow, and this can be seen in the field with a close look. In most birds, however, differences in eye color are more likely to reflect a difference in age.

Complicating factors. In some birds that are sexually dimorphic in color pattern, older females may begin to take on some of the colors of males. This is well known in ducks, in which old or senescent females may develop colors like those of the male but with the pattern more blended or muted. Something similar may happen in orioles, cardueline finches, and some other birds, with older females gradually developing brighter colors. In the latter cases, they may not ever approach the pattern of the adult male, but they might be more likely to be mistaken for young males. Conversely, it has been suggested that adult males in the Red Crossbill complex may occasionally molt from a brick red plumage to a yellow plumage, in which case they could easily be mistaken for females.

Northern Gannets may not be in full adult plumage until they are seven years old. Young Brown Creepers may be indistinguishable from adults by the time they are six months old. Most birds fall closer to the latter extreme than to the former, but there are many species in which we can distinguish ages up through at least the first year and a half, with a careful study.

The special category of juvenile plumage. (See Chapter 4 for an explanation of why I do not use the spelling "juvenal" here.) This is the first full plumage that a bird wears — technically its first basic plumage, but it is different in many ways from basic plumages in subsequent years. Whether this juvenile plumage is worn for only a few days before it begins to be replaced, as in the case of some songbirds, or for many months, as in the case of some gulls, jaegers, shorebirds, and raptors, it very often has a unique appearance that will have a profound effect on the field identification of the species.

On small songbirds that wear juvenile plumage only very briefly, such as warblers, the body feathers of this first plumage may have a very flimsy and weak structure. These young birds may leave the nest when they are barely able to fly at all. Humans who see them might wonder why they would not stay in the nest until they are stronger, but "the safety of the nest" is often a very vulnerable place; these birds may be better off getting out of the nest as quickly as possible so that they won't be sitting targets for predators. So their juvenile plumage is grown in a rush, the birds leave the nest, and within a few days they begin to grow their formative (or "first-winter") plumage to replace this flimsy first coat.

On juveniles such as these, the plumage pattern is often different from that of later stages, typically with more camouflage. Often it shows fewer bright colors and more streaking or spotting. Such birds can be truly mystifying to the birder who chances upon one. However, juveniles as young as

The first time a birder sees a young juvenile Mourning Dove, it can be a source of major confusion: shorter-tailed than the adult at first, it has a scaly pattern on the upperparts and wings and spots on the chest. Such birds sometimes have been misidentified as Common Ground-Doves or Inca Doves.

this are often still being fed by the parents, and if we watch from a distance we may see the adults come in. Lacking that kind of confirmation, the wing pattern provides a good clue: typically these birds do not replace the wing feathers during the preformative molt, so wing pattern is likely to be the same on juveniles as it is on first-winter birds.

There are other small birds in which the juveniles are patterned just like the adults (such as most of the chickadees) or that differ mainly in having pale edgings on many of the feathers of the upperparts (such as some flycatchers). In these birds, juveniles may be separated from adults in summer by the much fresher condition of the plumage.

On many large birds that keep juvenile plumage longer, for a period of months, this plumage is marked by having very distinct pale edges to the feathers in various tracts, such as the scapulars, coverts, and tertials, even if older birds or basic plumage lacks these contrasting edges. For examples of this kind of juvenile plumage, see the chapters on loons, sandpipers, gulls, terns, and jaegers. With a little experience, it becomes possible to instantly pick out the juvenile birds in these groups, and often they can be identified as juveniles much more quickly than they can be identified to species.

Being aware of the distinctive juvenile plumages and having a general idea of how to recognize them is one of the most important steps that a birder can take in developing advanced skills.

Shapes of flight feathers as an age character. In a great many species of birds, the tips of the individual tail feathers of juveniles are shaped differently from those of older birds. Among most passerines and near-passerines, and in many groups of larger birds as well, the juvenile tail feathers are narrower and more tapered toward the tip, while those of adults are more truncate, or broadly squared off across the tip. When such differences are present, they usually are most apparent on the outer two or three pairs of tail feathers. Bird banders are often tuned in to this difference, which is usually quite subtle but can be distinctive with experience. It varies among species, of course, and in a few groups of birds it can be noticeable enough that it might be seen in the field. The shape difference can be obvious in cuckoos, for example, but in most of these there are differences in the pattern, as well as the shape, of the outer tail feathers. In some finches the difference might be seen in the field at close range, such as at a feeder.

In most birds, even when they can be examined in the hand, the shape difference in tail feathers can be used only for the extremes, and many will appear to have an intermediate shape. But many birds retain the juvenile tail feathers for most of their first year of life, so until the feathers become worn, this is a characteristic worth looking for.

Some groups of birds show other kinds of age-specific differences in the shapes of tail feathers. Many juvenile hummingbirds have outer tail feathers that are broader than those of adults, and the same is true of some terns and of some other birds.

Very often the primaries and secondaries also are shaped differently between age groups, and again those of juveniles tend to be narrower and more tapered than those of adults. With experience and a good view, this may be visible in the field on some birds, such as some of the birds of prey.

Various other differences in feather shapes between age groups have been noticed. For example, in Ruddy Turnstone and Black Turnstone, the scapulars of juveniles are much smaller than those of adults, and this can give a different appearance to the pattern of the upperparts.

Fault bars. With a close view of the larger flight feathers, we may be able to see slight variations in the color or structure of the vanes of the feather. If the bird was subjected to some kind of stress, including a scarcity of food, while the feather was growing, the effect may show up as a slightly paler line or a narrow area of weaker structure in the vane. These effects are referred to as fault bars or growth bars; they are easiest to see on a bird's tail, and they are occasionally useful in aging birds. When juveniles are growing the tail feathers for the first time, all the feathers grow simultaneously; so any stress that causes a visible fault bar will be in about the same position on all the feathers. When adults of most birds are molting the tail feathers, they replace them only a pair at a time, so any visible fault bars will be in different positions on different tail feathers. Therefore, a noticeable fault bar running straight across the tail is often an indication of a bird that still has its juvenile tail feathers. This is not foolproof, because if an adult has its tail feathers pulled out through some mishap, the new feathers will grow in more or less simultaneously, and any visible fault bars will be lined up like those of juveniles.

Here's an exceptionally clear example of fault bars in the tail of a Gray Catbird. The position of this line indicates that all of these feathers were growing simultaneously and that some kind of stress had a significant effect on the bird when the feathers were partly grown.

Molt Limits. When the molt of a set of large feathers is interrupted or incomplete, we can often see a contrast between the newly replaced feathers and the older retained ones. These lines of visible contrast between old and new feathers are called molt limits, and they are sometimes significant in determining a bird's age.

This is especially true in many songbirds, in which the adults have a complete prebasic molt but juveniles often have only a partial preformative molt. This partial molt by young birds varies by species and by individual, but in some cases the molt will replace some of the greater coverts (always starting from the innermost), some or all of the median coverts, and sometimes one or two of the tertials. In these situations, the replaced feathers may look visibly fresher than the retained juvenile feathers next to them.

If we know the typical pattern of preformative and first prealternate molt in a species, we may be able to pick out young birds from adults by such molt limits. One pitfall to be aware of, however, is the possibility of "pseudolimits." In some birds, the innermost greater coverts, those protecting the bases of the tertials, are larger and have a slightly different color or pattern than the rest of the greater coverts, and this difference can suggest the effect of a molt limit.

Molt limits will not work for birds that replace all the greater coverts in either the preformative or first prealternate molt. But in some such birds, even though the secondary coverts have been replaced, the older, worn primary coverts are retained.

Inset:
detail of
greater
coverts

This male Bay-breasted Warbler, photographed in May, is a one-year-old bird in its first alternate plumage. In addition to some slight color differences, it differs from the typical adult male in showing a molt limit clearly in the greater coverts on the wing.

One-year-old male   Adult male

A comparison of the spread wings of male Indigo Buntings in first alternate plumage (one year old) and definitive alternate plumage (adult). The secondary coverts have been replaced on the young bird, but the flight feathers and the primary coverts have not, and the difference on the primary coverts is especially striking. Because of the way the wing folds up, it is difficult to see the primary coverts well in the field, but with practice we may be able to see extreme differences such as those illustrated here even when the wing is folded.

Eye colors and bill colors. It's a very common phenomenon for juvenile birds to have different eye colors than adults of their species. This is quite noticeable in the field for some, such as some large gulls that are pale-eyed as adults, and some birds of prey; see also the comments regarding scaup, loons, and accipiters in this book. For many smaller birds, the change is much more subtle. In Gray Catbird, for example, the iris color changes gradually from gray or gray-brown in juveniles to deep rich chestnut in adults, but this is hard to see in the field. We may notice the changes more readily in species that have unusual eye colors as adults, such as Red-eyed and White-eyed vireos; in those cases, the name refers to adults, since young birds have duller eye colors.

In quite a few passerines, the inside of the bill, especially the roof of the mouth, is paler in young birds; this is true of many jays and crows, some thrashers and thrushes, the Yellow-breasted Chat, and other birds. Of course, this hardly constitutes a field mark. But on a few birds, the paler color affects the visible exterior of the bill as well. Juvenile Brown Jays have yellow bills, juveniles of the western population of Mexican Jays have pink bills, and adults of both have black bills. It may take many months for the bills of these young birds to turn completely black, so this provides a quick way to pick out immatures in a flock through at least the first winter.

GEOGRAPHIC VARIATION AND THE SUBSPECIES PROBLEM

Over one-third of all North American bird species, and the majority of those with broad ranges, show at least some amount of geographic variation — that is, they look slightly different from one region to another. The basic idea of this is easy to understand. The big problems begin when we try to classify this variation and to put names on the component forms.

When our modern system of naming species was developed by the Swedish naturalist Carolus Linnaeus, a quarter of a millennium ago, it was assumed that "the species" was an immutable type and that every individual of a species would look essentially the same. To give an example: Linnaeus formally described the White Wagtail to science in 1758 and gave it the scientific name *Motacilla alba.* Several decades later, John Gould pointed out that the birds in Britain looked different from the ones Linnaeus had described, so he named them *Motacilla yarrellii.* Other scientists, looking more closely at the wagtails elsewhere in Europe and Asia, gave them other names: *Motacilla dukhunensis, Motacilla personata, Motacilla baicalensis.* Under the typological approach that prevailed, if a population of birds looked different, it must be a different species.

Eventually it was noticed that some of these "species" blended gradually where their ranges came in contact. It was concluded that they must be varieties of the same species, so they were reclassified as subspecies, designated by having a scientific name of three words, not two. The British bird became *Motacilla alba yarrellii.* The original north European bird described by Linnaeus became *Motacilla alba alba,* or the nominate subspecies.

By the beginning of the twentieth century, explorer-naturalists hoping to discover new species were already finding that most of the easy ones had been picked off. But with the concept of subspecies available, the floodgates were opened anew, and anyone who looked closely enough could find local variations that could be described as new subspecies. Dozens of subspecies were described for widespread, variable birds such as Horned Lark and Song Sparrow (but many of these would be considered only dubiously distinct by later researchers).

For a time in the 1930s, when bird listing was first becoming a serious pursuit in North America, birders kept life lists, year lists, etc., that counted subspecies as well as species. Often these determinations were based solely on range, as detailed in the *American Ornithologists' Union Check-list of North American Birds,* which included subspecies at the time. A birder who traveled through central and southern Florida in summer and saw Red-winged Blackbirds along the way could add the subspecies *mearnsi* and *floridanus* to his life list, even if these birds seemed to look essentially identical to the Red-wings of the subspecies *phoeniceus* back home in Pennsylvania.

This approach of listing every possible named subspecies, whether it could be recognized or not, gradually came to be seen as pointless. By the 1950s, listers were just keeping lists of species. The pendulum managed to swing from one extreme to the other, and by the 1970s, many birders were largely unaware of any kind of geographic variation within species. Today we seem to be getting back to a healthy balance, with birders being aware of how species vary but not placing too much importance on subspecies names.

What is a subspecies? Whole books have been written to try to define species and subspecies, so the capsule discussion below is necessarily an extreme simplification. Under the Biological Species Concept (the species definition still used by most ornithologists), a species will be reproductively isolated from other species — that is, if they come in contact, there will be relatively little interbreeding between them. For example, Hairy Woodpecker and Downy Woodpecker are remarkably similar to each other except in size and voice, but they occur side by side over most of this continent without ever hybridizing. Subspecies (also often called "races" in ornithological slang) are variations within a species, and they are not reproductively isolated: where one subspecies of Hairy Woodpecker meets another, they will interbreed so freely that one will blend smoothly into the next.

Hairy Woodpecker is a good bird to use as an example. Where I live in Ohio, the Hairies belong to the nominate subspecies, *Picoides villosus villosus*. (That doesn't mean that they are the "most typical" population; it just means that the species was described to science based on birds belonging to this general population, and other subspecies were named later.) Now imagine that we have convinced ten of these *P. v. villosus* from Ohio to perch quietly in front of us, and we have called in ten Hairy Woodpeckers from far to the south of us — say, southern Alabama — and ten from far to the north, in northern Quebec. Viewing them side by side, we'll see that the Alabama birds are smaller on average, with smaller white spots on the wings and slightly grayer underparts. The northern Quebec birds will look noticeably larger on average than the Ohio birds, and their white markings may look even brighter. With this direct comparison, we won't be surprised to learn that these have been named as different subspecies: the Alabama birds belong to the widespread southern race *P. v. auduboni,* while the northern Quebec birds belong to the widespread far northern and western race *P. v. septentrionalis.*

However, the difference is apparent mainly because we are comparing samples from distinctly different regions. If we were to walk from Ohio to Alabama, looking at Hairy Woodpeckers along the way, we would never see an obvious break — there would never be a point where we noticed a switch from one subspecies to another. Instead, the change would be subtle and gradual. This is called "clinal" variation, and drawing lines between subspecies in such a cline is always going to be arbitrary.

Furthermore, if we look closely at our sample of Hairy Woodpeckers from Ohio, we'll see that they are variable: some slightly larger, some smaller, some a little grayer below, some whiter. Does that mean that we are seeing stray individuals from other subspecies? No, it merely demonstrates the variability of any local population and hints at the danger of trying to identify subspecies in the field.

The shift from one subspecies to another does not always occur gradually over a long distance. It happens that way with Hairy Woodpeckers in the East because there is no break in their habitat, thus nothing to interrupt the free mixing of populations. In the West, where good woodpecker habitat is broken up by deserts and grasslands, differences among subspecies may be more pronounced. The resident Hairies in the isolated mountains of southeastern Arizona and southwestern New Mexico (race *P. v. icastus*) are small and tinged with brown, and they have almost no white spots on the wing coverts. Some populations along the Pacific Coast are similar.

Another example of the effects of geographic isolation occurs in the East. If we traveled north from Ohio to northern Quebec, the shift to larger and whiter Hairy Woodpeckers would occur so gradually that we would never notice. However, if we then traveled east and crossed over to the island of Newfoundland, the change in Hairy Woodpeckers would be abrupt and obvious. The subspecies there, *P. v. terraenovae,* usually has irregular black bars and spots breaking up the white stripe on the back, and it mostly lacks white spots on the wing coverts. There are probably occasional Hairies from the mainland that stray to Newfoundland and breed with the locals, introducing more variability into that population, but for the most part these birds are isolated and probably have been diverging from the mainland stock for a long time.

Notice that there is a geographic element in how a subspecies is defined. We don't just apply the name *P. v. auduboni* to any Hairy Woodpecker anwhere that looks small and dingy below; we apply that name to a population in the southern U.S. that typically looks that way. And every valid subspecies has its own breeding range. Separate species may overlap extensively in their breeding ranges, but where subspecies meet, they blend. If two different forms overlap without interbreeding, they will be considered full species. Of course, this applies only in the breeding season. At other times of year, different subspecies of migratory birds may mix freely. In the western U.S. in winter, for example, we often see three or four different-looking subspecies of Dark-eyed Juncos in the same flock, but in summer each goes to its own separate breeding range.

Opinions differ as to the value of having named subspecies. Some scientists in the past went to extremes of putting names on every local variation. Some today consider subspecies unnecessary. In their view, we could simply note that eastern Hairy Woodpeckers tend to be smaller and dingier toward the south, without putting a separate name on the southernmost birds (and without the thorny problem of deciding where to draw the dividing line). Most ornithologists are in between these extremes; they will continue to use names for subspecies, but only if the subspecies are reasonably distinctive.

A criterion widely used today is that for a subspecies to be considered valid, at least 75 percent of the individuals from the core of its range should be distinguishable from 100 percent of the individuals of other subspecies. This is a fairly rigorous test, but even in applying it, authorities often disagree as to which subspecies are valid. And the flip side of this criterion is that up to 25 percent of the individuals are *not* distinguishable from other subspecies, even when examined in the hand. Obviously, identifying such subtle birds in the field could hardly be considered reliable.

A practical approach to subspecies for birders. What does all this mean for birders in the field? I suggest that it's important for birders to be keenly aware of the fact that geographic variation exists, and to be alert for examples of it. But I also suggest that we shouldn't be too eager to put names on subspecies.

When David Sibley's first bird guide was published, some experts were upset that it included no subspecies names. Sibley illustrated geographic variation quite well, but he labeled the pictures just with general terms for their nesting ranges. Starting in the mid-1980s, serious birders had gotten a strong taste of scientific names for subspecies from the National Geographic field guides, and they wanted more. But Sibley's approach made perfect sense. He illustrated a typical Hairy Woodpecker from the Pacific Coast and labeled it "Pacific." Labeling it as one of the subspecies, such as *"sitkensis,"* would have required an additional explanation of the fact that the subspecies *harrisii, picoideus,* and *hyloscopus* could look very similar — or it would have resulted in birders misidentifying these other forms as *sitkensis.* Either would have defeated the basic purpose of the field guide.

There are some well-marked subspecies with scientific names that are well known to serious birders, and I don't suggest abandoning those. For example, the distinctive Short-billed Dowitchers nesting in central Canada are widely known by their subspecies name, *hendersoni,* and there's no need to call them the "prairie" population. But in most cases, using a simple English term for a group of subspecies will be better than the false precision of applying a scientific name that may not be correct.

Currently the best single source of information on subspecies of North American birds can be found in the two volumes of Peter Pyle's *Identification Guide,* mentioned at the beginning of this chapter. Pyle gives capsule accounts of the distribution and characteristics of all subspecies that seem worthy of recognition. Birders should be aware, though, that many subspecies cannot be identified from these accounts, even when examined and measured in the hand, and certainly most can't be identified in the field.

With a combination of reference works, including the descriptions in Pyle and the illustrations in field guides, birders may be able to gain a good overview of the geographic variation in widespread birds. And with attention and caution, we may be able to apply some subspecies names, or some group names, to some of the birds we see. A good rule of thumb is to avoid false precision. For example, we shouldn't say that a Dark-eyed Junco belongs to "the Oregon subspecies" without checking: is that a subspecies? (Actually there are at least five or six subspecies included in the "Oregon Junco" group.) We shouldn't claim that a migrant Hermit Thrush belongs to the race *guttatus* unless we know what other subspecies are possible, how they differ, and how much they vary (and if we do know those things, we'll know that we can't separate *guttatus* from several other similar forms in the field, except on the breeding grounds). In these cases, if we say that it's "a Dark-eyed Junco of the Oregon subspecies group" or "a Hermit Thrush showing the characters of *guttatus* or similar subspecies," it may sound as if we are waffling, but in fact we'll be reflecting the actual status of the birds and respecting the limits of what is possible in the field.

COLOR MORPHS

Relatively few North American bird species exhibit the phenomenon of polymorphism — the existence of more than one color morph — but these few species are scattered across a number of different families of birds, and some of them are well known and frequently seen.

The term "color phase" is sometimes used, but technically this is incorrect. The word "phase" implies an element of time (as in phases of the moon), but true color morphs are not temporary but permanent. Dark morph and white morph Reddish Egrets, for example, are easily distinguished from the time they hatch, as the fuzzy down that covers them is either gray or white, presaging the plumage they will wear later. The word "phase" might be used correctly for temporary plumage appearances, such as the patchy "calico phase" that the Little Blue Heron goes through during its molt from white juvenile plumage to dark adult plumage, but the term has been misused so much that it may be best to avoid it altogether.

Color morphs have a long history of causing confusion for birders and ornithologists alike. Some morphs were originally regarded as separate species; for example, the dark morph of the Snow Goose was treated as a full species, "Blue Goose," until the 1970s. In other cases, they were thought to represent different age groups or different sexes. A pattern that often holds is that the different morphs are usually not distributed randomly within the range of the species. Eastern Screech-Owl has both gray and rufous morphs, and some intermediate brown birds as well, and the occurrence of these morphs is far from uniform. In some areas near the northern edge of the species range, the rufous morph makes up less than 20 percent of the total population, while in some areas of the south it can be more than 70 percent. Intermediate or brown birds make up less than 10 percent of the population in most areas, but in Florida they can be up to 40 percent.

There is some evidence that the rufous morph of Eastern Screech-Owl fares better than the gray morph in warm, humid climates and that it is not so well adapted to cold or very dry climates, which would fit with the observed distribution.

When a particular color type has a very localized distribution, it may be debatable whether it is a morph or a subspecies. Such an unresolved question involves the "Great White Heron" in southern Florida and the Caribbean. It was treated as a full species until the 1970s, then lumped with Great Blue Heron. Some scientists regard it as merely a white morph of the Great Blue, but it actually differs in average measurements as well as in color, and it seems to replace the Great Blue rather abruptly in southernmost Florida rather than cropping up within the population there, as a true color morph should.

In some cases, polymorphism occurs in some populations of a species but not in others; Red-tailed Hawk is one well-known example. It is also possible for a species to be polymorphic only at certain ages. Juvenile Long-tailed Jaegers have distinct color morphs, but adults are all of the light morph. Such variations add to the range of interesting phenomena that we get to observe in the field.

An intriguing polymorphic bird often overlooked by birders is the White-throated Sparrow. This species has two color morphs distinguished by the color of the head stripes, black and white vs. brown and tan. Many birders assume that the tan-striped birds are merely immatures, but individuals will be either white-striped or tan-striped throughout their adult lives. Each morph includes roughly equal numbers of both sexes, and mated pairs are virtually always one white-striped with one tan-striped bird. The remarkable thing is that there are distinct behavioral differences between the two morphs, with tan-striped males tending to be less forceful and white-striped females acting more "macho" than their counterparts. For example, tan-striped females seldom sing, but white-striped females often do.

HYBRIDS

As I mentioned briefly in Chapter 1, most distinct species of birds seldom interbreed in the wild. In most cases, hybrids are at a distinct disadvantage, so there is strong pressure of natural selection against such interbreeding. But it does happen often enough that an active birder will eventually see some wild bird hybrids. In some regions, and with some groups of birds, they are actually common.

On practically any beach in Oregon you should be able to find Western Gull × Glaucous-winged Gull hybrids; in some nesting colonies in that region, hybrids and backcrosses actually outnumber either of the parental types. A backcross is the result of a mating between a hybrid and one of the parental types, and its appearance will generally be closer to that of the latter. In a situation such as the one involving these two gulls, where interbreeding has been going on for some time, the population may include everything from "pure" Western to "pure" Glaucous-winged, and every stage in between. (Incidentally, some birders are under the impression that hybrids are usually sterile, but this is not true; most bird hybrids are fertile and readily produce backcrosses when they mate with one of the parental types.)

In southeastern Canada and the northeastern U.S. in winter, any large concentration of Mallards and American Black Ducks is likely to include at least a few hybrids between the two. In forests of the Pacific northwest, where the breeding ranges of Townsend's and Hermit warblers meet, hybrids between the two are common. On the western Great Plains, just east of the Rockies, several east-west pairs of birds meet in the wooded corridors along river valleys. An alert birder there in summer may see hybrids between Indigo and Lazuli buntings, Baltimore and Bullock's orioles, Rose-breasted and Black-headed grosbeaks, and other related pairs. In the same area, incidentally, the Northern Flickers show every possible stage between the eastern "Yellow-shafted" subspecies group and the western "Red-shafted" subspecies group. Crosses such as this, between subspecies, are generally referred to as intergrades, not hybrids.

In addition to particular species pairs and certain geographic areas where hybridization is prevalent, there are also some taxonomic groups in which it is frequent. Among the gulls, ducks, and hummingbirds, interbreeding between species is far more common than it is in most bird families.

The most common hybrid combinations are unlikely to cause serious identification problems most of the time, because birders are well aware of them and know to watch out for them. Bigger challenges are caused by rare hybrid combinations. There have been literally hundreds of such examples documented among wild birds in North America alone, some of them known from only a single example, such as the Cerulean Warbler × Black-and-white Warbler once found in Louisiana. Identifying such a bird with certainty in the field could be an extreme challenge.

Hybrids often look intermediate between the parental species, but not always, or not always in an obvious way. The combination of the genetic material from two species can produce pattern elements unlike either of the parents. Sometimes the markings and voice will point to an obvious identification for a hybrid,

This apparent hybrid between Spotted Towhee and Green-tailed Towhee was a male on territory in Arizona, within the breeding range of Spotted but south of the range of Green-tailed. It gave call notes of both species, but its song sounded intermediate between the two. The streaks on its sides were not typical of either parent species.

but when the evidence is more ambiguous, the only way to be certain may be to test its DNA. Often it will be possible to mist-net such a bird, measure and photograph it in hand, take a few feathers for DNA testing, and release it unharmed. Without such confirmation, it may be best to identify such birds as "apparent hybrids."

Finally, some birds of odd appearance that might suggest hybrid origin actually may be "pure" individuals of one species, affected by some kind of abnormal pigmentation, as discussed next.

BIRDS WITH ABNORMAL COLORS

If we spend enough time looking at wild birds, eventually we'll see some with abnormal colors: birds that are white or mostly white, exceptionally dark birds, birds that have yellow where they should have red. Abnormal coloration in birds is not just a feature of plumage, as it may also affect the skin, eyes, bill, or legs and feet. What follows is a very brief and simplified overview of a complicated subject.

Part of the difficulty in discussing this subject lies in the fact that there is no universally accepted set of terms for these abnormalities of color. Another problem is that, even if we know about all the abnormalities of pigmentation that produce these odd-looking birds, we can't necessarily tell which aberration is responsible for the looks of a particular individual just by looking at it. So my aim here is to give a simple outline of what produces the coloring in birds and how it can go awry. It is more important to understand the basics of these abnormal colors than it is to be able to put names on the conditions.

The most common pigments in birds are melanins of two basic kinds (eumelanin and phaeomelanin), which produce most of the black, gray, brown, rufous, and buff tones in birds, and carotenoids, which produce most of the red, orange, and yellow tones. There are various other pigments that are less common. (There are also feather colors that are structural, involving no pigment at all: iridescent blue and green on feathers, for example, are caused by tiny transparent structures that reflect back only certain bright colors, while the underlying pigment of the feather is dark and dull.) For a field observer trying to understand abnormal colors, the melanins and carotenoids are enough to deal with.

Pure albino birds are those that lack all melanin in the feathers, eyes, and skin. They are not necessarily pure white, however; colors produced by carotenoids may be present in their normal positions. Thus, an albino adult male American Goldfinch in breeding plumage might appear mostly yellow, but all the normally black areas of the wings, tail, and forehead would be replaced by white. A true albino would be recognized by its pink eyes: the eyes are actually colorless, with the pink supplied by blood showing through. Adult albinos are seldom seen in the wild because their survival is usually poor. The lack of melanin in their plumage often makes their feathers weaker, their white color often makes them more conspicuous to predators, but most importantly the lack of melanin in their eyes gives them poor eyesight. Actual albinos born in the wild seldom make it to adulthood. Since the term "albino" refers to a complete lack of melanin, the term "partial albino" is now widely considered an impossibility. Birders generally should avoid the terms "albino" and "albinism" for things we see in the field.

Although birds lacking all melanin seldom last long in the wild, it is common to see birds showing a partial lack of melanin in areas of the feathers, skin, bill, or legs and feet. The effect may vary from a few scattered white feathers to a bird with entirely white feathers and mostly white skin, although the eyes generally have normal coloration. It is also possible, as mentioned above, for a bird in this condition to have yellow or red in the usual areas of the plumage for its species; and if the bill or legs are lacking melanin, they may not necessarily be white if those areas also contain other pigments. Terms for this condition include **amelanism** (using the prefix "a-" meaning "without" or "lacking") or **leucism** (with a hard "c"). Rather than "partially albinistic," a patchy white bird could be called partially leucistic or partially amelanistic.

This Swainson's Thrush exhibits partial leucism. Some of its feathers are white (typically leucism affects an entire feather, not parts of a feather), and the lack of melanin in the bill reveals an underlying yellow color. Leucism may be affecting the skin as well, since the narrow orbital ring looks brighter yellow than usual, perhaps reflecting a lack of melanin there.

When leucism or amelanism has a genetic basis, it will usually last for the life of the bird, and the same feathers will grow in white in each succeeding molt. But it's also possible for amelanism to have an environmental cause, with something like poor nutrition, disease, or some other extreme stress in the bird's environment causing certain feathers to grow in without pigment. In those cases, the white feathers may be replaced by normally colored feathers at the time of the next molt, if the bird's condition has improved in the meantime. Partial amelanism that's induced by temporary stress may produce a bird with a symmetrical pattern of white feathers: the same flight feathers in both wings may be white, for example, since the same feathers in both wings will be growing in at the same time. Partial amelanism that's genetic is far less likely to look symmetrical; the white will be distributed more unevenly.

It is also possible for melanin to be reduced, rather than lacking, in the plumage or other areas. This condition generally produces a faded or washed-out appearance. The effects are variable, with some birds looking only a little paler than normal individuals, others looking

An unusual aberration gave this Turkey Vulture pale flight feathers in just one wing. The fresher feathers in the affected wing appear pale gray or beige, not pure white, so the condition may be dilution or schizochroism, not leucism — in other words, the melanin in these feathers is apparently reduced, not lacking. The older, more worn feathers appear pure white, probably because of the effects of bleaching or fading on feathers that were pale to begin with. The molt seems to be roughly symmetrical — the bird is replacing p7 (the seventh primary) on the normal wing and apparently p8 (and others?) on the affected wing. The excessive wear and fraying on the white primaries here offers a graphic indication of how melanin helps to strengthen the feathers: we can easily see that the feathers with reduced melanin are in much worse shape.

nearly white but with a "ghost" of the normal pattern. This condition is sometimes called **dilution** or **hypomelanism.** Feathers in this condition may be very susceptible to bleaching in the sun, so a bird that starts off looking simply pale after a molt may look very white after a few months.

In some birds, only one of the types of melanin is affected, and this can produce a wide variety of different appearances, most of them paler or duller than the normal looks of the species. Eumelanin is mostly responsible for blacks and browns, while phaeomelanin mostly produces rufous colors, and precise combinations of both melanins in all dark feathers create the normal colors that we usually see. If the plumage is lacking eumelanin, the normally dark areas may look rufous, buff, or almost white. If the plumage is lacking phaeomelanin, normally reddish areas may look gray or dull black. Birds that are lacking one of the two melanins may be called **schizochroistic,** but it can be hard to distinguish this aberration from others in which one or both melanins are simply reduced or incompletely expressed.

This White-throated Sparrow had its head and foreparts unusually dark, but otherwise it looked normal. It was seen with other White-throateds and was identical in shape, behavior, and callnotes. Some observers wondered if it could be a hybrid, but a better explanation is that it was a melanistic individual — in other words, one with an excess of melanin in the plumage.

Some birds have an excess of melanin (of one or both kinds) in the plumage or elsewhere, making them darker than normal. The affected areas may be blackish or, if only phaeomelanin is increased, dark reddish brown. Birds with this condition may be called **melanistic** or **hypermelanistic.** Most of the time this could be considered a relatively rare condition, seen less often than leucism.

In some cases, if the darker color gives the bird some kind of advantage so that the genes for this condition are passed on to many offspring, a regular dark morph may develop from such an aberration.

In some cases, a bird looks odd because of some abnormality of the carotenoid pigments. This can be manifested in many ways, but the effects are seen on areas that are normally red, yellow, or orange. It produces common variations, such as male House Finches with orange or yellow instead of red, and such striking birds as bright yellow male Northern Cardinals. Carotenoids are much more suscep-

In this banding station photo, a normal Magnolia Warbler is compared to one displaying some form of carotenism, with all of the yellow pigment lacking. In a superficial view in the field, the "white Magnolia" might be identified as a Yellow-rumped Warbler or as a hybrid of some sort.

tible to the effects of diet than melanins or other pigments. The well-known example of zoo flamingos turning white without the proper diet reflects this phenomenon: the pink in their plumage is derived from carotenoids in their normal food. Diet can make colors brighter, too: Cedar Waxwings may have orange tail tips, not yellow, if they feed on large amounts of certain fruits while the tail feathers are growing. But not all such effects are thought to have anything to do with diet, of course. This whole class of abnormal colors could be lumped under the general term **carotenism.**

For birders interested in field identification, there's an obvious advantage to knowing about these color abnormalities in birds. If we know that they exist, we're much less likely to be thrown off when we happen to encounter one in the field. When we see a bird that looks (for example) like a robin with a white head, we can more quickly figure out that that's exactly what it is, and we can just enjoy it rather than searching through the field guide for a species that doesn't exist.

In the area of the Antarctic Peninsula, according to one estimate, about one out of every 114,000 Adelie Penguins is pale like this. Such penguins have been called leucistic, but many like this individual have the melanin reduced, not lacking, in the plumage of the upperparts; they might better be called diluted or possibly schizochroistic.

7. TECHNIQUES AND RESOURCES FOR LEARNING BIRD IDENTIFICATION

For learning to identify birds, there is no substitute for experience. But not all experience is equal. A day in the field can be tremendously educational or it can provide very little insight at all, and the difference is largely in what you make of it. You can direct your own experience of learning to recognize birds.

Of course, this is all provided that you *want* to learn about identification. No two people have exactly the same approach to birding; some will be content to watch the graceful flight of gulls or the active flitting of warblers without ever knowing what kinds they are. And of course there is nothing wrong with that! But most people reading a book called *Advanced Birding* will want to put names on birds, and becoming truly skilled at identification requires a conscious decision that you want to do that.

Birders often measure a day's success by the size of their list or by the rarity of the birds they've found. But to really learn identification, you may need to take a break from that kind of thinking. I often have spent hours in the field looking intensely at just two or three species. My total species lists for such days would have been pitifully small, but I didn't care, because the learning experiences have been huge.

This chapter is devoted to specific advice on how to go about learning field identification. In addition to discussing field techniques, I also offer some thoughts on how to make the most of the many resources and references available for birders today.

NOTE-TAKING AND SKETCHING AS WAYS OF SEEING

One of the most powerful sets of birding equipment that you can get is also among the least expensive. Although it can be a great advantage to have reference books, binoculars, telescopes, cameras, digital devices, and high-tech apps, none of these will improve your birding skill as much as carrying a pencil and a pad of paper, and using them.

Some of the sharpest ID experts I've met have been birders who regularly sketched birds in the field. These have included a few professional artists and others who never would have considered having drawings published: the point of the sketching was not to produce a work of art or of illustration, but to truly see what was there.

Many people are hesitant to try this, fearing that their results will look bad. But it's such a valuable exercise that it's worth overcoming the inhibition and attempting the sketches. You don't have to show anyone your sketches. The point, though, is to sketch the bird while it's actually in front of you, not to try to remember later what it looked like. If you take the latter approach, your sketches will look more generic or more like published illustrations.

For best results on your first attempts, find some bird that is relatively still (like a duck or heron sitting on shore, a flycatcher or hawk on a perch), and study the bird carefully before starting to draw. Work on its overall shape first before zooming in on details. If you have a spotting scope on a tripod, you can look back and forth from the scope to your paper to check your accuracy. If your first attempt at the bird's shape doesn't look right and you start to correct it, or do it over, you have already learned something about the bird's appearance. And the learning will go on for as long as you continue to refine your sketch.

As cameras improve and basic bird photography becomes easier, fewer birders are interested in sketching or taking detailed field notes. Some tell me that they're taking notes with their cameras. It's true that a good series of photos of a mystery bird can be extremely valuable, revealing details that no one would have noticed. But as a learning exercise, taking photos can't compare to the act of sketching. Process the images through your eyes and brain, rather than through a lens, and you are far more likely to understand and remember what you've seen.

A page from my sketchbook with sketches and notes on Chinese Grey Shrike. There's nothing artistic about the drawings, but the process of making them helped me to see more details. Notes in the margins add points not easily illustrated.

THE BIRD FEEDER AS A LEARNING TOOL

I have known some very serious birders who would never consider putting up a bird feeder at home. "I'm not a feeder-watcher, I'm a field birder," is a line that I've heard more than once. But for improving one's birding skills, there is tremendous value in looking at the birds at a feeder outside the window. Not for learning field marks for a lot of species, but for coming to understand how much variation there can be within one species. A feeder visited by nothing but House Finches can be a powerful learning tool for the avid birder.

In fact, House Finch is a perfect subject for study. Most birders don't look closely at House Finches at all. They can identify the species at a glance, usually, so they don't do anything more than glance. But any birder could increase his skill and his understanding of bird variation by looking closely at House Finches every day of the year. Their individual variation is remarkable. Not just the fact that the occasional male is orange or yellow instead of red. Look more closely. No two males are the same in the extent of the red color on the head and chest. No two females are the same in the pattern of striping below or the strength of pattern on the head. And every individual changes subtly in appearance every day, as the plumage gradually becomes worn and then is replaced at the next molt. The crisp wing bars of fall become gradually narrower and duller as spring passes into summer; the soft red of the males may actually become brighter, more garish, as the feathers become worn. By summer, when the adults may look ratty and drab, juveniles appear on the scene, and the sharp fresh appearance of their wings and tail (and the fluffy, loose appearance of their body plumage) makes them stand out instantly from the faded adults.

Not just another pretty face, but a serious opportunity for year-round study.

Another opportunity for study at the feeder comes in the form of the occasional large flock of birds that descends to gobble the food. If you're lucky, this might be a flock of Evening Grosbeaks or redpolls; if you're in the same boat as most of us, it's more likely to be a flock of starlings or blackbirds. Regardless, the approach is the same: look closely at the members of the flock and you'll find that no two are exactly alike. Find the two most similar birds in the flock, and invariably you'll spot some difference between them. This kind of close study is a terrific way to increase your powers of observation, knowledge of bird topography, and awareness of detail.

LEARNING TO RECOGNIZE BIRD VOICES

Beginning birders are often amazed at the ability of experts to identify hundreds of bird species by their voices. Experienced birders, on the other hand, may take such an ability for granted. Innate talent (such as an ability to discern subtle tone differences) may make the learning process easier for some people, but in fact anyone can learn to recognize many bird voices with a little effort. The main thing required is a conscious decision to pay attention to bird voices.

Any method that forces you to analyze a vocalization may help you to remember it. Here is a demonstration of a method that I use. With a complex vocalization, such as a song, I try to "draw" a rough "sonagram" of what it sounds like, showing where the pitch seems to rise, fall, or remain steady. I try to fit letters to the syllables of the song; these are usually nonsense sounds, but if the song suggests actual words, I'll write them down — there's nothing wrong with writing the song of White-throated Sparrow as "Oh, sweet, Kimberly-Kimberly-Kimberly," and it's more memorable that way. Finally, I'll try to describe the tone quality of each part of the song.

To create a permanent record of the song, it would be better to record it, of course, but that's not the point of this exercise. The point is to *learn* the song. Just as sketching or describing birds forces you to see them more clearly than if you had photographed them, describing their voices in detail forces you to hear them more clearly. In fact, you can go through this same kind of exercise with recordings of voices; I have done that many times myself, listening to published or online recordings of voices and trying to diagram or describe them, as a way of working out and remembering subtle differences.

Sources for bird voices. Many collections of bird voices have been published on CDs, with new ones appearing all the time. More recently, some online sources have made it possible to listen to thousands of recordings of bird voices. Most of the bird species of the world are now available in this fashion, and for some North American species there are literally hundreds of cuts available.

The Macaulay Library of Natural Sounds, at the Cornell Laboratory of Ornithology, is easily searched by species. Their worldwide holdings are impressive, and for North America their selection is unmatched: macaulaylibrary.org.

An independent, cooperative collection, with a fair number of North American birds but particularly strong for the tropics, is Xeno-Canto: www.xeno-canto.org.

A site with fairly good coverage for North America, especially for eastern species, is the Borror Laboratory of Bioacoustics at Ohio State University: blb.biosci.ohio-state.edu.

Learning bird voices from recordings is not the same as learning them in the field. Listening to recordings, we lose the context: for example, we don't get the fact that the Red-eyed Vireo is in the treetops and singing constantly, while the Ovenbird is low in the understory and singing less frequently. For me, personally, learning new bird voices from recordings is difficult, and they don't stick with me very well. But for birds that I have heard in the field, I find that listening to recordings is an excellent way to review and to retain what I've learned.

Learning flight calls. An exciting area of recent advances in bird ID involves nocturnal flight calls. Many birds migrate at night, and many of the songbirds are quite vocal while they are flying. A birder who stands outside in a quiet place on a relatively calm night in spring or fall may hear these night flight calls drifting down from high overhead. Some of these calls are easily identified: the dripping-water sound of Swainson's Thrush, for example, or the electric-buzzer note of Dickcissel. But many of the warblers, sparrows, and other small birds give high, thin notes that sound extremely similar until one listens closely.

Although some of the most distinctive nocturnal flight calls have been recognized for decades, many of the most subtle ones have been worked out only recently through ground-breaking research done by Bill Evans and others.

At the moment, the best single resource for learning them is a multimedia CD-ROM, *Flight Calls of Migratory Birds (Eastern North American Landbirds)* by Bill Evans and Michael O'Brien. This disk contains not only audio recordings, but also spectrograms and discussion. In listening to recordings of notes that are so similar, I find it extremely helpful to look at the spectrograms. The differences among the calls are often much easier to see in these visual representations than they are to hear, but if I can see what the differences should be, it makes it easier to pick them out when I listen again.

USING RESOURCES AND REFERENCES

Field guides and other books. Most field guides used by birders today are still illustrated with paintings, so birders need to have a sense of the accuracy of the guides they carry. Artists vary in knowledge of birds and attention to detail. Paintings by David Sibley almost invariably are extremely accurate and convey many elements of shape, posture, and markings that may not be mentioned in the accompanying text; they are worthy of close study. The same could be said for a number of other artists, especially European bird painters like Killian Mullarney, Lars Jonsson, and Dan Zetterstrom. Some other artists may be less careful, and details in their paintings should not be taken as gospel.

The artistic quality or the level of detail in a bird painting may not provide a good measure of its accuracy. Sophie Webb's color plates for *A Guide to the Birds of Mexico and Northern Central America* (Howell and Webb 1995) were regarded by some birders as looking a bit rough, but in fact they were highly accurate, and they represented a major step forward in showing Mexican birds as they appear in the field. Another aesthetic issue involves the consistency of illustrations throughout a field guide. The National Geographic bird guides have work by multiple illustrators, sometimes on the same page, and some birders are put off by that; but world-class experts Jon Dunn and Jonathan Alderfer work closely with the artists, and the illustrations in these books are reliable and accurate despite differences in style.

Of course, a field guide is not just a collection of pictures. Unfortunately, many birders who buy additional guides will mainly glance at the illustrations when trying to figure out a mystery bird, so they fail to get the full benefit of the text. Consider two recent guides illustrated with photos: *The Smithsonian Field Guide to the Birds of North America,* by Ted Floyd (2008), and the *National Wildlife Federation Field Guide to Birds of North America,* by Ned Brinkley (2007). Their real value for serious birders is in their words, because Floyd and Brinkley are both highly experienced birders and they manage to pack a lot of original information into the limited text space. A birder who gets these books and only looks at the pictures is seriously missing out.

Online sources. For bird ID, as for most subjects, the Internet has a huge amount of information. And as for any other subject, the quality and reliability of that information is highly variable. Any search of bird images online will quickly turn up many that are misidentified. A search for Web pages about identification may turn up some that are sketchy and possibly misleading, as well as some that are thorough, accurate, and informative. The challenge is to tell the difference.

In the future we'll probably see more thorough and detailed web-based resources on identification. For the time being, such material is scattered. The best bet for reliability is to find online copies of articles that have appeared already in a print publication, such as American Birding Association's *Birding* magazine, because printed periodicals usually require some kind of review process. A few websites are also produced with care; one that often carries excellent ID pieces (with an emphasis on Britain and Europe, but many for North America as well) is Surfbirds: www.surfbirds.com. Online discussion groups about identification usually feature some comments by genuine experts and some comments that are way off base. For the most part, ID material online should be approached with caution.

Identifying birds from photographs. This presents a challenge that is often strikingly different from identifying the same birds in life. There are many ways in which photos can be misleading, and it's important to know about these when we are trying to learn by looking at photos that already have been identified.

Size can be very misleading in photos. In particular, beware of comparing sizes of birds that are nearer or farther away in the picture. The foreshortening effect of a view through a telephoto lens can make it seem that a bird in the background or foreground is much closer to the subject bird than it really is.

Lighting can have a major effect on colors, of course, and our eyes don't seem to compensate for this in photos as well as in real life. Shadows on white areas can look blue, and I have heard birders seriously discussing photos of birds with blue bellies, when the birds were obviously white below. I'm sure those same birders would have had no problem figuring out that the blue was an illusion if they had looked at the birds in life. In a similar vein, a bird photographed against a bright sky may be misinterpreted to be genuinely dark, and a bird photographed in evening light may be thought to be more warmly colored than it really is. It's as if we believe the photos more than we believe our own eyes. Any time we're looking at bird photos, we need to ask: are those the bird's real colors, or are we seeing the effects of lighting?

In soft focus, limited pale areas surrounded by dark can appear to expand. White wing bars on dark wings, for example, or a white eye-ring on a dark head, can look much wider and brighter if a photo is slightly out of focus. On the other hand, digital sharpening of a photo can create the illusion of markings that weren't there at all — such as dark lines separating areas of different colors. Photographs can lie in a variety of ways, and we always need to take them with a grain of salt.

Bird-banding as a learning opportunity. Scattered throughout North America are research sites where birds are captured and banded. The capture usually involves mist-nets or traps, and each bird is held only briefly before a uniquely numbered, lightweight metal band is placed on one leg; then the bird is released unharmed. The band allows the bird to be individually identified if it is captured again. Banding has produced a tremendous amount of information about the migrations and longevity of wild birds, and it continues to be a valuable research method. But for those working at the banding sites, it also offers the opportunity to look closely, if briefly, at many birds. If you can arrange to volunteer to help at a banding station, you may get to learn details that would never catch your eye under normal field conditions.

As part of the process, banders are required to identify each bird, of course, not only to species, but to age and sex if possible. This requires looking at a number of fine details. Some such details are not useful in the field — the degree of ossification of the skull, for example. But many things about the molt or wear of the plumage, fine details of feather patterns, eye colors, etc., most easily seen with birds in hand, may be applied in the field with close views.

Birders must remember that banding stations are doing serious work and that the birds cannot be held any longer than necessary just for the sake of our ID studies. If we volunteer at a banding site, we have an obligation to be genuinely helpful and not to place any additional stress on the birds, or on the banders! But with consideration and common sense, birders who frequent banding stations may learn a lot there.

Visiting museum collections. Scientific collections of bird specimens can be treasure troves of information for really serious students of bird identification. With my lifelong interest in ID, I have spent literally thousands of hours looking closely at specimens in many universities and natural history museums throughout North America. Stuffed birds lying in specimen trays don't look like live birds in the wild, obviously, but most details of their feathers look the same. A good collection offers an unparalleled chance to look at details on many individuals, making comparisons of birds from different seasons and different regions, getting a sense for the degree of variation in each species.

As with any other resource, there are some pitfalls to looking at museum specimens. Even in the best collections, I occasionally find a specimen that is misidentified to species. More often, the labeling as to sex, age, or subspecies may be incorrect, particularly for specimens that were taken long ago (as many of them were, of course, in a different era of ornithology). So a bird labeled as an "adult female," for example, might not be, unless the label also indicates how the collector determined that.

In a collection that has been well cared for, the colors of most feathers may remain essentially unchanged for decades or even centuries, but some colors are subject to change. In particular, some browns may gradually become more reddish with age, a process known as "foxing" of the plumage. Old specimens that appear unusually reddish brown may result from this phenomenon.

Specimen collections are not open to curiosity seekers or the general public, but a birder with a serious and specific ID question often can arrange access to a museum or university collection. I have found the curators of such collections to be unfailingly courteous and often keenly interested in my questions, whether I wanted to look at variation in juvenile jaegers, signs of molt in flycatchers, back patterns in warblers, or something else.

Unfortunately, with the modern focus on molecular biology, some universities and museums fail to recognize that specimen collections are still tremendously important. Much of the recent progress on learning about molt and geographic variation has come from study of these collections, and there are many more questions waiting to be answered. Birders who make use of collections (which, by extension, includes everyone who uses any kind of advanced ID reference) should support the continued maintenance and staffing of such collections, for the good of ornithology.

FIELD EXERCISES FOR IMPROVING YOUR IDENTIFICATION SKILLS

For a few years after the first edition of *Advanced Birding* was published, I taught a series of ID workshops organized through Victor Emanuel Nature Tours. Since these events lasted several days, we had time to really explore concepts of identification. For our time in the field, so that we wouldn't just go birding without focus, I introduced "assignments" or "exercises" each day. Our workshop classes handled these as a group, but if you're birding by yourself, you can give yourself assignments like this, with good results.

Find a bird with a complicated pattern and describe it in words. One of the best subject species for this exercise was Killdeer; on a couple of occasions, we spent more than half an hour trying to describe clearly and accurately the complicated face pattern of the ordinary, everyday Killdeer. How could we really convey the shape of those white patches on the face? What was the difference between those two black neck rings, and why did they seem to keep changing? One man complained at the outset that this was unnecessary, that Killdeer was an easy bird to identify, and I couldn't disagree with the latter point. But after going through the Killdeer exercise, people remarked on how much more they were noticing the face patterns of other plovers, like Semipalmated and Piping plovers, that we found in the same area.

Describe how you would identify this bird without looking at its color or markings. Usually when I posed this challenge, I had to explain it. I would say, I know this bird is easy to identify, but imagine for a moment that it isn't. Imagine that it lacks all pigment, that we're looking at a completely white bird. How would we know what species it is?

When I would ask that question regarding some striking bird — say, a male Vermilion Flycatcher, flaming red with black trim — the reaction from the group often started out somewhat amused or exasperated, as if I were wasting their time. But then people would start to offer suggestions. Well, it's perched in the open. It's in an open habitat with grass and scattered short trees. It just flew down to catch an insect in midair, near the ground, and then came back to the same perch; that's a flycatcher kind of thing to do. Flying down like that for a low insect, maybe not all flycatchers do that? It's perching kind of horizontally, like a kingbird, but it keeps dipping its tail, like a phoebe. It's a phoebe type of tail action but it looks too short-tailed to be a phoebe. The bill looks small, maybe smaller than on most flycatchers. . . . On and on, as the birders rose to the challenge, looking past the bright colors to see the whole bird.

Okay, but aside from those brilliant colors, how would you identify it?

Find a bird that can't be identified with certainty. This was another challenge that produced some exasperation. Looking for a bird that *can't* be identified — isn't that the opposite of what we're trying to do here? But as we pursued this in the field, it sparked good discussion of the ways that we often name birds by assumption. We were seeing distant dark ibises and assuming they were White-faced, because Glossy Ibis is rare in Texas, but in fact we had only made definite identifications on a few that came close. We had identified nearby meadowlarks as Eastern Meadowlarks by hearing their callnotes, but we were seeing distant ones that we honestly couldn't identify — there could have been the odd Western and we wouldn't have known it. Once people got into the spirit of the question, they were coming up with all kinds of possibilities, with distant grackles, ducks, and even vultures for which we could not rule out other possible (but unlikely) species.

Fill out a checklist, not of species, but of parts of the bird. For this, I had to make up a new checklist for the group. It was like a bird checklist, but instead of species names it had bird topography terms such as "scapulars," "lesser coverts," "median coverts," and so on, with a blank line after each term. During the course of a day in the field, we found birds with distinctive colors or markings for each of these. Thus, during a good study of a perched Vesper Sparrow we might determine that the rusty color on its shoulder was limited to the lesser coverts, so we'd fill in that line. A scope view of a male Red-winged Blackbird might reveal that the buff edging on the red shoulder patch was confined to the median coverts, so that would go on the list. This turned out to be an excellent exercise both for reviewing the parts of the bird and for learning to see details.

Notice some new or unfamiliar thing about a familiar bird. This turned out to be one of the most popular exercises. The "new things" noticed ran the gamut from the dots on the coverts of a Carolina Wren to the head-bobbing behavior of an American Kestrel. What all had in common was that they required the birders to look a little more closely, to increase their powers of observation. I ran into one birder six years after she had taken the workshop, and she told me that she still tried to find one new thing about a familiar bird on every trip into the field.

Don't count your list. This might seem like an odd suggestion, but I'm serious. Any time we measure anything that can be affected by our own actions, the very fact that we're measuring it can alter our behavior. If we step on the scale twice a day, it may affect our behavior at the fridge; if we calculate our gas mileage every time we fill up, it may affect our driving. Likewise, if we count up our list of bird species at the end of every field trip, it can alter our birding — we may go out of our way to pick up a few more species, rather than spending more time studying the birds we have found. I'm not saying that we shouldn't keep notes on the birds we've seen, just that on a day when we really want to study identification, we need to de-emphasize the species total.

LEARNING TO IDENTIFY WATERFOWL

The general public might understand the term "waterfowl" to signify any bird found near the water. But for birders and ornithologists, the term denotes members of the family Anatidae, the ducks, geese, and swans. These birds make up a conspicuous element in the birdlife of most regions of North America, and indeed most regions of the world, although they are most diverse in the temperate zones.

Most species of waterfowl are relatively easy to identify, at least part of the time. But within this family there are some serious challenges. In fact, the majority of waterfowl species, especially among the ducks, can be hard to identify in certain plumages. In order to come to grips with these birds, it is more important to understand some basics than it is to memorize a series of field marks.

Overview of the problem. Swans, geese, and ducks all present problems in identification, but the challenges are different for each group.

With feathers all white (adults) or brownish gray (juveniles), swans have no plumage marks to distinguish them, so identification must revolve around details of size and shape, and especially the structure of the bill and the arrangement of feathering around the bill's base. Young birds are especially problematic. The feathering around the base of the

On these young Trumpeter Swans in late August, the arrangement of feathering around the base of the bill is not yet fully developed and not a useful field mark.

bill may not be a reliable field mark on these birds at first. In body size they may be slightly smaller than adults for many months, and this can affect our impressions of the ratio of bill size to body size. With Trumpeter Swans now being reintroduced widely in North America, the potential for confusion between Tundra and Trumpeter swans will continue to be a problem.

Among the swans and geese (and whistling-ducks), but not the true ducks, sexes are similar and both parents take part in raising the young. Whereas young ducks become independent rather quickly, young swans and geese may remain with their parents for months, and it has been shown that young geese of some species may be part of the same flock as their parents for several years. This tight cohesion of family units and flocks has led to the formation of many distinct local populations among ducks. Some of these populations have presented challenges for taxonomists as well as for field birders; classifying the various groups into subspecies, or even species, has been problematic. In North America, the great variation among populations of "white-cheeked

geese" has been recognized for some time, but the split of Canada and Cackling geese was made only recently, and there is still controversy about how to classify the subspecies of each. The subspecific identity of Canada Geese in much of the northern U.S. is now hopelessly muddled because of the widespread introduction of resident flocks, often consisting mainly of stock from the "Giant" Canada Goose *(B. c. maxima)*.

Cackling Goose is now recognized as a species distinct from Canada Goose, but we have only a foggy idea of subspecific variation within these two species.

The other big challenge on this continent involves interbreeding between Snow Goose and Ross's Goose; separating these two would be relatively simple if not for all the hybrids and backcrosses confusing the picture.

Whistling-ducks make up a distinct subfamily. Despite the name, they are more closely related to geese and swans than to any of the true ducks. In the whistling-ducks, as in geese and swans but unlike most

Adult Black-bellied Whistling-Ducks: ID is not a problem.

true ducks, the sexes are similar, and males take part in raising the young. Whistling-ducks are quite vocal, especially in flight, and they have very distinctive shapes and patterns. Aside from occasional confusion caused by young Black-bellied Whistling-Ducks with gray bills, they pose no challenges for birders.

Most of the identification challenges among North American waterfowl involve the true ducks, and the rest of this chapter will be devoted to them.

Among the true ducks, as a rule, males play no part in caring for the eggs or young. In most species, males have gaudy plumages for most of the year, while females are colored and patterned for camouflage. Many of the females are difficult to identify, especially at a distance. Males also become quite challenging during a period centered on late summer when they wear a dull plumage, the so-called eclipse plumage, that makes them less conspicuous while they go through the flightless stage of their wing molt.

Most true ducks apparently pair up on the wintering grounds or during migration, with males following their mates back to the females' nesting grounds and then leaving around the time the eggs are laid. With males often breeding in a different area every year, there is much genetic mixing of populations, so ducks are less likely than geese to develop distinctive local forms. (There are exceptions among relatively sedentary ducks with large breeding ranges, such as Common Eider.)

With male ducks putting most of their reproductive energy into courtship, and females not dependent on the help of males to raise the young, ducks succeed in producing hybrids more often than most wild birds. The ever-present possibility of hybrids adds to the challenge of identifying a duck that doesn't quite match the expected species.

A final complication results from the fact that exotic waterfowl from all over the world are kept in captivity in North America. Often these are kept in open-air situations, and if the owners fail to keep their wings clipped, these birds may wander far away and show up in natural habitats. A duck that is not readily identified might turn out to be such an escapee. Furthermore, since bird species in captivity tend to interbreed more often than birds in the wild, these collections of exotic waterfowl may produce some bizarre hybrid combinations involving species that would never come in contact in a natural state.

LEARNING THE GROUPS OF DUCKS

Separating ducks from other swimming birds is an early challenge for new birders. Grebes, loons, gallinules, even cormorants may mislead newcomers. Most of these have strikingly different bill shapes from ducks. American Coot is probably the non-duck that is confused with the ducks most often, but the high frontal shield on its bill and its habit of bobbing its rounded head as it swims are distinctive. Swans and geese are more similar to ducks, naturally, since they belong to the same family, but their size, patterns, and bill shapes are enough to separate them as distinct groups.

With more than three dozen species occurring regularly in North America, ducks present us with enough diversity to be confusing to new birders. In order to make sense of this variety, it is useful to think of ducks in terms of the groups that they represent. The summaries below focus mostly on field impressions of the groups, not technical aspects. Unless you are already familiar with most of these species, you may find it helpful to follow along with your favorite field guide, looking at illustrations, range maps, and descriptions for the species within each of these groups.

Typical dabbling ducks. All currently classified in the genus *Anas*. In the water, these find their food near the water's surface, swimming forward with the bill partly submerged, or upending with tail up and bill down to reach the bottom in shallow waters. They also will forage on land, walking on shores or flying out to fields to feed on waste grain. When taking flight, they are able to spring up directly from the water or land without

male Cinnamon Teal

the running start required by most diving ducks. Within this group there are some subgroups, such as the Mallard's closest relatives, and some names that do not represent actual taxonomic groups: for example, "teal" is a term applied to the smallest dabblers, but Green-winged Teal is not a close relative of Blue-winged and Cinnamon teal. Most dabblers are quite vocal for much of the year; calls of males are quite distinctive, while those of females tend toward more generic quacks.

Wood Duck. Not closely related to the typical dabbling ducks, but forages like them, dabbling at the water's surface (often eating acorns in flooded forests) or occasionally upending. May feed on waste grain in open fields and may live in very open marshes, but also found on small ponds or rivers inside forests, and often seen perching high in trees. In the air, the long broad tail is distinctive, and so is the habit of turning the head to look around in flight more than most ducks. Both males and females have distinctive voices.

female Wood Duck

The preceding birds may dive underwater in situations of extreme stress, as when attacked by a bird of prey, but they normally do not dive to seek food underwater. All of the remaining groups of ducks do at least some of their foraging underwater and are loosely classified as "diving ducks," a term that encompasses a wide diversity.

Pochards (genus *Aythya*). These common and widespread ducks (scaup, Redhead, Canvasback, Ring-necked, and others) are compact divers, often seen on lakes and ponds as well as coastal bays. (Ring-necked Duck in particular is often on small tree-lined ponds, while Redhead is often on very shallow marshes, foraging like a dabbling duck.) Winter flocks of some species can contain hundreds or even thousands of birds. In all of these, adult males are patterned in solid blocks of color, females and younger birds are rel-

male Ring-necked Duck

atively smooth brown or gray, without the strong feather patterns of typical dabblers. Head and bill shapes are very distinctive. Generally quiet at most times of year, although males of some species are quite vocal in spring.

Eiders. These are mostly large, bulky diving ducks of northern coastal areas (Steller's Eider is smaller and less stout than the others). Adult males are very ornate, females and young males are plain, and all have bulky bodies and thick plumage. Un-

adult male King Eider

like most ducks, eider males take more than a year to achieve full adult plumage, and young males present a variety of challenging appearances. Three of the species have feathering extending forward onto the bill, but Steller's Eider does not, and females and young males of this species might even be passed off as odd dabbling ducks.

Harlequin Duck. A distinctive small duck, nesting mostly along rocky, fast-flowing streams and wintering mostly along rocky coastlines. Usually seen only in small concentrations, seldom in large flocks. Tends to fly low, with fast wingbeats. Males make high-pitched squeaking calls.

female Harlequin Duck

Scoters. Large, dark, heavy-bodied ducks, nesting in the north and mostly wintering at sea. Often in flocks at sea, bobbing on the waves or flying low over the water, but may appear as singles or small groups on inland waters. As with eiders, male scoters take more than a year to attain full adult plumage, and young males can present some challenges in identification. Bill shapes, and the arrangement of feathering at the base of the bill, are very distinctive at close range. Generally silent at most times of year, although males in breeding season have interesting calls.

male Surf Scoter

Long-tailed Duck. A hardy northern duck, nesting on Arctic tundra and mostly wintering at sea in cold climates, with only a few stragglers coming farther south and inland. Compact and slim, with a small bill and (in males) a long tail. Often in very large flocks and very vocal for most of the year, far more so than most diving ducks. In the air, it may be recognized by its slim, elongated shape, fast flight, and solidly dark wings. It shows more obvious seasonal change in plumage than most ducks.

Long-tailed Duck, adult male in winter

Goldeneyes and Bufflehead. Strongly patterned divers with puffy heads and short bills. Common mainly in the north, they usually nest in cavities. They tend to be found on the open waters of lakes, bays, or rivers, not in marshes, and their winter flocks tend to be small — usually no more than a few dozen birds together. These three species fly with fast wingbeats, and the wings of the two goldeneye species make a whistling sound in flight.

male Common Goldeneye

Mergansers. These are our only ducks that specialize in eating fish, swimming rapidly underwater to catch them. The relatively long, narrow bills of mergansers have saw-toothed tomia (cutting edges of the

male
Hooded Merganser

mandibles), undoubtedly helping them to hold on to slippery fish. Mergansers in flight have a very linear and horizontal look, with the bill, neck, body, and tail all appearing to lie along the same straight line. Hooded Merganser in particular has a long-tailed look and very fast wingbeats.

Stifftails.   Ruddy Duck and Masked Duck are our representatives of this odd group, known by their compact size, short necks, large flat bills, and the long tail feathers that are often raised above the water. With relatively small wings for their size, they fly with very rapid wingbeats and often seem reluctant to fly. Ruddies gather in tight flocks on open water and often seem very lethargic, sitting still on the water for hours at a time. Masked Duck, a tropical species scarce in our area, is more of a marsh bird, often hiding in dense cover around shallow ponds. Stifftails appear to be on a different cycle of plumage color than most ducks, with males molting into their brightest colors in spring, not in fall. They tend to be silent most of the time except during courtship.

male Ruddy Duck in
alternate plumage

WHAT TO LOOK FOR IN IDENTIFYING DUCKS

Habitat and behavior. Choice of habitat and behavioral characteristics are almost never diagnostic for any species of duck, but these aspects are often very helpful in suggesting what species are likely.

We often see many species of ducks associating on the same body of water, and this mixing may lead us to overlook the fact that every species has a particular habitat type that it favors. Generally speaking, of course, dabbling ducks are found in shallow waters where they can reach the bottom by dipping their heads underwater or tipping up, while diving ducks may be found on much deeper waters. There are exceptions: American Wigeon is a dabbler but is sometimes on deep waters, where it may steal food from diving birds when they come to the surface. Redhead is a diving duck but often feeds at the surface; flocks may be found on very shallow lagoons in winter, even on flooded farm fields in migration.

Within these broad categories of shallow and deep waters, species have further preferences. Northern Shoveler, Cinnamon Teal, and Blue-winged Teal favor very shallow, muddy areas, where they use their broad bills to strain tiny food items from the murky waters. Ring-necked Duck and Hooded Merganser are more likely than most other divers to be found on tree-lined ponds. Mergansers generally seek out clear water where they can see to pursue fish, while Harlequin Ducks favor the roiled, turbulent water near wave-pounded coastal rocks and in rushing streams.

Foraging behavior is often a clue. Diving ducks may dip their heads underwater but they rarely upend with head down and tail up in the manner of a typical dabbler. Dabbling ducks may dive underwater when panicked, but they do not dive habitually for food. Among divers, some go underwater with a noticeable forward leap, while others slide below the surface with less effort. Most

A male Northern Pintail upending to reach for the bottom of a shallow pond.

A female Hooded Merganser beginning an underwater dive with a forward leap, wings folded against her body.

divers go underwater with the wings held tightly against the body. A few, however, spread their wings slightly just as or just before they go under; Surf Scoter and White-winged Scoter do this, while Black Scoter does not, and with practice this distinction can be seen at a distance.

Flocking behavior can be a clue in some cases. Some of the diving ducks such as scaup, may form very tightly packed flocks (or "rafts") on open water, the birds resting close together and all facing the same direction, into the breeze. Other ducks, such as Green-winged Teal, do not form such large or tight flocks even where they are abundant.

Flight behavior is also an important point, discussed in more detail under the section on identifying ducks in flight on p. 152.

Head shape and bill shape. Structure and silhouette are important field marks for all groups of birds, of course, but the ducks are particularly illuminating on the value of head shape and bill shape specifically for field identification. With a few exceptions (such as the Mallard's close relatives), almost all the North American ducks could be identified on this single aspect of their appearance. In fact, this is one of the most important points in separating some especially difficult species pairs or groups, such as Greater and Lesser scaup, Common and Barrow's goldeneyes, and female Blue-winged and Cinnamon teal.

Typical adult female Barrow's Goldeneye (left) and Common Goldeneye (right) are distinguished by bill color, but variation in both can make this tricky on some individuals, and young birds may be simply dark-billed for at least part of their first winter. Head shape and bill shape offer additional clues. To simply say that Barrow's has a "steeper" forehead is not very helpful; it's easier to see the difference if we look at the angle formed by an imaginary line along the lower edge of the bill vs. another imaginary line resting on the forehead. On Barrow's, these lines can be almost perpendicular. On Common, the angle tends to be much more shallow. In addition, the bill of Barrow's is shorter, more stubby and triangular, with a more blunt tip. Its head often looks more elongated, or more "puffy" toward the rear. Head shape may not be fully formed on young goldeneyes until they are several months old, however.

The apparent shape of a duck's head results from a combination of the shape of the skull, the length of the feathers on various parts of the head, and the way the feathers are being held at a given moment. The effects of the latter are usually subtle, although some male ducks raise their head feathers in a most exaggerated way as part of courtship displays. Hooded Merganser is our most extreme example of this, but even male Gadwalls in courtship puff out their foreheads in a conspicuous way. On the other hand, a bird that is alert or alarmed may sleek down its feathers, making the head appear narrower. The feathers also may be flattened against the head just before or just after a dive. So a momentary view (or a single photo) of a duck may give a misleading impression of its head shape.

Bill details. Along with head shape and bill shape, the color of the bill is among the easiest field marks for many female ducks. For example, the bill pattern of the female Gadwall, with a neatly edged black center and orange on the sides, is one of its most distinctive points. However, many species of ducks show different bill colors between males and females, and there are also many variations by age and season. The bright pinkish yellow bill of the female Barrow's Goldeneye is conspicuous in winter and spring, but from early summer into fall its bill is dark gray. In those few species in which the sexes are similar in plumage, bill color is often helpful in telling them apart.

The overall shape of the bill, combined with head shape, makes for an important field mark at a distance. At closer range, fine details of bill structure may be important. The exact size and shape of the nail on the bill is useful for separating some similar species (such as the scaup treated in the next chapter). Even the position of the nostril on the bill can be a significant point for some species.

On Red-breasted Merganser, the nostril is close to the base of the bill, while on Common Merganser it is closer to the center. This can be a useful distinction on some problematic individuals.

Eye colors. Given a close view, the color of the iris is always worth noting. Only occasionally is it significant for species identification. For example, the iris is red in the male Common Pochard (rare in North America), pale yellow in the similar male Redhead. The red iris of an adult male Cinnamon Teal would be a useful confirming point on a bird in full eclipse (alternate) plumage, when its usual flamboyant feather colors would be muted. Iris color is also an indication of age for some ducks; most of the species that have pale eyes as adults (such as goldeneyes and scaup) are darker-eyed as juveniles.

Leg and foot colors. Of course most views of ducks don't allow us to see their feet, but in a few cases, foot color is a useful mark. For example, female Blue-winged Teal can look similar to female Green-winged Teal and Garganey, but the feet are yellow to greenish in the Blue-winged, gray in the other two species. If we get a view of the feet on an unidentified duck, it is worthwhile to take careful note of their color.

Pattern details on dull-plumaged birds. The patterns of female, juvenile, and eclipse-plumaged ducks are so much less distinctive than those of bright-plumaged adult males that birders may subconsciously conclude that it's hopeless to look for field marks on these dull birds. But in fact, these subtly patterned ducks do have many markings that are helpful in identification, especially at close range.

Face pattern is somewhat more variable on females of most ducks than on males, but still worth studying. The very plain-faced look of female Northern Pintail or American Wigeon is noticeably different from the more patterned look of female Mallard or Gadwall. The contrast of the dark eye-line is usually obvious on female Blue-winged Teal, less so on female Green-winged Teal, and obscure on female Cinnamon Teal. The pale area near the base of the bill on female Ring-necked Duck is differently shaped and less contrasted than the white face patch shown by females of either scaup species.

Other areas of the plumage also hold significant field marks. On female Green-winged Teal, the whitish to buff stripe along the lateral undertail coverts forms a mark that may be visible at long distance. One of the most reliable ways to tell female Eurasian Wigeon from American Wigeon is that the axillars ("wingpits") are gray on the Eurasian, bright white on the American. While it might seem that it would be difficult to get a good look at the axillars, many kinds of ducks (including wigeon) will occasionally pause while swimming, rear up to an upright position, and flap the wings slowly a few times.

At close range, even the patterns of individual feathers can be important for identification. Fortunately, on birds as large as ducks, feather details can be seen at some distance, especially through a telescope.

Comparing the male Mottled Duck (left) and male American Black Duck, the latter is obviously a darker bird, but it would be harder to make this judgment if we saw the birds separately. However, the body feathers of the American Black Duck are not only darker in ground color, they also have a different pattern, lacking the internal pale markings that show on many of the body feathers of the Mottled Duck.

Pattern elements in distant views. Of course, waterfowl are often seen at a great distance, where reference to any kind of fine detail is out of the question. It's helpful to be aware of the fact that different elements of pattern are more obvious at different distances; some markings that seem insignificant on a close bird may become much more obvious when the bird is far away. For example, on a male Red-breasted Merganser at close range, the white neck ring is just one of many markings we might notice; but when the bird is very distant, this may stand out as the single most conspicuous mark.

If we saw just one of these ducks at such a distance, we might be uncertain of its identity. But viewing them in a tightly packed flock, with the same pattern elements repeated over and over, we can be more confident of what we're seeing. The shape of the birds (with squarish heads and with some tails raised), the large yellow-orange knob at the base of the bill on the males, and the contrast of pale cheek and dark cap on the females all point to Black Scoter.

Voices. We are seldom in a situation in which the voice of an individual duck will be the key to its identification. In fact, typically we see ducks in concentrations where it's a challenge to see which bird is making which call. Still, many ducks have distinctive voices, and knowing them may allow us to pick out some species before we spot them.

Identifying ducks in flight. Ducks of many species do a lot of flying around between wetlands, or between feeding and roosting areas, or even flying around and landing in the same spot as part of their social interaction, so we may often see them in the air. Identifying them in that situation generally involves some different clues from identifying them on the water.

Seen at a great distance, some ducks are actually much easier to identify in flight. Wing patterns are among the most distinctive aspects for some plumages of some species. For others, distinctive shapes are more easily appreciated in the air than on the water. A female Gadwall at 300 yards will just look like an obscure plain duck until it takes to the air, showing the white patch on its secondaries; a distant female Northern Pintail may not look strikingly different in silhouette from other ducks while swimming, but in flight its elegant elongated shape will become apparent.

Even field guides that illustrate all the duck species in flight often fail to convey their shapes very well, so that aspect is most easily learned in the field. Wing patterns are well illustrated in most books, however. In almost

Northern Pintails in a linear flock, looking elegant and streamlined.

all cases, the most important field marks on a duck's wing are on the upperside. Underwing patterns are generally less distinctive, but the contrast between the underwing and the sides of the body may offer helpful clues.

Flight action varies by species. As a general rule, and as we might expect, smaller ducks have faster wingbeats. In a given size range, however, diving ducks have faster wingbeats than dabbling ducks — they have heavier wing-loading, with heavier bodies for the size of their wings. Some small divers, such as Bufflehead, Hooded Merganser, and Ruddy Duck, have wingbeats that appear faster than those of any dabbling duck. Small dabblers such as Green-winged Teal look fast in flight but don't appear to be working as hard to stay airborne as the small divers.

A male Gadwall (left) and female Redhead in flight. These ducks have roughly the same overall length of the head and body combined, but the Redhead, a diving duck, has shorter wings and a more bulky body than the Gadwall, a dabbling duck. The heavier wing-loading of the Redhead is apparent in its faster wingbeats and more labored flight.

Flock structure in flight can be a clue in some cases. Teal are sometimes seen in tightly packed flocks, twisting and turning rapidly in flight. Pintails and some other dabbling ducks may fly in long straggling lines, often quite high. Scoters and eiders also may fly in lines, usually low over the sea.

Ducks often fly in mixed flocks, but the mixing is not random, as the various species tend to stick with their own kind. A typical sight would be a flock of 20 Mallards with two pairs of American Black Ducks mixed in and three American Wigeon straggling just

Blue-winged Teal in flight: tightly clustered, fast, with strong pattern.

behind, or a flock of 30 Lesser Scaup accompanied by two pairs of Redheads. Since most ducks pair up on the wintering grounds or on northward migration, many ducks will be in pairs even in midwinter. In scanning a flying flock for different species, in most cases they will stand out for having at least a slightly different size, shape, and flight action, as well as different patterns.

Wing patterns. The pattern of the upperside of the wing, as seen on ducks in flight or ducks preening and stretching, is often significant for identification. To understand such field marks, it's useful to understand how different groups of feathers create the pattern that we're seeing.

On the female Mallard's wing, the only distinct pattern centers on the "speculum," the patch of color on the secondaries. At a distance this looks like a blue rectangle with black edges, bordered in front and behind by white stripes. A close view shows how this pattern is formed. Each secondary (except a few of the innermost and outermost) is mostly iridescent blue, with a white tip set off by a black subterminal band. Overlapping the bases of the secondaries, most of the greater coverts have black tips set off from the brown base of each feather by a white subterminal band. So the speculum pattern is created by markings on both the secondaries and greater coverts.

On the wing of the male Blue-winged Teal, the speculum is not the most noticeable part of the pattern. The bird does have iridescent green on the secondaries, brightest on the inner ones, with the outer secondaries being mostly black with a slight gloss. This inconspicuous green speculum is set off toward the front by a white stripe formed by the tips of the greater coverts; these white tips become progressively longer on the outer greater coverts, so the white stripe becomes broader outward toward the bend of the wing. The median, lesser, and marginal coverts are all pale blue, forming a patch that is very conspicuous in flight and that gives the bird its name. This blue patch is sometimes referred to, incorrectly, as a blue "speculum," but that term should be reserved for patches of color centered on the secondaries.

FURTHER CONSIDERATIONS IN DUCK IDENTIFICATION

Molt patterns of ducks. The molts and plumage sequences of ducks were long thought to be unique. Recent studies have clarified how they relate to the molts of other birds. Most ducks exhibit a Complex Alternate Strategy in molting (see descriptions in Chapter 4), with an alternate plumage in addition to the basic plumage in each annual cycle and with a formative plumage in the first cycle. Because the molts bring about such a change in appearance of the birds (especially the males), a knowledge of the timing of the molts and plumages is essential for understanding what we see at different seasons.

The traditional view of duck plumages, based mainly on looking at the sharply patterned males, has been that most species molt into a bright "breeding plumage" in fall, wear this plumage through the winter and spring, and then molt into a drab "eclipse plumage" in summer. Males in eclipse look much like females of their species, while the eclipse plumage of females is less differentiated from their appearance at other seasons. While in this more camouflaged eclipse plumage, the birds undergo a synchronous molt of the flight feathers in late summer, dropping all the primaries and secondaries at once and becoming flightless for a period of weeks until the new flight feathers grow in. Once the birds are capable of flight again, they molt into the brightly colored plumage again, generally in early fall.

In most other kinds of birds, the bright "breeding plumage" is identified as alternate plumage, so there was a long-standing assumption that this was the case with ducks as well — that they wore alternate plumage in winter and spring and that the "eclipse plumage" of summer was equivalent to the basic plumage of other birds. Recent studies by Peter Pyle and others have suggested otherwise. The molt into "eclipse" in summer is often incomplete, which is more typical of a prealternate molt. The complete molt of the flight feathers in late summer leads into a complete molt of the head and body feathers in late summer and fall, and this complete molt (typical of a prebasic molt) produces the brightly colored plumage that the males will wear through the winter and spring, which should be considered the basic plumage.

Once we adjust to this way of thinking, it is not hard to accept the idea that the plumage aspect of ducks is the reverse of that shown by most birds. But many older references (and some fairly recent ones) still use the opposite terminology. To communicate with other birders and field ornithologists, for the foreseeable future, it may be necessary to clarify what we mean by referring to "basic (bright) plumage" and "alternate (eclipse) plumage" in ducks.

An adult male Mallard in eclipse plumage (alternate plumage) in late summer. Its plumage suggests that of a female, but it has a suffusion of brighter color in some areas of the plumage, and its male bill color is a good giveaway. A similar plumage at another season would indicate something else going on and shouldn't be called "eclipse."

Unlike the situation with most birds, male and female ducks differ significantly in the timing of their prealternate molt. Females begin this partial body and head molt in spring, even in early spring, commencing on arrival at the breeding grounds or even before. They are then occupied with nesting and caring for young for one to three months before their prebasic molt begins with the simultaneous loss of all their flight feathers, and they usually go through this phase of their prebasic molt in the same general area where they have nested.

Males hold their bright basic plumage later in the spring than females and do not generally begin the prealternate molt into "eclipse" body plumage until early summer. By the time they begin to molt, males generally have abandoned their mates, and they may have departed the breeding area altogether. Males of many ducks migrate to specific molting areas in summer, often far from where the females are nesting. (Male Canvasbacks, for example, may migrate hundreds of miles north of the nesting areas, to large lakes where they may be safer from predators during their vulnerable period.) Their molt to alternate (eclipse) plumage usually is followed immediately by the beginning of their prebasic molt, the loss of the flight feathers. For both females and males, the flightless period may last from three to five weeks, and they usually won't begin to molt the head and body feathers to attain bright basic plumage until after they are able to fly again.

For most ducks, the molt to basic plumage is largely completed before they migrate south in fall, but there are exceptions. For example, Blue-winged Teal and Garganey, and to a lesser extent Cinnamon Teal and Northern Shoveler, may migrate south while the head and body are still mostly in alternate aspect.

Young ducks of most species undergo a preformative molt in fall, usually on a timing roughly similar to the prebasic body molt of adults of their species. Among dabbling ducks, most males in their first winter look recognizably similar to adult males but with a dusty or brownish tinge, while most male diving ducks in their first winter look intermediate between the plumage patterns of adult females and males, gradually acquiring a more male-like appearance later in the winter. Young male eiders and scoters develop adult plumage more slowly than most other ducks.

This male Surf Scoter, as seen in March, had been hatched the previous summer. It will not attain full adult plumage for another year and a half.

The stifftails (Ruddy and Masked ducks) differ from our other true ducks in wearing basic and alternate plumages each for roughly half the year and having the brightly colored breeding aspect of males in alternate plumage, from spring to fall, not basic plumage.

It was long thought that Long-tailed Duck had a unique additional molt each year, giving it a supplemental plumage not shared by other ducks. More recent studies suggest that the molts of Long-tailed Duck are just unusually protracted, lasting for several months, and that feathers growing in during different parts of the same molt may look different. Still, even without invoking an extra molt, this species does change in looks more than most ducks in the course of a year. For purposes of field observation it does appear to have more different plumages, and its seasonal change is harder to understand without detailed study.

Knowledge of the molt strategy of ducks can be useful in several ways in understanding what we're seeing. For example, the seeming scarcity of male Blue-winged Teal in fall is an artifact of their late molt. Even after the flight feathers are grown, the rest of their prebasic molt may be delayed to late fall. Because male ducks may undertake a molt migration away from the nesting grounds, it is possible for a species to be breeding in an area even if we see no males there in midsummer, so we can't guess the identities of female ducks on the basis of the males that are present.

One plumage anomaly to be aware of is the fact that older females of some species of ducks may acquire a plumage similar to that of the male. Generally their colors will be duller and less contrasting than those of actual males, but the difference is not always obvious. An odd-looking "male" duck might be one of these older females.

Wild hybrids. Ducks and hummingbirds are different in most ways. But in both groups, males tend to be far more ornately marked than females, the pair bond is relatively brief, and males take no part in raising the young. In both groups, males are somewhat indiscriminate in their pursuit of females. Probably as a result of these lifestyle issues, interbreeding between species is not as rare in these groups as in most birds. Many different hybrid combinations have been noted among North American ducks, and some hybrid combinations are rather frequent; Mallard × American Black Duck hybrids are common in the northeast.

A hybrid male Mallard × Northern Pintail. In shape, pattern, and color, this individual looks perfectly intermediate between the parent species, making its identity easy to guess. Not all hybrids are so straightforward.

Most female hybrids probably go undetected if seen at a distance; even if studied closely by alert observers, they may be simply misidentified as one of the parent species. Male hybrids are usually more noticeable. Generally they combine the characteristics of the parent species, but not necessarily in an obvious way.

One famous odd example involves hybrid Northern Pintail × Green-winged Teal that showed a head pattern superficially like that of a male Baikal Teal.

Even though hybrids occur frequently, we should not be too quick to assume that an odd plumage is necessarily a result of interbreeding. For example, many younger male Northern Shovelers show an irregular whitish crescent on the face, and such birds are sometimes misidentified as hybrids between Northern Shoveler and Blue-winged Teal.

Of course, many waterfowl are kept in captivity. In large collections of exotic waterfowl, interbreeding may be rampant and practically any hybrid combination may be produced.

Potential escapees. With so many waterfowl from around the world being kept in zoos and private collections in North America, practically any species might escape and show up anywhere. A duck or goose that doesn't quite match anything in your field guide might be such an escapee, a species from another continent. This doesn't mean that we need to memorize field marks for all the waterfowl of the world, just that we shouldn't be too quick to apply a North American species name to a bird that doesn't quite add up.

Domesticated and feral ducks. Most domestic ducks are descended from either Mallard or Muscovy, and after hundreds of generations, most are obviously different from the original wild types. Many such birds live in a feral state around park ponds and other urban wetlands, but they may also wander to wild situations.

Especially with Mallards in parts of the U.S. and Canada, we see every possible stage between pure wild types and domestic forms. In some areas it is impossible to draw the line between wild and feral Mallard populations. A close look at male Mallards in city parks will show that many of them have odd markings: they may lack the white neck ring, for example, or lack the dark rufous on the chest. Patterns of feral female Mallards may not be so obviously "wrong." With both sexes, a common giveaway is size: the domesticated birds tend to be noticeably larger than the wild types.

9. THE SCAUP

Species treated in detail:

GREATER SCAUP *Aythya marila*
LESSER SCAUP *Aythya affinis*

The problem. These two species of diving ducks are widespread and often common. Both species are possible practically everywhere in North America, but there are many situations in which one of them is far less numerous or less likely than the other. They are often seen at a distance on large bodies of water, and this leads to identification problems, because the two are practically identical in pattern. The size difference between them is not strikingly obvious even when they are together. When they are seen separately (as often happens), size is no help at all in identification. Furthermore, two of the best-known field marks are potentially misleading: the color of the head gloss in males varies with light conditions, and the extension of the white wing stripe from the secondaries onto the primaries is variable on both species.

PRELIMINARY POINTS

Patterns of occurrence. The two species overlap broadly in range, but differ in their centers of abundance. Greater Scaup breeds mainly in Alaska and in northwest and north-central Canada. Lesser Scaup is more widespread in summer, from eastern Alaska through much of western Canada and the western U.S., locally into eastern Canada. In winter, Greater Scaup is often the more numerous of the two on coastal waters, especially in the north, and becomes rare toward the south. Lesser Scaup can be found on coastal bays in winter but is also very common far inland on lakes and reservoirs, and its winter distribution is centered much farther south than that of Greater Scaup.

Where both species occur in numbers, they tend to flock with their own kind rather than mixing randomly, but it is not unusual to find a few individuals of one species mixed in with a flock of the other.

Seasonal change. Scaup are mainly seen by birders and illustrated in field guides in their bright basic plumage (which males wear for most of the year, females for about half the year). Males of both species wear alternate ("eclipse") plumage from midsummer into early fall; in this plumage they look somewhat like winter females but have a dingier appearance, much less white around the base of the bill, and sometimes paler upperparts. Females wear an alternate ("summer" or "eclipse") plumage from spring into early to midfall; this is not strongly different from their basic plumage, but the bill may become darker, the white patch around the base of the bill may become smaller and/or less sharply defined, and a diffuse white spot or crescent usually appears on the ear coverts. Some females (especially Greaters?) may show traces of this white ear spot all winter.

female Greater Scaup
in alternate plumage

Age variations. Young scaup in their first fall and winter may be molting almost continuously, gradually replacing the head and body feathers. During their first fall, therefore, their plumage patterns can be highly variable, but by early winter they can be readily identified to sex. First-winter males are patterned approximately like adult males but are much duller: the head has little gloss, the back pattern is coarser, and the flanks may be darker. First-winter females are much like adult females but tend to have less white feathering around the base of the bill. In both sexes of both species the eye is brown in young birds, lightening to yellow in adults (with the process generally faster in males).

The value of practice. Birders experienced with scaup may identify most individuals quickly, on the basis of impressions that are based largely on head shape and bill shape. This chapter describes and illustrates these points, as a guide to what to look for, but there is no substitute for practice in seeing the differences. If you are fortunate enough to visit a lake or bay where both species are present, it would be most worthwhile to spend a few hours with a telescope studying their head and bill shapes from all angles, watching the apparent changes in head shape in both species. This kind of study will prepare you for identifying the scaup when only one species or the other is present.

SCAUP IN WINTER AND SPRING

Greater Scaup, females

Greater Scaup, males

Lesser Scaup, females

Lesser Scaup, males

FIELD MARKS: GREATER SCAUP VS. LESSER SCAUP

Head shape. The apparent head shape of any bird changes to some extent as the feathers are raised or depressed. Nevertheless, I find head shape to be the most consistently useful character for scaup. Of the two species, Lesser Scaup has longer, thicker feathering on the crown, and this creates the appearance of a peak or a point toward the rear of the crown. On Greater Scaup the highest point of the crown is a more smoothly rounded peak toward the front of the head. This may seem like a subtle character, but with practice it can be seen even on sleeping birds.

The head of Greater Scaup tends to look longer (front to back) and not as tall as that of Lesser Scaup. When seen from the front or back, the head of Greater Scaup tends to look wider. Greater also may occasionally appear to have a thicker neck, but variations in position make this almost impossible to use.

Greater Scaup seldom appears to have the Lesser's high, peaked head shape, even temporarily; but the peak on the Lesser's crown is often sleeked down, briefly, just before or after a dive. To avoid being misled by such momentary variations, watch the birds for a few minutes to get a sense for their overall head shape when relaxed. Either species of scaup may also appear to have an odd head shape when in the midst of molting head feathers, and an extended study will not help as much with these birds.

As shown by this female Greater Scaup, the difference in head shape can be seen even on sleeping birds.

Bill shape. This character is less variable but more subtle than head shape. The bill of the Greater looks a little deeper at the base and larger, proportionately, than that of the Lesser. Viewed from the side, the upper outline of the bill makes a slightly straighter line on Greater Scaup, a slightly more concave line on Lesser Scaup, especially toward the base. Viewed from the front, Greater Scaup also may appear to have a wider bill. Again, these relative differences are useless unless we have direct comparisons between the species or a lot of comparative experience.

Size of bill nail. In keeping with the larger bill of Greater Scaup, the nail at the tip of its upper mandible is noticeably and proportionately

Despite the slight difference in angle, a difference in the bill nail between the two species is easily seen here.

male
Greater
Scaup

male
Lesser
Scaup

larger than that of Lesser Scaup. This is visible only at fairly close range, but at least on males, the pattern of the bill tip may add to the effect: on Lesser, the nail is black, sharply outlined against the pale blue; on Greater, the black often spreads out somewhat beyond the nail and onto the surface of the bill tip. This seems to be more variable in females and harder to see at any rate, since their bills tend to be darker overall.

Wing pattern. This is one of the better field marks for scaup, not requiring as much comparative experience as the subtleties of head and bill shapes. Of course, wing pattern can be seen only on flying birds and occasionally when a bird on the water raises its wings. As illustrated in most standard field guides, the white wing stripe on Greater Scaup typically extends out from the secondaries onto about the inner six primaries, so that this white stripe stretches more than halfway from the bend in the wing to the wingtip. In Lesser Scaup, the white stripe typically extends only across the secondaries and cuts off sharply at the primaries, which are gray. Unfortunately there are a few exceptions, and about 5 percent of scaup show a wing pattern that is intermediate or approaches the condition of the opposite species. Lessers with "extra" white are mostly adult males, and Greaters that have less extensive white than average are mostly females. Keeping that in mind will help to resolve the identities of some problematic scaup.

On this male Lesser Scaup, contrast between white on the secondaries and gray on the primaries is obvious.

On these Greater Scaup in flight, the white wing stripe does not appear to extend all the way to the wingtip; the important thing is the lack of a clear change in the stripe's color between the secondaries and primaries.

Seen in harsh light conditions, the primaries on this Lesser Scaup look only a little darker than the secondaries, and in a brief view this bird might suggest the wing pattern of Greater Scaup.

This female Greater Scaup shows only a slight extension of the white wing stripe from the secondaries onto the primaries. Females average slightly less white in the wing than males.

Color of head gloss. Any birder who has noticed that drake Mallards can look purple-headed in some lights will realize that there are dangers in relying on iridescent head colors as field marks. We should never use apparent head color as a major field mark for a lone male scaup, or even for groups of them at a distance or in low light. But we shouldn't dismiss head color entirely, either. There are times when we can see both species together in good direct sunlight, and the head sheen on adult males — greenish in Greaters, purple in Lessers — may be obvious and may serve as a good quick field mark.

Flank pattern. On adult male Greaters, the flank feathers are often a nearly immaculate white. On adult male Lessers, these feathers often have extensive fine vermiculations of gray, which are almost never visible as such in the field but may give the flank a clouded appearance. (Young male Greaters during their first winter also may have the flanks clouded or dusted with gray or brown.) Because light conditions affect this so much, the whiter flanks of male Greater Scaup are rarely helpful in identification of lone birds. But when numbers of both species are seen together in good light, this may be another quick field mark for separating the males.

Back pattern. The backs and scapulars of adult males of both species are finely barred with black and white zigzags that blend to a pale gray when seen at a distance. These markings are narrower and more intricate in Greater Scaup than in Lesser (and narrower still in European populations of Greater), and this can be a minor supporting character at close range. However, first-winter males of either species may have coarser markings than adult males.

Size. Greater Scaup average nearly 10 percent larger than Lessers, with males averaging a little larger than females in both species. But there is enough variation in both species that the largest Lessers are about the same size as the smallest Greaters. Because of this variation, and because of the extreme difficulty of judging the size of a bird on open water, the size difference is no aid to identification when the two species are seen separately, and only a minor point when they can be directly compared.

Face pattern in females. Comparing the same ages and the same stages of plumage, female Greater Scaup tend to have slightly more white feathering around the base of the bill than female Lesser Scaup. The difference is slight and it is often overshadowed by individual variation, so this is usually not helpful for identification.

COMPARISONS TO OTHER SPECIES AND HYBRIDS

Other diving ducks. Differences in head shape, head pattern, and bill pattern should separate female scaup from females of Ring-necked Duck and Redhead most of the time, although they may require closer study on birds in alternate ("eclipse") plumage in summer. Potentially more similar is the female Tufted Duck *(Aythya fuligula)*, a rare visitor to North America. Occasional female Tufteds have fairly extensive white feathering around the base of the bill, sometimes suggesting the face pattern of female scaup. The trace of a small tuft at the rear of the crown on female Tufted might suggest the head shape of Lesser Scaup. Of course, given the rarity of the species in North America, observers are unlikely to run across a Tufted Duck here that closely resembles a scaup; but if such a bird were seen, one of the best marks would be the broad black band at the tip of the bill in Tufted Duck.

Not all Tufted Ducks look like the classic pictures in field guides. Identification of this bird was helped by the fact that it was photographed in Japan, but a bird like this among diving ducks in North America might be easy to overlook.

Hybrids involving other species. More than members of most bird families, different species of ducks sometimes interbreed. Among the pochards (genus *Aythya*), the group to which the scaup belong, several different hybrid combinations have been recorded. European birders have discovered that Common Pochard × Tufted Duck hybrids can be very similar to Lesser Scaup, but this hybrid combination is very unlikely to turn up in North America. However, there are a number of records of hybrids involving one of the scaup and another species of diving duck, such as Ring-necked Duck, and these hybrids can look like very odd scaup. The possibility of such birds should be kept in mind when we see individuals that don't quite match either scaup species.

Hybrids between the two scaup species. Given the amount of interbreeding between species in this genus, it would be astounding if Greater and Lesser scaup did not interbreed at least occasionally. Indeed, there are records of probable hybrids. It is unlikely that such a hybrid could be identified with certainty in the field. However, the possible existence of such birds gives us another reason to leave some individual scaup unidentified, as we won't be able to prove that they are not hybrids.

10. THE WINTER LOONS

Species treated in detail:

RED-THROATED LOON *Gavia stellata*
PACIFIC LOON *Gavia pacifica*
ARCTIC LOON *Gavia arctica*
COMMON LOON *Gavia immer*
YELLOW-BILLED LOON *Gavia adamsii*

The problem. Immature loons and adults in basic plumage are all superficially similar, gray-brown above and whitish below. In the past, treatments of their identification emphasized bill shape above all else. Although bill shape is important, it is also variable and potentially misleading. Relative differences in bill size are hard to judge without direct comparison or a lot of comparative experience. Some other characters useful in identification, such as face pattern, back pattern, and flank pattern, are also subject to variation related to the bird's age (and subject to misinterpretation). Since swimming loons are often seen at great distance, it can be hard to build a case for identifying one out of range. Problems often surround reports of Pacific Loons in the East, Red-throated Loons inland, and Yellow-billed or Arctic loons practically anywhere.

PRELIMINARY POINTS

Molt and plumage sequences. Loons take three or four years to reach full adult plumage, molting on a Simple Alternate Strategy, with basic and alternate plumages each year and with no preformative molt inserted in the first cycle.

Unlike most birds, loons molt all the flight feathers of the wings synchronously, becoming flightless for a period of a few weeks until the new primaries and secondaries are grown. The timing of this flightless period differs among species and among different ages of the same species. In Red-throated Loon, this wing molt occurs in summer in one-year-old birds, in late summer to early fall in two-year-olds or nonbreeding adults, and in early fall in breeding adults, and it is continuous with the rest of the prebasic molt. In the other four species, this wing molt occurs in summer in one-year-old birds but during late winter or early spring in older birds; although it is considered part of the prebasic molt, its timing in spring means that it may overlap with the prealternate molt of head and body feathers. The rest of the prebasic molt (in which the birds acquire their duller "winter" or basic plumage) occurs in fall.

Adult Common Loon in February, with all the flight feathers of the wings molting synchronously.

Age variations. Winter loons are variable in appearance, sometimes enough so to affect their identification to species. Some of this variability is caused by differences among age groups. Loons migrate south for the first time in juvenile plumage, and their first molt (considered to be a prealternate molt) is a limited one, beginning in late fall or winter. Loons in their first winter look distinctly different from older birds, while those in their second winter are more similar to adults.

In the four larger species (Pacific, Arctic, Common, and Yellow-billed), juveniles or first-cycle birds in their first winter have the feathers of the back and scapulars rounded at the tips, with well-defined pale edges producing a conspicuous scalloped effect. On adults these feathers are broader and more square-tipped, with the pale edges faint, diffuse, or lacking. On the smallest species, Red-throated Loon, the upperparts are dark gray with small pale spots on all winter birds. There are age-related differences in the shape and shade of these spots, but usually a better indication of the first-winter birds is the pattern of the face and foreneck, with much dirty gray streaking rather than clean white.

Immature loons in summer look different from breeding adults. At one year old (in first alternate plumage), Red-throated Loons may have some mottled reddish and gray on the throat and neck, but the four larger species just look like duller versions of their winter appearance. Most of these birds remain south of the breeding range for their first summer. Birders who encounter these dull summer loons may assume that there is something wrong with them, as they appear to be in "winter plumage" and they are unable to fly for at least part of the summer, but this is just the normal condition for these first-summer birds. Most two-year-old birds in summer (in second alternate plumage) appear to be in partial breeding plumage, with the bright patterns of the head and body mottled or incomplete. In their third summer, many will look just like breeding adults, but some still have some pale mottling breaking up the pattern.

In addition to plumage changes with age, the iris color of loons gradually develops from brown to red as they mature. Bill color also becomes darker gray in older birds (except in Yellow-billed Loon), and there is also seasonal change in bill color, becoming blackish in summer, gray in winter.

WHAT TO LOOK AT ON DULL-PLUMAGED LOONS

The discussion here covers all plumages other than the bright alternate plumages of adults, including subadult birds in summer as well as winter birds.

Overall size, shape, and posture. The size of a lone loon on the water can be difficult to judge, but when multiple individuals are present, size differences can be helpful. It's important to be aware that there is much size variation in all five species, and some overlap in size. Yellow-billed Loon averages larger than Common Loon, for example, but the largest Commons are bigger than some Yellow-billeds; Arctic Loon averages larger than Pacific Loon, but the largest Pacifics are bigger than the smallest Arctics. In all five species, males average slightly larger than females.

With experience, the shape and posture are also very helpful characters, even though they can appear to change from moment to moment. For example, Red-throated Loon tends to look slim, small-headed, and relatively long-necked. Yellow-billed Loon is superficially like Common Loon in shape, but its thicker neck and larger bill may make the head seem proportionately small.

Apparent head shape varies with the arrangement of the feathers, and the forehead can look steep or flattened on any of the species, but some general tendencies are helpful. Red-throated Loon often has the forehead feathers sleeked down flat and the feathers at the rear of the crown raised, so that the head looks somewhat peaked at the rear. The effect of a steep forehead tends to be more pronounced in the larger species, with Yellow-billed Loon appearing to have an exaggerated bump on the forehead at times.

In addition to having a lower mandible that often appears to angle up toward the tip, Red-throated and Yellow-billed loons often swim with the bill pointed slightly above horizontal, while the other three species usually hold their bills more horizontally.

Bill shape. Given close views, bill shape is helpful in identifying all loons, but it's important to be aware of variation within each species. Bills of males average thicker and longer than those of females. In Red-throated Loon, the female's bill tends to look slightly angled upward toward the tip, while the male's bill tends to look straighter. Age differences in bill shape are not apparent in the smaller loons, but young Common Loons and especially Yellow-billed Loons during their first winter may not have the fully developed bill shape of the adult.

Neck pattern. In a distant view of a dull-plumaged loon, when bill shape and other points are hard to see, the pattern on the side of the neck can provide a good quick separation of the species. In Common and Yellow-billed loons, the side of the neck has a zigzag pattern, with indentations of white extending back toward the dark hindneck and with two extensions of dark feathering coming forward. On Pacific and Arctic loons these zigzags are lacking; there is a sharply contrasting vertical separation between the dark hindneck and whitish foreneck, and one area of dark feathering extends forward at the base of the neck, about the level of the back. Red-throated Loon has the foreneck and sides of the neck extensively white in adults, more washed with gray in younger birds, but there is no zigzag pattern, usually no sharp line of contrast, and only one area of dark feathering extending forward at the base of the neck. All of these patterns can become obscure when the birds are in very worn condition, as on some summering individuals at southern latitudes.

Face pattern. Dull-plumaged loons are generally white on the throat and foreneck and some shade of gray or gray-brown on the crown and nape. But the division between dark and light on the face provides important clues for identification and should be noted with care. Particular points to notice include the amount of white or pale area immediately surrounding the eye, the darkness of the forehead, and the pattern of the ear coverts, which may be a blend zone or may show strong contrast. Pacific and Arctic loons often show a dark area extending slightly forward from the dark hindneck, just under the pale ear coverts, and they may show a dark "chinstrap" across the base of the throat, two points that are usually lacking on other loons.

Nape color and contrast. With a good view and good light, it is worth noting the color of the nape and the degree to which it contrasts with the back. On adult Pacific Loons, the nape is often a pale silvery gray that looks distinctly paler than the blackish back. On juvenile Common Loons, the nape is often dark brownish gray and may look darker than the pale-edged back feathers. Yellow-billed Loons often look distinctly pale brown on the nape. These characters are never diagnostic by themselves, but they can add to the overall look of each species.

Flank pattern. The presence of a white patch on the flanks, showing prominently above the waterline on the swimming bird, is one of the major field marks for separating Arctic Loon from Pacific Loon. Unfortunately, the unique nature of this mark has been exaggerated, leading to some serious errors. Common Loon and especially Red-throated Loon in winter also can show a lot of white on the flanks, and such birds have been misidentified as Arctics by birders relying too much on this one point. Even Pacific Loon can show prominent white on the flanks at times, especially when it rolls partially onto its side to preen, as loons often do.

SPECIES ACCOUNTS

RED-THROATED LOON is common in winter on the Atlantic and Pacific coasts but is less common southward; regular on the Great Lakes, but otherwise mostly rare to casual inland and on the Gulf Coast. Sometimes confused with Pacific Loon, seldom with Common Loon.

This species has an *unpatterned neck,* and the division between dark and light is not nearly so sharply defined as on Pacific Loon. It usually has a pale-looking face with *white or pale gray surrounding the eye.* The neck and lower part of the face are usually mostly white on winter adults, but on juveniles those areas are invaded by gray mottling or streaking; some juvenile Red-throateds seen in early winter are almost entirely dirty gray on the head and neck. Right at the base of the neck, an area of dark feathering extends forward into the whitish of the chest. The forehead may be quite pale on adults but is usually darker on juveniles (as dark as, or even somewhat darker than, the rest of the crown). At close range,

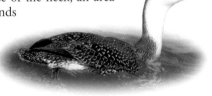

A typical view of an adult Red-throated Loon in midwinter (early February).

the hindneck and crown show a finely streaked effect (especially on adults) that is not apparent on other loons. (Note, however, that other loons can temporarily seem to be streaked on the nape when the feathers are wet.)

In winter adults the upper back and scapular feathers are rounded at the tips, dark glossy gray, each feather with a pair of small, well-defined, round white spots near the tip. In juveniles these feathers are more pointed at the tips, dull dusty gray, with a pair of dull white spots tending to converge toward the point. This detail of age difference is not apparent except at very close range, but it does tend to make the juveniles look duller and less distinctly spotted above. From midwinter on, the juvenile feathers on the upperparts be-

Red-throated Loon in early February. A bird with this much gray on the foreneck is probably a juvenile/first-cycle bird.

come mixed with incoming alternate feathers that may be plainer or may have differently shaped spots, so the appearance becomes more irregular. Some bird guides have emphasized "white spots on the back" as a field mark for Red-throated Loon, but this is helpful only if the bird is close enough for actual feather details to be seen, as juveniles and incompletely molted adults of all four other species can have pale markings on the upperparts.

Bill shape is distinctive on some birds. The bill averages smaller than in other loons, although it overlaps in length and thickness with that of Pacific Loon. On female Red-throated Loons, the culmen (upper ridge of the bill) tends to be straight or even slightly concave and the lower edge of the lower mandible angles up slightly to meet it, giving the bill a slightly upturned appearance. On the male, the bill tends to be longer and straighter, approaching the bill shape of some female Pacific Loons. However, Red-throateds often swim with the bill held slightly above horizontal, enhancing the illusion that the bill is upturned.

Photographed in May, this Red-throated Loon is probably in first alternate plumage. Unlike the larger loons, many Red-throateds at this age show more of the adult pattern.

Head shape varies with the arrangement of feathers. Red-throated Loon occasionally shows a steep forehead like that of the larger species, but usually its forehead looks very flat and the crown appears smoothly rounded or slightly peaked toward the rear.

PACIFIC LOON is abundant in winter along the Pacific Coast, rare inland, and casual to accidental in the East. In its Pacific wintering areas it tends to forage in deeper water than the other loons; so that while it may be the most numerous loon species offshore, it may be the one least often seen in harbors and along the immediate shoreline. It has been confused with both Common and Red-throated loons but is actually quite different from either. By far the most similar species is Arctic Loon, generally rare in North America.

Pacific Loon in all nonbreeding plumages has the side of the neck marked with a *sharp vertical division* between dark and light, with dark jutting forward at the base of the neck into the white chest. The dark area of the hindneck also usually extends forward in a point just below the edge of the ear coverts; on many birds, especially adults, there is a dark "chin strap" crossing the base of the throat below this, a feature not apparent on other loons (except on some Arctics). Face pattern is distinctive: Pacifics (and Arctics) are the only loons that consistently have *no* white or pale area above or in front of the eye; the dark gray of the crown extends down to enclose the eye. The ear coverts may be white like the throat, contrasting sharply with the gray crown, but more often they are partly invaded or clouded with gray.

Adult Pacific Loon in basic plumage (December). The gray nape, dark "chin-strap," and sharp vertical division on the neck are all apparent here.

A typical juvenile Pacific Loon in early winter.

A dark forehead and paler nape (silvery gray in adults, duller in juveniles) are typical of Pacific Loon, but other loons may also have the nape paler than the forehead. Contrast with the pale nape helps to emphasize the dark-backed appearance: adult Pacifics (and Arctics) are blacker-backed than other winter loons, although they have white spots on the wing coverts (usually concealed on swimming birds) and early or late in the winter they may have old or new squarish white spots on the scapulars (from breeding plumage).

However, juvenile Pacifics do have pale edgings on the upperpart feathers, so they do not look as blackish above as adults.

Pacific Loon consistently has a thinner bill than the Common Loon, *lacking* a very obvious gonydeal angle on

Photographed in early November, this juvenile Pacific Loon shows more obvious pale edgings on the upperparts than would be expected in midwinter.

the lower mandible. Its bill averages thicker than that of Red-throated Loon, but there is overlap. Pacific Loon typically carries its head and bill held horizontally, not tilted up as the Red-throated often does. Its appearance of head shape varies with the position of the feathers; often its head appears more smoothly rounded than that of Common Loon, but it can also appear to have a steep, angular forehead.

ARCTIC LOON is regular in small numbers in western Alaska in summer. Visiting birders often see a few along the shorelines of the Seward Peninsula, and small numbers are seen regularly at St. Lawrence Island in early summer. These birds normally winter in Asia, but a handful of individuals have been found in winter south of Alaska on our Pacific Coast. The birds reaching western Alaska (and presumably those found farther south) belong to the Siberian race, *G. a. viridigularis*. The race from western Eurasia, *G. a. arctica* (known as Black-throated Diver in Europe), might possibly stray to northeastern North America, but the notes below apply to the Siberian/Alaskan birds unless stated otherwise.

Arctic and Pacific loons were considered to belong to the same species until the 1980s, and they are very similar in all plumages. Arctic averages larger overall and larger-billed than Pacific, and although there is overlap, an Arctic swimming with Pacifics will usually look like a bigger bird — the largest Arctics overlap in size with the smallest Common Loons. Arctic may also have a more bulky, angular-looking head, again suggesting Common.

Juvenile and winter Arctics are very similar in plumage pattern to Pacifics, but they tend to be darker gray on the nape and crown and often whiter on the ear coverts, creating a more contrasting look to the head. A dark "chinstrap" is sometimes present (although it may be faint) on adult Arctics and usually lacking on juveniles; on Pacific Loon this mark is usually obvious on adults but tends to be faint or lacking on juveniles, so this is only a minor supporting characteristic.

An Arctic Loon, probably a one-year-old bird, in California in May. Some characters such as head shape and overall bulk are only "soft" criteria, but they would lead us to look twice at this bird. The very prominent white flanks on this individual, clearly visible when it is floating in a normal posture, help to confirm the identification.

The most consistent difference involves the *flank pattern*. On Arctic Loon, the femoral tract of feathers is mostly white. When the bird is swimming in a normal posture, this creates a white patch on the rear flanks, extending up from the waterline to the level of the wings. On Pacific Loon, the flanks are mostly dark. Some white may extend up above the waterline on its flanks at least part of the time, and this can change from moment to moment, so this point must be studied carefully over a period of time to be sure that a bird matches the pattern of the Arctic. Red-throated and Common loons also frequently show white on the flanks, so this field mark should not be over-interpreted, and it should always be used in conjunction with other characters.

While the other loon species are easily identified in breeding plumage, Arctic and Pacific loons continue to be quite similar in this stage. They may be seen in the same areas in western Alaska in summer, where Pacific is numerous and Arctic is uncommon but regular.

The features of size and shape are good clues in summer as well, and the white flank patch of Arctic continues to be apparent. The nape is generally dark gray in Arctic, pale silvery gray in Pacific. With a close view, Arctics in western Alaska have greenish iridescence on the black throat patch, while the iridescence on Pacifics is dull purple. (However, Arctics breeding in Europe also have purplish sheen on the black throat; and of course this can be just as tricky as iridescent colors on many other birds.) The black and white stripes on the side of the neck are wider on Arctics and so are more conspicuous at a distance.

Arctic Loon

Pacific Loon

In places where loons are regularly seen in flight in western Alaska, such as along the coast of the Seward Peninsula and at the northwest point of St. Lawrence Island, Arctic and Pacific loons in full breeding plumage may be separated by their flank patterns. Pacifics have dark gray feathering extending back along the length of the flanks, while on Arctics the white from the belly extends high up on the flanks just behind the wings.

COMMON LOON is the most widespread loon in North America, the one most frequently seen inland and often the most numerous in coastal areas as well. Because it is so widely available, it makes a good basis for comparison to other loons, and birders should make an effort to study it and get to know its variations. The Common Loon has been mistaken for each of the other four loon species at times, even though it is really similar only to the Yellow-billed.

Common Loons in midwinter to show shape, pattern on side of neck, and relatively plain upperparts of adult (above) compared to the scalloped effect on a juvenile (below).

The Common Loon in all nonbreeding plumages has a *patterned neck*: a single or double indentation of whitish back into the dark hindneck,

and a single or double dark half-collar extending forward into the white at the base of the neck. Yellow-billed Loon has a similar pattern but this is a good distinction from all the other loons. Face pattern is also important: Common Loon has white *around the eye* — not always surrounding the eye completely, but with at least some pale area separating the eye from the darkness of the crown. (In juveniles, the area *below* the eye is often washed with gray.) As an extension of the dark area of the crown and hindneck, the ear

This Common Loon in November is probably in second basic plumage, with some plain gray feathers on the back but with others showing too much pale edging for an adult.

coverts are usually fairly dark. This region includes some diffuse lighter and darker areas, so the division between the ear coverts and the white throat may appear irregular and indefinite. The hindneck often looks darker than the back, especially on juveniles with their extensive pale feather edges on the back.

The bill is heavier, thicker, and shows a more pronounced gonydeal angle than those of the smaller species. (Young Common Loons, however, may have slightly smaller bills than adults, so a smaller-billed loon seen with Commons may not necessarily be a different species.) The Common typically carries its head and bill held horizontally, and the neck may often appear somewhat slumped.

Photographed at the end of February, this Common Loon is already showing some alternate plumage coming in on the upperparts, and its bill is already turning black. Most are not so advanced at this early date in the spring. Such individual variations in timing contribute to the variation in appearance of loons at any given season.

YELLOW-BILLED LOON winters regularly in southern Alaskan waters and in very small numbers along the coast south to Washington. Stragglers reach California almost annually, and others have appeared in winter or migration on lakes and reservoirs in the interior of the continent, south to Texas and east to Pennsylvania. Away from Alaska and western Canada, this species should be identified with caution. Yellow-billed most resembles Common Loon, with patterned neck and heavy bill, but it averages even larger and bulkier so it is unlikely to be confused with Pacific or Red-throated.

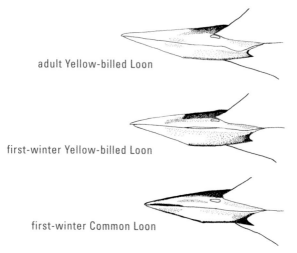

adult Yellow-billed Loon

first-winter Yellow-billed Loon

first-winter Common Loon

The "upturned" appearance of the bill on Yellow-billed Loon requires some additional discussion. The "upturn" is mostly an illusion, because the angle in the lower mandible (gonydeal angle) is only slightly more pronounced in Yellow-billed than in Common Loon. The culmen of the adult Yellow-billed usually is nearly straight, making the lower mandible appear more angled by comparison, but juveniles may have more decurved culmens, so their bill shape can be less distinctive. However, Yellow-bills of both age groups often hold the bill tilted above the horizontal, adding to the "upturned" look.

Here are some other aspects of bill shape that can be seen at close range. In adult Yellow-bills the cutting edge of the upper mandible dips somewhat near the base, producing a "smile." In juvenile Yellow-bills this may not be evident at first. These young birds may go through a stage during development of the bill when a long narrow gap appears between the mandibles (but on rare occasions this occurs in Common Loon as well). In all age groups, the lower edge of the lower mandible near the base is usually slightly convex in the Yellow-billed, slightly concave in the Common. The chin feathering extends a little farther forward on Yellow-billed than on Common Loon.

Paleness of the bill, in itself, is not a good field mark. Many winter Commons, especially juveniles, have very pale bills; most winter Yellow-billeds have at least some duskiness near the base of the bill; and some juvenile Yellow-billeds during their first autumn can have mostly dark bills that lighten gradually as the season goes on. However, the *pale culmen* (upper ridge of the upper mandible) is diagnostic for Yellow-billed. In Common Loon the culmen is dark to the tip, or to very near the tip, but in Yellow-billed the culmen is pale for at least the outer half, usually the outer two-thirds, with only the basal section dark. A close view or careful study is necessary to verify this mark, because the dark culmen area on a Common tends to become very narrow toward the tip of the bill and may be hard to see against a background of dark water.

Yellow-billeds tend to be paler and browner on the head and neck than Common Loons and to have a wider whitish area above and in front of the eye. The area of the ear-coverts is generally paler than the center of the crown and nape, but in the middle of this pale region there is usually a darker ear spot, which may be noticeable at long range. On Common Loon, by comparison, the diffuse darker areas on the sides of the head seldom create the impression of an isolated dark ear spot. Another subtle distinction on

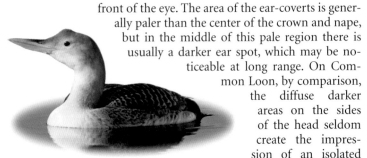

juvenile Yellow-billed Loon in early winter.

the face is that the Yellow-billed has a proportionately *smaller eye* than Common Loon; believe it or not, this actually can be noticed in the field, and it contributes to a different facial expression.

With experience or with direct comparison, observers might notice that Yellow-billed Loon tends to look thicker-necked than Common Loon. The thick neck and large bill may make its head look less bulky and massive than it really is. As with other loons,

Photographed in May and showing no sign of breeding plumage, this Yellow-billed Loon is undoubtedly young, probably a first-cycle bird.

the silhouette of its body while swimming appears to change; but it sometimes appears that the highest point of the back is located farther back on the Yellow-billed, near the midpoint of the body, and farther forward on Common Loon.

IDENTIFYING LOONS IN FLIGHT

Observers in seawatch situations often must distinguish among two or more species of loons that may be passing in flight at a distance. If the birds are in breeding plumage, a number of pattern differences may be evident; but young birds and winter birds are essentially grayish above and whitish below and must be identified mainly by flight silhouette.

Away from Alaska and northwest Canada, virtually all the loons will be Common, Red-throated, or Pacific, so this discussion treats only those three species; Arctic Loon is very similar to Pacific, and Yellow-billed is very similar to Common Loon.

Red-throated Loon is smaller and more slender than the others, and with its slender head and bill and with its thin feet trailing behind the tail, it looks attenuated at both ends. Its neck, head, and feet often droop below the level of the body, an effect not usually seen on the other loons. When its neck is drooping, its head and bill are still pointed straight ahead; by comparison, when Common Loon angles its neck down, its head and bill are also pointing down, and this usually lasts only a short time.

Pacific Loon looks thicker-necked and thicker-headed than the Red-throated Loon, and its trailing feet may look more solid but they are still not obviously large. It tends to hold the neck and feet straighter, not drooping.

On Common Loon in flight, the large head is often obvious and the large feet may be even more so; it often flies with the toes spread, making the feet look large and paddle-like as they trail beyond the end of the short tail. Unlike the smaller loons, Common often flies with its bill noticeably opened.

11. LEARNING TO IDENTIFY SEABIRDS

For most birders in North America, the seabirds are the final frontier, the last group with which we come to grips. Even for birders living in coastal areas, it takes a special effort to see many seabirds; for those who live inland, a seabird trip involves much time and expense. There are some coastal points where birders with time, patience, and telescopes can see fair numbers of seabirds from shore, but most successful seabirding involves pelagic boat trips, introducing a kind of birding that is unfamiliar and even uncomfortable for many. Perhaps it's no wonder that relatively few people are really good at seabird identification.

Fortunately, there are now many organized pelagic trips in coastal regions, and these trips feature expert leaders who know the birds and will point them out. This changes the equation for new birders going offshore. The operative question is no longer, "Will I know what the bird is?" Instead, it is more nuanced: "When the leaders tell me what the bird is, will I be able to appreciate what makes it distinctive?" This chapter is intended to help birders rise to this kind of challenge.

Overview of the problem. The term "seabird" has no precise definition, but I use it here for those birds that may spend months on the open ocean, coming to land mainly to raise their young. On the North American list, this category would include a few gulls and terns (such as kittiwakes, Sabine's Gull, and Bridled Tern), all the jaegers and skuas, two of the phalaropes, and all of the alcid family (although some of the latter, such as the guillemots, may spend most of their lives quite close to shore). It also would include groups such as frigatebirds, tropicbirds, and boobies and gannets. For most birders, however, the most challenging seabirds are the ones most specialized for pelagic life: members of the order Procellariiformes, the shearwaters, petrels, storm-petrels, and albatrosses. These birds may be profoundly unfamiliar to birders who have not spent time offshore.

Members of this order nest mainly on islands. The majority of the species known for North American waters do not nest anywhere near this continent. (Some of our most common offshore visitors, such as Wilson's Storm-Petrel and Sooty, Pink-footed, and Great shearwaters, nest entirely on islands well south of the equator.) Many of these birds visit their nesting sites mainly at night, where they may recognize their mates by location, and by voice: largely silent at sea, they are often very noisy around nesting colonies. Some may identify their own species partly by smell. One result of all this is that the birds can recognize each other without reference to field marks that would be apparent to us. So as we might expect, some species seem extremely similar from our viewpoint. Some of our toughest ID problems — for example, Sooty vs. Short-tailed shearwaters — are among these birds that are undoubtedly distinct from each other, but may not look it.

The fact that they nest on islands also creates the potential for isolated populations that may diverge over time. As a result, there are questions about the status of various forms. For example, the number of albatross species in the world may be as few as 13 or as many as 25, or even more, depending on how some forms are classified. Similar questions attach to some small shearwaters, such as Audubon's, Manx, and Little, which may be just widespread and variable or may be complexes of several species. Birders need to be alert to the possibility of recent splits that are not reflected in their field guides.

POINTS TO CONSIDER IN IDENTIFYING SEABIRDS

How to study ahead of time. If you lack experience with seabirds, you'll certainly want to study your field guides before going on a pelagic trip. But for effective study, don't spend a lot of time trying to memorize field marks for particular species. Instead, pay close attention to the *names* of all the seabirds possible in the area where you're going, and try to get a sense of the general appearance of those birds. Then you'll know what to look for when a new bird name is called. If someone spots an Ashy Storm-Petrel, for example, you'll look for a small dark bird, fluttering about erratically over the water. If the cry goes up for a Cook's Petrel, you'll look for a slim-winged, fast-flying bird, swooping over the waves in high arcs. If a Cassin's Auklet is called, you'll expect a rotund little bird, flying low, with fast whirring beats of its short wings. This kind of general idea of what to expect will be much more useful than trying to memorize details of pattern for every species.

It's important to study the names partly because your fellow pelagic birders may get certain ones wrong. "Petrel" and "storm-petrel" mean very different things: the true petrels belong to the family Procellari-idae, and they are fast, stiff-winged fliers related to the shearwaters; storm-petrels belong to the family Hydrobatidae, and they are relatively small birds that usually flutter about close to the surface. Unfortunately, birders sometimes shorten the names of the latter birds during informal conversation. If someone calls out, "Wilson's Petrel," what they really mean is "Wilson's Storm-Petrel," and if you've studied the names enough, you'll be able to make the conversion and look for the right kind of bird.

Focus on flight action and shapes. For identifying seabirds at sea, the single most important aspect is also the one that is impossible to illustrate and most difficult to describe: the flight action of each species. This action is the product of several factors, especially the bird's body size and wing shape. But size of a lone bird against water or sky can be impossible to judge, and details of shape can be hard to see at a distance, while the characteristic wing motion of a species may be detected practically as far away as the bird can be seen.

Weather conditions can affect flight action, of course. Although many seabirds are masters of the air, their behavior will be different in gusty winds than in a flat calm. Still, some elements of flight are consistent. The best way to commit a bird's flight action to memory is to watch and describe it in your own words. Are the wingbeats fast, medium, slow? Are the wingbeats deep or shallow? Do the wings seem stiff or is the motion more fluid, and do the wings bend at the wrist? Does the bird alternate wingbeats with glides, and if so, in what pattern?

It can be useful to try to compare a seabird's flight style to that of a familiar landbird. For example, to say that Wilson's Storm-Petrel flies "like a Purple Martin" while Leach's Storm-Petrel flies "like a nighthawk" is almost a cliché now in those areas along the Atlantic Coast where these are the only two expected species of their family. But once we're clued in to this difference, we can separate these two at a distance of hundreds of yards, much farther than we could see any other kind of detail.

"Like a Purple Martin": corny, perhaps, but it works.

With a better view, details of shape become extremely important. Tail length, head shape, and precise shape of the wings can be especially significant. If the tips of the feet extend beyond the tip of the tail in flight, that is worth noting. On swimming birds, head shape and bill shape may be studied more easily. Some of these points can be gleaned from good illustrations, but many of them, again, are best learned in the field.

To use flight action and shape for ID requires practice, and you can make a conscious effort to practice. Some birders on pelagic trips stand idly between sightings of rare birds, or scan the horizon for the next rarity. If you're the trip leader you have a responsibility to scan for new finds, but if you're a participant, you can use this time productively to study common birds. So what if there's nothing visible but Sooty Shearwaters or Northern Gannets? Get to know them better. Watch with binoculars and without, watch how flight action changes under different conditions, watch the effects of lighting and distance.

Notice the effects of molt. As we might expect, molt of the flight feathers can have a major effect on appearance of these birds. It usually doesn't change their wing action in a major way — presumably they've developed molt strategies that allow them to maintain their full powers in the air — but it can change their flight silhouette, making the wingtips appear more rounded, or making the tail look shorter. It can also appear to change their wing pattern: for example, if certain coverts are missing, exposing the bases of other feathers, it can create the look of white patches in otherwise dark wings.

Normal wear on the plumage also affects the looks of some seabirds. Many of the dark storm-petrels show slightly paler greater coverts on the upperside of the wing, forming a pale "carpal bar."

This Cook's Petrel in July is near the end of its molt, with outer primaries partially grown, changing the apparent shape and pattern of the wingtip.

These feathers apparently fade faster than the rest of the plumage, so that the pale bar across the wing becomes more pronounced as the plumage becomes more worn.

Rhinoceros Auklets in flight off southern California in March.

12. LEARNING TO IDENTIFY HERONS AND EGRETS

Only about a dozen species in the heron family occur regularly in North America. Their identification is made more challenging by the existence of various color morphs and age-related plumages; and because most of them are large strong-flying birds, a number of vagrant species from other continents have made it to North America, adding to the mix and to the potential confusion. In a number of cases, the best-known field marks may involve colors of the bill, face, and legs, all of which are subject to some variation. Structural points may be more reliable, but take more time to learn.

The terms "heron" and "egret" do not attach to distinct taxonomic groups — they have been applied almost interchangeably, with "egret" more often used for the all-white species — and we shouldn't allow the names to affect our sense of which species will be most similar. Little Blue Heron and Snowy Egret are probably close relatives, for example, while Great Egret is more closely related to Great Blue Heron.

POINTS TO CONSIDER IN IDENTIFYING HERONS AND EGRETS

Studying shapes. Structure is significant for ID in all groups of birds, but its importance is especially pronounced for egrets and herons with all-white plumage. Since the colors of the bill, facial skin, legs, and feet can vary, and since field marks on the plumage are lacking, details of shape emerge as the main identification characters.

Learning shapes of herons and egrets will take a flexible outlook, because most can greatly change their silhouette by extending or folding their long necks. Still, with practice we can distinguish the statuesque proportions of Great Egret from the more dainty shape of Snowy Egret, for example, much farther away than we can see bill colors.

At close range, look at leg and neck length relative to body size, and study the precise shape of the bill. Even closely similar species often differ in average bill shape: for example, Little Egret and juvenile Little Blue Heron are quite similar to Snowy Egret, but the bill of Little Egret tends to be slightly longer and thicker, that of Little Blue Heron appears thicker at the base and subtly more downcurved.

Foraging behaviors. Although this is a "soft" criterion, the typical foraging behavior of various species is often a good way to pick them out. The Reddish Egret is famous for its habit of lurching about erratically in the shallows, dodging left and right, pausing to spread its wings suddenly. Snowy Egret is also a very active forager, if somewhat less flamboyant. Little Blue Heron, by contrast, tends to be very sedate in foraging, often standing still with its neck outstretched, leaning forward, looking down at the water. This can be the easiest way to pick out juvenile Little Blues at a distance, where they would be easy to pass off as Snowy Egrets.

Juvenile Little Blue Heron: much like a Snowy Egret in size and shape, but its typical foraging posture is different.

Seasonal changes in plumage. Adult herons and egrets have only one molt per year, so they achieve "breeding plumage" without going through a prealternate molt. The long ornamental plumes that species such as Snowy Egret and Great Egret show in breeding season actually come in during the prebasic molt in fall and grow very slowly, reaching their full glory the following spring. More unusual is the breeding aspect of Cattle Egret: the buff patches that it develops on the plumes of the crown, breast, and back apparently come from a systematic staining of the existing feathers, rather than new feathers growing in, although the process is not well understood.

Seasonal changes in bare parts. Colors of the bill, bare facial skin, legs, and feet are often among the best-publicized field marks for various herons and egrets, but these colors change with the season. For a variable period around the peak of courtship, the bare facial skin of Snowy Egret changes from yellow to red-orange. The bare facial skin and base of the bill on Tricolored Heron change from dull yellow to bright blue. The legs and feet on Black-crowned Night-Heron change from dull yellow to coral-pink. Some such changes occur in most of our species, even in those that birders may take for granted without a second look, such as Great Blue Heron. Awareness of this can help us avoid being confused when we see familiar species at different times of year.

13. LEARNING TO IDENTIFY
THE DIURNAL RAPTORS

Perhaps more than any other group of birds, the hawks, eagles, and falcons have their own constituency, with many devoted hawk watchers who have little interest in other birds. Identification techniques for raptors have developed along their own independent lines among the hawk watchers, and their approach has contributed greatly to the recent movement toward "birding by impression." This approach — taking in general impressions of shape and actions, rather than fine details of structure or plumage — is well suited to the situation at a typical hawk watch site. There the migrating birds pass at a distance, a few at a time, and observers can practice their impressions over and over. When a bird goes by unidentified it's not a big deal, because another will come along soon enough.

The lessons learned at a hawk watch site sometimes can be applied to identifying raptors at other times and places, but often the challenges of raptor identification in "normal" birding are quite different. The raptors are fewer and they are seen in a wider variety of situations: not all flying in the same direction, but hunting, soaring, or perched. Learning to recognize them under these circumstances can almost seem like learning a completely different set of birds.

The terms "raptors" and "birds of prey" often include the owls as well as the hawks, eagles, and falcons. For the rest of this chapter I will be talking about just the hawks, kites, and eagles (family Accipitridae), Osprey (family Pandionidae), falcons and caracaras (family Falconidae), and New World vultures (family Cathartidae — which might not be related to hawks). This is mostly to save the trouble of having to say "diurnal raptors" every time to exclude the owls from the discussion.

Overview of the problem. One part of the challenge with raptors, admittedly, may be a psychological one. Except at concentration points for migration, we may not see many raptors in the course of a day, so there may be more subconscious pressure to put a name on each one. And there may be a sense that we *should* be able to name these birds: after all, we're talking about big, obvious raptors, out in the open, not obscure little sparrows diving into thickets. It's helpful to keep in mind that some raptors are genuinely difficult to identify, even with a good view.

Variation within each species is a big contributing factor. In almost all the diurnal raptor species in North America, juveniles are colored and patterned differently from adults. They can be subtly different in shape as well: in some species, the large flight feathers of the wings and tail are slightly longer in juveniles than in adults, changing the flight silhouette. In some species, birds in their second annual cycle can look somewhat intermediate between juveniles and adults, adding to the variation that we see in the field.

Color morphs also present a major complication in some raptors. The incidence of morphs differs by species, so few generalizations are possible; the observer must learn the particulars for each species separately. In addition, some species have a substantial amount of geographic variation; a birder who knows Red-shouldered Hawks in the northeastern U.S. may be startled by the small pale-headed populations in Florida or by the richly colored populations in California, where the juveniles look utterly different from those in the East. There is even geographic variation in the incidence of color morphs. Red-tailed Hawks in the eastern U.S. and Canada mostly look quite similar to each other, but in the West they are far more variable, ranging from chocolate brown to rufous to very pale, even within the same local population. A dark morph of Broad-winged Hawk occurs regularly at the western edge of the species' breeding range, but is almost unknown from populations farther east.

Finally, birds that look very different and distinctive in flight can look confusingly similar when they sit down. Even birds as different as female Northern Harrier, Red-tailed Hawk, and immature Peregrine Falcon may just look like brown lumps when perched.

DISTINGUISHING AMONG THE GROUPS OF RAPTORS

When it comes to identifying raptors, unlike many other groups of birds, the importance of breaking them down into subgroups has long been recognized. Practically every field guide includes an obligatory page comparing buteos to accipiters to falcons, with a nod to other groups such as harriers and eagles. Since that information is so widely available, there is little reason for me to repeat it here. The notes that follow cover just a few problem areas and miscellaneous points regarding the groups of raptors.

Kites as a group. The term "kite" is applied to a number of raptors around the world, not all of them related. Most have a buoyant, floating flight (the paper kite was named for the bird, not the other way around), but otherwise they have little in common. The five species of kites in North America north of Mexico belong to five different genera, with different lifestyles, and all give very different impressions in the field. For example, illustrations make it appear that White-tailed and Mississippi kites are very similar in shape; but White-tailed Kite feeds mainly on rodents that it catches by plunging to the ground, while Mississippi Kite feeds mainly on large insects that it catches in midair, and as one might expect, their flight styles are different. For identification purposes, it is better to think of each of the kite species individually rather than as members of a group.

Slow and floppy in the air, the Snail Kite flies about as fast as you would expect of a raptor that preys on snails.

Eagles as a group. The term "eagle" is used even more loosely than "kite" for unrelated raptors all over the world. Bald Eagle and Golden Eagle are the two largest species in the Accipitridae that are widespread in North America, but other than size they do not have much in common. Bald Eagle belongs to the genus *Haliaeetus,* along with sea-eagles and fish-eagles from around the world (including White-tailed Eagle and Steller's Sea-Eagle, both rare in North America). Golden Eagle belongs to a different worldwide group, the genus *Aquila,* not at all related to the sea-eagles. Shape differences between them, such as the Bald Eagle's much larger bill and the Golden Eagle's longer tail, may make more sense if we realize that these birds are not close relatives.

The long broad wings say "eagle," but the big head and relatively short tail on this sub-adult Bald Eagle make it look quite unlike the (unrelated) Golden Eagle.

Confusion between accipiters and other groups. Beginners soon learn that the accipiters have short wings and long tails and fly with a rapid flap-flap-glide action. This is generally true, but some other raptors can fit this description, at least part of the time. As detailed in the next chapter, some buteos fly with a similar action; Red-shouldered Hawk and Gray Hawk can look especially accipiterlike in flight. In fact, an old name for Gray Hawk was Mexican Goshawk. Conversely, juvenile Northern Goshawks are occasionally passed off as young Buteos. The more pointed wingtips of falcons usually distinguish them easily from accipiters, but Northern Goshawk is sometimes mistaken for Gyrfalcon, and a Merlin hunting along the edge of the woods might be confused with Sharp-shinned Hawk or Cooper's Hawk.

It's good to develop the habit of quickly assigning an unknown raptor to a particular group. But then if its field marks do not seem to add up, we may have to reconsider whether we've placed it in the right group in the first place.

POINTS TO CONSIDER IN IDENTIFYING RAPTORS

Using shape and behavior to identify raptors by impression. Looking at shapes is important in identifying all groups of birds, but it is especially critical for raptors and especially when they are seen in flight. Even for a beginner, the different shapes of the basic groups should be apparent. With more experience, practically every species of raptor in North America can be distinguished by its flight silhouette. This is an acquired skill; the more time you spend looking at hawks in flight (or studying lots and lots of photos of them), the easier it will become to appreciate subtle differences in shape.

The reason it takes a lot of field time (or a lot of photos) to learn raptor flight silhouettes is because their apparent wing and tail shapes often change from moment to moment as they adjust to flying conditions. A Red-tailed Hawk soaring will

Male Northern Harrier in flight. This species typically flies low while foraging, so one directly overhead might be confusing, but its shape is unlike that of any other North American bird.

appear to have broadly rounded wingtips and tail, but when it goes into a steep glide, its wingtips look pointed and its tail looks narrow. Despite this variation, however, each species is different. A flying Ferruginous Hawk will not look the same shape as a flying Broad-winged Hawk, no matter what it does. With practice, we can learn the range of flight silhouettes for each species.

Flight behavior is equally important in identifying birds by impression, despite the fact that it is even more variable. To an even greater extent than shape, this is something that must be learned through experience. The best way to learn it is to spend more time on birds of known identity. When you see a flying raptor that is relatively easy to identify, rather than lowering the binoculars and looking for another bird, focus on that raptor and watch to see what it does. Try to come up with a verbal description of its flight action. If it is soaring, are the wings held flat or in some other position? If it is flapping, how deep and how fast are the wingbeats, and how long does it flap before it breaks into a glide? Your description might not make sense to anyone but you, but the effort of describing the flight action will help to fix it in your mind.

A good behavioral field mark for distant Merlins is their habit of going out of their way to harass other birds of prey, as if these snappy little falcons had an excess of attitude and energy. Here a Merlin makes a pass at a Sharp-shinned Hawk, demonstrating their similarity in size and their differences in shape and markings.

The size of a flying raptor seldom can be determined directly, because there is seldom anything right next to it for comparison: even if another bird is flying nearby, we can't always tell whether the other bird is closer to us or farther away. But a bird's size often can be inferred indirectly from its shape and its flight action. Peregrine Falcon and American Kestrel are both falcons, of course, but they are not exactly the same shape; the Peregrine has the broader wings, broader tail base, and more muscular shoulders of a larger bird, and this difference can be seen at a long distance. Northern Goshawk and Sharp-shinned Hawk are both accipiters, but their flight action is different; the Goshawk has the deeper, more powerful wingbeats of a larger bird, and this is easy to see with practice.

Using plumage characters to identify raptors by details. No matter how confident we are in identifying raptors by impressions, plumage details are also important, and they become essential in any record of a raptor outside its normal range.

Some birders who have spent a lot of time in hawkwatch situations, identifying distant raptors by shape and actions, have told me that they have a mental block about looking closely at plumage. If you find yourself in this position, a good antidote is to make a detailed study of one variable species. There has been some outstanding work done recently on variation in Red-tailed Hawk, and this widespread and common raptor is a perfect subject for study. The "Harlan's" form, nesting in Alaska and wintering mainly in the south-central U.S., formerly considered a separate species, is astonishingly variable in some aspects of plumage. So are some populations of Red-tails in the West. Eastern Red-tails are not so obviously variable, but there are still enough differences among individuals to reward a close study. Some time spent looking closely at the details of Red-tails will pay off in greater awareness of the fine points of plumage on other raptors.

Some plumage characters will be visible on perched birds, and things like details of head pattern and the patterns of the individual scapular feathers are well worth studying on these birds. The precise pattern of the underparts is also significant. However, many of the most important points, especially of wing and tail patterns, will be most evident

Photographed in Colorado in December, this juvenile dark morph "Harlan's" Red-tailed Hawk is a fairly "typical" individual — if there is such a thing in this variable species! Notice that its long outer primaries are barred all the way out to the tips. The secondaries are strongly barred, with the subterminal bar looking thickest, but the actual tips of the feathers are paler. The tips of all the flight feathers are slightly more pointed on this juvenile than they would be on an adult. These are a few examples of the kinds of fine details we would look for if we were trying to confirm a bird like this outside its normal range.

when the birds are flying, which adds to the difficulty of seeing these points well. This is a situation in which photographing the birds may be more helpful than sketching them, unless you are a practiced artist with quick-draw skills. If a raptor flies overhead and you are able to fire off a number of quick photos, you may be able to pick out a lot of details in a careful study after the fact. (Just make sure you keep the shots of different individuals separated, or you may never figure out what's going on with their variation!)

In assessing details on the spread wings and tail, it's helpful to consider one feather group at a time. It is not very informative simply to note that the flight feathers are barred. Consider whether the inner and outer primaries are marked differently and whether the barring extends out to the tips of the outer primaries (on most birds, it doesn't) and all the way to the visible bases of the feathers. A number of distinctions are possible in the patterns of individual tail feathers. If the tail is barred, it's important to note whether all the bars are roughly the same thickness, or if one near the tip is broader than the others. With practice, we can learn to take in a large number of small details in even a brief view.

Molt and plumage sequences. Most of the diurnal raptors have only one molt per annual cycle, so as adults they are always in basic plumage. During their first year of life, many individuals of some species have a limited preformative molt of body feathers. For example, a Red-tailed Hawk might leave the nest in juvenile plumage in June and its first prebasic molt might not begin until the following February or March; but in the intervening time, between about September and March, it might undergo a preformative molt. This molt could involve up to 20 percent of its body feathers or it could be absent altogether, varying by individual. (Therefore, the question whether the Red-tailed molts on a Simple Basic Strategy or Complex Basic Strategy is a matter of opinion and depends on how much importance we place on that limited preformative molt — one more example of why birders should not get too hung up on these definitions.) For field observation, the significant thing is that Red-taileds will look essentially unchanged, with their juvenile tail color (brown in most instances), throughout their first winter, and will not be actively molting flight feathers until sometime in spring.

Timing of the prebasic molt varies with age. In one-year-old raptors it often begins early in spring and continues gradually through the summer, completing in early fall. In adults it often begins in mid- to late spring, with a few primaries and some other feathers molted before the birds start nesting; then the process may be suspended until after the nesting season, completing in late fall.

In the Accipitridae, especially in the larger species, the annual molt may be incomplete — the birds may not replace all the large flight feathers each year. Some of the largest species replace only a few of the primaries and secondaries each year, so they may have three, four, or even five generations of flight feathers in their wings, each in a different stage of wear. They may also have two "waves" of molt proceeding out through the primaries (this is the "stepwise molt" or *Staffelmauser* described on pp. 86–87). In adults, the difference between a freshly molted feather and one retained from a year earlier may not be obvious, but it can be very noticeable when a bird in its second plumage cycle retains some juvenile flight feathers, which often have a different pattern.

Molt of the flight feathers in falcons is generally complete, but its pattern is different from that of members of the Accipitridae. Their molt of both the primaries and the secondaries begins in the middle of the tract and proceeds outward in both directions: in other words, the first primary to be replaced is usually around p5, and the last to be replaced will be the innermost and outermost, p1 and p10. Therefore, falcons in molt can exhibit some odd wing shapes unlike those of most birds.

In most of the raptors, birds older than one year look superficially similar to adults; but with a closer look, second-cycle birds often show some distinctions from older birds. When they can be examined in the hand, it is possible to determine the ages of some raptors up to five years by the condition of the flight feathers. These distinctions are interesting in their own right but they are subtle enough that they should not affect identification to species in most cases. Among North American raptors, the extreme in age differences is provided by Bald Eagle, with at least five age classes that can be distinguished with a fair degree of accuracy by markings alone.

Geographic variation. Most raptors do not show enough geographic variation within North America to be noticeable in the field, but the few that do (Red-tailed and Red-shouldered hawks, Merlin, Peregrine Falcon) can cause serious confusion for observers. Many experienced eastern birders have been tripped up when they encountered western Red-tailed Hawks for the first time. The Arctic-breeding race of Peregrine Falcon, *F. p. tundrius,* which occurs widely in migration, is relatively small and pale, and it can be puzzling to birders who are familiar with the birds nesting farther south. The distinctive populations of Merlins are illustrated in most field guides; even so, I have seen the pale brown female of the prairie subspecies, *F. c. richardsoni,* misidentified as a Prairie Falcon more than once.

Color morphs. At least seven species of raptors in North America regularly show different color morphs: Short-tailed Hawk, Broad-winged Hawk, Swainson's Hawk, Red-tailed Hawk, Rough-legged Hawk, Ferruginous Hawk, and Gyrfalcon. (In addition, Hook-billed Kite has a dark morph in tropical regions, but this form has rarely been found in the limited Texas population.) It is important to understand that these color morphs are different from the kinds of variation in appearance that are caused by age, sex, or geographic differences. With that said, however, there are definite geographic trends in the occurrence of many of these color morphs. The white morph of the Gyrfalcon, for example, is more frequent in the northernmost populations, such as those in Greenland. In Red-tailed, Swainson's, Broad-winged, and Ferruginous hawks, the dark morph is more numerous in the western parts of their breeding ranges. Rough-legged Hawk may show the opposite tendency, with more dark birds toward the east. The strength of the trend is not the same for all species; dark Swainson's Hawks are a little less frequent toward the east than they are in the far West, but in Broad-winged Hawk, the dark morph is almost unknown away from the extreme western edge of the breeding range. Birders who are very familiar with birds like Broad-winged or Red-tailed hawks in the East may be thrown off the first time they encounter one of the dark-morph birds.

Rough-legged Hawk exhibits complex variation, with light and dark color morphs and with different plumages by age and sex. This light-morph bird, with a relatively lightly marked belly and with multiple bands near the tip of the tail feathers, is almost certainly a male, but research has shown that some adults of both sexes show some elements of the "wrong" pattern.

Even in species that are not considered polymorphic and not known to have a regular dark morph, rare melanistic individuals may occur; this has been documented in Northern Harrier, Osprey, and Sharp-shinned Hawk, for example.

LEARNING TO IDENTIFY RAPTORS AT MIGRATION HOTSPOTS

The process of recognizing birds at an established hawk watch is a specialized art. In addition to all the usual clues of shape and flight style, species often have specific ways that they interact with the topography of a particular site — the way certain species tend to follow certain ridges, for example, or how close to the shoreline they fly, or how high they tend to be on approach. For this reason, even hawk watchers with a lot of experience at one site may be disoriented at first when they go to a new site and may have to spend some time recalibrating their impressions before they feel comfortable making snap calls again.

Many hawk migration hotspots are sites for long-term monitoring projects. The counts of passing birds, maintained consistently over periods of years, are important for understanding the raptors' population dynamics. Most official hawk counters are very dedicated and skilled individuals who work long hours, and their first responsibility is to keep an accurate count, not entertain visitors. A basic rule of hawk watch etiquette is that you don't distract or interrupt the official counter. At some places and times, especially on slow days, the counters might be happy to talk to you about the identification of passing birds, or there might be other experts there who will offer guidance. But if not, there's nothing to be done about it, and it's best to just quietly try to work out the birds for yourself. In many ways this can be the most rewarding approach anyway, since hard-won lessons are more likely to be remembered.

14. THE ACCIPITERS

Species treated in detail:

SHARP-SHINNED HAWK *Accipiter striatus*
COOPER'S HAWK *Accipiter cooperii*
NORTHERN GOSHAWK *Accipiter gentilis*

The problem. The bird-hunting hawks of the genus *Accipiter* are the most consistently difficult to identify of North American raptors. The adult Northern Goshawk has a distinctive plumage pattern, but adults of the other two species are patterned almost alike, and immatures of all three species are very similar to each other. Size differences are not very helpful as field marks, partly because size is so difficult to judge in the field, and partly because size variations within each species are nearly as great as the size differences between any two of them. The often-quoted field mark of tail shape is subject to some confusing variation, and other differences in flight silhouette may vary from moment to moment depending upon the flying conditions. To top off the problem, accipiters (except during active migration) tend to stay inside the forest more than most hawks, making them harder to see well.

PRELIMINARY POINTS

The need for caution. As recently as a generation ago, some ornithologists were insisting that most accipiters could not be identified in the field at all. They pointed out that every well-known field mark, taken by itself, was subject to exceptions or variations that obliterated the differences among species. This extreme view has been altered by further study of identification, but the need for caution is still apparent. Accipiters can be named with confidence only if a whole suite of characters are seen, and seen well. No single field mark is foolproof by itself. No expert, no matter how experienced, can name every bird seen — some views of accipiters are just too distant or too brief. There will be many cases in which the correct answer is "I don't know."

The value of practice. To identify these birds by shape and flight style, adding up to their "gestalt" or "impression," requires some comparative experience. If we can get to one of those favored spots on a coast, lake shore, or ridge where raptors concentrate in migration, it is a very valuable exercise to study as many accipiters as possible, constantly analyzing and refining our impressions. But when we try to use this experience elsewhere, we have to remember that the surroundings can have a huge effect: an accipiter nesting or wintering in the woods will not behave like one cruising down a ridge or a beach, and the impressions that it gives may be utterly different.

Molt, plumage sequence, and age differences. Juvenile accipiters differ from adults most obviously in being brown above, not gray, and in having the underparts mostly streaked, not barred. Accipiters wear juvenile plumage for about a year, from the time they leave the nest until the time of their first prebasic molt, which occurs in late spring and summer of their second calendar year. Some individuals have a partial preformative molt during their first winter to early spring, and in some Sharp-shinneds this can include a good number of body feathers, but in most birds this molt is apparently lacking.

Overall brown color, streaked chest, and pale eyes all indicate that this Sharp-shinned Hawk is a juvenile.

After the end of their first prebasic molt, in late summer to fall of their second year, the second-cycle plumage of accipiters is usually very similar to that of adults. Signs of immaturity that often show up in second-cycle birds include retained brown juvenile feathers on the lesser coverts and the rump; some birds have a few retained juvenile tail feathers or secondaries, looking worn and brown and contrasting with the rest of the flight feathers. However, the field marks that work for adults should apply equally well to second-cycle birds.

In older birds, the annual prebasic molt occurs generally between late spring and midfall; if they are nesting, the birds may replace some feathers early in the breeding season, then suspend the molt until after their young are independent. The annual molt is often incomplete, and some flight feathers may be retained for more than one year; so the presence of a few older, worn flight feathers in the wings or tail does not convey much information about the bird's age.

Iris color in juveniles is grayish (some Goshawks) to yellow, the eyes gradually becoming more orange to red in full adults. The eyes tend to be a deeper red in adult males, more orange in adult females, so eye color is a function of both age and sex.

GENERAL FIELD MARKS — ALL AGES

Size. In the hand, size is virtually diagnostic: there is essentially no overlap in size among the species. (Taking wing length as a standard, the smallest male Cooper's may have the same measurement as the largest female Sharp-shinneds, but these Cooper's will still be longer-tailed.) In the field, size alone can rarely be used for identification. But since direct comparisons are sometimes possible, I include a graph of relative sizes.

In all three species, females average noticeably larger than males; in Sharp-shinned Hawk, all females are larger than all males. I show the separate data here only to indicate the amount of size variation within each species. Unless you are a raptor specialist with lots of experience, I don't recommend trying to guess the ages of lone accipiters in the field. However, it can be obvious when both members of a pair are seen together, such as near a nest.

male Sharp-shinned

female Sharp-shinned

male Cooper's

female Cooper's

male Goshawk

female Goshawk

Here is a size comparison of adult accipiters, representing the total length of each, from tip of bill to tip of tail. The stepped-down section at the end of each bar shows the range from the smallest to the largest birds in each category; most individuals will fall between the extremes shown. Notice the great amount of variation within each species, practically overshadowing the differences among the species, demonstrating that size alone is a poor field mark for these birds.

Tail shape. This is often quoted as the single best mark for separating Sharp-shinned and Cooper's hawks, but it is also often a source of error and a cause of misidentifications. The truth is that tail shape is a useful difference between the two, at least part of the time, but because it varies it should be used with great caution.

On Cooper's Hawk, when the tail is full-grown and not molting or overly worn, the outer pairs of tail feathers are progressively shorter than the central pair; the tail looks more or less smoothly rounded, whether it is folded or spread. On Sharp-shinned Hawk all the tail feathers are roughly the same length, so that when the tail is folded it appears square-tipped, slightly rounded, or slightly notched. When the tail is fanned widely, the tip looks rounded, of course, but not as much so as on a Cooper's in the same position. The appearance of "corners" on the tail remains subtly more evident on the Sharp-shinned, because the outer tail feathers themselves are more smoothly rounded at the tip on Cooper's, while the Sharp-shinned tends to have more definite angles on the outer corners of these feathers. The Northern Goshawk's tail is somewhat rounded at the tip, intermediate between the shapes of the other two species.

Molt must be considered in any discussion of tail shape. Depending on age, accipiters may be replacing tail feathers any time in summer to early fall; until this molt is completed, they may have misleading tail shapes. If the central tail feathers are missing or not full-grown, an otherwise rounded tail may look notched or square-tipped. If the outer feathers are not full-grown, the tail will look more rounded than normal. Usually a tail in molt will look somewhat irregular in shape, alerting the observer that something is amiss.

Relative wing and tail lengths. If the human eye were capable of accurately gauging body size, wing length, and tail length on a flying accipiter, we might detect the following proportions. In relation to body size, Cooper's has a proportionately longer tail while Sharp-shinned has proportionately longer wings. Comparing the two larger species, Cooper's has slightly shorter wings relative to its body size, but the Goshawk's tail is proportionately quite a bit shorter (by about 10 percent on average).

In actual practice, the eye tends to analyze mainly tail length, comparing it to an overall impression of size, which is based mostly on wingspread. Therefore, Cooper's Hawk looks proportionately longer-tailed than the other two; with practice, this is a very helpful point. The bulky, rather broad-winged Goshawk looks distinctly short-tailed for an accipiter.

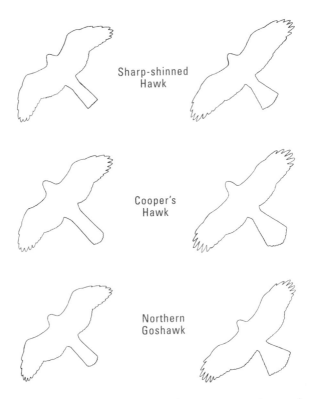

Sharp-shinned
Hawk

Cooper's
Hawk

Northern
Goshawk

Flight silhouettes. Here the great size differences among the species are ignored. They are all intentionally drawn the *same* approximate size, scaled by wingspread, to emphasize the differences in *shape*.

Sharp-shinned Hawk. The head is relatively small and the wings are often held with the "wrist" somewhat forward, so that the head hardly projects beyond the leading edge of the wings. The tail is square-tipped or slightly notched when folded and appears moderately rounded when spread.

Cooper's Hawk. The wings are relatively short — so that here, scaled to the same wingspread as the other two, the bird looks large-bodied and long-tailed. The head is large and the leading edge of the wing is usually held "flatter" than in the Sharp-shinned; the head projects well out in front of the wings. The tail is rounded, more obviously so when spread.

Northern Goshawk. As in Sharp-shinned, the head barely projects out in front of the leading edge of the wings, but the head seems broader at the base, with a thick neck resting on more muscular shoulders. The tail is short and somewhat rounded at the tip. When soaring, this species has a silhouette much like that of a buteo.

Head size and extension. For experienced hawk watchers, the relatively larger head is a good way to distinguish a Cooper's from a Sharp-shinned Hawk. This distinction is especially apparent in flight because of the usual wing positions of each species. The Sharp-shinned tends to hold the "wrist" farther forward, so the head barely extends in front of the wings. Cooper's tends to hold the wings with the leading edge appearing straighter or "flatter" in outline, so the longer head extends well out in front of the wings. The Goshawk is usually closer to the posture of Sharp-shinned in this character. Of course, even when the bird is gliding its wing position can change from one moment to the next, so a brief look can be misleading. But with a reasonably long view and some prior experience, this is a very good mark.

Judging head size on perched birds is more difficult; but with a good view, the eye on the small head of the Sharp-shinned looks relatively large and centrally positioned on the face. The eye of Cooper's is actually a bit larger, but because of the size of the head it looks relatively smaller and seems to be positioned farther forward on the face. The head of the Sharp-shinned also tends to look more rounded, that of Cooper's slightly more squarish, or with the hint of a "corner" at the back edge of the crown.

Leg thickness. With a good view of a perched accipiter, the thickness of the exposed tarsus is a helpful mark. On the Sharp-shinned the tarsus is thin, almost pencil-like, and this makes the bird look proportionately long-legged. The tarsus of Cooper's is at least twice as thick, so it does not look nearly as long in proportion. The Goshawk's tarsus is very thick, often making the bird look short-legged for its size.

Flight style. If a beginner tries to name distant accipiters by the way they fly and uses these impressions as a basis for comparison with other accipiters, it may reinforce initial errors and make it harder to actually learn the birds. But for an observer with a lot of comparative experience, the flight actions of these three will serve as major field marks for separating them. These actions are best learned by watching a lot of birds of known identity. Beginners should focus on identifying the birds by more concrete marks, and then study the flight style of those birds that already have been named with certainty. With experience, some behavioral differences will start to become apparent.

When they are out in the open, all three accipiters may fly with a repeated pattern of several quick flaps followed by a glide. The wingbeats of Sharp-shinned Hawk are very rapid, and the bird appears buoyant in flight, easily shifted around by crosswinds; its flight may suggest that of a butterfly, not a comparison we would be likely to make with the larger accipiters. Cooper's Hawk looks heavier, with slightly slower wingbeats; it seems less likely to be pushed around by the wind, and it may use its longer tail more actively in maneuvering. The wingbeats of Northern Goshawk are still slower, and its flight looks more powerful, purposeful, and direct. Of course, these descriptions will not have a lot of meaning until you have watched the birds yourself, studying and comparing their flight styles.

PLUMAGE DIFFERENCES — ADULTS

Overall color. In Cooper's and Sharp-shinned hawks, males average slightly more colorful than females. They tend to be brighter blue-gray above, not dull brownish gray, and the fine barring on their underparts tends to be a brighter reddish. Occasionally this is relevant in identification; a bird that seems mid-sized and looks very colorful may be more likely a male Cooper's than a female Sharp-shinned, but this is only a minor supporting point at best. The female Cooper's is not only larger than the male but also a bit duller overall, and sometimes one of these big females can look quite grayish in the field, suggesting the general colors of a Goshawk.

Back and cap color. There is no useful difference among the species in the blue-gray tone of the upperparts, although in all three species the females average slightly duller and browner above than the males. However, crown color and contrast can help to separate Cooper's and Sharp-shinned hawks. Cooper's has a dark gray to blackish cap, usually contrasting with the paler nape and upper back. The crown of the Sharp-shinned is slaty blue (males) or dusky gray (females), sometimes a little darker than the upper back but not showing a line of sharp contrast. The Goshawk's head pattern is very different, with a blackish cap and ear coverts setting off a white supercilium.

Adult female Cooper's Hawk. The dusky cap contrasts with the paler nape and back; on an adult male, the contrast would be even more pronounced.

Tail pattern. In fall, when the birds are in fresh plumage, Cooper's

Hawk has a broader white band at the tip of the tail than Sharp-shinned Hawk. The difference is most apparent from above (or looking from the back at a perched bird), but it can also be discerned from below. Use of this field mark requires some practice, because the narrow white terminal band on an adult Sharp-shinned's tail can stand out conspicuously against the blackish subterminal band; the mark of a Cooper's is the width of this band, not its mere presence. As with any pale marking located on the tips of feathers, wear on the plumage makes this character less reliable by spring; by early summer, shortly before the molt begins, either species may be left with virtually no white tip on the tail.

Goshawks can have white tail tips nearly as broad proportionately as those of Cooper's. A field mark that is occasionally useful is that the dark crossbands on the tail of the adult Goshawk usually show far less contrast than those of the two smaller species, so that in some views the tail can appear practically uniform.

PLUMAGE DIFFERENCES — JUVENILES

Superficially all three species are similar in juvenile plumage, but there are a number of ways in which they differ. With a good view, observers can consider all of the following points in addition to the aspects of shape discussed earlier in this chapter.

Tail tip. As in adults, juvenile Cooper's Hawks in fresh plumage have broader white tips to the tail feathers than do Sharp-shinneds. This mark must be used with caution, however, because in juvenile Sharp-shinneds (unlike adults) there is usually a noticeable pale area beyond the last dark subterminal crossband on each tail feather. This can be very tricky when seen from below: light coming through this pale area can make the tail look very broadly pale-tipped when seen in bright sunlight. Seen from above, however, the actual narrow white tip to the juvenile Sharp-shinned's tail is made even less noticeable by this medium gray area, which separates the white from direct contrast against the last dark tail band. Juvenile Goshawks have proportionately more white at the tail tip than Sharp-shinneds but less than fresh-plumaged Cooper's Hawks.

Because of wear, this field mark becomes difficult to use for juveniles after late fall. A few young Cooper's Hawks may continue to show substantial white even into the spring, but a very narrow white tail tip in spring means nothing, as it could simply result from wear.

adults

juveniles

These figures show Sharp-shinned Hawks in various flight positions. Notice how tail shape and especially wing shape vary according to momentary positions; the extension of the head in front of the wings also seems to vary a lot. A generally compact shape is usually evident in flight, but not always, and sometimes the birds can have almost a lanky or rangy look. See the text for details about plumage characters for both adults and juveniles. On the juveniles, in particular, notice how much the pattern of the underside of the body can appear to vary.

Tail banding. On each feather of a juvenile Goshawk's tail, each dark crossband is shaped like a shallow V or chevron across the inner vane of the feather. When the tail is fully spread it shows a neat zigzag pattern, especially as seen from below. On the other two species, the crossbands on most of the tail feathers run straight across, so that the fully spread tail shows a more evenly banded effect. When the tail is not spread this difference is not apparent from below, because the outermost tail feathers may have irregular patterns in all three species.

The juvenile Goshawk's tail bands are often made even more conspicuous by narrow pale margins that set them off from the ground color of the rest of the tail; these are usually best developed on the upperside but may also show on the underside of the tail. The other two species only rarely show traces of this effect on a few tail feathers.

Breast pattern. Typical juvenile Cooper's Hawks have the breast rather narrowly and sharply striped with blackish brown on a whitish background. On typical juvenile Sharp-shinneds, the streaks tend to be broader, more teardrop-shaped, and paler brown or dull reddish brown on a more buffy white background, and the streaking usually extends farther down onto the belly than on Cooper's. But this difference is useful only for well-marked individuals at one extreme or the other. Both species are variable, and Sharp-shinneds in particular may approach rather closely the pattern of the typical Cooper's. The streaks of the juvenile Goshawk are heavy and sharply defined like those of the typical Cooper's; they usually extend well down onto the belly and show up as heavy spots on the flanks and thighs.

Undertail coverts. On juveniles of all three species the undertail coverts are basically white. On Sharp-shinned Hawks they are always unmarked; on Cooper's they are usually unmarked but sometimes lightly streaked; and on Goshawk juveniles they almost always show heavy streaks or spots, at least near the tips of the feathers.

Back pattern. The upper back and scapulars may appear more uniform on juvenile Sharp-shinneds than on Cooper's; the feather edgings tend to be narrower and darker (chestnut to rufous) on Sharp-shinned, broader and often paler (rufous to buff) on Cooper's. White areas are more often apparent on the back of Cooper's Hawk, although the Sharp-shinned also has concealed white areas on the back that show up prominently if the feathers are disarranged. This difference between the species is slight and variable, however.

The juvenile Goshawk tends to be paler and more variegated above than the other two, with edgings of buff, pale rufous, and whitish.

Head pattern. The juvenile Goshawk has a whitish supercilium that usually broadens behind the eye. On some individuals this is quite conspicuous. However, juvenile Cooper's and Sharp-shinned hawks also have light supercilia. Usually these are narrow, but on some birds (especially some Sharp-shinneds) they are as broad and as noticeable as on some Goshawks. Juveniles of some other woodland hawks, such as Red-shouldered and Broad-winged, also show pale supercilia, and

Juvenile Cooper's Hawks seen in a variety of flight positions. Note the consistently long-tailed and large-headed look. See text for a detailed discussion of plumage characters.

Juvenile Northern Goshawks in flight. With their bulky body shape and broad wings, they often look strikingly different from the smaller accipiters. Some plumage characters, such as tail pattern and the spots on the undertail coverts, may be obvious or obscure depending on position.

they are sometimes misidentified as Goshawks on that basis. So this element of head pattern should be used with caution, as a supporting mark rather than a main clue.

The crown tends to be more solidly dark in juvenile Sharp-shinned, more strongly variegated with light and dark in Goshawk, with Cooper's intermediate between these extremes. However, this too is variable in all three species. Some juvenile Cooper's Hawks are distinctive in having the face strongly tinged tawny-buff or rufous, an effect not usually seen on the other two species.

COMPARING ACCIPITERS TO OTHER SPECIES

Although the main ID contenders for accipiters are other accipiters, they are occasionally confused with other species, even by birders with some experience. In areas where birders don't get to see many Merlins, these compact, fast-flying falcons are sometimes mistaken for Sharp-shinned Hawks. Male Merlins are blue-gray above, like adult Sharp-shinneds, while females and young are browner above and streaked below, like immatures, and the shape differences may not be obvious in a quick view. Juvenile Northern Goshawks are sometimes mistaken for buteos, especially for young Red-shouldered Hawks. In all of these cases there are many potential field marks to separate the species, and the important thing is just to be aware of the possibility of error.

Separating juvenile Northern Goshawks from juvenile Gyrfalcons is potentially more challenging. Their shapes in flight can be surprisingly similar, as the Gyr's wingtips are not as pointed as those of smaller falcons. The Gyrfalcon's tail is densely and evenly barred, a pattern quite unlike the bold zigzags on the Goshawk's tail. The difference in tail shape is more subtle, but when folded, the Gyrfalcon's tail appears to narrow toward the tip, while the Goshawk's appears to broaden somewhat toward the tip. The Gyrfalcon's tail is roughly square-tipped when folded, slightly rounded when spread, while the Goshawk's tail is distinctly rounded or somewhat wedge-shaped at the tip (more obviously so when spread). With good light, the juvenile Goshawk is a warm brown all over, while even the brownest juvenile Gyrfalcons have a distinct gray cast. Finally, with a good view, the legs, feet, and cere (fleshy area at the base of the bill) are blue-gray in juvenile Gyrs, yellow in all ages of Goshawks (and in adult Gyrfalcons); the eyes vary from pale gray to yellow in juvenile Goshawks, but all ages of Gyrfalcons have dark eyes.

15. LEARNING TO IDENTIFY SHOREBIRDS

Not every bird found at the shore is a shorebird; not every shorebird is found at the shore. For birders in North America, "shorebird" is a taxonomic term, denoting members of the sandpiper and plover families, plus a few related families within the order Charadriiformes. Many of these birds nest on tundra or grasslands, and some spend their lives on dry open plains. Still, the majority of species spend the majority of their time near the water's edge, so the group term is appropriate.

Their habitats are often ephemeral — changing by the hour in tidal flats, or by the day around some inland waters — so shorebirds must be mobile, and in fact most are strong, graceful fliers. Some members of this group are among the most impressive long-distance migrants in the world, traveling annually from the Arctic practically to the edge of the Antarctic and back. Only a few are found nesting at middle latitudes of southern Canada and the lower 48 states. Most of them breed in the far north and many winter south of the United States, so for most birders on this continent, these birds are seen primarily in migration. Their great mobility means that they can turn up almost anywhere, and the chance of finding something unexpected is part of the allure of shorebird watching.

Overview of the problem. Most shorebirds wear a muted palette of grays and browns. Some are more brightly patterned in the breeding season, with accents of rusty and black, but overall they are not colorful. A simple description of grayish brown above and whitish below would apply to most shorebirds most of the year. This overall similarity makes it hard for new birders to find a good starting point.

With a closer view, most species show seasonal variations in plumage, often quite extensive. In many species, the adult basic, adult alternate, and juvenile plumages are so different as to suggest three different species. Furthermore, many that we see on stopovers during spring and fall migrations are in transition from one plumage to another, adding to the wide variation in appearance of each species. If we just look at the birds' color patterns, the diversity can seem overwhelming.

To add to the challenge, but also to add to the excitement, many North American shorebirds have counterparts in Europe and Asia that may look very similar in some plumages — and these counterparts may stray to this continent, at least on rare occasions. So when we see a shorebird that looks a bit odd, it could just be a normal variation on one of the local species, or it could be a wanderer from halfway around the globe.

PRELIMINARY POINTS

Plumages of shorebirds. Most species in this group exhibit the Complex Alternate Strategy in molting, with adults having distinct basic and alternate plumages in each annual cycle and with young birds having a formative plumage in the first winter that is usually quite similar to the adult basic plumage.

Many shorebird species look strikingly different in different plumages, as demonstrated by these Sanderlings. Basic plumage tends to be the plainest in many species, with relatively unpatterned upperparts; like many other shorebirds, Sanderlings may be in basic plumage not only during the winter months but for more than half the year. Alternate plumage often shows brighter colors or stronger pattern, especially around the head and chest. In Sanderlings, full alternate plumage is usually seen only from late spring through midsummer. Juvenile plumage often has a sharp pattern on the back, scapulars, and wings, the individual feathers having dark centers and crisp pale lines or spots along the edges.

The timing of the molts varies among species, and even among populations of the same species, and it seems to be interrelated with the timing of the migration and the region where the birds spend the winter. Although there are many exceptions, as a general rule, the birds that migrate the farthest tend to have the preformative and prebasic molt stretched out over a longer period of time; the molts may begin during stopovers on fall migration, but they are often completed on the wintering grounds, by sometime in late winter. Their prealternate molts in spring are variable, and they may take place largely during stopovers on northward migration. By contrast, many shorebirds that migrate only short distances will complete the preformative and prebasic molts in early fall, and their prealternate molts may take place largely on the wintering grounds before spring migration.

The plumage sequence of American Golden-Plover, which nests in the Arctic and winters in southern South America, provides a good example of the long-distance type. Adults may molt some body feathers on the breeding grounds in summer but most of their body molt occurs after they start south, and they molt the flight feathers of the wings on the wintering grounds. Young birds migrate south in essentially full juvenile plumage, and they undergo most of their complete preformative molt on the wintering grounds. In spring, adults and young birds mostly start north in basic and formative plumages, and much of their molt into bright alternate plumage takes place at stopover sites during spring migration. Birders in Texas in early spring may be surprised to see large numbers of golden-plovers in "winter" plumage, but this is the normal occurrence; those plovers will molt to alternate or "breeding" plumage during their spring stopovers, before they reach the Arctic.

Photographed in April in Texas, this American Golden-Plover has already come thousands of miles north from its wintering grounds, and it is still almost entirely in basic plumage; it will molt into its alternate plumage during this spring stopover, before continuing on to the Arctic.

The Dunlin provides a good example of the plumage sequence of a short-distance migrant. In late summer, most adults move from their nesting grounds on Arctic tundra to nearby coastal areas of the far north and complete most of their molt there before migrating south. Juveniles likewise go to staging areas and go through a partial preformative molt in late summer and early fall before migrating south, so birders in southern Canada and the lower 48 states seldom get to see Dunlins in full juvenile plumage. In late winter, both adults and young birds have a partial prealternate molt, mostly on the wintering grounds before they start north.

Differences in timing of molt are sometimes helpful in identification; for example, see the discussion of this point for Western and Semipalmated sandpipers in the next chapter.

HOW TO LOOK AT SHOREBIRDS

For a beginner, a brief visit to a mudflat teeming with shorebirds can be confusing and disheartening. At first glance all the shorebirds seem to look essentially the same, while if we look more closely, it seems that every individual looks different. Either way, it seems unlikely that we'll be able to make sense of what we're seeing.

It is possible to set out systematically to learn to identify shorebirds. Anyone who is really skilled at this group of birds has probably done exactly that. The distinctions among shorebird species are often subtle, it's true, but with enough attention and practice, they sort themselves out beautifully. Here are some strategies for learning them.

Try to get close. After you get to know the shorebirds well, you may be able to recognize them at very long distances. But if you're just getting started, those distant gray and brown shapes may not tell you anything. To increase your chances of figuring out what you're seeing, try to get close looks at the birds.

In the interior of the continent, places with large concentrations of shorebirds are few and far between, but there are many situations that attract a decent handful: ponds, flooded fields, sewage treatment plants. If you can find a place where you can get close views of a few shorebirds, that can be more valuable than driving a long distance to one of the major hotspots.

In a coastal situation with tidal mudflats, low tide may reveal a thousand shorebirds scattered widely over the flats, a mile away. Just before or after high tide there may be fewer birds, but they are likely to be much closer to solid ground. Close looks at a few dozen will be more valuable than distant views of hundreds.

Shorebird study is one situation in which a telescope is practically essential. A decent spotting scope and tripod will make a huge difference in your attempt to learn to identify these birds.

One thing that I often do, after studying an interesting shorebird through the scope, is to look at it through binoculars for a while, and then spend some time watching it with the naked eye. This has the same effect as seeing the bird farther and farther away, and it's good training for recognizing shorebirds at a distance.

Calibrate to something identifiable. Any time you look at a mixed concentration of shorebirds, some probably will be easier to identify than others. It may be tempting to zero in on the unknown birds immediately and try to puzzle them out. A better approach is to focus on being sure you know what the "obvious" birds are, and then build from there, making comparisons back to the known birds. If you can be sure that some of the birds present are Sanderlings, for example, you can compare them to other birds that look smaller, larger, or about the same size, and you can compare things like bill shape and overall plumage color. But you need that identifiable bird as a starting point. Whether it's a Ruddy Turnstone with its thick orange legs or a Semipalmated Plover with its dark back and single neck ring, go for something easy and sure at the start.

Try for size comparisons. This follows from the previous point. Unlike many groups of birds, in which the birds are usually seen singly and it is hard to judge their size, shorebirds are often in mixed groups and there is often another bird close by for a direct size comparison. This can be very helpful, especially after you build up a sense of the relative sizes of various species. For example, if a yellowlegs blends in and seems to disappear among a flock of dowitchers, it's probably a Lesser Yellowlegs, because Greater Yellowlegs tends to be conspicuously larger. A gray sandpiper on the beach in winter that looks a little smaller than the Black-bellied Plovers may be a Red Knot, because Dunlins and "peeps" would look much smaller and Willet would be larger. The size of a lone shorebird can be very misleading, so size should not be given such importance unless comparisons are possible.

When we get a direct comparison between two birds like Dunlin and Least Sandpiper, the difference in size can be striking.

Focus on the common species. Especially when you know that rare strays are possible, it's tempting to scan quickly through the shorebirds looking for such rarities, and to pay scant attention to the more common birds. But in the long run, you can't hope to identify most rare shorebirds unless you have a solid grounding in the more common species.

Learning these birds and reinforcing our impressions of them can be an ongoing process. Even after years of birding, I still spend time every year carefully watching Least Sandpipers, Black-bellied Plovers, and other common species (as well as all of the uncommon or rare ones that I can find), trying to refresh my familiarity with their subtleties of shape, behavior, and plumage.

Make the most of each season. There are different advantages to studying shorebirds at different times of year. During the winter the birds are all in formative or basic plumage, generally their drabbest plumage of the year, and they may not look very distinctive. But there are fewer species present in North America at that time than during migration, because some (such as Pectoral, Baird's, and White-rumped sandpipers, for example) spend the winter far to the south of us, so it's easier to narrow down the identification of the birds we see.

During spring migration, many shorebirds are at least partly in alternate plumage and may be much easier to recognize. A Dunlin with red back and black belly patch, or a Stilt Sandpiper with barred underparts, can be named instantly on the basis of color pattern. But this is exactly the season to learn the shapes and behaviors of these birds: since we can identify them quickly and confidently by their markings, we can concentrate on studying every aspect of their silhouettes and foraging actions, so that we'll still be able to recognize them when we see them again in plainer garb.

Late summer is one of the most interesting times to study shorebirds. For many species, southward migration begins very early: a few adults start to show up south of the breeding grounds by the end of June. Some of these might be birds that failed in their first nesting attempt and that did not have time, in the brief Arctic summer, to make a second attempt. Regardless, by early July, adults of many shorebird species are moving south. By the end of July or early August, juvenile shorebirds are also showing up south of the breeding grounds. Timing varies by species, of course, and some (such as Purple Sandpiper) may not begin to move south until October. But for many shorebirds, August is a prime time to see adults and juveniles side by side, the adults worn and fading or starting to molt, the juveniles bright and crisp in their new plumage. You can learn a tremendous amount about shorebirds, and about changes in plumage, by putting in some serious scope time at the mudflats in late summer and early fall.

LEARNING THE GROUPS OF SHOREBIRDS

The diversity of shorebirds can be even more daunting on the pages of a field guide than it is in the field — especially a guide that includes all the rare strays, because at least 90 species of shorebirds have been recorded in North America. However, nearly one-third of those could be considered extremely rare visitors anywhere in the U.S. or Canada; and about a dozen more are moderately rare, or are regular only on the islands of western Alaska. Fewer than 50 species could be regarded as common and widespread on this continent. That is still a substantial number to learn, with plenty of challenges. But the shorebirds will not seem so difficult if we break them down into manageable groups.

In the discussion that follows, I have organized the shorebirds by their relationships and by their similarity in the field. In discussing their habitat preferences and flocking behavior, I'm referring only to what they do during migration and winter. During the nesting season, of course, the flocks break up, and many species move into different habitat, with tundra favored by most of the northern types.

In this section I ignore a couple of families that are usually included among the shorebirds: thick-knees (family Burhinidae) and pratin-coles (family Glareolidae). Both are recorded in North America only as accidental strays, and they are so distinctive that no one would mistake them for other shorebirds. With those omitted, the shorebird fauna in our area includes five families. The first three listed below are so distinctive that they pose little challenge in identification.

Jaçanas (family Jacanidae). These odd tropical shorebirds have small heads and short straight bills. Their very long toes enable them to walk on floating vegetation, such as lily pads, and they are usually found at marshy ponds rather than mudflats or other typical shorebird haunts. One species, Northern Jaçana, is a rare stray into Texas and extremely rare elsewhere in our southernmost states. The brown-and-white juvenile might possibly be mistaken for something like a Wilson's Phalarope — until it spreads its wings, showing brilliant yellow flight feathers.

Northern Jaçana

Oystercatchers (family Haematopodidae). Very distinctive shorebirds with stout bodies, thick legs, short necks, and long bladelike bills, oystercatchers are strictly coastal in North America. Patterned in solid black and white, with colorful bills and piping call notes, they are unlikely to be mistaken for any other shorebirds. The only potential identification challenge is in southern California, where Black Oystercatcher × American Oystercatcher hybrids occur rarely.

Avocets and stilts (family Recurvirostridae). These shorebirds are elongated in every way, with long thin legs, long necks, long narrow wings, and long, very thin bills. They forage mostly in shallow water in very open habitats, the American Avocet sweeping its bill tip just below the surface, the Black-necked Stilt often picking at things on the surface. Stilts are usually in small loose flocks, while avocets may be in larger, tightly packed flocks where they are common; both can be very noisy when alarmed.

Black-necked
Stilt

Plovers (family Charadriidae). Plovers in general are compact birds, with short straight bills, short necks, and fairly short legs. Unlike many shorebirds, plovers typically seek their food visually rather than probing in mud or water, and their behavior reflects this: when foraging they run a few steps and then pause, run and pause, a repeated action that may mark them from far away. Because they are generally not probing in mud, some species can live in relatively dry surroundings, such as sandy beaches, or even open fields far from water. Most species, however, are most commonly found at mudflats and other "typical" shorebird sites.

Golden and Black-bellied plovers (genus *Pluvialis*) are four species of medium-sized shorebirds that nest on northern tundra and mostly migrate long distances, spending the nonbreeding season on open fields, mudflats, and beaches. The feathers of their upperparts are patterned, and they have clear, whistled callnotes.

American
Golden-
Plover

The "banded" plovers (genus *Charadrius*) are mostly smaller; they include six that are regular and widespread and another six that are rare in North America. The feathers of their upperparts are mostly plain, and most have at least a partial neck ring in some plumages, although this is obscure on Mountain Plover. The Semipalmated Plover nests in the far north, but the others occur mainly at temperate latitudes, including several that nest on sandy beaches along our coastlines.

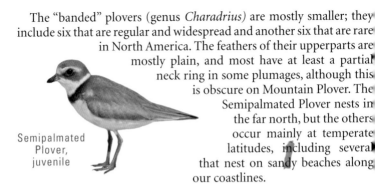

Semipalmated Plover, juvenile

Sandpipers (family Scolopacidae). This family includes most of the North American shorebirds and most of the shorebird identification challenges.

The listing below does not follow any official checklist order. I kept close relatives together and mostly kept members of the same genus together, but beyond that I did not try to reflect relationships among the various genera; the list is arranged to make sense for observers in the field. For example, dowitchers have very long bills, as do snipe and woodcocks, and may be somewhat related, but their behavior is so different that there is no reason to group them together here.

Group 1. Genus *Tringa* and allied groups. Classic members of the genus *Tringa* are the yellowlegs. These trim, elegant sandpipers have long legs, rather long necks, and long thin bills. They forage mostly in shallow water near mudflats or open marshes, wading about actively and mostly picking at items on or near the water's surface. Often they are sociable in migration and winter but they do not form tight flocks like some shorebirds. When excited, they often bob their heads. Solitary Sandpiper is like a scaled-down version of the yellowlegs, usually seen singly and often on small bodies of water such as creeks or ponds; when it is at more typical shorebird sites, it usually lurks along the edge.

Greater Yellowlegs

The Willet is now placed in this genus also; it is a bulkier bird with a heavier bill, common on marshes and mudflats, especially in the West. Also now placed in *Tringa* is the Wandering Tattler, another head-bobbing sandpiper, more compact and shorter-legged than the yellowlegs. It frequents rocky Pacific shorelines. A few rare stray sandpipers from Eurasia are also classified in *Tringa;* they are recognizably similar either to yellowlegs, Solitary Sandpiper, or Wandering Tattler.

The Spotted Sandpiper (genus *Actitis*) is similar to *Tringa* and is sometimes mistaken for Solitary Sandpiper. It also favors small ponds and creeks, although it also occurs on tidal flats and coastal rocks. It is shorter-legged than most *Tringa* and tends to bob its tail rather than its head. Spotted Sandpipers seldom form flocks, even where common; when flushed they fly away singly, with shallow, stiff wingbeats. The Old World Common Sandpiper, rare in North America, is very similar to Spotted Sandpiper. The odd Terek Sandpiper (genus *Xenus),* another rare visitor (mainly to Alaska), has shape and behavior somewhat similar to smaller members of the genus *Tringa.*

Spotted Sandpiper
in basic plumage

Group 2. Dowitchers. The two species of dowitchers are often difficult to tell apart, but relatively easy to separate from other shorebirds. These are stout-bodied, short-necked, long-billed sandpipers that forage by wading slowly in shallow water, probing straight down into the submerged mud with their bills. They are usually seen in flocks, often with a dozen to several dozen birds standing very close together, with their bills completely submerged and also very often with their heads partly underwater as they methodically probe the mud.

Above: Short-billed Dowitcher, race *hendersoni,* in alternate plumage. Below: a typical view of a feeding flock of Long-billed Dowitchers.

Group 3. Genus *Calidris*. This group includes nineteen species on the North American list, although six of those could be considered rare. Members of the genus are mostly medium-sized to small sandpipers, nesting on northern tundra and migrating moderate to long distances, and mostly found in flocks outside the nesting season. It is useful to break the genus down further:

"Peeps" or "stints" include seven species of the smallest sandpipers, three nesting mainly in North America and four mainly in Eurasia; they are covered in detail in the next chapter. The three common peeps in the New World — Least, Semipalmated, and Western sandpipers — are very common and widespread, and getting to know them is an essential part of learning the shorebirds.

Dunlin and Sanderling are both a little larger than the peeps, although they might be confused with them. These two are found mainly in coastal areas in migration and winter, and they are common and widespread on North American coastlines at most times of year; it is worthwhile to learn them in all their plumages.

Sanderling molting into alternate plumage

The larger *Calidris* species are a varied lot, but most are recognizable as "scaled-up" versions of the peeps. White-rumped and Baird's sandpipers are like "stealth sandpipers," only slightly larger than the peeps and easy to overlook, but their very long-winged silhouettes give them away. Pectoral Sandpiper is a bit larger still, like a Least Sandpiper on steroids, especially the larger male, while Red Knot and Purple and Rock sandpipers are more distinctive but still recognizably similar in structure to other members of the genus.

Now classified in *Calidris* but giving a very different impression in the field is Stilt Sandpiper. In shape this bird suggests a somewhat less elegant version of a yellowlegs, but with a long bill that appears to droop slightly at the tip. In behavior it is very much like a dowitcher, wading slowly and probing straight down with its bill. It often associates with dowitchers, where it may be picked out by its slimmer build and longer legs.

Stilt Sandpiper

Group 4. Odd sandpipers allied to the genus *Calidris*. Two very rare visitors, Spoon-billed Sandpiper and Broad-billed Sandpiper, are probably related to *Calidris*. In a genus by itself is the Ruff, a strange bird that somewhat resembles a bulky Stilt Sandpiper or a stretched-out Pectoral Sandpiper; in some situations, it might be passed off as a yellowlegs with an odd bill. More easily recognized is another unique species, Buff-breasted Sandpiper, which has a small dovelike head, short bill, and distinctive color pattern. This sandpiper is only a casual visitor to most standard shorebird sites, as migrants are usually found in open grassy areas, dry flats, or even plowed fields.

Buff-breasted Sandpiper

Group 5. Turnstones and Surfbird. At one time these were treated as a subfamily of the plovers, but they are now recognized as slightly odd sandpipers. They are stocky, compact birds, built rather

Ruddy Turnstone

like musclebound versions of *Calidris*, with strong legs and short, distinctively shaped bills. Often they are in small flocks on rocky shorelines, although Ruddy Turnstone is also common on mudflats and on sandy beaches.

Group 6. Large sandpipers. This category includes a couple of groups of distinctive birds.

Curlews (genus *Numenius*) vary from medium-sized to very large for shorebirds. Their bills vary by size, from fairly short to extremely long, and all are at least slightly downcurved. All eight of the world's species have been recorded in North America, but two are now possibly extinct and another three are very rare visitors to this continent. In migration and winter, Long-billed Curlew may be on mudflats or in dry open fields, but Whimbrel is usually near water.

Long-billed Curlew

Related to the curlews is Upland Sandpiper, an odd bird with a short bill, small head, and long tail, living in grasslands and rarely found in typical shorebird habitats.

The four species of godwits (genus *Limosa*) are very large sandpipers that are recognized by their long legs, moderately long necks, and long bills that vary from straight to slightly upcurved. All have loud, rather harsh call notes. Migrants forage in flocks on coastal mudflats, marshes, and flooded fields.

Marbled Godwit

Group 7. Snipes. These sandpipers are adapted to live as marsh birds, with cryptic patterns, long bills, and short legs. Only Wilson's Snipe is likely to be seen in North America. It may be found lurking around the edges of typical shorebird sites, if there is enough marsh vegetation, and occasionally it ventures out onto the mudflats, but it never occurs in flocks. If alarmed, it makes off in rapid, zigzag flight, giving a hoarse scraping call note.

Group 8. Woodcocks. Living in woodlands by day and coming out into damp fields at night, the American Woodcock is a round-bodied, short-legged, long-billed curiosity. It is unlikely to be confused with other shorebirds, or to be seen with them.

Group 9. Phalaropes. Long considered to make up a separate family, these are now recognized as a distinctive subfamily among the sandpipers. Medium-small and compact, with thin, straight bills, they are best recognized by their foraging behavior: they mostly feed while swimming, often spinning in circles and picking lightly at the surface. Red-necked and Red phalaropes winter at sea and are very aquatic at all seasons. Wilson's Phalarope, which winters in South America, usually forages while swimming also; but it may be seen foraging on mudflats at times, actively dashing in pursuit of insects, and it may be puzzling to observers who expect to see phalaropes swimming.

female Red Phalarope in alternate plumage

WHAT TO LOOK FOR IN IDENTIFYING SHOREBIRDS

Overall shape and behavior. Experienced birders may be able to name most shorebirds at a glance, not by tallying up field marks but by a quick impression of the birds' shapes and the ways that they are foraging. Part of this comes only with experience, of course, but you can speed up the process by reading about the birds and looking at lots of good illustrations, and then by careful observation in the field. When confronted with an unfamiliar shorebird, rather than zeroing in on markings or colors, take a minute to consider its actions, shape, and comparative size. You should be able to quickly rule out some of the groups described above, narrowing your choices considerably.

Clues of habitat and season. Often we can see more than a dozen species of shorebirds together at the same spot, but that doesn't mean that they all favor exactly the same habitat. Each species has its own particular habitat preference, which may be reflected in how each one uses the niches available at a site. If several types of small sandpipers are present, for example, the Western Sandpipers might be wading belly-deep in water, while the Least Sandpipers might be picking along the muddy margins; the Baird's Sandpipers might be wandering on higher and drier areas of the flats, away from the water, while the Pectoral Sandpipers might be among the marsh vegetation or out on grassy areas of the flats. There is overlap, of course, and they frequently forage in the "wrong" places, but these tendencies provide useful clues.

Timing is also very helpful. A good local bird book or annotated checklist that gives details of seasonal occurrence can get you on the right track with some difficult birds. In areas of the interior where both dowitcher species occur only as migrants, their peak passage usually differs, with Long-billeds tending to come through earlier in spring and later in fall than Short-billeds. This is never a totally reliable distinction, but it helps to know what timing is expected for your local area.

Fine details of shapes. As you develop more familiarity with shorebirds, you'll be able to appreciate more subtle points of their structure. Things like the length of the legs or neck may be obvious, but head shape and body shape are also important. The position of the wingtips relative to the tip of the tail can be significant, and the number of primary tips visible beyond the end of the tertials is an important point for some tough species pairs.

Bill shape. This is an element in identifying every shorebird, and for some difficult groups it provides a critical field mark. Bill length may be an obvious thing to notice, but in addition, the shape of the tip, the thickness, and any degree of curvature are worth noting. In many of the sandpipers, females average longer-billed than males (although this is reversed in some, such as Pectoral Sandpiper and Ruff, in which the males are larger overall). This can have an impact on distinguishing species. Females of the western populations of Short-billed Dowitcher, for example, have the same average bill length as male Long-billed Dowitchers, rendering this point useless in identification.

Separating age classes. In late summer and fall, it is imperative to think about the age class of any unknown shorebird. At that season, for most, it will be easy to separate the fresh-plumaged juveniles from the worn, fading, or molting adults. Often it is easier to separate plumage classes than it is to separate species, and it makes for a critical first step. As an example of how this applies, Least Sandpipers in late summer are sometimes misidentified as Little Stints — because the *juvenile* Least has colors superficially like those of the alternate-plumaged *adult* Little Stint. Birders who look at plumage condition and determine the age class of the bird will not fall into this error.

Fine details of plumage. For many of the most challenging identifications among shorebirds, it becomes necessary to examine very fine details, including patterns of individual feathers. For example, the patterns of the tertials are important for separating juvenile dowitchers, and the patterns of the scapulars are helpful in identifying some of the "peeps." To use these marks, of course, we have to be able to recognize these feather groups. So an important part of learning the shorebirds is to study elements of "bird topography" as detailed in Chapter 3.

Short-billed Dowitchers and
one Lesser Yellowlegs

Flight silhouette and action. In some situations, especially when we are birding in marshes where visbility is limited, some of the shorebirds present may be seen only in the air. By looking at their shapes and their wing actions, we can often identify them at least to group, and even to species.

Flight patterns. With good views of shorebirds in the air, we can see some elements of pattern that are not visible when they are on the ground. Many species have a white stripe on the upperside of the wing, formed by white tips to the greater coverts and/or white bases to the flight feathers, and the presence or absence of such a stripe can be a significant field mark. Many species have a white area on the rump or uppertail coverts that is hidden by the folded wings when the bird is standing, but shows up well when the bird flies. Black-bellied Plover and American Golden-Plover in basic plumage may look superficially very similar to each other when standing, but when they fly, their flight patterns are distinctive as far away as the birds can be seen.

A Black-bellied Plover in basic plumage offers far more field marks in flight than it does standing still.

Voices. On the breeding grounds, most shorebirds give complex territorial songs, often on the wing in elaborate flight displays. Birders who get to spend time on northern tundra in summer may learn to recognize many of these songs. Brief bursts of song may be heard from some shorebirds on migration, but for the most part, we are more likely to hear shorter call notes from migrants and wintering birds.

Learning the calls of shorebirds can be a challenge. It takes a lot of concentration to be sure which birds on a crowded mudflat are making which calls. But learning them is well worthwhile. When I am looking at large concentrations of shorebirds, I often hear the uncommon species before I see them, especially if they are flying over or just arriving. Some shorebirds are more easily identified by voice than by any visual point; for a few species in certain plumages, voice may be the only reliable distinction.

Leg color. Many bird guides in the past pointed to leg color as a major field mark for various shorebirds, but at an advanced level, it is only a minor clue. It is fairly common for a shorebird to have the "wrong" leg color, and it is very common for the legs to be discolored by mud or muck. Leg color should be considered a supporting field mark at best, not a main point for separating difficult species.

16. THE SMALL *CALIDRIS* SANDPIPERS

Species treated in detail:

SEMIPALMATED SANDPIPER *Calidris pusilla*
WESTERN SANDPIPER *Calidris mauri*
LEAST SANDPIPER *Calidris minutilla*

Supplemental notes on:

RED-NECKED STINT *Calidris ruficollis*
LITTLE STINT *Calidris minuta*
TEMMINCK'S STINT *Calidris temminckii*
LONG-TOED STINT *Calidris subminuta*

The problem. These three — popularly known as "peeps" — are our smallest shorebirds, literally smaller than some sparrows. Seeing their field marks at a distance can be challenging. Even with a close view, however, they can remain difficult. All vary with age and season, and a large amount of individual variation adds to the potential confusion. With experience, birders soon learn to separate Least Sandpiper from Semi and Western (and to say "Semi" instead of "Semipalmated," thus saving energy and space). However, separating the latter two can be much more difficult.

Semi and Western are close relatives, similar at all seasons. For years, birders separated them mainly on bill length — even though the average difference involved mere millimeters, and even though they were known to overlap. That bubble burst in the 1970s, when it was pointed out that the hundreds of Semis reported on Christmas Bird Counts in North America were probably ALL misidentified: they were probably all Westerns, since practically all real Semis spend the winter farther south. Admittedly, winter is by far the most difficult season for separating these two species. At other seasons, in alternate and juvenile plumages, they have characters of colors and markings that can be diagnostic. But these characters must be applied with caution, with an appreciation for how much these birds vary and how rapidly their appearance can change with the season.

A final complicating factor in separating these three small *Calidris* is the need to rule out other sandpipers. Even moderately experienced birders sometimes confuse these birds with other common species of sandpipers that are only a little larger. And even very experienced birders may run into difficulties when trying to rule out some extremely similar Eurasian species that are rare visitors in North America. The search for these rarities might be considered one of the payoffs for studying the small sandpipers in the first place, but it has also led many birders into errors.

PRELIMINARY POINTS

Ruling out other likely species. Among other common North American sandpipers, several are only a little larger than the three featured in this chapter. The difference can be subtle even when they are seen together, and size alone is useless for telling them apart when they are seen separately.

Baird's and White-rumped sandpipers average about an inch to an inch and a half longer (from tip of bill to tip of tail) than the three small "peeps."

With a side-by-side comparison, the size difference is evident, but differences in shape are more useful. Baird's and White-rumped have a more elongated and horizontal look when standing, and their notably long wingtips extend past the tip of the tail. Both have medium-long, straight, fine-tipped bills, not matching the typical bill shape of any of the three "peeps."

Juvenile Baird's Sandpiper in September: more muted head pattern and less variegated upperparts than Least Sandpiper, in addition to more obvious shape differences.

Baird's tends to be quite brown overall, suggesting the general color of Least Sandpiper, while some elements of plumage pattern on White-rumped suggest Western Sandpiper, but many differences are evident with a closer study.

Pectoral Sandpiper can be 50 percent taller and more than three

juvenile Pectoral Sandpiper in September

times the bulk of Least Sandpiper, but its pattern is very similar, and lone birds without anything nearby for size comparison can be momentarily confusing. Female Pectorals average significantly smaller than males, and even though they are still much larger than Leasts, they may be the ones most likely to cause confusion.

Birders lacking a lot of winter shorebird experience may have trouble telling winter Western Sandpipers and Dunlins apart: both are grayish above, with rather long, droop-tipped bills. Winter Dunlins are typically darker on the chest and face, but shape is a better criterion, as Dunlins are proportionately bigger-headed and have higher shoulders, giving them a "hunchback" appearance when feeding.

Ruling out rare species. This chapter features three of the seven smallest species of *Calidris*. The other four — Red-necked, Little, Temminck's, and Long-toed stints — occur mainly in the Old World, but all might be possible as rare strays anywhere in North America. The possibility of finding these rarities has led many birders to look more closely at our three "peeps," but the great variation in plumage of our species has led to many false alarms, as birders have zeroed in on individuals that looked so different that they "had to be" some other species.

The only real defense against this kind of problem is to become thoroughly familiar with our three species. This is a process that takes some time and serious study. Developing the ability to distinguish among our three "peeps" in all their variations is a good preparation for picking out vagrant stints. But it's best to assume that, while you are in this process, you won't be so unlucky as to find one of these vagrants. Remember that an odd-looking bird among our regular "peeps" is almost always going to be a variation on one of the common species, not a stray from overseas.

Incidentally, there is no difference between the categories of "stints" and "peeps" (except that the latter is sort of a silly name). Long-toed Stint is probably the closest relative of Least Sandpiper, while Western and Semipalmated sandpipers are probably reasonably close relatives of Red-necked and Little stints. To say that a small sandpiper "looks like a stint" (as has happened during outbreaks of "stint fever" in local birding communities) is really meaningless. Birders need to avoid placing too much importance on the difference in name.

Foot structure and leg color. The name "Semipalmated," clearly coined in the era when birds were examined in the hand, means "partially webbed," and it refers to slight webbing between the toes, shared by Semipalmated and Western sandpipers but not any of the other *Calidris* species. This character is difficult to see in the field, requiring a very close look. Unfortunately, many birders make their first effort to see webbing (or lack of it) when they have found a small sandpiper that they suspect to be either Red-necked Stint or Little Stint, and they are trying to rule out the two North American look-alikes. Birders who want to seek stints should make it a project first to look closely

A closeup of the right foot of an adult Semipalmated Sandpiper, showing the limited webbing between the bases of the toes typical of this species and Western Sandpiper. It should be evident that this webbing could be difficult to see under normal field conditions. The hind toe, angled away from us, is not visible in this view. Notice also that the leg and foot color is not actually black, but more of a dark olive.

at the feet of definite Semis and Westerns, to get a sense of how hard it is to see that webbing, so that they will have a basis for comparison when they start to look at the feet of suspected stints.

It's also worthwhile to study leg and foot color on "peeps" that are already identified. The breakdown of yellow legs on Least vs. black on Semi and Western is an oversimplification. The legs of Leasts can vary, while those of Semi and Western are often olive or brown instead of black. Seeing this variation on known birds can lead to a healthy skepticism about trusting leg color too much on mystery birds.

IDENTIFYING LEAST SANDPIPER

Because Western and Semipalmated sandpipers are much more similar to each other than they are to Least Sandpiper, it's useful to separate that species out first before tackling the really difficult pair. Least Sandpiper is one of the most generally distributed shorebirds in North America, common in migration practically everywhere, including many small ponds and stream edges where few other sandpipers are found regularly. Getting to know this species thoroughly is a worthwhile project and an essential part of becoming a skilled birder.

In keeping with its tiny size, Least Sandpiper has a very compact shape, small-headed and short-necked, but it can occasionally look more elongated and rangy when it is actively feeding. Its bill is fairly short and straight, tapered to a fairly fine point at the tip, and the tip often appears angled slightly downward; some yellow sometimes shows at the base of the lower mandible. The legs vary from yellow to greenish to yellowish brown. The toes lack webbing at the base, and they can look surprisingly long for the size of the bird; it is worthwhile to study the foot structure so as to have a basis for comparison with other species.

molting to first alternate, May

beginning molt to alternate, April

unusually pale juvenile, September

full alternate plumage, May

two examples of juvenile plumage, August

Examples of Least Sandpipers in alternate and juvenile plumages. Although this species always looks browner than Western or Semipalmated sandpipers, its overall appearance is exceptionally variable, from brightly marked to dark and plain, depending on viewing conditions and on the seasonal plumage. Although Least Sandpiper is usually depicted in a furtive, half-crouching posture, and often does look that way in the field, it also can look more stretched out, upright, and active when it is foraging. Birders who want to be good at shorebird identification should spend time looking closely at Least Sandpipers at all times of year, to develop a good awareness of their variability.

Least Sandpipers begin their preformative and prebasic molt in late summer, at stopover sites on their southward migration, and may complete the molt either at such stopovers or after arrival on wintering grounds. Those wintering in the tropics may molt later, but those that remain in warmer regions of the U.S. for the winter are likely to be in full basic or formative plumage by November. First-winter and adult winter birds (in formative and basic plumages, respectively) are superficially very similar, relatively dark dusky brown above with blackish feather centers, and with a dusky brown wash across the chest. The crown and ear coverts are rather uniform dull brown with vague darker streaks, and the pale supercilium does not contrast much. In plumage, winter Leasts look much darker and browner overall than Westerns or Semis at that season.

Least Sandpiper in basic plumage (from October or November through March, sometimes extending earlier or later) is a relatively uniform dark grayish brown above and on the chest.

The prealternate molt occurs between February and May and may start on the wintering grounds but also may occur mostly at stopover sites on northward migration. Leasts in fresh alternate plumage are brighter than winter birds. The head and back are a paler, warmer brown, and some of the scapulars, coverts, and tertials have contrasting edges of rufous or white. These colors are affected by wear on the breeding grounds, and by July these birds look much duller, with the colorful feather edgings mostly gone. Some adult Leasts begin their fall migration by late June, and the first southbound migrants (possibly failed breeders) appear in the lower 48 states by the beginning of July, typically in worn alternate plumage.

Juveniles are very brightly colored at first. Birders who are accustomed to the dark brown look of winter Leasts, or even the colors of spring adults, may be stunned the first time they get a good view of a juvenile. The first southbound juveniles to show up south of the breeding range, in late July, may look practically orange overall. This initial blush of color fades very rapidly, but through August and September juveniles are readily recognized by the edgings of chestnut, white, rufous, and buff on the scapulars, coverts, and tertials. White edges on some sets of scapulars may line up to form conspicuous white stripes down the back, or these may be more obscure. The chest is often more sharply and finely streaked than on adults, and the ground color of the chest varies from pale brown to white; some juveniles look much paler and more sparsely marked below than adults.

The common call of Least Sandpiper, given especially in flight, is a thin, drawn-out *kreeet* or *kreeyeet*. This distinctive note may be recognized at a long distance once learned, and it is a good way to pick out flocks flying overhead, even at night.

IDENTIFYING SEMIPALMATED AND WESTERN SANDPIPERS

Having built a thorough familiarity with Least Sandpiper, so as to take it out of the equation quickly, we're still faced with the challenge of separating Semi and Western.

Western Sandpiper breeds mostly in western Alaska and winters commonly on the coastlines of North America, including the Gulf and southern Atlantic coasts, and from there south to extreme northwestern South America. As a migrant, it is most common west of the Great Plains, although it also occurs widely in the East. Semipalmated Sandpiper breeds from Alaska to eastern Canada and winters mostly from southern Mexico south, with major concentrations on the northeastern coast of South America. As a migrant, it is most common from the Great Plains eastward.

At most places in North America, both species are possible in migration; but at most places and times, one is predictably much more numerous than the other. Knowing the expected local status of each is a tremendous advantage in working out what we are seeing. If we can consult a good state or provincial bird book or a local annotated list, we'll know whether we should be looking for the odd juvenile Semi among lots of Westerns, a few Westerns among larger numbers of Semis, or some other combination.

Bill shape. The typical bill shapes of these two are visibly different, and this can allow for rapid identification of some individuals. The classic Semi bill is short, straight, blunt, deep at the base, and slightly expanded or even slightly bulbous at the tip. The classic Western bill looks thinner at the tip, partly because the bill averages longer; it may be subtly less deep at the base, and it is often somewhat drooped at the tip. With practice, the extremes are readily recognized.

Unfortunately, there is much variation. In both species, females average longer-billed than males. There is also a geographic trend in bill length in Semi, with the longest-billed individuals at the eastern end of the breeding range. Some female Semis from eastern Canada are distinctly longer-billed than some male Westerns. Throughout their range, many individuals will be "too close to call" on this character. However, the Semis that migrate through western North America are likely to be among the shortest-billed individuals, which is some help to birders there.

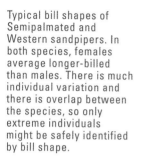
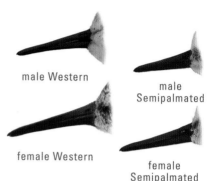

Typical bill shapes of Semipalmated and Western sandpipers. In both species, females average longer-billed than males. There is much individual variation and there is overlap between the species, so only extreme individuals might be safely identified by bill shape.

male Western

male Semipalmated

female Western

female Semipalmated

Voice. Small sandpipers are capable of making a wide variety of call-notes, and flocks may give off a constant low chatter of random noises. Generally the loudest and most recognizable calls are those given in flight. Even the flight calls can vary a lot, but Western and Semi do differ in their most typical calls. Western gives a *kreeip* less drawn out and with a more "strained" or "squeezed" quality than the call of Least Sandpiper. Semi has a short, rough *cherrt* that sounds lower-pitched. Both species vary a lot, unfortunately, with Western also giving a lower *chrk* and Semi also giving a *chiet* that is higher and thinner than its most common calls. Because of this variation, single callnotes can't be considered diagnostic, and even with a lot of comparative experience, voice is only a supporting character in separating the species.

Overall shape and behavior. Shape differences between the two species are slight. Western tends to average slightly longer-legged and tends to have a slightly larger, more squarish-looking head, contributing to a more "front-heavy" appearance. Semi looks a little more compact in most dimensions and has a slightly more rounded head, but its wing-tips are at least as long (relative to its size) as those of Western. Feeding behavior is quite variable in both. There is a slight tendency for Semi to do more deliberate picking at the surface while Western does more probing (as we might expect from the difference in bill length). Western is more often found wading belly-deep in water.

This nice juxtaposition shows (from front to back) juvenile Western, Least, and Semipalmated sandpipers. The Least is clearly darker and browner than the other two. Bill shape differences between the Western and Semi are hardly obvious, but the Semi's more contrasting face shows well here. The photo was taken in New Jersey on September 23, and the difference in molt between the Western and Semi is striking: the Western already has replaced most upper scapulars and upper back feathers, while the Semi apparently has not begun to replace any of these feathers yet. There is individual variation in this (and some juvenile Semis do show much molt by late September), but the difference shown here is typical.

Plumage characters — juveniles. Some very fresh juveniles of both species can look very bright, with a wash or bloom of orange-buff or almost peach color to the plumage, but this color fades very quickly and is not often seen away from the breeding grounds. Southbound migrant juvenile Semis begin to show up in southern Canada and the lower 48 states around the first of August; juvenile Westerns may arrive in the Pacific Northwest in late July, but farther east the first ones usually appear in early August. Peak numbers of migrant juveniles are usually seen in late August and September, but it is worthwhile to get out and see them as early as possible in August, when their plumage is fresh and the differences between the species are most obvious. This is also the time when the differences between the fresh juveniles and the worn adults are most striking, so it's a very educational time to be looking at the birds.

The fresh juvenile Semi gives the first impression of being *all one color,* a beautiful soft buffy gray, with some individuals having a pale rufous suffusion throughout. On closer inspection, this overall unicolored look turns out to be made up of buffy white or pale rufous-buff edgings to the gray feathers of the wings, scapulars, back, and head. By comparison, the fresh juvenile Western has a *two-colored* look. At first it is chestnut-rufous and pale buffy gray; later it becomes more simply rufous and gray. The key is the *contrast* between the upper two rows of scapulars (which are black with deep chestnut edges) and the two lower rows (which are extensively gray, with black "anchor" marks). The upper scapulars stand out as a contrastingly dark patch, the most richly colored part of the bird.

Facial expression is a good mark on typical birds. The Semi usually shows a little more contrast. It has darker lores and ear coverts and a more contrasting dark cap, helping to set off a narrow pale eye-ring and making the pale supercilium stand out. These aspects, combined with the short bill, give the typical juvenile Semi a vaguely "ploverlike" face. The Western generally has a paler face. Although the forward part of the Western's supercilium is usually wider and its forehead is whiter, they do not stand out because there is less contrast. Western has less of a "capped" look, and its eye-ring is usually inconspicuous.

Examples of juvenile Semipalmated (left) and Western (right) sandpipers. Their overall appearance will be changing gradually from the time they first arrive south of the breeding grounds in late July or early August, with colors becoming duller and Westerns beginning to molt.

By late August or early September, wear and fading have begun to make the colors of these juveniles slightly duller, their pale edges narrower. By this time, also, juvenile Westerns may have begun to molt. As the strongly patterned upperpart feathers are replaced by the plainer gray feathers of formative (first-winter) plumage, these Westerns begin to take on a grayer and plainer appearance, but the contrast between this gray and the retained rufous continues to look different from any plumage of Semi. Often the last feathers molted are the forward scapulars, so that a young Western most of the way through preformative molt may be mostly gray with a spot of rufous on the shoulder.

Juvenile Semis molt later in fall than Westerns, on average. Many Semis are still in complete juvenile plumage in late September when many young Westerns are far along in preformative molt. By late September, of course, it may take a closer look to see the difference between juvenile plumage that is faded and that which has been replaced by plainer feathers. To be able to recognize these birds in the latter part of the season, it is tremendously helpful to go shorebirding regularly from late July into the fall — that way you can watch the gradual change in appearance of these sandpipers.

Plumage characters — adults in alternate plumage. Both species go through the prealternate molt in late winter and early spring, largely on the wintering grounds, although some may finish this molt at stopover sites on migration.

Alternate-plumaged adults of these two are usually fairly easy to separate. Birders who rely on a sense of overall color may misidentify some Semis as Westerns: although it's true that Western generally has brighter colors, some Semis are more warmly colored than others and may look pale rufous around the upperparts, face, and sides of the crown. However, such birds are likely to have an overall brown cast. The rufous color on Western is brighter and shows more con-

Adults in alternate plumage. The classic Western in full alternate is much more heavily marked than Semipalmated, but many Westerns do not develop such strong markings. Semis in full alternate are variable in overall color. Some have an overall brownish gray tone, while others develop much more of a rusty wash on the head and upperparts, suggesting the colors of a dull Western.

rast against the rest of the plumage — rufous scapulars against gray wing coverts, rufous face markings against pale gray nape and breast. Western in this plumage also usually has a paler look to the face, with a wider and cleaner supercilium. Both species have some dark arrow-head-shaped marks on the underparts, but on Western these marks typically are larger and more conspicuous and extend much farther down on the flanks.

Plumage characters — winter birds. Many Western Sandpipers spend the winter along the warmer coastlines of North America, so birds seen here in August may already be on their wintering grounds. Semipal-mated Sandpipers almost all winter to the south of the U.S. (with only a few known to stay through the winter in southern Florida). This probably contributes to the difference in timing of their molts. Many Westerns may be in full formative or basic plumages by sometime in October. Semis undergo most of their preformative and prebasic molts after they are already south of us, so birds in full "winter" plumage are not often seen in North America.

Identifying such birds in winter is a serious challenge. Bill shape would be useful only for those at the short-billed extreme. Plumage differences in winter are slight and variable: Semi tends to be slightly browner and darker above, and its face and forehead may be darker. The narrow eye-ring may continue to be a little more noticeable on winter Semi than on Western. The sides of the chest may tend to be slightly more sharply marked with fine streaks in Western, more blurred in Semi. None of these points is diagnostic. A birder who finds a suspected Semi in midwinter should try to photograph it thoroughly and record its voice if possible.

Western Sandpipers in basic plumage, as seen in January. Semipalmated Sandpipers at the same season would be almost identical; see text for a discussion of their minor differences.

BRIEF NOTES ON VAGRANT STINTS

In addition to the three small *Calidris* featured here, there are four spe
cies found mainly in the Old World. All four occur in Alaska at varying
degrees of rarity, and all have been recorded as strays in southern Can
ada or the lower 48 states. Red-necked Stint is regular in small number
in western and northern Alaska, and both Red-necked and Long-toed
can be fairly common as migrants on the western Alaskan islands, bu
otherwise all four of these species should be identified with great cau
tion anywhere in North America. These notes should be considered
just a brief overview of what to look for on these birds, and any sus
pected stint should be studied, described, and photographed in detail.

RED-NECKED STINT is regular in small numbers in western and north
ern Alaska in summer and a fairly common migrant on the islands o
western Alaska, especially the outer Aleutians. South of Alaska it is ver
rare, but virtually annual in occurrence somewhere, mainly along th
Pacific and Atlantic coasts. These records generally involve adults in
July or August, still showing enough alternate plumage to be easily rec
ognized; there are also some spring records of adults, mainly in May
Records of juveniles have been surprisingly lacking, perhaps becaus
identification is so difficult.

In structure, Red-necked suggests Semipalmated Sandpiper, but i
averages even shorter-billed than Semi and its bill usually has a narrow

adult,
early June

juvenile,
August

adult,
late June

Red-necked Stints in adult alternate plumage and in juvenile plumage.
Overall structure, including wing and tail length and bill shape, are worth
noting even on the bright-plumaged birds.

fine tip. Red-necked has slightly longer wings and tail on average, and slightly shorter legs on average, giving it a subtly different shape. And of course Red-necked lacks the webbing between the bases of the toes (although as discussed earlier, this is a difficult mark to use). Its legs are blackish and its typical callnote is similar to that of the Semi.

Adults in full alternate plumage are very unlikely to be confused with our regular "peep" species, but can be similar to adult Little Stint (see under that species). Frequently, however, adult Sanderlings in their briefly held alternate plumage are mistaken for Red-necked Stints. Sanderling is a different shape, with large head, short neck, and very stout bill. It rarely approaches the Red-necked Stint's pattern of clear, unmarked rufous across the sides and front of the neck. For a technical detail to be checked at close range, Sanderling lacks the hind toe, while all the stints and "peeps" have it.

Juvenile Red-necked can be very similar to juvenile Semipalmated Sandpiper. It usually shows extensive pale rufous edges on the upper scapulars and somewhat duller pale edges on the lower scapulars, while the coverts and tertials are mostly gray; this gives it more of a bicolored overall appearance than most Semis.

Adults in basic plumage are very drab and grayish above and are suggestive of Semipalmated Sandpiper, differing mainly in structure.

LITTLE STINT is a rare migrant on islands of western Alaska and very rare elsewhere in North America. Recently there have been records almost annually of vagrants in the lower 48 states or southern Canada, mostly of adults in mid- to late summer.

Structurally this species is much like Red-necked Stint, averaging slightly longer-legged but with similar bill shape. Its legs are blackish, and like Red-necked it lacks webbing between the toes. Its typical callnote, a high, emphatic *kit* or *chit*, can be a good field character.

adult Little Stints in alternate plumage

May

June

May

Adults in alternate plumage are marked with bright orange-rufous on the upperparts, head, and sides of the chest. They are brighter overall than the North American "peeps" but superficially they resemble Red-necked Stint. The distribution of rufous is different: on the upperparts, this color extends to the tertial edges and coverts, while on Red-necked in alternate plumage, bright rufous on the scapulars and back usually contrasts with much grayer coverts and tertials. On the sides of the neck and chest, Red-necked Stint usually has an *unspotted* area of clear rufous, with dark spots beginning at the lower edge of that. On Little Stint, the sides of the upper chest may be washed with a similar orange-rufous, but this area is overlaid with dark spots. Little Stint is often brightest rufous on the ear coverts, and its throat is usually extensively white.

In late summer, Least Sandpipers in bright juvenile plumage are sometimes mistaken for adult Little Stints, demonstrating again the importance of aging shorebirds in order to get the species right.

There have been a few North American records of juveniles away from Alaska, mostly in early fall along the Pacific Coast. These usually look like very bright juvenile Semis, or like brighter versions of juvenile Red-neckeds, with extensive white, buff, or rusty edges on the scapulars, coverts, and tertials. The crown pattern is often distinctive, with a dark central strip and with the sides of the crown much paler (often appearing to be invaded by a "split supercilium").

Basic plumage is very similar to that of Red-necked Stint.

LONG-TOED STINT is a common migrant on the western Aleutians, rare elsewhere in western Alaska, and only an accidental visitor south of Alaska along the Pacific Coast.

This species is similar to Least Sandpiper in most ways. It averages a bit longer-legged and often looks longer-necked. Its bill may average slightly shorter, and a pale area at the base of the lower mandible may be more evident, but essentially its bill is quite similar to that of Least. It has yellowish legs. Its toes are distinctly longer than those of Least Sandpiper, but this won't be evident without some experience, because Least can also look surprisingly long-toed for its size. A difference in feeding posture is sometimes noted: since Long-toed has longer legs, it may have to lean farther forward when foraging. The typical call is a rolled *trrrrr*, much lower-pitched than that of Least Sandpiper.

Adults in alternate plumage average more colorful above than Least Sandpiper and often are more lightly marked at the center of the chest. Their face pattern tends to be brighter and cleaner, with a broader pale fore part of the supercilium, and with the ear coverts often paler.

On juveniles, the difference in face pattern is more pronounced, with a bright pale forward section of the supercilium contrasting with the dark center of the forehead, a very narrow dark area on the lores, and often pale ear coverts, making the dark eye look more isolated. The scapulars of juvenile Leasts often have a more scalloped look, with widely rounded black centers and narrow rufous edges, while those of juvenile Long-toeds often have a more striped look, with broad black central stripes and broad, straight rufous edges.

juvenile Long-toed Stint

TEMMINCK'S STINT is a rare migrant on islands of western Alaska, accidental on the mainland and on the Pacific Coast south of Alaska.

In some ways this is the most distinctive stint. It has a bill shape similar to that of Least Sandpiper (but often shorter), slim and fine-tipped, often with a slight droop at the tip, and it has yellowish legs. It has long wingtips, but they don't extend past the tail tip because Temminck's has a longer tail than the other small Calidris. It is also unique in having white outer tail feathers. This point is visible only in flight, and only with a careful view, because all of the other species have conspicuous white on the lateral uppertail coverts, and pale gray outer tail feathers. Its typical call is a dry trill, *trtrtrtrtr,* often given repeatedly when flushed; the other species give calls that are superficially similar.

In all plumages, Temminck's looks relatively plain and uniform above. It shows little face pattern except for a narrow white eye-ring. Adults in alternate plumage show at least some scapulars with blackish centers and rufous or whitish edges. Juveniles have very plain-looking upperparts with narrow pale edges to the larger feathers, creating a subtle scaly pattern. In all plumages there is a gray-brown wash across the chest, broken up somewhat by streaking in alternate plumage.

Temminck's Stint in basic plumage

17. LEARNING TO IDENTIFY GULLS

In some ways, gulls are the ultimate birds for people interested in field identification. Entire books and innumerable articles have been devoted to identifying gulls, and every winter the birding listserves erupt with arguments about problematic individuals that have been studied and photographed somewhere. Gulls are large and they live out in the open, where they are easy to study. Their feathers are large enough that we can study patterns of individual feathers, but their behaviors and shapes tempt us to identify them by more impressionistic clues as well. Their molts create very obvious changes in their appearance, so that their plumage cycles are easy to see but often challenging to understand. The amount of age-related and individual variation in every species is remarkable, hybrids are frequently encountered, and individuals often stray far from their normal ranges. For field ID maniacs, gulls are almost perfect. If only their voices were more interesting, we would hardly need any other birds.

Birders who want to be confident about naming gulls have to go through a learning process, hence this chapter's emphasis on learning. Of course, most of us would like to skip that process, to have a reference that would allow us to go out "cold" and name every gull by matching it to a picture. Unfortunately, it doesn't work that way.

Gulls are just too variable for that approach. All go through various plumages before they reach adulthood, so even though there are only a little more than two dozen species in North America, they present nearly 200 distinctly different plumages. And each of these is affected by a large amount of variation. Most gulls are gradually and continuously changing in appearance throughout at least their first two years of life, and no two individuals look exactly alike even at the same age. And then there are numerous hybrid combinations, all of which also are changing with age and season. No book, no matter how many illustrations it has, can show every possible variation.

In other words, there will never be a quick solution that will allow the beginner to identify every gull immediately. If we want to identify gulls tomorrow, we have to take the time today to learn the basics — to genuinely *learn* the gulls.

APPROACHES TO GULL STUDY

As with any complicated subject, you can make the gull ID learning process easier and faster by adopting specific strategies. The essential point is that it requires a conscious decision that you want to learn. With a concerted effort, you can have a good handle on gull ID within a couple of years. Conversely, you can be an active birder for 50 years without ever knowing the gulls well if you merely stop periodically to glance through flocks for "something different." That approach is backwards, because for learning, the focus should be on those birds that are "not different" — the majority of the birds in the flock, what are they, and why?

Think of gulls as opportunities. A gull that can't be identified immediately could be a source of frustration, but it doesn't have to be. Many birders make the assumption that our first step, on spotting a new bird, should be to identify it to species, and then fill in other information about it. But with an odd gull, it's good to turn that around: see how much we can determine about it *before* we name the species. This can be far less aggravating and more informative.

So, for example, we've spotted a big brown gull and we're not sure what kind it is. No problem — what else can we tell about it? For example, what exactly is the color pattern of the bill? How fresh or worn is the plumage? Do the scapulars all have roughly the same pattern, or are some of them being replaced in a molt? What is the pattern of the tertials? If the wings and tail are spread (with the bird preening or flying), so much the better. Does the tail contrast with the uppertail coverts? Are the inner primaries marked differently than the outer primaries? And so on. If we don't succeed in putting a species name on it, that's not a disaster; even the world's top gull experts can't identify every individual. And even without naming it, we have gotten the benefit of practicing our observational skills and refreshing our ability to recognize the various feather groups.

In fact, even if you don't like gulls, you could think of them as excellent "practice birds" for developing the perceptions that will help you identify other birds.

Start in winter. Unless you are in a region where no water remains unfrozen through the cold months, winter (especially early to midwinter) is the best time to get serious about learning the gulls. That is when most are in their freshest plumage and when the distinctions among the various age groups are most apparent. During late summer and fall, and to a lesser extent in spring, their patterns are complicated by molt.

In early to midsummer, the plumage of some young gulls may become incredibly worn and faded, so that it is hard to see any markings at all.

Admittedly, full adult gulls in late spring and early summer will be in breeding plumage and easy to identify with a good look. Studying these birds can be a good way to learn shapes and sizes and some aspects of adult pattern that will be the same all year. But immature gulls in early summer can look terrible, and beginners might want to steer clear of them, except in situations where they can be safely identified by direct size and shape comparisons to adults of their species.

Build a familiarity with common species. The temptation to look for rarities is strong, of course, and the ability to recognize rare gulls is one of the payoffs for learning the common ones. But the desire to find rarities can hamper our learning process if it makes us skim over the common birds instead of studying them.

At most places and times in North America, only a few species of gulls are common. At some sites on the Atlantic Coast, there may be hardly anything but Herring Gulls. That's great: the American Herring Gull is one of the most variable birds in the world, and it merits a huge amount of close study. There are places on the Pacific Coast where there may be nothing but Western Gulls on the beach. Excellent: that's a chance to study variation in this species without being distracted by others. In some inland areas, it may be a surprise to see anything but a Ring-billed. That's fine: we can learn by studying Ring-billeds at all seasons. We can even study them in small increments daily, in the parking lot at the mall, or while waiting in line at the drive-through, building up our mental library of variation and seasonal change in the species.

Herring Gulls in their first year of life are like snowflakes: no two of them look the same. This first-cycle American Herring Gull in February shows wonderful pattern on many different feather groups, and we could easily spend several minutes just studying details of this one bird. Getting to know Herring Gulls better is a worthwhile project for birders at all skill levels.

From a mindset of bird-listing, it can seem boring to have just one kind of gull around. From the standpoint of learning identification, it's a golden opportunity to get to know that one species thoroughly, to have it as a baseline for comparison to others.

Develop an awareness of each individual's stage in life. As a beginner, baffled by gulls, I made a mental distinction between those with "clean" plumage (which I considered to be adults) and those with "messy" plumage (which I assumed to be immatures, and perhaps unidentifiable). It seemed odd to me that I didn't see adult gulls in early winter. Later I came to realize that there was seasonal change in the appearance of all gulls. At the simplest level, all of those that had black hoods in summer would lose most of the black in winter, and almost all of those that had white heads in summer would gain some dark head markings in winter. As I gained more experience with the gulls, other and more subtle points of seasonal variation became apparent.

As discussed at great length in this chapter, all species of gulls go through changes between juvenile plumage and adulthood, some more extensive than others. Learning the basic elements of the plumage sequences is an essential part of being able to identify gulls to species. Indeed, it is sometimes easier to tell the age of a gull than to tell what species it is. Gulls may look "clean" or "messy" for a variety of reasons, and a worn adult will not look the same as a molting juvenile, for example. If you spend enough time studying plumage sequences and seasonal changes of gulls, it becomes second nature to think about these aspects with every bird you see.

Seeing this bird in late October, beginners might focus on the messy dark marks around the head and the dark bill spot and assume that it must be an immature. But in fact, adult American Herring Gulls typically have these features in winter. The clean pattern of the wingtips, upperparts, and tail indicate that the bird is an adult. A few dark marks on the upper back may mean some feathers are still being replaced at the end of the prebasic molt. A more obvious sign of this molt is the short primary extension, the wingtips barely extending past the end of the tail, giving the bird an oddly stubby look: the bird looks this way because it is nearing the end of the molt of the primaries and the outermost ones are not yet full-grown. With experience, it becomes easy to interpret features like this.

Look at flying birds. Many of the most important marks involve details of wing and tail patterns that are seldom visible except in flight. If you spend time with gull flocks, you should concentrate at least as much on the flying birds as on those that are sitting still; you'll learn more that way and you'll enhance your skill at seeing detail on all flying birds.

PLUMAGE SEQUENCES OF GULLS

In the twenty years since the first edition of *Advanced Birding* was published, there have been great advances in our understanding of the molts and plumage sequences of gulls. I have to point out, though, that greater understanding doesn't necessarily mean that the subject is any easier to understand!

In the first edition I wrote an account of the plumage sequence of Ring-billed Gull. The account reflected what was common knowledge at the time, but it turns out that it was partly wrong; I wrote about Ring-billeds being in their "first winter" plumage, for example, at a season when they are probably in the middle of their first prealternate molt. Some other gulls that we used to consider to be in "first winter" plumage probably don't have one, instead holding full juvenile plumage for several months. So in looking at the changing appearance of gulls through the seasons, we now have to interpret what we're seeing in the light of some new concepts of molt.

Terms such as "first-winter," "second-summer," etc., are no longer considered useful. With the realization that many of the birds may be in prealternate molt in fall, or that prealternate and prebasic molts may overlap in many birds, the distinction between "winter" and "summer" plumages is blurred, especially in younger birds. It is more informative and helpful to think of the gulls in terms of plumage cycles. The first cycle begins when the bird leaves the nest in its juvenile/first basic plumage; the second cycle begins when the bird begins its second prebasic molt, less than a year later (this is considered the second prebasic molt because the act of growing its first set of feathers is designated as the first). A bird may be molting into what we would have called a "winter" plumage in early June, so these seasonal terms are best abandoned. Referring to a given appearance as "second-cycle" will be understood by anyone with a serious interest in gulls.

The designation of species as "two-year gulls," "three-year gulls," and "four-year gulls" is still useful for indicating how long it takes for each species to reach full adult plumage. Two-year gulls are among the smallest species; they look distinctly different from adults during their first cycle, but after their second prebasic molt is completed they look like adults. Most three-year gulls are medium-sized; first-cycle birds look very different from adults, second-cycle birds are generally much more adultlike, and after the third prebasic molt they are in adult plumage. Four-year gulls are mostly among the largest species. First- and second-cycle birds in this group look very different from adults, third-cycle birds are quite variable but usually look mostly adultlike, and some fourth-cycle individuals still show traces of immaturity, reflecting the fact that there is more room for variability in these longer plumage sequences. Still, these designations of two-, three-, and four-year gulls are a useful way to remember how many different age classes of each species we can expect to see.

Plumage sequence of Ring-billed Gull. The following treatment will take a Ring-billed Gull from fledging to adulthood, with the molts and sequence of plumages illustrated. I start the sequence in 2010, so that the bird is one year old in 2011, two years old in 2012, and so on.

August 2010. Full juvenile plumage usually lasts a short time; within a month or two, most begin to molt. Often, as on this bird, some scapulars, head feathers, and feathers of the underparts are among the first to be replaced. This molt is now considered a long, gradual prealternate molt, not a preformative molt, and it may continue from August to the following April.

July 2010. Juvenile plumage. Fresh juveniles, recently fledged, are heavily marked with dark brown, looking quite different from any later stage. Their bills may be all dark at first, although pink soon begins to develop at the base.

October 2010. These three first-cycle birds are all roughly the same age and in the process of a gradual prealternate molt, but they differ in the number of scapulars and other body feathers that have been replaced. Much of the variation in appearance of young gulls is owing to variation in timing of the molt.

January 2011. The bird may still be gradually molting body feathers, but the overall appearance seems to show less change after the scapulars and upper back feathers are replaced with smooth gray and after most of the dark brown spots on the underparts are lost.

April 2011. The body and head plumage are looking fairly clean. Some birds replace some inner coverts, but this individual apparently has not; the coverts are very worn and have faded or bleached to whitish. On this bird the bill is already more yellow than pink, and it appears that the iris is just starting to turn paler. Even if the first prealternate molt is still going on, the second prebasic molt starts around this time.

June 2011. The bird is now showing extreme wear and fading on the coverts, which now look white and frayed, and the primaries and tail are also faded and abraded. In flight, we can see that the second prebasic molt has begun, as the innermost primaries on both wings are missing.

July 2011. As the bird glides past, we can see that it is well along in the second prebasic molt. The inner primaries (and inner primary coverts) are new, the outer ones are old, and apparently a couple of central primaries are missing.

August 2011. In the latter stages of second prebasic molt, the outermost primaries are still being replaced, but the best clues to age are eye color and bill pattern. The bird looks much more similar to the adult than to the juvenile birds that have just appeared on the scene.

October 2011. With the prebasic molt complete, the bird is now a clean example of a second-cycle Ring-billed. As is typical with three-year gulls, the second-cycle birds look superficially similar to adults and might be overlooked in a casual view. Distinctive points include a variable subterminal black tail band (usually a series of spots, not a complete band); more extensive black in the outer primaries, with only one small white "mirror" or none; black markings on the primary coverts; a few extra dark marks elsewhere on the wings; and usually a wider black ring on the bill. Although the bird appears to be in complete second basic plumage, the second prealternate molt may have begun already; this molt will have only a limited impact on the bird's overall appearance during the winter.

May 2012. The second prealternate molt is finished and the bird is in complete second alternate plumage. It looks much like a breeding adult, but still has the extra dark marks in the wings and tail from the previous winter. On the standing bird, the most obvious sign of age is the black wingtip, mostly lacking white spots. Around this time, the bird will begin its third prebasic molt.

August 2012. Now in third prebasic molt, the bird shows big white spots on the incoming primaries, while the old outermost primary (solid black, but in worn condition) has not been dropped yet.

January 2013. In third basic plumage the bird is essentially adult, although older birds tend to show more white in the wingtips.

May 2013. The bird went through the prealternate molt in late winter and early spring, replacing only head and body feathers. It is now in adult alternate plumage, although the prebasic molt will begin soon.

September 2013. The bird is now in the latter stages of its fourth prebasic molt. The outermost primaries are just growing in and are too short to be visible on the folded wing, and this makes the wingtip look distinctly odd

February 2014. Now in its fourth cycle or in fourth basic plumage, the bird may show more white in the wingtip than third-cycle adults, but otherwise its appearance is essentially unchanged. From now on, its only changes will be seasonal.

Overview of other typical plumage sequences. The preceding account of Ring-billed Gull describes the usual molt and plumage sequence of a typical three-year gull. There are a number of other species that have very similar sequences, but there are also some different patterns that apply to other species. Here are notes on the most important differences to know about.

Two molts in the first cycle. As noted in the preceding pages, the first molt of Ring-billed Gull is considered to be a long, protracted, prealternate molt, starting within a month or two after the bird leaves the nest and continued in a gradual way until the following spring. It is assumed that as a rule, a given feather is not replaced more than once during this cycle. But in some of the small gulls, there is a preformative molt in fall, creating a formative plumage worn for at least part of the first winter, followed by a first prealternate molt in the spring. Bonaparte's Gull is a good example of this, and something similar happens with Black-headed, Little, and Laughing gulls.

August   November

Juvenile Bonaparte's Gulls are heavily marked with warm pale brown when they are in fresh plumage, but these colorful tones are soon lost in the preformative molt, and by late fall they are monochrome gray, black, and white in their formative (first-winter) plumage. A first prealternate molt will follow in the spring.

Juvenile plumage held for several months. In the examples of Ring-billed and Bonaparte's gulls, juvenile plumage begins to be replaced within a month or two after the bird fledges, by late summer or early fall. But there are some species that hold juvenile plumage much longer. Some of the large "white-winged" gulls, such as Glaucous, Iceland, and Thayer's, may not start to replace any feathers until sometime in late fall, winter, or even early spring, in a limited prealternate molt. Something like this may also happen in some common species such as Herring, Great Black-backed, or Glaucous-winged gulls, in which some individuals in late fall or even midwinter still show essentially complete juvenile plumage. It's useful for birders to be aware of this, to know that for some species there may not be any significant change in plumage on first-cycle birds from summer to winter, other than some wear on the plumage. This also demonstrates why a term such as "first-winter plumage" can be meaningless or at least misleading for some gulls.

This Thayer's Gull in November is still in virtually complete juvenile plumage.

Two complete molts per year. Franklin's Gull is unique among our gulls in having two complete or near-complete molts in each annual cycle as an adult. Young birds start off with only a partial preformative molt, and the first and second prealternate molts may be partial or incomplete, but thereafter most birds have a complete prebasic molt on or near the breeding grounds in late summer or early fall, and a complete or near-complete prealternate molt in late winter on the wintering grounds. Franklin's is more of a long-distance migrant than most of our gulls, spending the winter mostly along the west coast of South America, and it has an exceptional amount of white in the wingtip; a few individuals fail to replace the outermost one or two primaries in the prealternate molt, and their wingtip patterns in summer may look odd because of wear and a reduced amount of white.

adult Franklin's Gull in basic plumage (October)

Only one molt per annual cycle. Also unique is Ivory Gull, which has only one molt per year. A bird with this molt pattern is always in basic plumage, of course, and the molt is always a prebasic molt. In adult Ivory Gulls the molt may begin in late spring, suspend during the most active part of caring for the young in the nest, and then resume in late summer. It's interesting that this bird, living in such an extreme environment, has developed a molt strategy unique in its family, but it doesn't affect identification of the species.

Uncertainty in aging large gulls. In the small two-year gulls, except when a bird is in some kind of aberrant or delayed molt, there is never a question as to whether a bird is in its first cycle or an adult cycle. Aging of three-year gulls is also usually straightforward, as the differences between first-cycle, second-cycle, and adult birds is usually pronounced. But in the four-year gulls, there is often a lot of variation in the plumages of birds in their second, third, and fourth cycles, so the age of an individual may be open to question.

At least one study in Britain found that Herring Gulls of a known age — birds that had been banded as nestlings — did not always match the appearance expected of their age group.

Birds known to be in their third cycle could look more like the typical appearance of second-cycle or fourth-cycle birds. This kind of variation may well apply to other large gulls as well. Not only can the plumage vary substantially, but there is a large amount of individual variation in the timing of the change in bill color, eye color, and leg color. In identifying young four-year gulls, it is better to refer to them as "second-cycle type," etc., rather than to make concrete statements about their ages.

Several aspects of plumage suggest that this Herring Gull, photographed in April, is in its first cycle, with the molt that initiates the second cycle about to begin. (For example, the primaries appear to be narrowly pointed, not as rounded as they would be on older birds.) However, its bill pattern is unusually advanced for such a young bird. Such conflicting evidence is noted often with large four-year gulls, making their identification to age open to question.

Understand the ratios of age groups. In viewing three-year gulls, such as Ring-billed Gull, it is possible to separate three age groups in winter: first-cycle, second-cycle, and adult. With four-year gulls, such as American Herring Gull, it is usually possible to separate at least four age classes in winter: first-cycle, second-cycle, third-cycle, and adult. Sometimes even fourth-cycle birds may differ slightly from full adults. At first thought, one might expect all of these age classes to be about equally common, but the reality that we see in the field is different. With Ring-billed Gull, generally we see far fewer second-cycle birds than we do of either first-cycle or adult. With Herring Gull, the third-cycle birds are generally the least numerous, with somewhat more second-cycle, but it is the first-cycle and adult birds that are most common.

With a little more thought, the reasons become apparent. Life in the wild poses many hazards, even for a tough bird like a Herring Gull, and inexperienced young birds are especially vulnerable. Many of those first-cycle Herrings will not survive long enough to see their second winter, and even fewer will survive to their third winter. Somewhat fewer than that will make it to the fourth winter, of course, but at that point the Herring Gull is in adult plumage, and the combination of fourth-winter with all subsequent winter plumages (the birds may live more than twenty years) makes the adult plumage relatively common.

A further complication is that different age groups may have different patterns of dispersal. Among some northerly species, immatures may move farther south than adults: Glaucous Gulls wintering in the southern U.S., and Ivory Gulls that get as far south as southern Canada, are often first-winter birds. During the breeding season, adults may be concentrated near the nesting colonies, while younger birds may be much more widely dispersed. So the ratio of the various age groups at a given locality may be different from the ratio in the population as a whole.

Most Glaucous Gulls found south of their normal range, like this first-cycle bird in Florida, are young ones, not adults.

WHAT TO LOOK AT IN IDENTIFYING GULLS

A novice looking at a gull may see nothing but a big gray or brown bird, while an experienced gull watcher may see an abundance of interesting details. Here are some specific suggestions for what to look for.

Size. The overall size of a gull is a very important point, but of course a difficult thing to judge on a lone bird. Fortunately, gulls are often seen in concentrations where it is possible to make direct comparisons. Male gulls average slightly larger than females of the same species; the difference is usually negligible on the small species, but can be noticeable on the largest ones. There is also individual variation in size, so a bird in a flock that looks slightly larger or smaller may just be a variant individual.

Structure. Many aspects of gull structure will be discussed separately below, such as bill shape, leg length, and primary extension. But the overall structure or shape of the gull is worth noticing as well. Overall shape often reflects the bird's size; even with nothing around them for comparison, we would guess that the slim, petite shape of Bonaparte's Gull reflected a smaller bird than the bulky, blocky structure of Yellow-footed Gull.

first-cycle Yellow-footed Gull in February

Facial expression. Most field guides say little or nothing about the facial expressions of gulls, putting more emphasis on solid plumage characters. However, I find that in practice I use the facial expressions a lot, as a major part of the overall impression of each gull species. The precise shape of the bill (and its pattern), the typical shape of the head, the size and position of the eye, and the typical pattern of dark markings on the head of an immature or winter-plumaged bird all combine to create a characteristic expression that allows us to identify many common gulls very quickly. Ring-billed Gull, for example, tends to look more "gentle" and "cute" than American Herring Gull, which has more of an imperious expression. Western Gull seems sleepy or slow, perhaps because of the combination of its bulky bill and relatively small eyes. These kinds of things are hard to communicate (and if you try, it's hard to get anyone to take you seriously), but I find that I very often name a gull first on the basis of its face and then look for other field marks to back this up.

Bill shape. The precise shape of the bill is a critical point and always worth studying closely, both on birds of known identity and on mystery gulls. However, there is variation within species. In keeping with their overall larger size, males tend to have slightly longer and thicker bills. In the smallest species the difference is hardly visible even with a direct comparison, but in large gulls it may be very noticeable. Since precise bill shape is often a character for separating some very similar species, this sex difference in bill shape can have a serious impact.

By looking closely at gulls, we can develop an awareness of the subtleties of their bill shapes. The length of the bill and the depth at the base combine to create an impression of its thickness. The prominence of the gonydeal angle is an important clue for some species.

Bill color. The color and pattern of the bill are always worth noting. Most gulls show a change in bill color with age (with darker bills generally in younger birds) and most show at least some seasonal change in bill color of adults. Variation in the timing and extent of such change adds up to a lot of apparent individual variation in bill color and pattern. Still, such bill details are often significant field marks. For example, first-cycle Lesser Black-backed Gulls in winter usually have all-black bills, while first-cycle American Herring Gulls in winter tend to have more of a pale or fleshy base to the bill. First-cycle nominate Iceland Gulls usually develop a more visible pinkish area at the base of the bill than first-cycle Kumlien's Iceland Gulls. There are exceptions, so bill color should never be used as a diagnostic mark on its own, but it is often a useful clue.

Bill color and pattern are subject to individual and seasonal variation. The adult Herring Gull at the peak of the breeding season has a bright yellow bill with a red spot on the lower mandible, but on winter adults the yellow becomes duller, a dusky partial band usually develops, and the base of the bill often becomes pinkish.

Head shape. The exact shape of the head has a strong influence on the "facial expression" noted earlier. In the large species, there are subtle differences between females and males. Males have proportionately larger heads, usually with a more shallowly sloping forehead, while females tend to have more rounded heads. It is seldom safe to judge the sex of a lone bird on this basis, but it may be noticeable when members of a mated pair are together, and it can affect the use of head shape as a field mark for separating species. Depending on how the bird is holding its feathers, the head can look more rounded when the feathers are fluffed out, smaller and narrower when the feathers are sleeked down, as in alarm. This in turn can change the impression of bill size: when the feathers are flattened down, the head looks smaller and the bill can look relatively larger.

Orbital ring color. The narrow ring of bare skin immediately surrounding the eye is often contrastingly colored, and its exact color can be useful in some identifications. It is often much more noticeable in the breeding season, when it may become swollen and brightly colored, while at other times of year it may be dark and dull.

Eye color. The iris is dark in most juvenile gulls, but in many the iris becomes paler as the birds mature. Eye color is often a useful field mark for adult gulls, but at least in some species it is variable. Adult Ring-billed Gull seems to always (or virtually always?) have pale yellow eyes, but in adult Mew Gull the eyes vary from dark brown (usually) to dull yellow. Adult California Gulls almost always have dark brown eyes, but they can be dull yellow. Because of the potential for this kind of variation, eye color is never diagnostic, but it is always worth noting.

Leg length and color. In most cases, the length of the legs is not a significant field mark. Some northern species, such as Ivory Gull and the two kittiwakes, have notably short legs. Minor differences between species may be noticed; for example, Laughing Gull often looks longer-legged than Franklin's Gull (but it is elongated in other aspects as well). Gulls in general tend to look longer-legged in hot weather: they flatten their feathers against their bodies instead of fluffing them out, so their bodies look slimmer, their bellies look farther above the ground, and the legs seem longer as a result.

Leg color varies with age in many gulls, often starting off some shade of pink even if the adult leg color is going to be yellow or olive. Leg color is often a significant field mark for adults but it is not infallible; there are frequent cases of adult gulls having the "wrong" leg color, so it should not be used as the sole field mark. However, typical colors often provide a quick way of picking out species. Among a flock of Herring Gulls, for example, a Thayer's Gull may stand out partly because its legs are so bright.

Adult Yellow-footed Gull differs from Western Gull most obviously in leg and foot color. But some Westerns can have yellow legs also, so to be sure of the ID, we should also note this bird's very bulbous-tipped bill with a very large red gonydeal spot. The worn white primary tips on this January bird are suggestive also, since Western typically molts later and would have fresher primaries in January.

Wing shape. Before we delve into all the details of wing pattern, we should note that gulls also differ in wing *shape*. Some aspects of shape are best noted in flight, such as the difference between the long pointed wings of Laughing Gull and the wings of Franklin's Gull, appearing slightly shorter and more rounded at the tip. On standing birds, the length of the wingtip is worth noting in a couple of ways. One is the primary extension: the extension of the wingtip past the tips of the tertials. The other is the extension of the wingtip past the tip of the tail. The latter can be measured in a way if we can determine which primary tip comes closest to falling even with the tip of the tail, but this requires careful attention to the structure of the wingtip, to see whether the longest primary is the outermost (p10) or whether p10 is hidden by a longer p9.

Wing pattern. This is so important that it requires some extended consideration. Different areas of the wing are important at different ages, and different points can be seen on sitting birds as opposed to flying birds. On younger birds, it becomes worthwhile to discuss some of the major feather groups separately, to avoid missing some critical points.

Wing pattern on adults and near-adults. On adult gulls in general the coverts are uniform (usually some shade of gray) and the secondaries are relatively unmarked, so the only real pattern is on the wingtips. Many adult gulls have black or dark gray on the outer primaries, often broken up with a pattern of white, and the differences among species in these patterns are significant for identification. With a good look at the spread wing, it's important to note the number and size of

any white spots enclosed within the dark wingtip and whether these spots are isolated or connected to pale areas toward the bases of the feathers. These dark primaries may also have white spots at the tips, but these may wear away and disappear by a few months after the molt is completed.

Many aspects of wing pattern are more easily discerned from the upperside of the wing, but the size of the white "mirrors" in the outer primaries and the number of primaries with black at the tip can be seen from below as well. On this adult Mew Gull in February, we can see a narrow black mark near the tip of p5 and a broader black band setting off a white tip on p6. On p7 and p8 we can see large white or translucent spots that are set off by black only on the distal side (toward the tip), and on p9 and p10 there are very large white spots that are mostly surrounded by black. With practice, we can see much of this kind of detail even on a moving bird in active flight.

Near-adult birds (second-cycle birds in three-year gulls, and third-cycle birds in four-year gulls) often have wing patterns suggestive of adults, but with fewer and smaller white spots in the outer primaries, with extra dark markings on the primary coverts, and often with some extra dark or brown marks on the secondaries or greater coverts.

Some of the small gulls (such as Little and Bonaparte's gulls) have such different wing patterns as adults that the descriptions above do not apply to them.

Young birds: primaries. Unlike adults, most young gulls do not have interesting wingtip patterns. The pattern of the primaries overall is still worth noting. On some, the primaries as a group look rather uniformly dark, while in others, the inner primaries are distinctly paler than the outer ones, creating a pale area partway out the trailing edge of the wing. There are also a number of species in which first-cycle birds have much paler primaries, such as Iceland, Glaucous-winged, and Glaucous gulls; these all have paler wingtips as adults as well. On some of these, especially Thayer's Gull, the tips of the primaries may look generally darker when the wing is folded than when it is spread.

For separating first-cycle from later plumages of gulls, it's good to know that the primaries tend to be more narrowly pointed on the first cycle, more rounded in later plumages. The same thing applies to the secondaries, but the difference is not so pronounced there.

Secondaries and greater coverts. Many young gulls in flight show a contrast between the secondaries and the greater coverts. This is worth watching for and worth analyzing when it is seen. Often the secondaries are mostly dark, especially on first-cycle birds, so the pattern of the greater coverts will determine the degree of contrast. The color and pattern of the greater coverts may change as the season progresses, especially in first-cycle birds, often becoming very worn and fading all the way to white while the secondaries show less change in appearance.

On this first-cycle Great Black-backed Gull in late October, we can see many details on the spread wing. The greater coverts are obvious here, with strong pale checkering showing up on the inner ones, helping to set off the blackish secondaries.

On this second-cycle American Herring Gull in February, the greater coverts are obvious as a group of pale brown feathers, with a little more gray showing on the innermost ones. The tertials are much darker, a dark dusky brownish at the base with whitish markings toward the tip.

On this first-cycle Lesser Black-backed Gull in February, the greater coverts are clearly visible on the lowest, forward part of the wing. The innermost ones show some white checkering, but the outer greater coverts are mostly solid brown with whitish edges.

The secondaries are mostly or entirely hidden most of the time when the gull is standing or swimming, of course, but the greater coverts remain visible and their pattern can be important in identification until they become worn or faded.

The black diagonal bar across the inner part of the wing on this juvenile Black-legged Kittiwake is mostly on the lesser coverts, but it extends back to take in the innermost median coverts as well.

Median and lesser coverts. These rows of coverts are not as broad as the greater coverts, but they are still readily discernible in flight. They are usually visible on the folded wing as well, although the forward part of the wing may be partly covered up by scapulars or by breast feathers overlapping the wing. In many of the medium-sized and large gulls, the individual coverts on first-cycle birds have dark centers and pale edges; the patterns are not usually helpful for identification, although there are some differences among species, such as the more pointed dark feather centers on Ring-billed Gull compared to the more rounded centers on Mew Gull. However, the condition of the coverts can give a quick read on whether the plumage is fresh, worn, or molting, because the effects of wear show up clearly on these feathers. Some of the small gulls have distinctive dark bands across the inner part of the wing, involving these feather groups.

Tertials. The tertials, essentially the innermost secondaries, often are not very noticeable in flight, because the longest scapulars may fan out to cover them when the wings are spread. But on standing or swimming gulls, the tertials are obvious, and their patterns are always worth noting. For example, first-cycle Thayer's and Kumlien's gulls can be very similar, and one of the most consistent differences between them is in tertial pattern: tending to have more solidly or evenly dark centers on Thayer's, often more checkered or barred on Kumlien's.

Underwing. In general, the pattern is less distinct on the underside of the wing than on the upperside. But with a good view of a gull from below, it's important to note the overall pattern of the wing-linings. In some cases involving large gulls, this provides a clue to the age of the bird. For example, on first-cycle and second-cycle Great Black-backed Gulls, the wing-linings are mostly brown, while on third-cycle and adult birds of this species, the wing-linings are mostly white.

Underwing pattern is most important on some of the relatively rare small gulls. Black-headed Gull is superficially similar to Bonaparte's Gull in many respects, but the dusky inner webs of the central primaries create a very dark area on the underwing, unlike anything shown by Bonaparte's. Adult Little Gulls have blackish on the wing-linings and the undersides of the flight feathers, and adult Ross's Gulls are medium gray in those areas. These patterns are distinctive, but in certain lights, even a white underwing may look dark because of the effect of shadows. By studying many Bonaparte's Gulls in flight to see how their underwings appear in varying light conditions, we can be prepared to recognize the difference in Black-headed Gull when we see it.

Many things about wing pattern can change on worn or molting birds. This first-cycle Slaty-backed Gull in June has much of the plumage worn and bleached by the sun, and the whitish greater coverts show extreme contrast against the secondaries, which are still blackish.

This one-year-old Red-legged Kittiwake in mid-July is in latter stages of its second prebasic molt; primaries 1 through 6 are new, p7 is growing, p8 appears to be missing, and p9 and p10 are old. The bird still shows dusky marks from first-cycle plumages on the primary coverts and lesser coverts, most of which will probably be lost by the time the molt is complete.

This adult Black-headed Gull in late August is near the end of the prebasic molt. The only old primary remaining on the near wing is p10, the outermost (apparently dropped already from the far wing). On the underside of the far wing, notice the dark inner webs of the primaries, giving a very different underwing pattern from that of Bonaparte's Gull.

Scapular pattern. Adult gulls almost always have unmarked scapulars, but on immatures they are often strongly patterned, and these are such large feathers that they have a significant impact on the bird's overall appearance. Unfortunately, the patterns of the scapulars are seldom diagnostic for separating similar species. They may be more useful for indicating stages of molt. For example, in American Herring Gull and some other large species, the juvenile scapulars have solidly dark brown centers and relatively narrow pale edges; when these are replaced in the first molt, the replacement feathers are usually paler and grayer, with dark central marks or bars.

Tail pattern. Unlike the situation in many groups of birds, the length and shape of the tail seldom serve as useful field characters for gulls. But the pattern of the tail is often useful in identifying young birds.

Almost all of our gulls have all-white tails as adults (with the exceptions of Heermann's Gull and the vagrant Black-tailed and Belcher's gulls). Almost all of our gulls have at least some dark markings on the tail in their youngest stages (the odd exception is Red-legged Kittiwake). In identifying young gulls, the pattern of the tail is always worth noting, and in detail. To see the full tail pattern we have to see it spread, when the bird is either preening extensively or flying. If there is a dark band on the tail, note whether it is at the tip of the feathers (a terminal band) or set back from the tip (a subterminal band). If the tail looks all dark, take a closer look to see if the outermost feathers might have paler markings. In looking at the tail pattern, be sure to make distinctions between the tail feathers themselves and the uppertail coverts, or you could be thrown way off on some birds.

On this first-cycle Bonaparte's Gull in April, the very narrow white tips to the tail feathers are mostly worn away, so that the black tail band appears to be a terminal band, not subterminal. This kind of variation with wear should be expected.

Assessing tones of gray. The precise shade of gray of the upperparts is often a field character for separating gull species, but this point is easily misinterpreted. As discussed in Chapter 2, effects of lighting can alter our perceptions of gray in an extreme way. Gulls standing on snow or ice may give the illusion of being extremely dark-backed, while in other situations, bright sunlight may make the birds look washed out and pale above, so we should be cautious about judging gray tones without direct comparisons. Even when gulls are side by side, in some lights, a bird turned at a different angle may appear lighter or darker.

ISSUES AND PROBLEM AREAS IN GULL IDENTIFICATION

Changes in distribution and status. One tricky but fascinating aspect of gull watching is the fact that the distribution of species changes over time, sometimes in major ways. The recent history of Lesser Black-backed Gull in North America is a prime example of this. First recorded on this continent in 1934, the species was still a rare visitor as recently as the 1970s, with only a handful recorded in most winters. Numbers increased rapidly during the 1980s and 1990s, and the wintering population now certainly numbers in the low thousands. It is now easy to find dozens in a day at several points along the Atlantic Seaboard, even hundreds at a couple of spots. Lesser Black-backeds have become regular in small numbers on the Great Lakes, and a few show up regularly throughout the interior, even a few west of the Rockies.

This expansion of the wintering population undoubtedly reflects the changing status of the species in Iceland, where it first began breeding in the late 1920s and has increased rapidly in numbers since the 1970s. Iceland's position far out in the North Atlantic makes it a much more likely source than birds coming all the way from Europe. There is also a growing population nesting in western Greenland since 1990, and by the time you read this there may be thriving colonies of Lesser Black-backeds in North America. The status is changing so fast that any older reference may give a misleading impression of what to expect.

adult Lesser Black-backed Gull in February

Many other gulls are going through changes in distribution or have within the last few decades. As recently as the 1920s, Great Black-backed Gulls were not known to nest south of Maine; now they nest commonly along the coast south to the Carolinas. Little Gull was long considered only a rare visitor from Eurasia, but since the 1960s it has been found nesting at a number of sites from the Great Lakes north to Hudson Bay. Black-headed Gull was not found in North America until 1930, but now it nests locally in the northeast, and large numbers spend the winter in eastern Canada. Kelp Gulls from the coasts of South America appeared around the Gulf of Mexico in the 1980s, nested several times on islands off the Louisiana coast, and strayed as far inland as the Great Lakes. Slaty-backed Gull was known in North America only from western Alaska until 1983, when a wintering bird was found in Missouri; now there have been records all over southern Canada and the lower 48 states, and birders actively look for it in winter. Other notable changes in distribution, sometimes only temporary, have involved several other species, from American Herring and Laughing gulls to Ross's Gull.

The significance of all this for field birders is twofold. First, we can't necessarily make assumptions about what is expected; that odd gull that we find is probably just a variation on something common, but it could be a bird from another continent, in the process of invading and not in the field guides yet. Second, by staying alert and keeping good records, we can add to the scientific knowledge of the dynamics of gull distribution.

Hybrid situations. There are some situations in North America where hybrid gulls are actually common, and there are a number of hybrid combinations that are seen regularly. Without an awareness of these, birders are likely to be mystified or to make many misidentifications when they run across such birds. Some birders have a general bias against hybrids, perhaps because they don't "count" on lists, but ignoring such birds won't make them go away. We're better off acknowledging their existence and seeking to understand how they fit into the picture.

Glaucous-winged Gull is unique among North American birds in the extent to which it interbreeds with multiple other species. It interbreeds abundantly with Western Gull in Washington and Oregon, commonly with Herring Gull in southeastern and southcoastal Alaska, regularly with Glaucous Gull in southwestern Alaska, and at least fairly often with Slaty-backed Gull in eastern Siberia. With so many genes from other species entering from all directions, we might wonder whether there is such a thing as a "pure" Glaucous-winged Gull anywhere. But at the core of the range (especially coastal British Columbia) there is a standard Glaucous-winged with a consistent appearance, and with care it can be separated from obvious hybrids.

Glaucous-winged Gull × Western Gull. At the southern end of the Glaucous-winged's range, the extent of its interbreeding with Western Gull is remarkable. Along the coast in Washington and Oregon there are breeding colonies in which hybrids outnumber both "pure" parental types combined. Interbreeding and backcrossing are rampant, and it is possible to find birds that look like every possible stage from pure Glaucous-winged to pure Western, if such can even be defined. Introgression (the spread of genes through the population) affects birds well to the south and north of this hybrid zone, and it is possible to find slightly pale Westerns and slightly dark Glaucous-wingeds breeding south to northern California and north to central British Columbia, respectively. Hybrids winter commonly to central and southern California, and wanderers reach Alaska as well.

Glaucous-winged and Western are very similar in structure, so shape is of little aid in identifying hybrids. Adults differ in dorsal color — pale gray with gray-patterned wingtips in Glaucous-winged, dark gray with black-patterned wingtips in Western, and hybrids can be anywhere in between. The orbital ring is pink in Glaucous-winged, yellow in Western, and can be either or a mix of both in hybrids; in all of these birds, of course, it can be much duller in winter. The eyes are usually dark but sometimes pale in Glaucous-winged, usually very pale (but varying to medium-dark) in Western.

In basic plumage, Glaucous-winged adults often develop heavy gray-brown markings on the head and neck; these have a horizontally barred effect, different from the lengthwise streaking shown by many winter gulls. Adult Westerns usually develop only faint streaking on the head at most, and some remain purely white-headed through the winter. Another difference is that the bill often remains brighter yellow through the winter on adult Western, while the bright yellow bill of the breeding Glaucous-winged, as with many other gulls, becomes duller and paler in winter and develops a dusky subterminal spot. Even with all of these differences, in some cases it just isn't possible to separate variants of the parental species from intermediates that are close in appearance to one or the other.

Adult Western Gull in January (left) and Glaucous-winged Gull in February (right). In addition to the difference in upperparts and wingtip color, note that Western typically has pale eyes and yellow orbital ring, while Glaucous-winged typically has dark eyes and pink orbital ring. On this Western in midwinter the head is essentially unmarked white and the bill is bright yellow. This Glaucous-winged is relatively lightly marked on the head and neck — many have much darker markings there in winter — and its bill is duller than it will be in summer.

This is a reasonably typical example of a Glaucous-winged Gull × Western Gull hybrid in first-cycle plumage. It looks mostly similar to Western Gull, with a tail much too dark for any stage of Glaucous-winged, but its outer primaries are too pale for Western. Such birds are easy to overlook unless we focus on identifying every individual.

In a major hybrid zone such as the coast of Washington, hybrids do not necessarily look exactly intermediate between the parental forms. This adult gull looks very much like a Glaucous-winged in most ways, including the head markings, pink orbital ring, and dark eye. The only real giveaways of its mixed ancestry are the darkness of the wingtips and perhaps the darkness of the upperparts.

Younger stages also run the gamut between the typical appearances of the two species. First-cycle hybrids can be superficially very much like the appearance of first-cycle Thayer's Gull, even to the extent of having the outer primaries contrastingly darker brown on the outer vanes and paler on the inner vanes. Both hybrids and Thayer's Gulls are so variable in plumage in the first cycle that there are few really useful plumage characters to separate them; the best distinctions are bill size and shape, plus overall structure, with Thayer's being a smaller-billed and more slender bird.

Glaucous-winged Gull × American Herring Gull. These two interbreed commonly in southern Alaska, and hybrids are seen regularly south to California in winter, although they are undoubtedly often overlooked. The parental species differ somewhat in structure, American Herring Gull being a slimmer bird with a less bulbous-tipped bill. On adults, in addition to obvious points of wingtip color, Glaucous-winged has a pink orbital ring and usually dark eyes, while Herring has a yellow to orange orbital ring and usually pale yellow eyes. In basic plumage, the head and neck markings tend more to barring on Glaucous-winged, streaking on Herring. Adult hybrids are usually intermediate in multiple characters. The same is true for young birds, which are even easier to overlook, or perhaps to misidentify as Thayer's Gulls.

Glaucous Gull × Herring Gull. In its widespread range in the far north, Glaucous Gull overlaps with several forms that are currently considered part of the Herring Gull complex. In Iceland, interbreeding between European Herring and Glaucous gulls is very common, producing all manner of intermediate birds. Some such hybrids seen in northeastern North America may be from Iceland. Other such birds may be hybrids between Glaucous and American Herring Gulls from northern Canada, and some seen in Alaska might be hybrids between Glaucous and "Vega" Herring Gulls. With their combination of characters, some of these birds suggest Thayer's or Kumlien's gulls in pattern, but the hybrids are almost always noticeably larger and bulkier birds. Glaucous × Herring hybrids have sometimes been called "Nelson's Gulls," but I personally don't like the use of such a name; it implies that this hybrid combination has a special status, unlike the many other hybrid combinations that birders might see, and it implies a level of certainty that may not be warranted. For field identification, "probable Glaucous × Herring Gull hybrid" is probably a better term to use.

Photographed in western Alaska, this bird undoubtedly has Glaucous Gull as part of its ancestry, but the rest is uncertain; the dark in the wingtips may have come from Glaucous-winged Gull, but it could have come from Herring or Slaty-backed gulls, and the bird is likely a backcross rather than a first-generation hybrid.

Other common hybrid combinations. Many other species pairs are known to hybridize at least occasionally, producing a dizzying array of possible appearances. Often it will be impossible to be certain of the origins of such hybrids, but birders need to keep the existence of such birds in mind to avoid misidentifying them as other species. For example, Herring Gulls occasionally interbreed with Great Black-backed Gull and Lesser Black-backed Gull, and the resulting hybrids can bear a superficial resemblance to various other things. When we see a gull that doesn't quite add up, we should always consider the possibility of some hybrid.

The Thayer's/Kumlien's problem. Thayer's Gull has been causing confusion for ornithologists and birders alike, ever since it was described to science in 1915. For years it was treated as a subspecies of Herring Gull; that is clearly wrong, but its exact status is still controversial.

Thayer's appears to be the western/northern representative of a group of three closely related forms nesting in the Arctic. Its breeding range takes in several of the western and northern islands of the Canadian high Arctic, as well as the coast of northwest Greenland. Thayer's Gulls mostly winter in the Pacific Northwest, with fewer farther east. Kumlien's Gull, currently treated as a subspecies of Iceland Gull (*L. g. kumlieni*), nests mostly southeast of the breeding range of Thayer's, on southern Baffin Island and the northern edge of Hudson Bay, and winters mostly in eastern Canada and the northeastern U.S. The nominate Iceland Gull *(L. g. glaucoides)* nests in southwestern and southeastern Greenland and apparently winters mostly in nearby Arctic seas, with some going to Iceland.

Typical adults of these three forms differ clearly. Thayer's is the darkest, with gray upperparts averaging slightly darker than those of American Herring Gulls, and with blackish slate markings in the wingtips; it also averages larger and longer-billed than the other two. Adult nominate Iceland Gull is the palest, with upperparts averaging slightly paler than those of American Herring Gull and with the wingtips usually pure white. Adult Kumlien's Gull is intermediate between the other two. All three forms are quite variable in appearance at all ages, especially Thayer's and Kumlien's, so that drawing distinct lines between them is a challenge.

Thayer's Gull is exceptionally variable. Shown are an average winter adult and two fairly typical first-cycle birds.

In terms of their classification, the main challenge is that we don't know much about what happens where the breeding ranges of Thayer's and Kumlien's meet in the Canadian Arctic. All three forms nest in fairly small colonies, mostly on ledges of cliffs facing the sea, so the logistics of studying them where they nest are quite challenging. Some past studies are open to serious question, and follow-up studies have not really clarified the situation. We simply don't know to what extent there is interbreeding between birds that look like Thayer's and birds that look like Kumlien's. Without that knowledge, it is very difficult to interpret the variation that we see on the wintering grounds.

Expert opinion is divided about wintering birds. Most birds of this complex wintering on the Pacific Coast seem clearly referable to Thayer's Gull, and most in the northeast fit within the standard idea of

Kumlien's Gull. In both areas, however, there are problematic birds, and some birders suggest that many of the palest Thayer's and the darkest Kumlien's could also be interpreted as intermediates. In between these areas, on the southern Great Lakes where both Thayer's and Kumlien's are uncommon, some observers have reported numbers of seemingly intermediate birds. Until we know more about the taxonomic status of the forms involved, field identification of intermediate birds will be open to question. For the moment it is more useful to study and photograph such birds than it is to try to put names on them.

The Herring Gull complex. One of the more interesting things going on in the bird world is the changing perception of birds formerly lumped under the catch-all category of "Herring Gull."

All of those breeding on the North American mainland are classified under one subspecies, *L. a. smithsonianus*, even though there are some average differences between eastern and western birds. The situation is far more complicated in Europe and Asia, where up to fifteen distinct subspecies of similar large gulls occur. Three of those have long been split off as constituting Lesser Black-backed Gull, which overlaps in breeding range with a couple of Herring Gull forms with only rare interbreeding. The other dozen or so were long regarded as making up one variable species, which also included the North American population. More recently, as ornithologists focused on all these Eurasian forms, it became impossible to ignore the major differences among populations. Differences in leg color (yellow or pink), darkness of the upperparts, wingtip pattern, immature plumages, and other points have led to suggestions to split the old "Herring Gull" up into several species.

One such split already has been accepted by the American Ornithologists' Union: the Yellow-legged Gull *(Larus michahellis)*, native to southern and western Europe and to islands in the eastern Atlantic, has

This first-cycle gull standing on the beach in September might not draw a second glance, but it is a European Herring Gull — and it might be hard to confirm that, except for the fact that it was photographed in Europe. Field marks for separating many of the members of this complex are still being worked out, but undoubtedly they will get more attention in the future.

strayed to eastern North America a number of times. It is now included in a number of field guides aimed at experienced birders.

Although the AOU has not yet acted on the evidence, most European experts now regard the North American bird as a full species, American Herring Gull *(Larus smithsonianus)*. It would thus be distinct from the European Herring Gull *(L. argentatus)*, which strays regularly to Newfoundland and has been found at a number of other points in eastern North America. Most European authorities now also regard Vega Gull *(L. vegae)* as a distinct species. Vega Gull nests on St. Lawrence Island, Alaska, and occurs elsewhere in western Alaska, and has been found as a rare stray as far south as Texas. Most birders are not actively looking for it, because it is still not treated as a full species by the AOU, and full details for identifying it are still being worked out. It is possible that Vega Gulls are occurring widely in North America, as is true for Slaty-backed Gulls that come from the same general region.

Under a modern taxonomic treatment, therefore, the "Herring Gulls" on this continent are mostly American Herring Gulls, but at least three other species are known to occur, and there may be others. There is an old possible Alaska record of a bird that would now be regarded as the eastern subspecies of Heuglin's Gull from northern Russia, part of the whole Herring Gull complex. However, separating Heuglin's from Lesser Black-backed Gull in the field could be an extreme challenge, so it is possible that Heuglin's (and perhaps some other forms?) are occurring undetected in North America. The fact that there are still unanswered questions like this is part of the reason why many experienced birders find gulls endlessly fascinating.

18. LEARNING TO IDENTIFY TERNS

As a group, terns are beautiful, variable, and challenging. Many species are quite similar to each other, so there are many identification difficulties involved with this group. They are so often seen at a great distance — as flickering white shapes out over the water, or as hunched forms on unapproachable sandbars — that birders may fall into the habit of leaving them unidentified or, worse, of making careless assumptions as to what they are likely to be. Even many birders with long experience may make confident identifications only of adult terns at the height of the breeding season. Young birds and adults at other seasons may be only quasi-identified, marked down on the list based on assumptions as to what is probable.

Overview of the problem. With a close view, most adult terns in the breeding season can be recognized by details of bill shape and color. But these details are hard to see at a distance, and for young birds and for adults at other seasons they often do not apply. Most tern species are superficially very similar in overall pattern, and some of their best-known field marks are subject to variation with season and age; because of this variation, these field marks are easy to misuse or misinterpret. Some subadult stages and some molting terns look confusingly different from the plumages usually shown in field guides. Terns have some unique aspects of molt, which can make their seasonal changes in wing pattern harder to understand. Size and shape of the birds are good clues at all times, but size is very difficult to judge in the field, and it takes considerable experience to be able to identify terns by shape.

PRELIMINARY POINTS

Plumage sequences and ages of terns. Almost all North American terns show some seasonal change in appearance as adults, and all show some variations with age. Juvenile terns are distinctive: all show some kind of patterning on the back, scapulars, and/or the upperside of the wings that differs from the pattern of adults in those areas. Juveniles of many species have brown on the upperparts, lacking in all subsequent plumages, and many of the pale-backed species have strong dark markings above at that stage.

A juvenile Black Tern in early September: superficially like a winter adult, but with brown markings and scaly pattern on the upperparts.

A juvenile Caspian Tern in August, just beginning preformative molt, still showing neat black subterminal marks on many feathers of the upperparts.

The complete juvenile plumage is usually worn for only a short time, and the molt to replace it may begin by late summer. This molt starts later in some long-distance migrants that winter mostly south of the U.S., such as Common and Arctic terns, which may not begin to molt until late fall, after they have left our area. For other species, however, we can see the plumage changing in early fall with the onset of molt. This is considered a preformative molt in most species, it is usually complete, and it may last from early fall until late the following spring, overlapping extensively with the first prealternate molt in the spring. In some species there is then a limited presupplemental molt as well, before the next prebasic molt begins. (With two or more molts inserted in the first cycle, this is considered an example of Complex Alternate Strategy; see pp. 82–84.) In some species, such as Forster's Tern, there is only one molt inserted in the first cycle, and it is considered a prealternate molt.

In summer, one-year-old terns of almost all species, and two-year-old terns of most species — that is, birds in first alternate and second alternate plumages — look different from summer adults. Generally only small numbers of such birds are seen close to breeding colonies, and they may spend their first and second full summers near the wintering grounds. If we get a chance to study these summer immature terns, some may appear to be more "advanced" in plumage than others. There are some that look fairly similar to juveniles, but without the markings on the back and scapulars and with much wear on some wing feathers. There are others that look more like summer adults, but with extra white on the forehead and with extra dark markings on the wings. It might seem logical to assume that these represent first alternate and second alternate plumages, respectively, but studies of banded birds of known age have shown that it is not so simple, and it is probably not safe to try to age such birds on the basis of their overall appearance.

This Black Tern looks similar to a winter adult — but it was photographed in May. The mostly white underparts and the very worn outermost primaries suggest that it is probably in first alternate plumage.

Most terns have a remarkable molt pattern in which the inner primaries may be replaced twice, or even three times, during each annual cycle; see "Understanding upperwing pattern in terns" on the next page. Most tern species, especially those with long outer tail feathers, also molt most of the tail feathers twice per year, in the prebasic and prealternate molts. The outer tail feathers of basic plumage are often shorter and wider than those of alternate plumage, giving the bird a different shape at rest and in flight.

A note on "portlandica" plumages. Among the first terns to be examined closely by ornithologists were populations of Common, Arctic, and Roseate terns nesting in northeastern North America and northern Europe. Around such colonies in summer, virtually all the birds are in adult plumages. As a result, at one time, it seemed logical to assume that last year's fledglings were this year's breeders. Indeed, when the normal immature summer plumages of Arctic Tern were first detected, they were described to science as two new species, *Sterna pikei* and *Sterna portlandica*. We now understand that many immature terns simply remain on the wintering grounds throughout their first summer — and, depending on the species, often the second as well. Those individuals coming north with the adults may be relatively few. Only half a century ago, some astute birders were still puzzling over these birds and referring to them as representing the "portlandica plumage." Since we now know that these are a normal part of the plumage sequence and not some abnormal phase, I mention the term here only for historical interest, and I don't recommend its use.

Understanding upperwing pattern in terns. On many terns, there is a distinct contrast on the outer part of the wing, as seen from the upperside, with the inner primaries looking sharply paler than the outer ones. This can vary from one season to another, even on the same individual: the outermost primaries may look strikingly darker at some seasons, and much closer to the color of the inner primaries at other seasons. This also can vary among individuals, even those of the same age group seen at the same time of year. And there are some differences among species that can be relevant in identification. But to use this outer wing contrast as a field mark, it helps to understand how it is caused.

On this adult Least Tern in April we can see the outer seven primaries: p4 through p8 are very pale gray, while p9 and p10 are very dark. These patterns of contrast in the outer part of the wing are often important in identification.

The darkness of the upperside of a single primary feather in a tern's wing depends on two things: the darkness of the feather's ground color, and the amount of pale powdery "bloom" that covers it. Since this pale bloom will be gradually worn away over time, the feather is palest when it first grows in; if the ground color of the primary is dark, the feather will gradually become darker until the time it is next molted. (Tern primaries of the same age are not all of the same darkness, of course, because of differences among species in the tone of the feather's base color and in its original amount of pale bloom.)

So, as a general rule, when we are looking at terns with essentially pale gray wings, the primaries are darker when the feathers are older. This has a major effect on wing pattern because of the sequence of molt. Many of the terns have a remarkable molt pattern in which some of the inner primaries are replaced twice, or even three times, in the course of the annual cycle. As a result of this, there are some times of year when the outer primaries may be many months older than the inner primaries, and thus strikingly darker.

Common Tern provides a good illustration of how this works. In adults, the prebasic molt of the primaries begins in late summer or early fall, either on the breeding grounds or at some stopover site on migration. During this early stage of the molt, anywhere from one to four or five primaries will be replaced, one at a time, in the usual sequence beginning with the innermost (p1). The molt is then suspended while the tern continues its southward migration. After its arrival on the wintering grounds, the prebasic molt resumes where it left off, and the rest of the primaries are replaced, one by one, ending with the outermost (p10) usually in late winter.

The prealternate molt often begins before the prebasic molt is completed, sometime in midwinter. In this prealternate molt, some of the inner primaries will be replaced again (in the usual way, one at a time, beginning with the innermost). There can be a time at which the bird has molt going on at two points in the primaries at once, with for example the prebasic molt of p9 happening at the same time as the prealternate molt of p1. (Most Common Terns are south of the U.S. in winter, so North American birders get few opportunities to observe this pattern.) The number of primaries replaced in this prealternate molt can vary from three to seven, but five is a typical number, and the molt usually ends in mid- to late spring, often after the bird has started its northward migration. Remarkably, there may be another molt overlapping with the prealternate, a presupplemental molt in spring, in which a few of the innermost primaries may be replaced yet again.

From the standpoint of a field observer, the result of this odd molt sequence is that on adult Common Terns in early summer, the inner primaries are significantly newer (and paler) than the outer ones. Furthermore, because primary molt always progresses outward on the wing, the last of the inner primaries replaced in spring (and thus the freshest) is usually next to the oldest of the retained outer primaries from the previous molt, so the contrast is especially noticeable. In the case of Common Tern, it shows up as a narrow dark wedge running in from the trailing edge of the wing. This can be striking on some summer birds, and occasionally even more so in fall, when the outer primaries may be almost a year old. In late winter, when the prebasic molt is completing and all of the primaries are closer to the same age, no such dark wedge may be evident.

This immature Common Tern in May shows an example of the odd primary patterns that are possible because of the unique molts of terns. On this bird, the outermost, longest primaries (apparently p9 and p10) are extremely worn and frayed, then there are two that are much fresher (probably p7 and p8), and just basal to those is another primary that is apparently older and darker (probably p6). The uncertainty about which primaries we're seeing is because we don't know if one or more primaries might be missing altogether at the moment and because it's hard to see detail on the worn outermost feathers.

In the four similar species discussed in the next chapter, variations on this molt pattern produce visible differences in the wing pattern as seen in late spring and summer. Roseate Tern has a molt schedule similar to that of Common Tern but it usually replaces more of the inner primaries in the prealternate molt in late winter, retaining only about three of the old outer ones, so it has a much more limited dark area on the outer part of the wing. Forster's Tern has a less extensive molt than Common, replacing fewer of the inner primaries in the prealternate molt and lacking the extra presupplemental molt. Its outer primaries are paler to begin with, however, at least on adults, and do not darken as much with age, so adult Forster's in summer have the primaries very pale above. The adult Arctic Tern goes through its complete prebasic molt of the primaries during the winter in the southern hemisphere. Its prealternate molt sometimes includes one to three of the inner primaries, but often none of them are replaced; the upperside of the primaries will look relatively uniform on adult Arctics in summer.

These field marks will be repeated in the next chapter under each species, but if we understand the mechanisms by which these patterns are created, we can understand the wing patterns of other terns.

THE GENERA OF TERNS

For many years, most of the terns were classified by the American Ornithologists' Union as belonging to the genus *Sterna,* a diverse assemblage that included everything from the gull-sized Caspian Tern to the tiny Least Tern. On the basis of recent studies, they now have been divided into several genera, leaving no North American species in *Sterna* except for the four discussed in the next chapter. This change was made by the AOU so recently (2006) that the current names are not included in most field guides. The new classification is worth noting for birders because now it actually makes sense in the field: the genera now correspond to groups of terns that are recognizeably different. The following is a brief overview of the currently recognized genera of terns that occur regularly in North America.

Genus *Sterna*. Medium-sized terns. Under the current AOU classification, this genus now includes only Common, Forster's, Arctic, and Roseate terns. These could be considered "typical" terns, medium-sized and long-tailed. One or more species can be found practically everywhere in North America and can be seen flying and hovering over open water, plunge-diving headfirst into the water to catch small fish. These four terns are treated in detail in the next chapter.

Genus *Thalasseus*. Crested Terns. Royal Tern, Elegant Tern, and Sandwich Tern. These are large long-winged terns, with elongated feathers forming a loose crest at the back of the head. In North America they are most common in warmer southern climates, and almost exclusively coastal. When foraging they plunge-dive into the water, sometimes from a considerable height, often hovering in one spot before diving.

Royal
Tern

Genus *Hydroprogne*. Caspian Tern. Larger than the crested terns and probably not closely related to them. A heavy-billed, square-headed tern, with long broad wings, suggesting a gull more than a tern when seen in flight, and sometimes overlooked when it is resting on beaches with gulls. Widespread coastally and inland, it is usually seen in small numbers except at nesting colonies. In foraging it plunge-dives into the water, often hovering momentarily first.

Genus *Gelochelidon*. Gull-billed Tern. A unique tern, large-headed, thick-billed, long-legged, and short-tailed. In flight its wings look both broad and very long. It flies buoyantly, often catching insects in midair over marshes, also swooping down to pick up crabs or other creatures on beaches or from the surface of the water. In North America it occurs inland in Florida and at Salton Sea, California, but otherwise it is a coastal bird.

Genus *Sternula*. Least Tern. Smaller than our other terns, with slender body, slim wings, and stiff wingbeats. It forages by plunge-diving into the water. Mostly coastal, but also nests far inland in central regions of the continent. Strictly a summer resident in North America, wintering deep in the tropics.

Genus *Chlidonias*. Marsh terns. Black Tern is widespread in North America, while White-winged Tern and Whiskered Tern are rare visitors. These are medium-small, short-tailed terns, extensively dark below in breeding plumage. Buoyant in flight, they have relatively slow, shallow wingbeats, banking from side to side in flight. In foraging they dip down to pick items from the surface of water or land, sometimes catching insects in midair. They nest at inland marshes, but they migrate to spend the winter out at sea at tropical latitudes.

Black Tern,
adult in
alternate plumage

Genus *Onychoprion*. Dark-backed terns. Sooty Tern and Bridled Tern are tropical and subtropical, while Aleutian Tern nests in the Arctic and subarctic. All nest on islands and coasts and live at sea for part of the year. All have dark backs and white foreheads as adults in alternate plumage, and juveniles of all have heavily marked upperparts. In foraging, they typically swoop down to pluck prey items from the surface of the water rather than plunge-diving.

Genus *Anous*. Noddies. Brown Noddy and the rare Black Noddy are like terns in reverse, dark with pale caps, their tails roughly wedge-tipped. Strictly tropical, they nest on islands and range widely at sea and are seldom seen from the mainland in North America. Their flight is swift and direct, with deep wingbeats, and they usually forage by dipping to the surface of the water. Noddies are unlikely to be confused with other terns but might be mistaken for jaegers or other seabirds.

WHAT TO LOOK FOR IN IDENTIFYING TERNS

These points apply to terns in general. The next chapter, focusing on the four medium-sized *Sterna* terns, gives concrete examples of how these points can be used to separate the most difficult species.

Size and shape at rest. Some aspects of structure are most easily seen on standing birds. Head shape varies among species, both in obvious ways (such as crested vs. uncrested) and in more subtle ways. The size and shape of the head, combined with size and shape of the bill, have a major impact on the overall impression given by the bird.

The length of the tail, relative to the length of the wingtips, is always worth noting if it can be seen; the tail is often hidden by the wings on shorter-tailed species.

Leg length varies among species, with some (such as Arctic Tern) looking exceptionally short-legged, others (such as Gull-billed Tern) looking notably long-legged, and most falling somewhere in between. The appearance of leg length is affected by how the bird is holding its body feathers; if the feathers are fluffed out and the belly feathers are drooping, it can make any tern look very short-legged.

Size of a lone tern is usually impossible to judge accurately, but comparative sizes of tern species can be very useful in some situations. Flocks of terns in flight generally will turn out to be all of one species; but at rest on open beaches, multiple species of terns often will mix freely, and slight differences in size can be one easy way to pick out a different species.

Shape and actions in flight. With experience, these are among the best ways to identify terns, as all species have distinctive flight silhouettes and characteristic flight actions. Differences in head size and tail length among species may be more obvious in flight, making the wings appear to be set far forward or far back on the body, and making larger-headed or smaller-headed structure easier to see.

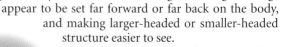

Differences in wing shape are noticeable in flight, and these are related to differences in flight action. For example, the marsh terns have relatively broad short wings to go with their compact bodies and short wide tails, and they look very buoyant in flight. Least Tern has very narrow wings, emphasizing the look of its slim, small body. In normal flight it has stiff, deep wingbeats, switching to stiff, rapid, shallow wingbeats when it is hovering over the water. The crested terns have long narrow wings, deep wingbeats, and strong, direct flight. The wings of Gull-billed tern are uniquely shaped, broad on the inner part (the secondaries and coverts), noticeably long on the outer part (the primaries), giving this species a buoyant and highly maneuverable flight action. Even the four species of medium-sized terns

The Sandwich Tern in flight is distinctive in shape, with its long slender bill, large head, and very long angular wings.

Caspian Tern in flight looks more similar to a gull than to other terns, with its heavy head, broad wings, and relatively slow, deep wingbeats.

discussed in the next chapter, similar though they are, have distinctive flight styles: for example, the stiff, shallow wingbeats of Roseate Tern provide the best way to pick it out at long distance.

It's important to keep in mind that the flight action of any bird can change in strong or gusty wind conditions. Also, most terns have courtship display flights, in which their actions may be very different from that of normal flight.

Foraging behavior. Typical foraging differs among groups of terns, and while any bird may occasionally forage in an unusual way, these broad patterns provide very helpful clues. The medium-sized terns, crested terns, Caspian Tern, and Least Tern all usually forage by plunge-diving headfirst into the water, capturing small fish (mostly) from just below the surface. They may dive from a considerable height above the water (especially the large species) or from very low, and they often hover before diving.

The dark-backed terns, marsh terns, and noddies usually forage by swooping down to pluck items from the water's surface with their bills, rather than plunging in headfirst. The marsh terns also will dip down to pick up small creatures from land or from marsh vegetation and will sometimes catch insects in midair; the latter is a common foraging behavior for Gull-billed Tern, another species that seldom or never plunge-dives into the water.

Any of these birds may employ unusual foraging behavior when unusual opportunities arise; medium-sized terns sometimes catch insects in midair, for example, and marsh terns occasionally make shallow plunge-dives, especially when wintering or migrating out at sea.

Bill shape and color. Even among very similar terns, subtle differences in bill shape contribute to the overall appearance of the species. This is described in some detail for the four in the next chapter, and it works for the other groups of terns as well. Indeed, bill shape is one of the main criteria for separating Elegant and Royal terns, a helpful point in separating Brown and Black noddies, and useful for separating Black Tern and White-winged Tern in some plumages. Male terns average slightly longer-billed than females, and the extremes might be noticeable on a few of the large species, so this could affect our perceptions of bill shape for some.

Bill color is important but subject to seasonal variation, more so in some species than others. The medium-sized terns and Least Tern have colorful bills in breeding season but become mostly or entirely dark-billed in winter. Conversely, their bills can become briefly even brighter at the peak of the breeding season: in the next chapter, see the comments about breeding Roseate and Common terns with excess red on the bill. The crested terns and Caspian Tern show less seasonal change, but their bills can be duller in winter. Bill color is tricky and variable on juveniles and generally should be used only as a minor supporting field mark. Some species that are black-billed as adults often show some pale coloration on the bill as juveniles, especially at the base.

One tricky element of bill color occurs with some Forster's and Common terns, at least, during some periods in fall or winter, when their bills can be all black with a small pale area at the tip. This is not illustrated in most field guides. Birders who focus on bill color to the exclusion of bill shape and other structural characters might confuse these with Sandwich Terns.

Underwing patterns. Because of the way the wing feathers overlap, in looking at the underside of a tern's spread wing we can see the long outermost primary in its entirety, but only the tips and inner vanes of the other primaries. The patterns of the tips of the individual primaries may seem like a minor point — but they create an overall pattern that is quite distinctive for some species, and that can be seen from a surprisingly great distance. For the four similar species treated in the next chapter, this is one of the most consistent points to learn, because that pattern is essentially the same for all ages. In fact, it is practically the only plumage character that works for all age groups at all seasons.

For the dark-backed terns, the wing-linings are white but the undersides of the flight feathers are at least partly dark, and the precise pattern is important to notice. The pattern of the under-wings also provides a significant field mark for the marsh terns.

The translucence of the wings is another field mark that is sometimes useful, but it is tricky to use and can be misleading.

Adult Aleutian Tern. From below, the dark secondaries provide an important field mark.

When terns are seen overhead against bright sunlight, some parts of their wings allow light to pass through while other parts do not; the translucent sections may appear to glow brightly while the other areas appear as dark shadows. Occasionally this is useful (as described for a couple of species in the next chapter), but only when conditions are perfect for it.

Upperwing pattern. See "Understanding upperwing pattern in terns" on p. 275. On most terns, the main thing to notice is the degree of contrast between the inner primaries and the (darker) outer primaries, and how many feathers are in the latter group. Some species, such as Least and Roseate terns, tend to have only two or three contrastingly dark outer primaries, giving the effect of a narrow dark leading edge on the outer part of the wing. Other species with more dark outer primaries may give a very different effect. This aspect of wing pattern is obvious on flying birds, but with a close study it can also be seen on standing birds. A worthwhile project is to practice seeing and identifying the individual primaries on standing terns, counting back from the longest (p10); depending on the position of the wings, we often can see seven or more of the primary tips and can get an accurate read on where the break between darker and paler feathers is located.

Tail shape and pattern. With a good view of the tail on a perched or flying tern, the degree to which it is forked — that is, the difference in length between the shortest central tail feathers and the longest outer tail feathers — is worth noticing. Tail length is important, too, although many species have only the outermost pair of tail feathers elongated, and if these feathers are broken or molting, it changes the appearance of total tail length. A number of species are also shorter-tailed in basic plumage than in alternate plumage, molting most of the tail feather twice per year.

Many terns have all-white tails as adults, but some have gray on the central tail feathers, or narrow areas of gray or black on the inner or outer vanes of the outermost tail feathers. These patterns can be hard to see in detail but they are worth focusing on if possible.

General tone of body plumage. In a number of cases, the shade of gray on the back or on the underparts is useful for separating similar species. Such field marks always must be used with caution, and preferably only when more than one species is present for direct comparison, because these shades of gray are so difficult to judge in isolation. Terns are often seen in situations of harsh and contrasting light conditions, making subtle differences in gray tones particularly unreliable.

Leg color. This provides a helpful field mark in some cases; for example, the legs and feet are usually black in juvenile Roseate Tern, usually reddish in juveniles of the other three medium-sized terns. But to use leg color as a field mark, we have to know about age-related and seasonal variation in each species. In many of the large terns, such as Gull-billed, Royal, and Caspian, the legs are pale at first and turn darker during the first autumn or winter. In many of the medium-sized and small terns, the legs are brightly colored on summer adults, duller or darker on winter adults. There is also individual variation: for example, most adult Royal Terns have black legs, but on a small percentage of adults the legs are orange.

Voice. Terns make a wide variety of sounds, and some of their alarm calls in particular can sound very similar, but most species have characteristic calls that are useful in identification. It may take considerable experience to be able to separate the calls of Common, Arctic, and Forster's terns, but some of the other species are more easily learned; Least, Roseate, Aleutian, and Elegant terns are examples of species with distinctive voices.

The calls of dependent juveniles often sound quite different from those of adults. In some of the large terns, such as Caspian and Royal, young birds may remain with their parents for months, following them on fall migration, and the striking difference in their voices often draws attention. A typical late-fall encounter on southern coastlines may involve an adult Caspian Tern in flight, giving its deep, growling call, following by a young bird giving a thin, weak whistle, sounding like an utterly different bird.

9. THE MEDIUM-SIZED TERNS

Species treated in detail:

COMMON TERN *Sterna hirundo*
ARCTIC TERN *Sterna paradisaea*
FORSTER'S TERN *Sterna forsteri*
ROSEATE TERN *Sterna dougallii*

The problem. These four species are superficially very similar to each other in size, shape, and pattern, to the extent that a careless description of one could apply to any of them. Typical adults in the breeding season, as described in all the field guides, can be identified by bill color. Unfortunately, not all individuals are typical, and reliance on bill color alone will lead to error in a certain percentage of cases. To compound the problem, some of the best-known additional field marks — such as darkness of the back, underparts, and wingtips, length of the tail, and others — are subject to variation and are easily misinterpreted. And those are merely the problems associated with identifying adults in breeding plumage. Variations with age and season make these terns potentially even more challenging to separate in other plumages.

PRELIMINARY POINTS

The preceding chapter gives an overview of identifying terns in general, including the characteristics of the various groups of terns. With a little experience, it is relatively easy to separate these four medium-sized terns from all the other tern species in North America. Separating these four from each other can be much more challenging, however, and working on them can increase our powers of birding perception. Common and Arctic terns are superficially so similar that British birders long used the generic term "Commic Tern" for unidentified ones seen at a distance. That term never became popular in North America, mainly because there is only a limited region where they overlap in numbers. Separating Common from Forster's Tern is a much more widespread challenge in North America, but with experience, the structural and plumage differences between these two are more apparent. Finally, Roseate Tern is the most distinctive of these four, but in some situations it also can be difficult to pick out from concentrations of Common or Arctic terns.

Terns have unique molts that have a major impact on their distinctive upperwing patterns. The preceding chapter gives a detailed discussion of these molts and of plumage sequences in terns. That chapter's overview of "what to look for" applies well to the four medium-sized terns in the present chapter. Here I will focus on a few things that are especially useful for all ages and then review one species at a time under the categories of adults and juveniles.

These terns provide the perfect example of the importance of looking at the whole bird. As detailed below, there is no single field mark that is totally diagnostic for any of these four. Any two of these species might be mistaken for each other, for different reasons, depending on which field marks we were using. But all four species differ in a variety of ways, and a holistic view that takes in all the differences is the best approach for really knowing them.

FIELD MARKS — ALL AGES

Underwing pattern. The pattern of the trailing edge of the outer primaries is practically the only field mark that works for all plumages, from full-grown juvenile on, so it merits close attention. Arctic Tern has narrow, sharply defined blackish tips to the outer seven or eight primaries; the effect is of a sharp, narrow black trailing edge to most of the outer part of the wing. The primaries and secondaries of Arctic Tern are almost entirely translucent when seen against a brightly lit sky, adding to its white-winged look overhead. Common Tern has broader dark tips to the outer five or six primaries; the resulting dark trailing edge is broader than that of Arctic but not as long and not quite so sharply demarcated. The Common Tern's wings show only a small area of translucence on the inner primaries, not always visible even with strong backlighting. Forster's Tern duplicates the pattern of Common but in slightly paler shades (medium gray instead of blackish gray); the difference is not usually apparent. The wings of Forster's show little or no translucence. Roseate Tern has no dark tips to the primaries: the blackish on its outermost primaries is confined to the outer vanes of the feathers. The trailing edge of its wing is entirely white, and this trailing edge can be conspicuously translucent.

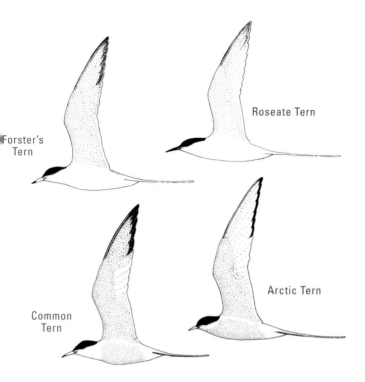

Forster's
Tern

Roseate Tern

Common
Tern

Arctic Tern

Flight silhouette and flight action. The combination of short bill, small head, and long tail gives a flying Arctic Tern the appearance of having its wings set far forward on its body. Its flight looks especially buoyant: the upstroke of the wings is quick, and the following downstroke is a slow, emphasized motion; the bird seems to float through the air. Common Tern has a larger head and shorter tail than Arctic, so in flight its wings appear to be set a little farther back on its body. Its action in flight looks less graceful than that of Arctic, with deep wingbeats that are emphasized equally on the upstroke and the downstroke. Forster's Tern is similar to Common in shape, but its bill and tail are somewhat longer and its wings are broader. Its wingbeats are usually shallower, slower, and more graceful than those of Common Tern. Roseate Tern has a long-looking head and a long bill. The outer tail feathers of adults in alternate plumage are also very long, but under some field conditions these can be hard to see (and on young birds the tail is much shorter), so the bird can actually look "front-heavy" much of the time. Roseate has relatively short wings and has the most distinctive flight of these four terns, with wingbeats that are shallow, fast, and stiff.

Bill shape and head shape. As in other terns, males average slightly longer-billed than females. But average differences in bill shape among these four species are often helpful, with experience and with a good view. Arctic Tern has the shortest bill on average, although many male Arctics are as long-billed as some female Commons. Common Tern averages longer-billed than Arctic but shorter-billed than the other two, and its bill narrows noticeably toward an attenuated tip. Forster's averages only slightly longer-billed than Common, but its bill is often noticeably *thicker* overall. Roseate Tern averages about the same bill length as Forster's, but in the field its bill often gives the appearance of being longer, probably because it averages narrower throughout and is often darker than in the other species.

Adult Common Tern in June. By building a good familiarity with the bill shape and head shape of one of these four terns, we develop a basis for comparison with the others.

Differences in head shape add to the impressions given by bill shapes. If Common has an "average" head shape for a tern of this size, then Arctic has a smaller, rounder head and shorter neck, emphasizing its compact appearance. Forster's looks large-headed, while Roseate's head is smaller but often has a more angular look.

Leg length. Of these four species, Arctic Tern looks notably short-legged, Forster's looks long-legged, and Common and Roseate terns look intermediate between the other two. This can be a useful additional point to check when flocks of terns are standing together.

Voice. Most terns have varied voices, and three of these four sound very similar in many of their usual calls, but with practice they may be separated. Common Tern's most typical call is a musical but grating *kreee-yarrrr*. It also gives varied shorter notes like *kip* and *kyeew*. Arctic Tern has a very similar *keee-yarrrr* call, usually sounding higher-pitched than that of Common, and also gives short notes like *kip* or *peek*. Many calls of Forster's Tern sound a little lower-pitched, with less of a ringing or far-carrying quality; it gives a hoarse *kyyarrr* call, not so clearly two-syllabled as in Common or Arctic, and more frequently gives short *kip* or *keck* calls. Roseate Tern is more distinctive, giving a *chivvyick* that varies in tone quality from musical to harsh; it also has shorter notes like *kyew*. In all four species, as in other terns, juveniles can sound noticeably different from adults.

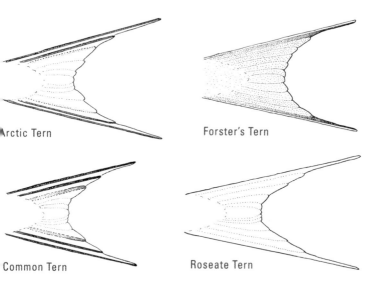

Arctic Tern

Forster's Tern

Common Tern

Roseate Tern

Tail patterns of adult terns in summer, as seen from the upperside, to show shapes and patterns. In adult Arctic Tern the tail is mostly white, but the narrow outer vanes of the outer tail feathers are dark gray; these dark edges are not apparent at a distance, and the bird may look white-tailed when seen overhead. Common Tern has blackish outer vanes on the outer tail feathers, which may show up a little more conspicuously than those of Arctic Tern and may be more apparent on birds overhead. In Forster's Tern the outer vane of the outermost tail feather is white, the inner vane of that feather is gray, and the rest of the tail is a very pale gray. Tail pattern is one of the best confirming marks for separating Common and Forster's at close range, but at a distance in bright light, either species may simply look white-tailed. The adult Roseate Tern really does have a pure white tail. Tail shapes also differ slightly. Note that these terns molt most or all of the tail feathers twice per year, and the outer tail feathers in basic plumage (winter) may be shorter than those of summer.

FIELD MARKS — ADULTS

Of these four species, only Forster's Tern is commonly seen in full basic plumage in North America, as it winters in good numbers in the southern states. The other three usually winter farther south, with only a very few Commons found in the southern states after early December. Adult Common, Forster's, and Roseate terns may begin their pre-basic molt on or near the breeding grounds, starting to acquire some white on the forehead and often replacing some inner primaries before the start of their fall migration, completing the molt on the wintering grounds; adult Arctic Terns generally do not even begin to molt until long after they are south of our latitudes. In all four species, the prealternate molt is generally completed before the birds arrive near the breeding grounds.

Therefore, birders in North America may see adult Forster's Terns in any plumage, adult Common and Roseate terns mostly in alternate plumage or in the early stages of prebasic molt, and adult Arctic Tern almost entirely in full alternate plumage. The following notes refer to alternate plumage unless stated otherwise.

Common Tern. In summer adults the bill is typically red to orange-red at the base and black at the tip. On some individuals, especially in late summer, the black is mostly or entirely lacking. During the fall the bill starts to turn darker, becoming mostly black with some dusky red at the base in winter.

The upperparts are medium gray, and in breeding plumage most adults have a wash of gray on the underparts as well; in some it can be as dark and extensive as on many Arctics, and if these happen to be individuals with all-red bills, the potential for misidentification is strong. Structural clues help: in addition to bill shape, Common has longer legs and shorter tail than Arctic. On a standing Common in summer, the tips of the outer tail feathers extend only to about the tips

adult Common Terns
in May and June

of the wings, while in the other three species, the tail extends beyond the wingtips.

Underwing pattern, as illustrated on p. 287, is good for distinguishing Common from Arctic and Roseate terns. Upperwing pattern is even more distinctive at a distance on summer adults in flight, with about five of the outer primaries (four to six, but five is typical) much darker than the inner ones. Where these darker and paler gray areas meet, there is a dark wedge pointing in from the trailing edge of the wing. This may become even more apparent in late summer (but it can be obscure on adults in midwinter, when the outer primaries are fresher and not so contrastingly dark). The dark wedge is a good mark for Common but not quite diagnostic, because Forster's at some stages of molt can have a suggestion of a similar dark wedge on the primaries. Adult Commons in winter have dark feathering on the lesser coverts, forming a dark "shoulder" or carpal bar, similar to that shown by younger birds.

With a good view of the tail, the dark outer vanes of the outer tail feathers are usually more visible than on Arctic Tern. Seen in flight, the gray back usually contrasts with the white rump and tail in Common and Arctic terns, while such contrast is usually less evident on Forster's and Roseate terns.

(These notes refer to the mainland North American population. An east Asian subspecies that occurs as a regular stray in western Alaska tends to be darker gray above and below, and it has a black bill even in breeding plumage.)

Arctic Tern. Adults seen in and near North America almost always have the bill entirely deep red (or with a slight dusky tip); in winter their bills are mostly black with some dark red at the base, but the color change usually does not begin until after they head south in fall.

adult Arctic Terns
in June

Both the upperparts and underparts on breeding adults are about the same shade of medium gray. On some the face is a contrasting white stripe between the black cap and gray throat, but on others the throat is whitish also, reducing the contrast. A standing Arctic Tern looks very short-legged, and in breeding plumage its outer tail feathers extend beyond the tips of the folded wings.

adult Arctic Terns in summer

Underwing pattern is a very good mark for Arctic Tern in all plumages if seen well. The upperwing tends to look uniform, with the uppersides of the primaries all looking the same shade of gray, unlike Common or Roseate in summer. The narrow dark outer vanes of the outermost tail feathers are harder to see than those of Common Tern, especially on birds overhead. With a good view of a summer adult Arctic flying low, the white rump and tail contrast noticeably with the gray back (as on Common, and more so than on Forster's or Roseate).

Forster's Tern. In summer adults the bill is typically orange to orange-red at the base and black at the tip; it tends more toward orange than the bill of Common Tern, and the color is often more noticeable because the bill is thicker. In winter the bill may be entirely black or may have dull orange-red at the base.

adult Forster's Tern in May

molting, early April

adult
Forster's Terns

May

April

The upperparts of adult Forster's Tern are about the same shade of gray as those of Common and Arctic, but its all-white underparts and pale wingtips give the bird a paler look overall. When standing, it looks noticeably long-legged, and its outer tail feathers extend beyond the tips of the wings in alternate plumage (not in basic plumage).

Underwing pattern looks similar to that of Common Tern, although the dark trailing edge to the outer primaries may look more diffuse. On the upperwing, the primaries usually look very pale, silvery or whitish gray, on summer adults. Toward late summer the outer primaries may become darker, but they seldom approach the degree of contrast shown by summer Commons. A good view of the tail reveals most of it as actually a very pale gray rather than white, with the outermost tail feathers gray on the inner vanes and white on the outer vanes, reversing the pattern shown by Common Tern. Because the rump and tail are tinged with pale gray rather than being pure white, Forster's usually shows less contrast between the back and rump than either Common or Arctic terns.

The head pattern of Forster's in winter, with black ear patches and whitish nape, is clearly different from the other species, which always have black across the nape in basic plumage. However, many winter Forster's have the nape gray, not black, and such birds are often misidentified as Common Terns. Any purported Common in midwinter should be identified by more than just head pattern.

adult Forster's Tern
in basic plumage

Roseate Tern. The adult's bill is mostly or entirely black for most of the year, but in spring and summer it develops some red at the base. During the height of the breeding season, the red area may increase until it occupies half the length of the bill, and this can be confusing for birders who don't expect it.

Roseate has slightly paler upperparts than the other three species, and it tends to look very pale overall. Its legs are of intermediate length, like those of Common Tern, but its more elongated shape (with longer bill and tail) may create the illusion that it is shorter-legged. When standing, its outermost tail feathers often extend well past the wingtips, an effect that is emphasized because the wings are shorter than in the other species.

Underwing pattern of Roseate is clearly different from the other three species, with no dark area on the trailing edge of the outer primaries. On the upperwing it shows a strong contrast between pale inner and dark outer primaries, like Common Tern, but the dark is restricted to only two or three feathers so it looks much more limited. The tail is all white (occasionally with slight dusky marks on the outermost tail feathers), long, and deeply forked. Because the back is relatively pale, flying birds do not show strong contrast between the back and the rump and tail.

On flying birds, not only is the pattern distinctive, but the flight action (with relatively shallow, stiff wingbeats) makes Roseate Tern easy to pick out for experienced observers.

adult Roseate Terns
in May

On this adult Roseate Tern overhead in April, we can see shadows of the dark outer vanes of the outer primaries, giving just a hint of a dark area along the trailing edge of the outer part of the wing. This is still very different from the appearance of the other species that have actual dark markings on the inner vanes of the outer primaries, creating a solid dark trailing edge.

FIELD MARKS — JUVENILES AND FIRST-WINTER BIRDS

When juveniles first become independent in summer, they can be confusing. Their bills may be shorter than those of adults at first, and they have shorter tails and shorter, more rounded wingtips, so their shapes may look oddly unfamiliar to birders who know the adults.

Common Tern. Like Arctic Tern but unlike Forster's and Roseate terns, this species generally does not start to molt until after its fall migration. The changes in its appearance during late summer and early fall of its first year seem to be more a function of wear and fading on the plumage. Common Tern has a more variegated wing pattern than the other three species in juvenile plumage. As seen from the upperside, it shows a broad blackish carpal bar along the leading edge of the wing,

juveniles in August and September

dark secondaries, and paler coverts separating these two dark bands. Underwing pattern, with a broad blackish trailing edge on the outer primaries, is like that of the adult. The forehead has a strong wash of pale brown at first, but this is rapidly lost through wear, leaving the forehead whitish against a sooty half-cap that crosses the rear crown and nape. The area immediately below the eye is often white, creating a different face pattern from the typical one of juvenile Arctic Tern. Barring or scaling on the lower back is apparent on fledglings, but wear soon makes this pattern obscure. On recently fledged juveniles the bill is extensively pink at the base, but by the time of southward migration the bill usually has become almost entirely black.

Arctic Tern. This species undergoes a preformative molt beginning in late fall of its first year, after migrating south, so young birds seen in North America should not be molting yet. On the upperside of the wing, the carpal bar is somewhat less striking than that of Common Tern, being narrower and not quite as dark. A more obvious difference involves the pale secondaries on the Arctic, paler than the coverts, often looking white in flight. Underwing pattern, with a long narrow black trailing edge on the primaries, is like that of the adult. The dark half-cap of Arctic is often a deeper and more solid black than that of Common and is usually more complete below the eye than that of Common

juveniles in July
and August

as well. The faint brown wash on the forehead and back, and the scaled effect on the lower back, are less apparent on Arctic than on Common and seem to be worn away more rapidly; at a comparable stage of development, Arctic tends to look more clean-cut than Common. Juvenile Arctic and Common both have dark outer edges to the tail, but on Arctic the tail is paler and the rump is whiter, often seeming to contrast more with the back. The juvenile Arctic has pink at the base of the lower mandible, usually much less extensive than on juvenile Common, and the bill may appear all black by the time of fall migration.

Forster's Tern. This species has less extensive molts than the other three in this chapter. While juveniles of the other three are beginning a complete preformative molt sometime in their first fall, young Forster's do not begin to molt the flight feathers until the following spring; the gradual molt of some head and body feathers that takes place during their first fall and winter appears to be a prealternate molt. Juvenile Forster's do not stand out as much as the young of the other species. Their upperwing pattern is more uniform than in the others at first, with only slightly darker secondaries and only a hint of a dark carpal bar. These dark markings on the wings may become more obvious as the winter goes on, and the wing may look more strongly patterned by spring, just as it is beginning to molt the flight feathers.

late summer

late fall

early fall

The underwing pattern on juvenile Forster's, with a broad dark trailing edge to the outer primaries, is like that of the adult and thus similar to that of Common Tern. The darkness of the nape is quite variable, but even birds with a lot of dark gray across the nape show the outlines of the black ear patches that will be prominent later. Tinges of buff and brown on the face and upperparts are obvious on very young Forster's Terns, and although this color is rapidly lost to wear and fading, it may still be apparent on some fall migrants. Juvenile Forster's Tern mostly lacks dark outer edges to the tail, although the inside of the tail fork is dark. The black bill usually shows a pale area at the base.

Roseate Tern. The upperwing of juvenile Roseate has a dark carpal bar, nearly as prominent as on Common Tern, and its secondaries are moderately dark. The white trailing edge on the primaries of Roseate, lacking a dark border, can be seen on the underside of the wing but is hard to discern from the upperside. On young juveniles, the nape, crown, face, and much of the forehead are dull blackish, making the head look darker overall than on the other juveniles. The forehead soon becomes whiter, as the preformative molt may be under way by August, but the lores may remain darker, and the birds continue to look dark-headed during fall migration. The upperparts are usually more heavily marked than on juveniles of the other three species, with barring or scalloping of black and brown that may be especially heavy on the rear scapulars. This pattern soon begins to be replaced in the preformative molt, but it shows up to some extent on most fall migrants. Juvenile Roseate also has a longer and whiter tail than the others, with only limited dark marking at the tip. It also has an all-black bill, and usually blackish legs, unlike the reddish to brown legs of the other three species.

juvenile Roseate
Terns in August

IDENTIFYING OLDER IMMATURES

As described in the previous chapter, young terns may take two and a half years to reach adult plumage. The intermediate plumages of one-year-old and two-year-old terns may be unfamiliar to birders. These younger individuals often stay on the wintering grounds through their first couple of summers or come north only partway to the breeding grounds. In some cases, birders may find flocks of young birds in summer, within the normal distribution of their species but far from any nesting colonies.

In general, these immatures have head patterns suggesting those of winter adults, although some look more like summer adults in most respects. Usually they have shorter outer tail feathers than summer adults, and usually they have some extra dark markings on the wings, such as on the primary coverts, tertials, or secondaries. One frequent clue is that the molt of their primaries is generally out of sync with that of the adults, and if we've trained ourselves to look at the primary patterns on standing and flying terns, this should be obvious.

This Common Tern looks superficially like a winter adult, but it was photographed in May. Excessive wear and some telltale dark areas on the wing coverts, as well as a dark area visible on the secondaries, indicate that it is a young bird. The pattern of the primaries — with somewhat fresher gray feathers between darker, worn feathers — would not be expected on an adult in May. Identification to species is by bill shape, leg length, and the presence of the dark bar on the lesser coverts. Compare this to the young Common on p. 276.

One tricky element is that immature Forster's Terns in summer (perhaps mostly two-year-olds) may show a complete black cap and still have very dark outer primaries; such birds could be confusing.

HYBRID TERNS

Unlike the situation with gulls, tern species seldom interbreed. However, instances of interbreeding have been recorded involving several combinations of these four terns. The only combination that seems to have occurred multiple times has involved Common and Roseate terns interbreeding in both North America and Europe. Birders can expect such hybrids to be intermediate between Common and Roseate in such matters as length and color of the bill, darkness of the back and wings, and length of the outermost tail feathers. The underside of the wingtip could be quite variable, depending on the patterns of individual primaries.

Apparent Common × Roseate hybrids have interbred successfully with each other and with parental types. It may be impossible to identify offspring of such pairings with certainty. But even where large numbers of Commons and Roseates nest in the same colonies, hybrids and intermediates make up only a tiny fraction of the population.

20. THE JAEGERS

Species treated in detail:

POMARINE JAEGER *Stercorarius pomarinus*
PARASITIC JAEGER *Stercorarius parasiticus*
LONG-TAILED JAEGER *Stercorarius longicaudus*

The problem. Although there are only three species of jaegers, telling them apart is a challenge that has many angles and complications.

Adult jaegers, despite the great variability of their plumage patterns, usually can be identified by the shapes of their protruding central tail feathers. However, Parasitic Jaegers with unusually long central tail feathers are often mistaken for Long-taileds; the same mistake has been made with adult Pomarines seen at odd angles. On the other hand, Long-tailed Jaegers with shorter central tail feathers are sometimes passed off as Parasitics. And in any of the three species, the central tail feathers may be broken off or missing, so knowledge of other field marks is essential.

Young birds are much more difficult. Jaegers probably take three to four years to reach adulthood, going through a series of distinct plumages. But despite some recent progress, the sequence of these plumages is still not well understood. Research on them is difficult, because the birds may spend their early years entirely at sea, not returning to the Arctic breeding grounds until they are nearing adulthood. Adding to the challenge, at every age there is a large amount of individual variation, which blurs the distinctions among age groups and among species. It becomes difficult to find any one field mark for one species that cannot be matched by some individuals of some age group of another one of the species.

There are two kinds of situations in which jaegers, especially immatures, pose problems for birders:

1. At sea. Viewing conditions cause much of the difficulty here. Strange light conditions, motion of the boat, and distance all work against the observer, making fine details almost impossible to see. On the positive side, a good boat trip may provide a number of encounters with jaegers. If some of those birds are "easy" adults, they can serve as a basis for comparing the shapes and flight styles of the others; and if some of the jaegers can be identified, birders may be more willing to let others go as simply unidentified, which is often the most accurate diagnosis.

2. Inland. Aside from their regular passage on the Great Lakes, a few jaegers turn up every year far inland in North America. These birds may remain at small lakes for several days, allowing fairly close approach and good views. But for inland observers who rarely see jaegers, such a bird can be a major source of frustration: it may remain unidentified (or uncertainly identified) even after a lengthy study. Because such a bird often represents a significant record wherever it turns up, an identification based on general size impressions is not likely to be accepted; more solid criteria are needed.

PRELIMINARY POINTS IN JAEGER IDENTIFICATION

Plumages and molts. Jaegers migrate south for the first time in full juvenile plumage. Their first complete molt (apparently a preformative molt) begins in late fall or winter (generally between November and January), with gradual replacement of the feathers continuing until late spring or summer, or even into early fall in the case of Pomarine Jaeger. One-year-old birds may or may not have a limited prealternate molt in spring. They then go into a complete prebasic molt, beginning sometime in late summer or fall and running to the following spring, when it may overlap with the partial prealternate molt. Subsequent molts run on approximately the same schedule, with a complete prebasic molt beginning sometime between late summer and midwinter and running into the following spring, and a partial prealternate molt in spring.

Individual variation in the timing of the molts (especially the prebasic molt) contributes to the great variation in the appearance of jaegers, even among individuals of the same age and species.

Changes in appearance with age and season. Jaegers show extreme changes in overall appearance from juvenile to adult, and even adults continue to show seasonal changes. After some general points below, applicable to all age groups, I discuss adults, juveniles, and older immatures separately. With the exception of some extreme dark-morph individuals, it should be possible almost always to distinguish among these age groups.

The seasonal change in adults has the result of making winter adults look more like the older stages of immatures. Adults in basic plumage usually have barred undertail coverts and uppertail coverts, often extensive barring on the sides and flanks, and often some pale feather edgings on the upperparts, and their head patterns become less well defined. All of these changes are more obvious in pale-morph adults than in dark adults. There is apparently some question about the molt of the central tail feathers — i.e., whether they are molted once or twice per year — but winter adults, at least in Long-tailed and Pomarine, seem to consistently have shorter central tail feathers than summer adults.

Color morphs. The existence of multiple color morphs adds to the complication, and fascination, of looking at jaegers. To understand the phenomenon, it's important to remember that the incidence of color morphs varies by age. Long-tailed Jaeger is especially interesting in that juveniles show a range of variation, including pale, intermediate, and dark morphs, but adults are all of the pale morph. These variations in frequency of the morphs are discussed separately in the accounts for each age group.

IDENTIFYING ALL AGE GROUPS

Size. Most books used by birders indicate a bird's size by a measurement of total length, from tip of the bill to tip of the tail. For jaegers, this can produce very misleading impressions of size, because of the varying lengths of the elongated central tail feathers. A short-tailed Pomarine Jaeger, for example, can be much shorter in this total length measurement than a Long-tailed Jaeger, even though the Pomarine is clearly a much larger bird.

Wingspread (the distance from one wingtip to the other when the wings are fully spread) is a very imprecise measurement, but for these birds it is a better indication of size for field use. Here are some comparisons of jaeger wingspans to those of some gulls:

wingspread of:	is about equal to that of:
Pomarine	Heermann's, or a little larger than Ring-billed, or a little smaller than California
Parasitic	Mew, or a little smaller than Ring-billed
Long-tailed	Laughing, or a little larger than Black-legged Kittiwake

These comparative wingspans are useful *only* with direct comparison, as when a jaeger is chasing a gull; it doesn't work with lone birds.

For example, it would take odd perceptions to say that a lone Pomarine Jaeger "looked about the size of a California Gull" — seen alone, the Pomarine's bulky shape and powerful flight actually create the impression of a much larger bird.

Bill shape. The precise shape of the bill is often a diagnostic characteristic for jaegers. Of course it is hard to see at a distance, but close-up photos often reveal bill shape quite well. This can be a critical point for some birds, especially for very worn immatures on which few plumage characters are visible.

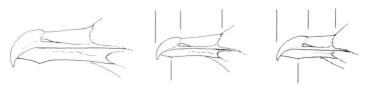

Pomarine
Jaeger

Parasitic
Jaeger

Long-tailed
Jaeger

Pomarine Jaeger has a long and heavy bill, with a heavy hooked nail at the tip of the upper mandible. The gonydeal angle on the lower mandible is usually prominent. The base of the bill is usually pale on Pomarines of all ages. Parasitic Jaeger is variable in bill size. Some large-billed individuals might suggest Pomarine, although they rarely show such an obvious gonydeal angle. Small-billed Parasitics might suggest Long-taileds. However, there are small but definite differences in bill shape between Long-tailed and Parasitic. On Long-tailed, the basal section of the upper mandible is shorter and the nail on the bill tip is longer than on Parasitic. Either of these factors would be obscure by itself, but the different ratio between them is noticeable. On the lower mandible, the distance from the tip back to the gonydeal angle (which can be hard to see) is longer on Long-tailed even though the bill is shorter, creating again a different ratio.

Shape and flight style. After we have had a lot of field experience with jaegers, we may find that we can identify many at a distance by their characteristic shape and flight action. Some published sources suggest that this is the best approach for everyone and may go on at length about naming the birds by general impressions alone. This does sound like a lot more fun than studying fine details of plumage and structure. Unfortunately, however, until we have done our own observing, reading other people's descriptions of a bird's shape and actions will not be very helpful. To recognize jaeger species by general impressions, we have to see the birds for ourselves and study them repeatedly.

When we see a jaeger that can be identified with certainty — a well-marked adult, for example — it's a good idea to watch it as long as possible, studying its shape and its actions in flight, and trying to store this image for comparison with other individuals.

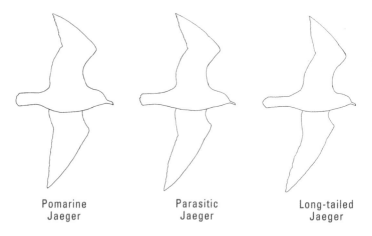

| Pomarine Jaeger | Parasitic Jaeger | Long-tailed Jaeger |

Although there are distinct differences in size among the three jaegers, here they are all drawn the *same* size — and with their elongated central tail feathers removed — to emphasize differences in their shapes.

In studying such birds of known identity, we might note the following. Pomarine looks heavier than the other two, with a bulky body, thick neck, and broad-based wings. Its wingbeats in normal flight are relatively slow and deep, like the action of a large gull. Parasitic is not so broad-winged and has a slimmer neck and body, although it often can look very bulky, at least temporarily. Its wingbeats in normal flight are quicker than those of Pomarine, often broken by short glides, and its flight action may bring to mind the flight of a falcon. Long-tailed has the slimmest body and smallest head of these three. The narrow wings contribute to the impression of a long tail, even when the elongated central feathers are broken or lacking. Its wingbeats in normal flight are buoyant, and the action may bring to mind a medium-sized tern. Any of the three species, of course, will "shift into high gear" when chasing other birds, changing their flight action and even changing the impression of their size and shape.

White primary shafts. In some older references, a lot of attention was focused on the number of primaries showing white shafts in each species. This in-hand character was subject to a lot of misinterpretation by birders, even in print. The distinction applies only to the shafts of the feathers, not to the surfaces of the feathers themselves. Because of the way the primaries overlap, none of the shafts except the outermost is visible from the underside of the wing, so this character has no effect on the amount of white or paleness visible on the primaries from below, and it has only very limited correlation with the amount of white surface area visible from above.

Occasionally, when problematic jaegers can be studied or photographed at close range, this can be a minor supporting character. Focusing on the upperside of the outermost primaries, Long-tailed shows two primary shafts (p9 and p10) that are white (or pale ivory) for most of their length. The shaft of the next feather inward (p8) varies from whitish to pale brown to dark brown, and on a very few individuals, the shaft of p7 is also whitish. The remaining primary shafts are dark brown; but because their surfaces are glossy, they may catch the light and momentarily look whitish, especially toward their bases.

In Parasitic Jaeger, the number of white primary shafts usually varies from three to six. In Pomarine Jaeger it is usually five or more. However, when the wing is less than fully spread and there is more overlap of the feathers, even a Pomarine may appear to have only one or two white primary shafts. The bottom line is that this character is potentially misleading in several ways, and it should be applied only when we can be sure of what we're seeing.

IDENTIFYING ADULT JAEGERS

As I mentioned at the beginning of this chapter, identifying adult jaegers solely by the shape of their extended central tail feathers can lead to errors at times. Furthermore, reliance on these feathers as the main field mark can leave us clueless when the central tail feathers are missing. As with other birds, identification of adult jaegers should be based on a holistic view of the whole bird.

Adult jaegers molt into a basic (winter) plumage that is less distinctly marked than the alternate (summer) plumage. This is a complication in describing adult plumages, but it does not add very much to the challenge of identifying them. Winter adults usually have barring on the rump and undertail coverts, narrow light barring on the back, more extensive and uneven dark markings on the underparts, and less sharply defined black caps than summer adults. (All of these points apply mostly to light-morph birds; dark birds show less change.) They may also have shorter central tail feathers than those of summer adults, although there is some question as to whether or not these central feathers are molted twice per year. In a number of ways, adults in basic plumage resemble subadult birds.

The molt to basic plumage takes place mostly after the adults have moved south from the breeding range; it may begin during fall migration, or it may be delayed until the birds have reached their wintering range. The molt to alternate plumage takes place mostly before spring migration. Long-tailed Jaeger — which migrates south relatively early and winters mainly south of the Equator — is very unlikely to be seen in full basic plumage in North American waters. Parasitic and especially Pomarine jaegers in basic or transitional plumages may be seen off the southern coastlines of the U.S. in winter.

The notes on adults below apply mainly to their appearance in late spring, summer, and early fall. I'll also refer occasionally to their basic (winter) plumage.

Color morphs. Most adult Pomarine Jaegers are of the light morph. Dark birds make up less than 10 percent of the population in most areas, although some local studies have reported proportions as high as 15 percent on Canada's Baffin Island and 20 percent in north-central Russia. Light-morph adult Pomarines are variable in appearance, but few birds are truly intermediate between light and dark morphs.

In adult Parasitic Jaegers, there is extreme geographic variation in the incidence of light and dark morphs. Dark birds can make up anywhere from 0 to 95 percent of a population. As a very general rule, dark birds are more numerous in the more southerly breeding populations and become rare in the northernmost populations. The dark morph may make up 50 percent or more of the breeding population in southern Greenland and southern Alaska, but it is rare in high Arctic Canada. In Parasitic Jaeger, a fair percentage of birds could be considered intermediate between the light and dark morphs.

In Long-tailed Jaeger, despite the variability of juveniles, adults are essentially all of the light morph. If a dark morph exists at all in adults of this species, it must be very rare. Birds breeding in the arctic regions of Europe and most of Asia are more extensively dark on the belly than those breeding in arctic America and eastern Siberia, a point to keep in mind when studying illustrations in European references.

Pattern of underparts. In summer, adult Long-tailed is the least variable of the three jaegers. Its throat and chest are white, with the gray from the undertail coverts extending forward as far as the belly or even the lower edge of the breast. In full basic plumage it may develop a dark chestband, but this plumage is unlikely to be seen in North America.

The underparts of adult Parasitic Jaegers vary from light (with or without a dark chestband) to very dark. But in alternate (summer) plumage, the underparts of this species tend to look smooth, without barring or mottling. The chestband may be complete, partial (limited to patches at the sides of the chest), or absent, but if present, it is a wash of smooth gray. By comparison, adult Pomarine is far less smoothly marked on the underparts. Light-morph adults often have dark barring along the sides and flanks, especially in females. The dark chestband, present in females and many males, tends to be mottled or barred, not smooth. The darkest adult Pomarines may look uniformly blackish brown, but with a close view they may show some mottling, not the smooth dark smoky gray of the darkest Parasitics.

Pomarine

Long-tailed

Parasitic

Head and chest patterns of typical light-morph adult jaegers.

Head pattern. The adult Long-tailed Jaeger in alternate plumage has a rather small black cap, sharply defined and neat in outline. The black is more extensive on the light-morph Pomarine, often creating the effect of a ragged-edged hood. The light-morph Parasitic is intermediate between the other two in shape of the cap, and its cap is blackish to charcoal and often looks less sharply defined at the edges.

The pattern of the malar area (extending back from the base of the lower mandible) contributes much to the overall head pattern of adults. In Long-tailed, only the base of this area is black, and the rest is white (or yellowish white) like the throat; the sharp edge of the black in the malar area connects evenly with the black edge of the cap. In light-morph Parasitic, the malar area is variable. It may be whitish with a gray smudge in the center, or it may be gray, shading toward black at the center, but it almost always pales somewhat toward the base of the bill. In adult Pomarine the entire malar tract typically is black, creating a "heavy-jawed" appearance and emphasizing the heavy bill.

In most adult Parasitics, the cap pales noticeably toward the base of the upper mandible, going from blackish at midcrown to smoky gray at the sides of the forehead to whitish at the point where the feathering meets the bill. This pattern does not occur in the other two species, although light Pomarines sometimes have a narrow light area where the feathers meet the upper mandible.

Color of upperparts. The darkness of the back and the upperside of the wings is variable in both Pomarine and Parasitic adults, but both species are very dark there, and Pomarine is often virtually black on the back. Adult Long-tailed is consistently medium gray on the back and wing coverts, paler than most Parasitics. On all three species the secondaries are black, but only on Long-tailed do the secondaries create an obvious dark trailing edge (because of the contrast against the paler coverts). This trailing edge rarely contrasts on Parasitic, and almost never on Pomarine.

Underwing pattern. Adult jaegers have solidly dark wing-linings (the underwing coverts and underprimary coverts). In Pomarine and Parasitic jaegers, the undersides of the bases of the primaries are almost always strikingly paler, creating a strong contrast. In adult and older immature Long-tailed Jaegers, the bases of the primaries are dark, so that no such contrast appears. Juveniles of all three species show pale primary bases from below, so this works only for Long-taileds that are past the juvenile stage.

White flash at base of primaries below: Parasitic has it, Long-tailed lacks it (after the juvenile stage, that is).

IDENTIFYING JUVENILE JAEGERS

To have any chance of identifying young jaegers correctly, the observer must understand the difference between "immature" and "juvenile." The notes in this section apply *only* to juveniles. Jaegers migrate south for the first time still in full juvenile plumage, not beginning their first molt until sometime between November and February. These juveniles differ in appearance from older immatures in some important ways.

Although there are exceptions, jaegers in far-inland areas show up mainly in fall, and most are either adults or juveniles, not immatures of intermediate age. Juvenile jaegers inland have been responsible for major debates and major learning experiences for local birders. In several cases, birders have studied, photographed, and identified a juvenile — only to find out later that the photos proved the bird to be not the species they had thought. (Obviously, sightings that are not backed up by photos may be open to considerable doubt, even if they can't be disproven.) Fortunately, juveniles may be somewhat easier to identify than some of the older immatures, and inland stray juveniles may be relatively tame, allowing close study.

General appearance of juveniles. Among autumn immature jaegers, juveniles are the ones with the neatest, cleanest look overall. Older immatures may be in molt, with a combination of old and new feathers in the wings, or feathers missing from the wings or tail, but juveniles are in uniformly fresh plumage. Their general color tends toward brown or gray-brown. Their dark upperparts and wings, except on the darkest individuals, have neatly arranged pale barring. Winter adults and older immatures may also have some pale bars on the back, but the pattern on the wings of juveniles is distinctive, with neat pale tips on the coverts creating a precise barred or scalloped effect (which carries over onto the scapulars).

A few of the darkest juveniles may lack nearly all pale markings and may look uniformly sooty all over. Identifying these birds as juveniles will be difficult, but with close views, the freshness of the plumage and the shape of the extended central tail feathers will provide clues. In Pomarine Jaeger, even the darkest juveniles usually show at least a little pale barring on the underwing coverts. Leg color may be helpful also: juveniles of all three species have the tarsus mostly pale, turning all black in adults of Pomarine and Parasitic but remaining at least partly pale in adult Long-tailed. Therefore, a very clean-looking but very dark bird with pale legs and black feet might be a very dark juvenile.

Pomarine
Jaegers

Parasitic
Jaegers

Long-tailed
Jaegers

Some representative plumages of juvenile jaegers. No set of illustrations
can cover the full range of possible variation; be sure to read the text for
a discussion of the important plumage characters of each species.

Bill shape and color. This is described on p. 303, under "Identifying all age groups," but it is often particularly helpful for lone juveniles found on shore or at inland waters, since they often can be approached for close studies. Note that juveniles of all three jaegers have the bill pale at the base, whereas on adult Parasitics and Long-taileds, the bill is mostly dark.

General plumage color. Although juvenile jaegers are at least as variable as adults, each of the three species has some general tendencies in color and pattern that can be very helpful in identification.

Juvenile Parasitic Jaeger tends to be the most colorful of the three, usually warm brown with edgings of rufous and golden-buff that give the back and wings a strongly scalloped effect. The underparts are usually barred (except on the darkest birds), but the bars are often very uneven or wavy except on the flanks. The head usually shows a pale nape and a streaked face. On some, the pale nape contrasts with a darker cap, creating a "collared" effect.

The majority of Parasitics are of the intermediate type described above, but some are much paler. They can be very pale-headed, in which case the head is usually strongly washed with buff or pale orange; the palest birds also show a considerable white flash on the upperside of the primaries. At the opposite extreme, a few juvenile Parasitics are so dark that the underwing coverts appear uniformly dark and the body plumage appears nearly so, perhaps with a slightly paler nape and with faint paler barring on the upper- and undertail coverts. Another variation involves a few intermediate juveniles that are much grayer, suggesting the typical color of juvenile Long-tailed Jaeger.

The juvenile Pomarine Jaeger generally shows less variation than juveniles of the other two species. It is typically brown in tone but duller and a little darker than the average Parasitic, and it usually has a fairly dark head. The bars and scalloping on its upperparts may be warm buff but they do not vary to bright rusty or orange-buff. The underparts are often vaguely barred, and sometimes the barring looks more even than the wavy markings of Parasitic. Only a minority of juvenile Pomarines are paler overall, with pale heads, or very dark overall.

The juvenile Long-tailed Jaeger tends to be much grayer than juveniles of the other two species. In overall tone it varies from very pale (looking white-headed) to very dark, and its pale areas may be washed with creamy yellow but it never shows the rich rusty tones of some Parasitics. Its upperparts are marked with whitish or creamy edgings, which often look straighter (less curved or scalloped) than the dorsal markings of the other two species. Most intermediate types have a large whitish patch in the center of the lower breast, contrasting with the smooth gray chest. Most have conspicuous black and white bars on the uppertail coverts and undertail coverts, although a very few of the darkest individuals may lack these.

Head pattern. Mentioned briefly above, this is frequently a good clue. On juvenile Parasitic the nape is usually a very pale brown or buff, and the nape and face usually have noticeable fine dark streaks. The malar area (next to the base of the lower mandible) is usually pale, creating little contrast against the pale base of the bill. On darker juveniles the nape usually continues to be paler than the rest of the head, often contrasting with a darker cap, and there may be a hint of a paler collar even on the darkest individuals. On juvenile Pomarine the head is usually somewhat darker and more uniform, and it may be lightly barred but it is almost never streaked. Darker feathering toward the front of the head means that the pale base of the bill often contrasts more. Some juvenile Pomarines are paler on the nape and crown and darker on the face, but they don't show the dark-capped, pale-collared effect of Parasitic. The juvenile Long-tailed varies in head pattern from very pale overall (grayish white or creamy) to very dark, almost black. Intermediate birds often show a vague dark cap contrasting with a paler nape, suggesting a common pattern on Parasitic but with a grayer look.

Primary tips. The great majority of juvenile Parasitic Jaegers (except a few of the darkest individuals) have buff tips on the outer primaries that look like conspicuous pale chevrons on the wingtip when the wing is folded. This is a very strong indication for Parasitic when seen well. Some Long-tailed and a few Pomarine juveniles have narrow pale fringes at the tips of the outer primaries, and sometimes these form pale crescents on the tip of the folded wing that can be seen in the field, so only the well-marked buff chevrons are indicative of Parasitic.

Typical pattern of the primary tips on juvenile Parasitic Jaeger.

Underwing pattern. Juveniles of all three species typically have the axillars and underwing coverts heavily barred. (The same is true of older immatures, and the lack of barring on the underwing coverts is one of the best distinguishing marks of adults.) On the darkest juveniles, the underwing barring can be mostly or entirely lacking; this happens more often on Parasitic than on the others, and even some intermediate juvenile Parasitics may lack barring there. On juvenile Pomarine and Long-tailed, the light barring on the underwing coverts may be so prominent that the underwing looks paler than the body; this effect is seen less often on Parasitic, on which the body and underwing are more likely to be the same general tone.

Seen from below, the bases of the primaries are contrastingly pale or whitish on Pomarine and Parasitic jaegers of all ages and on juvenile Long-tailed Jaegers, forming a white flash on the underwing. On most juvenile and immature Pomarine Jaegers the bases of the underprimary coverts are also white, contrasting with the dark tips to the underprimary coverts and forming a "double flash" on the underwing. Occasionally this can be a helpful mark. However, some Parasitic and Long-tailed juveniles show a suggestion of this mark, while on some Pomarines it is not obvious, so it becomes a matter of degree and may be hard to judge under some conditions.

Central tail feathers. Given a good view, preferably from directly above or below (not always the easiest angle to achieve), the shape of the central tail feathers on a juvenile jaeger makes an excellent clue. These central feathers extend slightly past the rest of the tail, and on fall juveniles the tail should still be in good condition and the shapes easy to discern.

| Pomarine | Parasitic | Long-tailed |
| Jaeger | Jaeger | Jaeger |

On Pomarine juveniles the central tail feathers barely extend past the others, and they are generally blunt, looking squarish or rounded with only slight points showing. The short, broad extension that they create may be overlooked altogether in a casual view. On Parasitic juveniles, the central feathers extend more obviously; they vary from slightly to noticeably longer and taper to a sharp point. On Long-tailed juveniles these feathers are often noticeably long, extending up to an inch past the rest of the tail. They may have fine spiky points, but their overall shape is distinctly rounded at the tip; these feathers often have whitish marks at the tip, which are usually lacking in the other two species. It is important to remember that these characters apply only to juveniles in their first autumn. After early winter, wear on the feathers will make these shapes unreliable, and in older birds the tail shapes are different.

Uppertail coverts and undertail coverts. The majority of juvenile jaegers have conspicuous barring on the tail coverts, but there are some helpful differences among the species. The barring is most variable in Parasitic Jaeger, on which the pale bars are pale buff to rich cinnamon-buff and are usually quite wavy or scalloped; the bars may be obscure or almost invisible on the darkest juveniles. On Pomarine the bars vary from dull whitish to buff and they usually run straight across the uppertail and undertail coverts, making a much more evenly barred effect, especially as seen from above. Even on very dark juvenile Pomarines, these pale bars are usually obvious. Juvenile Long-taileds usually show very obvious barring that tends toward black and white (or dark gray and cream), and the bars tend to run straight across the uppertail and undertail coverts. Even very dark juveniles usually show these pale bars, although they may be lacking on rare individuals.

IDENTIFYING OLDER IMMATURES

Like some of the large gulls, jaegers may take up to four years to reach adult plumage, although many are thought to look essentially adultlike in their third plumage cycle. Unlike most gulls, however, older immature jaegers are not easy to assign to age groups. Light-morph jaegers tend to become lighter and more adultlike in pattern as they mature, but telling the age of a given bird (between juvenile and full adult) will be at least partly guesswork.

It can also be a challenge to identify these intermediate-aged birds to species. Beyond juvenile plumage, young jaegers have the central tail feathers shaped like those of adults of their species, but usually much shorter. Bill shape continues to be an excellent ID character when it can be seen well, and light-morph birds start to show head patterns suggestive of the adult patterns from the second cycle onward. Young Long-tailed Jaegers, from second plumage cycle onward, lack the white at the base of the primaries on the underside of the wing, while the other two species continue to show this. Otherwise, because of their extreme variation, there are few plumage characters for separating the species.

Immature Pomarine Jaeger in September. Similar to some juveniles, but notice the longer central tail feathers.

Fortunately, these older immatures do not often show up inland. They tend to spend the first year or two of life out at sea, not returning to the breeding grounds until they approach adulthood, so they are unlikely to be migrating overland at this difficult age. Out at sea, they may be routinely identified (by observers familiar with all the jaegers) by their shape and flight style.

Some of the worst jaeger problems involve one-year-old Pomarine and Parasitic jaegers, perhaps with delayed molts, that show up on southern beaches in summer. These worn, ratty birds may show no useful plumage markings at all and their central tail feathers may be so worn that their shapes cannot be determined. The best approach with one of these birds is to try to get close-up photos that show the overall shape of the bird, its size compared to other birds if possible, and especially the shape of the bill.

COMPARISONS TO OTHER SPECIES

Skuas. Dark Pomarine Jaegers seen on offshore trips are sometimes misidentified as Great Skuas or South Polar Skuas by hopeful observers. However, the reverse almost never happens — a real skua is unlikely to be passed off as a mere jaeger.

Skuas are larger and bulkier than Pomarine Jaegers, even thicker-necked and more barrel-chested; their wings are very broad, and in normal flight they look more rounded at the tips. The breadth of the wings helps to accentuate the skuas' short-tailed look. Broad, crescent-shaped white patches at the base of the primaries are very conspicuous on both the upperside and the underside of the wings. Dark young Pomarines often have a great amount of white at the base of the primaries on the underside, but they seldom if ever show such extensive and well-defined white patches on the wings' upper surfaces.

Heermann's Gull. Odd as it might seem, this Pacific Coast species is sometimes mistaken for a jaeger. Heermann's Gull seems to be even pushier than most gulls, and is often seen chasing other species. Its overall grayish appearance is suggestive, and moreover it has an uncommon variant with white patches on the primary coverts, recalling the white primary bases often shown by jaegers. In a quick view, one of these dark Heermann's Gulls with a white wing flash can give a convincing impression of a jaeger, if only momentarily.

21. LEARNING TO IDENTIFY OWLS

Most birders probably would be glad to have the challenge of identifying owls. Typically, the challenge we face is a more basic one: finding any owls to identify in the first place. But because most birders have relatively few encounters with owls, often we are ill-prepared to identify these birds when we do find them.

Getting to hear and see owls is largely just a matter of making a serious attempt — going out to good habitat at night and trying for them. In a similar way, we can prepare for identifying owls by understanding some basic points about them and recognizing the potential for a few common pitfalls.

POINTS TO CONSIDER IN IDENTIFYING OWLS

Variations in voices. Field guides and other popular references usually describe only the most common vocalizations of owls. But as nocturnal birds that do a lot of their communicating by sound, most owl species have a wide variety of calls. If we keep that in mind, we can avoid being misled when we hear some of their less-frequent vocalizations.

The best-known call of Western Screech-Owl is an accelerating series of short hoots, in a "bouncing-ball" pattern. However, it also gives a long low trill, similar to the trill of Eastern Screech-Owl except that it is broken into two parts, one short and one long. Birders sometimes report hearing Westerns "giving the calls of both species" because they don't realize that this species has a trill. However, Western Screech-Owl also sometimes does a slow series of short notes that might suggest Ferruginous Pygmy-Owl, and it has a wide variety of other notes, even one that could be described as a screech!

If we're going out to seek particular owls, it's worthwhile to read detailed voice descriptions such as those in the online Birds of North America accounts, or to listen to compilations of recordings (see p. 134). But such sources may not include all vocalizations, so in pursuing owls in the field, we have to keep an open mind about what we hear.

Pitfalls of viewing conditions. Optical illusions may come into play when we look at birds under artificial light conditions at night. I regularly hear reports of "huge white owls" flying across roads in areas where neither Snowy Owl nor Barn Owl is likely to occur. In most cases, these probably represent normally colored Great Horned Owls seen briefly in the headlights. Impressions of size are often misleading when we see brightly illuminated objects in dark surroundings, and of course impressions of color may be even more so. If we're using a bright light to look at nocturnal birds, it's wise to calibrate our perceptions by looking at some closeup objects of known size and color, gradually shifting to looking at things farther away.

Variations in plumage. More than in most families of birds, owls are subject to much individual variation in overall color. This reaches its extreme in the strikingly distinct color morphs of Eastern Screech-Owls, but a number of other species are notably variable also. Northern and Ferruginous pygmy-owls have grayer and redder color morphs, while Flammulated Owl shows an almost continuous range of variation. In many species, females tend to be more heavily marked than males, and more reddish or buffy brown, while males tend to be more grayish. To top this off, there is also a lot of geographic variation in some species. Great Horned Owl, for example, varies regionally from dark dusky brown to reddish brown to pale gray. For all of these reasons, it's best not to rely too much on an owl's overall color as a field mark.

Juveniles and downy young. A few owl species have juvenile plumage patterns that are markedly different from those of adults — Boreal and Northern Saw-whet owls are examples — but in most species, the differences between juveniles and older birds are more subtle. Generally the juvenile body plumage is very soft and loose, and it often has a more muted pattern than that of the adults.

Birders sometimes may encounter downy young owls, too young to fly, in situations where the parent owls are not in evidence. Downy young Great Horned Owls sometimes cause confusion because they are whitish at first and they make rasping food-begging calls — superficially suggesting the appearance and sound of Barn Owl. In fact, second-hand reports of Barn Owls always should be treated with caution: sometimes they refer to these young Great Horneds, and sometimes they refer to adults of other species (Long-eared, Great Horned, or even screech-owls) that happen to be roosting in barns.

juvenile Great
Horned Owl

22. LEARNING TO IDENTIFY HUMMINGBIRDS

It goes without saying that hummingbirds are very popular. Millions of people, including many who don't know or care what species they are seeing, put out hummingbird feeders in order to enjoy the colors and behavior of these tiny gems. Birders appreciate hummers for the same reasons, and also for the potential for exciting records. Only about two dozen species of hummers have been found in North America north of Mexico, but virtually all of those species have been known to stray far outside their normal ranges on multiple occasions, so there is always the possibility of finding a rarity. In addition, hummingbirds provide worthwhile challenges in identification. Among the widespread North American species, most adult males are distinctive, but other plumages range from moderately to extremely difficult to identify. Studying them is a good way to sharpen our perceptions (especially for fine structural details) and increase our overall birding skill.

Overview of the problem. Because of their size and their hyperactive nature, it can be a major challenge just to see details on hummingbirds. But even with excellent views, many will remain tough to identify. The diagnostic points used for in-hand determinations often involve details of single feathers. Live birds in the wild offer additional clues of shape, behavior, and voice, but those clues are often subtle and require considerable practice.

To complicate the issue even more, there is considerable variation among plumages within most species — so that immature females, immature males, adult females, and adult males of a given species usually look noticeably different from each other. They may look more similar to the same plumages of a *different* species than they do to others of their own kind. So a bird that looks "obviously different" from the others in the neighborhood may simply represent a different age or sex class. Furthermore, males going from immaturity to adulthood can pass through confusing intermediate stages.

To add one more complication, hybrids among hummingbird species are not as rare as in most groups of birds, and these hybrids can be uniquely challenging to identify.

An approach to studying hummer identification. Hummingbirds challenge our powers of perception. The fine details and subtle differences that separate them will seem invisible at first and will become apparent only after a lot of comparative experience. If we start by going out with a field guide and simply matching hummingbirds to pictures, all of our identifications will be tinged with doubt and we will never really understand what we are seeing. To become really proficient at recognizing hummers, we have to dedicate some time to studying them and learning the basics of this specialized group.

The best way to study them is to stake out a position close to some well-attended hummingbird feeders, where a few hours can yield more good views than we might have in a year's worth of chance encounters "in the wild." A major advantage to watching at a feeder is that every bird is seen at the same distance and under the same light conditions, making it much easier to judge minor differences in size and color. It is worthwhile to get as close as possible without scaring the birds away and set up a telescope to try to see individual feather details.

The birder who really wants to learn hummer ID should dedicate blocks of time to watching well-attended hummingbird feeders — not just watching for "something good," but closely studying as many individuals as possible and learning to pick out the fine details.

This kind of study has its most obvious value in a situation where hummers are numerous and diverse. The Southwest in late summer is ideal for learning the basics of hummers, because not only are several species possible, but late summer offers both adults and young birds, doubling the number of possible plumages to study. But even at eastern feeders being visited by nothing but Ruby-throated Hummingbirds, this kind of concentrated study is worthwhile.

Paradoxically, most eastern birders do not know the Ruby-throat very well, because they haven't had to look or listen carefully to know what it was. It is a valuable exercise for eastern birders to apply this kind of careful study to the local Ruby-throats, considering all the points mentioned below under "things to look for." Such preparation will pay off later: when these birders encounter the diversity of hummers in the West for the first time, or spot a possible western vagrant in the East, they will have a solid basis for comparison.

PRELIMINARY CONSIDERATIONS

Molt and plumage sequences in hummingbirds. It was long considered that hummingbirds had only one molt per year as adults, a complete prebasic molt, performed on the wintering grounds. Young birds have an additional preformative molt in their first cycle, so the definition would have been that hummers show the complex basic strategy in molting. Recent research has revised this view. A detailed study by Donna Dittmann and Steven Cardiff showed that many Ruby-throated Hummingbirds are going through extensive body molt in summer, on the breeding grounds. Not only does this change our concept of molt in hummers, it's also a fine demonstration that things can be learned by close attention to common birds, even in the 21st century!

A new interpretation for Ruby-throated Hummingbird is that they molt on a Complex Alternate Strategy: adults have both prebasic and prealternate molts, and young birds have both a preformative and first prealternate molt. In adults, prebasic molt begins on the breeding grounds, with extensive replacement of head and body feathers; after fall migration, prebasic molt continues with molt of flight feathers. A prealternate molt, involving just head and body feathers, occurs in late winter (perhaps overlapping the end of prebasic molt) before spring migration. In juveniles, likewise, a preformative molt of head and body feathers may occur in late summer on the breeding grounds, with the preformative molt of the flight feathers occurring after the birds arrive on the wintering grounds, and then they probably have a partial prealternate molt of head and body feathers in late winter.

At this point it's not clear whether this timing would apply to other hummers, but it may well apply to the small migratory species (like the ones discussed in the next chapter). There is still plenty of room for study to clarify the molt patterns of other hummers.

For field observers, this understanding of molt means that we may see very worn-looking adults on the breeding grounds, more so than in fall migration. Young males, at least in some species, may begin to show some colorful gorget feathers when they are only a few weeks old, as part of the beginning of the preformative molt; they may replace the gorget feathers again in a prealternate molt before the beginning of the next breeding season.

It's important to remember that "breeding season" doesn't necessarily mean "summer." Anna's Hummingbird, for example, breeds in winter in most parts of its range, with nesting activity under way in December and peaking in February and March; it's no surprise that Anna's goes through its major prebasic molt mainly from June to October.

This juvenile male Black-chinned Hummingbird in early August has already begun to molt some head feathers, as shown by dark spots marking the edge of the gorget.

A detail of molt that might occasionally be noticed on photos of wintering hummers involves the end of their primary molt. As with many other birds, hummers replace the primaries in a regular sequence from the innermost toward the outermost (replacing the short inner ones faster than the long outer ones), but toward the end of this molt, they typically replace the outermost (p10) before the next-to-outermost (p9). This can create an odd shape of the wingtip for a period of a few weeks.

A sign of plumage wear that often shows up on female hummers during the breeding season is a "nest mark," an irregular dark area on the underparts. This is undoubtedly caused by abrasion against the edge of the nest during incubation, causing wear on the pale feathers and exposing their darker bases.

Age characteristics of hummingbirds. In most North American hummers, juveniles can be clearly distinguished from adults. First-cycle birds that have gone through part of the preformative molt may continue to be separable from adults, but by the time they are a year old they are essentially adultlike. In several species, second-cycle males are a little less brightly colored than older males: the gorget (the patch of iridescent feathers on the throat) may be less extensive, and some of the feathers may be gray rather than colorful. In species with colorful bills, like Broad-billed Hummingbird, the red may be less extensive on second-year birds than on older birds.

In general, juvenile hummingbirds resemble adult females. Juveniles of most have broad pale edges on the feathers of the upperparts (back, scapulars, nape, and crown), tending toward dull buff in most species, more rusty or cinnamon on members of the genus *Selasphorus*.

The outer tail feathers of juveniles may be patterned somewhat like those of adult females, but they are often slightly different in shape. Frequently these feathers are broader and more rounded in juvenile females, narrower in juvenile males, and intermediate in width in adult females. This variation should be kept in mind when trying to use the shapes of individual tail feathers for identification.

An age characteristic for use at close range is a difference in the texture of the bill. On adult hummers, the surface of the upper mandible is hard and smooth. On young juveniles, the surface is softer and has a series of long "grooves" or "corrugations" that gradually disappear over a period of months as the bird matures. On this young Violet-crowned Hummingbird in August, the grooves are apparent, especially toward the base of the bill. Notice also that the red on the bill is poorly developed so far, and the violet crown feathers have broad buff edges.

THINGS TO LOOK FOR WHEN STUDYING HUMMINGBIRDS

If we have positioned ourselves to study hummer identification, here are some of the points that we should be looking and listening for. The relative value of these points will vary depending on the species involved, so this list is not necessarily in order of importance.

Tail shape and pattern. The precise shapes and color patterns of individual rectrices (tail feathers) are among the most significant points for identifying, aging, and sexing many hummingbirds in the hand. Unfortunately, this level of detail can be difficult to see in the field. Most of the individual rectrices can't be seen clearly unless the tail is fanned or spread all the way. Hummers often hold their tails fully spread for a few seconds when they are hovering, especially as part of their aggressive interactions with each other, so we can often see this posture briefly. This is especially true when there are many birds gathered at feeders. If we've had enough practice and experience, we can get a fairly accurate idea of these details of rectrix shape and pattern, and then try to confirm our impressions by getting photographs of the bird(s) in question.

On this Black-chinned Hummingbird, the relatively pointed tip of the outermost tail feather (r5) and the amount of white on the tip of r3 not only help confirm the species, but also indicate that this is an adult female. Such tail details are often very useful in hummer ID.

While such fine details of individual feathers are challenging to see, the overall shape and color of the tail is somewhat more obvious and is also very useful for identification to the species level. For example, female and immature Costa's Hummingbirds tend to have the tail more rounded, less squared off, than those of the Black-chinned and Anna's hummingbirds, and with somewhat less black in the outer tail feathers. This kind of general difference might be seen even in a quick look when details can't be determined. In the next chapter I illustrate the overall tail shapes and patterns for several of the most confusing hummers in North America, but these characteristics are worth noting for every species.

On perched birds it's worthwhile to note the length of the tail, as indicated by where the tip of the tail falls relative to the tips of the wings. This may appear to change slightly from moment to moment as the bird shifts position, so it may be necessary to watch for a while to gauge this accurately. In most North American hummers, the tip of the tail extends at least slightly beyond the tips of the wings, while in only a few does it appear that the tail is shorter than the wingtips.

There are several species on which there are age and sex differences in the tail-to-wingtip ratio. For example, in Anna's and Costa's hummingbirds, the tails of the adult males usually extend beyond the wingtips, while on females and immatures the tip of the tail usually falls slightly short of the wingtips or falls even with them.

Bill shape and color. The length of the bill is an important field mark, and its degree of curvature and its thickness can be worth noting on some species. In many North American hummer species, adult females average slightly longer-billed than adult males. Young birds, when they first leave the nest, can be noticeably shorter-billed than adults of their species, and their bills may not be fully grown for a period of a few weeks, so this is a potentially tricky point in summer. Fortunately, such fledglings are usually easy to recognize as very young birds, so we can take that into account when considering their bill lengths.

Many of our hummers have bills that are slightly decurved. We generally don't notice this slight curvature — until we are in the Southwest and actively looking for the Lucifer Hummingbird, which has a curved bill as one of its famous field marks. As soon as we start looking for them, curve-billed hummers are suddenly everywhere. If we pay close attention to bill shapes from the start, we'll be familiar with the slight curvature of the bills of Ruby-throated, Black-chinned, and many other common species.

Lucifer Hummingbird, adult female — a hummer with a genuinely curved bill.

Most North American hummers have all-black bills, but a few have red or pink at the base of the bill. This can vary from those with the bill mostly red with a black tip (adults, especially adult males, of a few species) to those with just a slight amount of red at the base of the lower mandible (especially females and the young of a few species). The latter type of color can be very difficult to see without a close view. Note that birds sitting on red hummingbird feeders often appear to have a red or pink tinge on the lower mandible because of light reflecting up from below. Occasionally, even the bright hue of the throat of a male hummer can reflect some color onto the bill.

Color of the underparts. The general tone of the underparts is useful for separating out some broad groups of species, mainly among females and immatures. Confusingly plain female-plumaged hummers include four (Ruby-throated, Black-chinned, Anna's, Costa's) with no rufous in the tail and with no orange-buff on the underparts or with only a small buff area on the lower flanks, and four (Broad-tailed, Rufous, Allen's, Calliope) with at least some rufous in the tail and some orange-buff on the underparts. These two quartets of species are treated in some detail in the following chapter. But beyond these broad groups, it is worth looking at the color of the underparts in detail. Is there an orange-buff wash along the sides and flanks, and if so, how extensive is it? Are the underparts more generally white or gray? Are the sides and flanks marked with gray or green? These details can be critical for separating similar species.

Throat pattern. Among widespread North American hummers, adult males of most species have a well-defined patch of bright iridescent color on the throat (called the gorget), and adult females and immatures of most species do not, although females may have a few iridescent feathers in this area. The color of the gorget on adult males may look black or gray in poor light, or certain angles of light may make the colors look odd: iridescent red feathers, for example, often momentarily look gold or orange or green. So we may have to watch for a while to gauge this color accurately.

The exact pattern of the throat is often more important in identifying females and immatures, and it often holds clues as to the age and sex of an individual. In late summer, for example, the pattern of the throat usually differs among adult female, immature male, and immature female Rufous Hummingbirds, and it is usually easier to tell these three plumages apart than it is to tell Rufous from Allen's.

To use throat pattern in identification, we have to study it in detail. It isn't helpful to simply distinguish between "spotted" and "plain," for example. In particular, we need to note whether markings on the throat are evenly distributed or irregular. Immatures of some species have the throat neatly and evenly spotted, with dark centers and pale edges on individual

juvenile male Rufous
Hummingbird

feathers. This is different from the effect created when a plain-throated young male starts to molt in the gorget feathers of its adult plumage; that pattern is irregular, blotchy, and usually asymmetrical. Young males and adult females of some species may combine these two kinds of patterns, with an evenly spotted background and a few blotches of iridescent feathers. But if we're looking to identify the birds, we need to distinguish among these different kinds of spotting on the throat.

General color of upperparts. For most North American hummers, the answer here will be green, of course, but differences among species in the precise shade of green can be helpful for experienced birders.

Juveniles of most of our hummer species have pale edgings on the upperparts, ranging from pale grayish buff to cinnamon depending on the species, and these edgings can change the apparent overall color of the back when the bird is viewed from a distance. Up close, it is usually possible to see the basal color of the feathers and distinguish it from the pale edges.

Wing structure details. Nothing can be seen of the wings on a flying hummingbird, obviously, but on perched birds, the shapes of individual primaries are very important for separating some similar species. With a good side view of a perched hummer, preferably up close and through a telescope, it is possible to see and distinguish all ten primary feathers and to determine their shapes. In such a close study, the narrow inner primaries of the *Archilochus* species (Ruby-throated and

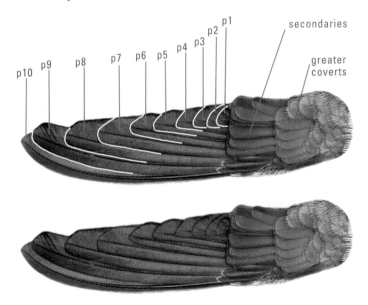

A close-up of the wing of a young female Black-chinned Hummingbird, as viewed from the upperside. In the upper diagram, the tips of all the primaries are outlined in white, and all ten primaries are labeled, from the innermost (p1) to outermost (p10).

Black-chinned) are clearly different from the broad inner primaries of the *Calypte* species (Anna's and Costa's). Differences in the shapes of the outermost primaries provide one of the best ways to tell Ruby-throated and Black-chinned apart. So it is worthwhile to practice seeing this level of fine detail on perched hummers.

It can be a challenge to see the outermost (tenth) primary on some birds, or even to be able to tell whether or not you are seeing it. Counting the primaries (starting from the innermost) will usually tell you whether you are seeing all ten, but of course a bird in molt may be missing one or more primaries on each wing. When the birds are in worn plumage, especially on females, the outermost primaries may be so worn at the tips that their original shapes can't be determined.

Face pattern. On drab female hummers, subtle differences in face patterns can provide helpful clues, but they also can provide some traps for the unwary. Many female hummers have a white spot behind the eye, sometimes elongated into a white or pale postocular stripe. On some, the long pale postocular stripe may not be sharply defined, but it has the effect of completely isolating a dark patch on the ear coverts; this is true of Costa's and Lucifer hummingbirds, for example. On some, this stripe can be well defined and conspicuous; female Broad-billed Hummingbirds are sometimes misidentified as White-eared Hummingbirds on this basis. Points to notice on face pattern include the presence or absence of a contrasting ear patch, pale spot, or stripe behind the eye, or pale area above the lores, and the degree of contrast between the throat and the face.

Head and body shape. In addition to bill and tail shapes, overall shape of the head and body are worth noting as well. These points are more subtle and changeable, as the bird shifts position or as it raises or lowers its head feathers. Still, experienced birders may notice that Costa's Hummingbird tends to look "potbellied," White-eared Hummingbird has a short, thick neck, and Magnificent Hummingbird often looks oddly flat-headed. Studying your local hummers, you may find other subtle shape clues that will be helpful in quick views.

Even without knowing the size of this female Magnificent Hummingbird, we can notice its elongated shape (with long bill, tail, and wings) and its very flat forehead and crown.

Behavior and posture. The posture and the actions of a foraging hummingbird can be very useful for separating some species. The detailed treatment in the next chapter includes some prime cases. For example, female Anna's Hummingbird can be superficially very similar to females of Costa's and Black-chinned hummingbirds, and all three may occur together in parts of the Southwest. But Anna's tends to hold its tail down and relatively still while hovering, and the other two species flip their tails up and down quite a bit while hovering, so often it is possible to separate these birds even at a glance. Not all species show such distinctive behaviors, but the foraging posture of an unidentified hummer is always worth noting.

Size. In general, size is only a minor field mark for hummers. Judging the size of a lone hummer can be very difficult, and a false impression can be very misleading, getting us off track from the correct identification. But in a situation at feeders, where birds can be studied in direct comparison, relative size becomes significant and worth noting.

Voice and other sounds. Typical callnotes are among the most important things to notice about many hummers. They are of little help in separating the two most difficult species pairs (Black-chinned vs. Ruby-throated and Rufous vs. Allen's), but in most cases these callnotes are significant for identification. Notes given by foraging or perched birds are easiest to categorize and learn. These callnotes may be slightly higher-pitched from males than from females in some species, but not enough to cause confusion in identification. Most hummers also give a variety of squealing and chattering notes during aggressive encounters, generally somewhat higher-pitched and buzzier than their simple callnotes, but these complex calls are harder to learn (and to describe).

In a few species of hummers in North America (as well as in many tropical species), males have distinct songs, given repeatedly from a perch as part of their territorial defense. These are worth knowing but seldom play a role in critical species identification.

Wing noise is also worth noting. Hummingbirds are so called because of the hum of rapidly beating wings of all species, audible at close range, but some do more than that. The most distinctive wing sound among North American hummers is the metallic trill of the adult male Broad-tailed, produced by the modified shape of the tenth primary. It makes this sound in forward flight but generally not when hovering. When the bird is in molt and the tenth primary is missing, the wing-trill is silenced. Adult males of Rufous and Allen's hummingbirds make a lower buzzing trill, also produced by the shape of the tenth primary, and also silenced when that feather is missing in molt.

Aside from adult males of these three *Selasphorus*, most of our hummers do not make distinctive wing noise. However, the humming sound produced by the wings of any hummingbird may sound different when the bird is molting or when the outer primaries are very worn, and this different sound may draw our attention at times.

ADDITIONAL CONSIDERATIONS

Discoloration and other misleading features. Hummingbirds may show unusual patches of color from being dusted with pollen. It is common to see hummers with spots of yellow on the forehead or throat or with red pollen on the face; sometimes they show persistent spots of yellow pollen on the bill or chest. These odd colors need not cause any confusion as long as we're aware of the possibility. Another type of temporary change involves female hummers during the breeding season: they often develop dark spots on the underparts, caused by wear against the edge of the nest during their incubation period.

An optical illusion that affects hummer identification is caused by light reflecting from red hummingbird feeders. A hummer perched or hovering at a feeder may appear to have the underparts suffused with red or buff because of the reflected light. Again, just being aware of the possibility of this illusion is a good defense against being misled.

Hummingbird hybrids. Hummingbird species interbreed far more often than members of most bird families. Since hummers establish no long-term pair bond and mating seems somewhat indiscriminate, practically any two species that overlap in range might interbreed occasionally. Sometimes the identity of the resulting hybrids seems evident, but more often such birds are correctly listed as "probable" identifications, unless a few feathers can be collected for DNA testing. The main point for field observers to remember is that such hybrids are always possible. A hummer that doesn't quite match the field marks of any one species always could be a hybrid, and without a detailed study it may have to be left unidentified.

This hummer in Arizona, no match for any known species, was thought to be a Berylline × Magnificent hybrid.

23. THE CHALLENGING SMALL HUMMINGBIRDS

Species treated in detail:

RUBY-THROATED HUMMINGBIRD *Archilochus colubris*
BLACK-CHINNED HUMMINGBIRD *Archilochus alexandri*
ANNA'S HUMMINGBIRD *Calypte anna*
COSTA'S HUMMINGBIRD *Calypte costae*
CALLIOPE HUMMINGBIRD *Stellula calliope*
BROAD-TAILED HUMMINGBIRD *Selasphorus platycercus*
RUFOUS HUMMINGBIRD *Selasphorus rufus*
ALLEN'S HUMMINGBIRD *Selasphorus sasin*

The problem. Small size, hyperactive behavior, and variation within species all contribute to the general difficulty of recognizing hummingbird species everywhere, but birders who travel in the American tropics soon find that most hummers there are relatively straightforward to identify. Only about two dozen of the world's 300-plus species of hummingbirds have ever been found in North America north of the Mexican border, but those two dozen include some of the most difficult identifications in the family, which hardly seems fair.

Adult males of North American hummer species are almost always distinctive, with the sticky exception of Allen's Hummingbird. But females and immatures within four of the genera can be very challenging. These break down into four species that are simply very plain above and below, generally lacking rusty or buff tones in the plumage (the species of *Archilochus* and *Calypte),* and four relatively plain species that have some rusty and buff tones in the body plumage and almost always in the tail as well (the species of *Selasphorus* and *Stellula).* These two groups will be treated separately in this chapter.

A number of basic considerations apply to identifying hummers in general, and these are discussed in detail in the preceding chapter. Reading that section would be good preparation for understanding the relatively brief treatment that follows.

GROUP 1. SMALL PLAIN SPECIES

These are four species of small to medium-sized hummers lacking any rufous in the tail and mostly lacking buff or rufous on the underparts. The species of *Archilochus* (Ruby-throated and Black-chinned hummingbirds) evidently are very close relatives, extremely similar in shape, pattern, and voice. Even adult males differ mainly in throat color. The species of *Calypte* (Anna's and Costa's hummingbirds) are slightly more distinct, but females and immatures of these two species can be confused with each other and with the two *Archilochus* as well. These four are much less likely to be mistaken for any other species.

With a close, detailed look, shapes of the primaries provide diagnostic clues for some members of this group; see the diagram on p. 333.

Adult males. Given reasonable views, adult males of these four species are unlikely to be misidentified.

The adult male Ruby-throated is superficially similar to the adult male Broad-tailed Hummingbird of the West: both have red throats and green upperparts. However, observers who are familiar with both are very unlikely to confuse the two. Ruby-throated tends to be slimmer, Broad-tailed is more chunky and has a larger tail. Ruby-throated has a black patch from the chin back to below the eye and looks dark-faced, with only a small isolated white spot behind the eye; Broad-tailed usually has a diffuse pale area surrounding the eye. Ruby-throated is slightly more orange-red on the throat and golden-green on the back, while Broad-tailed tends toward rose-red on the throat and blue-green on the back. For most of the year (except during molt) the wings of the adult male Broad-tailed make a shrill metallic trilling in flight.

BLACK-CHINNED HUMMINGBIRD — females, immatures. Common over much of the West and almost identical to the Ruby-throated of the East, the Black-chinned Hummingbird makes a good basis for comparison with other plain hummingbirds. In body size it is a little smaller than Anna's and a little larger than Costa's Hummingbird. The outer tail feathers are longer and wider than in Costa's, creating a less-rounded tail shape, and the outermost feathers are bluntly pointed at the tip in most (more rounded in immature females). The tail also looks more contrastingly patterned than that of Anna's, with more black and less gray in the outer feathers. When hovering, the Black-chinned usually flips and spreads the tail almost continuously. The bill averages slightly longer and heavier than that of Costa's, and proportionately longer than that of Anna's, and usually looks slightly decurved.

The throat varies from almost unmarked to lightly streaked (usually) to heavily marked with dusky, but any markings present tend to be spread evenly over the entire throat (except in molting young males that are developing the dark gorget). The dusky patch on the ear coverts often spreads out more than on female and immature Costa's, extending down onto the throat somewhat and often partly obscuring the pale line behind the eye. The underparts are mostly pale gray, washed slightly darker along the sides and with a small area of buff on the flanks. The common callnote, a descending *teew,* is very similar to that of Ruby-throated but different from that of any other western hummingbird.

juvenile   adult female

Juvenile and adult female Black-chinned Hummingbirds. Common and widespread in the West, this species makes a good basis for comparison with other small plain hummers. See text for details.

Juveniles can be either darker or paler gray below than adults, their bills are often shorter at first, and juvenile females may look more round-tailed than adults. Thus, some young birds can look confusingly similar to Costa's. Their voices, however, are quite distinctive.

RUBY-THROATED HUMMINGBIRD — females, immatures. This species is extremely similar to Black-chinned Hummingbird and is separated from Anna's and Costa's by the same criteria. Its normal range does not overlap with those of Anna's or Costa's hummers, so this ID problem comes up only when the possibility of vagrant occurrences is suspected. Separating Ruby-throated from Black-chinned is a serious challenge that birders face frequently in central and southern Texas and on the western Great Plains, as well as among scattered birds in the southeastern U.S. in winter.

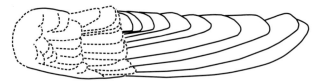

Black-chinned Hummingbird, young female

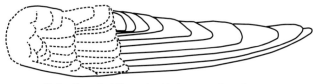

Ruby-throated Hummingbird, young female

Anna's Hummingbird, young female

Comparing primary shapes of Black-chinned, Ruby-throated, and Anna's hummingbirds. On the two *Archilochus* species (Black-chinned and Ruby-throated), the inner six primaries are narrower than the outer four, and the difference in width between p6 and p7 is particularly obvious. On Anna's (and on most hummingbirds), the inner primaries are not distinctly narrower, giving more of an appearance that the primaries are similar in shape and neatly stacked. Comparing the two *Archilochus* species, the outer primaries on Black-chinned tend to be more curved, broad, and blunt-tipped. On Ruby-throated, although p7 is distinctly broader than p6, the outer primaries in general are not as broad as on Black-chinned. This makes the outer part of the wingtip look more narrow and tapered on Ruby-throated, and the narrow tip of the outermost primary (p10) is a very good mark if it can be seen.

Note that in this illustration, the wings of the Black-chinned and Ruby-throated are shown in a more relaxed posture than the wing of Anna's, in order to show the individual feather shapes more clearly. Any of these species may hold the wing in more relaxed or more tightly folded positions, but the shapes of the individual feathers do not change.

In many cases, females and immatures of these two species are best left as *"Archilochus,* sp." But with close studies of typical individuals, these are points to look for. Ruby-throated tends to be a brighter green above and a more whitish gray below, showing more overall contrast. It tends to be greener on the crown and forehead, but this area is quite variable in both species. Ruby-throated averages shorter-billed than Black-chinned, but this must be used with caution, especially in summer: young birds of both species can be noticeably shorter-billed than adults at first. Behavior is sometimes a clue: Black-chinned usually flips and spreads its tail a lot while hovering, while Ruby-throated often holds its tail relatively still in the same situations; both species vary in their actions, so this is only a minor supporting character.

adult female
Ruby-throated Hummingbird

With a close study of a perched bird, the shapes of the primaries can provide the best confirmation (see illustration on p. 333). These differences are subtle, and they require a very good view of a perched bird. If you want to use primary shapes as a field mark, don't start when you have a suspected rarity in front of you; prepare by studying the primaries on whichever of these species is common in your area.

ANNA'S HUMMINGBIRD — females, immatures. Anna's is slightly larger and more solidly built than the others in this group. Its tail usually looks less rounded at the tip than the others' and shows less black, more gray, in the outer tail feathers. When hovering, Anna's usually holds its tail in line with the axis of its body, with relatively little flipping or spreading of the tail.

Its bill averages a little longer and heavier than that of Costa's and slightly shorter and straighter than that of Black-chinned. However, Anna's has a relatively large head, so it looks proportionately shorter-billed than Black-chinned, often noticeably so. The underparts are quite grayish, usually with an extensive wash of dull green on the sides. Adult females typically have some red spots on the throat, often concentrated in a patch on the center of the lower throat; sometimes this patch is so large that virtually the whole throat looks red, and a red-throated, green-crowned female may cause temporary confusion. The common callnote of Anna's is a dry, loud *tzick* or *kipp;* in excitement, the bird may run several notes together into a rapid chatter.

adult female,
March

adult male,
August

Anna's Hummingbirds. The male at left is actively molting head feathers
in August. Note the stocky overall shape and large-headed look. The female at right shows the overall dingy gray look of the underparts and the
substantial but squarish tail. On the folded wing of the male, notice that
there is no abrupt change in the width of the primaries between p6 and
p7, unlike the species of *Archilochus*.

Timing of molt can be a clue. Anna's nests mostly in late winter and
may be actively molting in summer, like Costa's Hummingbird but unlike the adults of most species.

Juvenile Anna's (especially those not long out of the nest) can differ
from adult females in confusing ways. They are smaller at first, and
their bills may be shorter. Their underparts may be paler at first, suggesting the pattern of a Costa's or Black-chinned, and they may lack the
red on the throat and green on the sides. Callnotes may be the only sure
way to identify some of these.

COSTA'S HUMMINGBIRD — females, immatures. This small hummer
of the desert regions often looks round-bodied or pot-bellied. The tail
of Costa's is proportionately short and visibly rounded at the tip, because the outer tail feathers themselves are short, narrow, and round-
tipped. When hovering, Costa's usually flips its tail up and down (like a
weaker version of the Black-chinned's tail action, but unlike the usual
behavior of Anna's). When perched, the wingtips extend beyond the
tip of the tail. Seen in profile, the bill looks notably thin (or flattened)
and slightly decurved.

In adult females and immature birds the back often has a pale or
grayish look, and the underparts are nearly white, paler than in similar
species. The throat is virtually unmarked white in adult females (occasionally with a few purple spots), but young males will show purple

coming in on the throat, often starting near the back corners of the gorget. A dusky patch on the ear coverts is well defined (though not large), set off by the whitish throat and a pale line behind the eye. Costa's also has a pale line above and in front of the eye, like many Anna's but unlike Black-chinned. The callnote of Costa's is a thin, hard *tik*; in excitement, the bird may run many notes together into a rapid ticking or dry twittering.

Since Costa's may nest very early in spring, adults may be in active molt in summer, like Anna's but unlike Black-chinned Hummingbird.

immature male,
August

adult female,
October

Female and immature male Costa's Hummingbirds, to show proportions, tail shape, and bill shape, as well as markings. The patch on the ear coverts varies from obscure to obvious, but the light area over the eye is always apparent. The overall pale look of the bird is characteristic, but some similar hummers can look as pale, especially in bright sunlight.

GROUP 2: THE *SELASPHORUS* COMPLEX

This group includes our three species of *Selasphorus* (Broad-tailed, Rufous, and Allen's hummingbirds) and the related Calliope Hummingbird. In this group, females and immatures show at least a trace of buff on the underparts and rufous in the tail. Adult males of Broad-tailed and Calliope are distinctive if seen well. Rufous and Allen's, however, are extraordinarily similar in all plumages, and even adult males can be problematic. In this section, I mostly treat these two species as a unit, under the name Rufous/Allen's Hummingbird, because most females and immatures cannot be separated in the field. Specifics for separating Rufous and Allen's from each other are at the end of this section.

RUFOUS/ALLEN'S HUMMINGBIRD — females, immatures. This combined category makes up the most widespread (and usually the most common) member of this complex. Its migrations are notably early. Northward migration (mostly along the Pacific Coast and through the southwestern deserts) is well under way by February; southbound birds are already common throughout the West, including well south of the breeding range, by early July. Because Rufous/Allen's is so numerous and because it is sized in between Broad-tailed and Calliope hummingbirds, it makes a good basis for comparison.

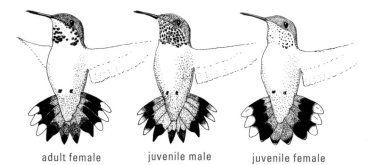

adult female   juvenile male   juvenile female

The hordes of "female-plumaged" hummingbirds seen in late summer show a lot of variation within species, and much of this is owing to age and sex differences. These three Rufous Hummingbirds show typical throat patterns, tail patterns, and shapes of tail feathers for three classes of birds. Allen's Hummingbirds are extremely similar, although within each age and sex class, the tail feathers average slightly narrower.

Plumage color and pattern vary with sex and age. Of the three categories considered here — adult females, immature males, and immature females — the immature males have the narrowest tail feathers and the greatest amount of rufous in the tail, while immature females have the broadest tail feathers and the least amount of rufous. The central tail feathers of immature females often appear all green in the field (because the limited rufous at the base may be hidden by the uppertail coverts). A rusty wash on the sides, flanks, and undertail coverts is variable in darkness and extent, but is usually more obvious and more contrasty than on Broad-tailed or Calliope. The throat may be lightly spotted with dusky (immature females), more heavily spotted with bronze and a little red (immature males), or blotched with red toward the center (adult females). The back and rump have variable amounts of rufous edging on the feathers.

immature male,
August

adult female,
August

Female and immature male Rufous Hummingbirds (Allen's is virtually identical), to provide examples of shape, throat pattern, flank color, and overall appearance. In late summer in mountains of the West, these are the common birds against which others are to be compared.

When hovering, Rufous/Allen's moves its tail very little and often holds its tail up almost horizontally, behaviors shared with Broad-tailed and Calliope. The callnote of Rufous/Allen's is a musical *chip*.

BROAD-TAILED HUMMINGBIRD — females, immatures. This is a species that actually has an appropriate name. In body size the Broad-tailed Hummingbird is not much larger than Rufous/Allen's, but its tail is much larger, and with practice you can see this in the field. The outer tail feathers are rufous toward the base, with this color most obvious on

Female Broad-tailed Hummingbirds. The size and length of the tail may or may not be obvious, depending on angle.

young males and least extensive on young females. A smooth wash of buff on the sides, flanks, and undertail coverts is usually paler than on most Rufous/Allen's; in the field, this may look more intensely rufous in some lights, or it may look washed out to white. Compared to Rufous/Allen's, the face tends to look more green or gray, less washed with rusty or buff, and it may show a more obvious eye-ring. The throat is evenly spotted with dusky; the spots may be very small and widely spaced on young females, larger and more densely packed on young males, with adult females usually between these extremes. Young males in molt will show rose-red feathers in a random pattern on the throat; some adult females also have rose-red feathers on the throat, typically concentrated at the center. The back is a rich green or blue-green; juveniles may show rufous edgings to some back and rump feathers, but apparently these wear off quickly. The callnote is a musical *chip* like that of Rufous/Allen's or slightly higher-pitched.

Broad-tailed Hummingbirds molt mainly on the wintering grounds, and some young males start migrating north in spring before their molt is complete. These young males can be confusing. In some, the outermost primaries are still molting, so they may not make the characteristic wing trill of adult males. In many, the gorget is incomplete, as these are among the last feathers to be molted. Some of these young male Broad-taileds in spring might even be confused with some plumages of Anna's Hummingbird, but tail shape and callnotes should separate them.

CALLIOPE HUMMINGBIRD — females, immatures. Small size alone is not enough for identifying this species, even in a situation in which direct comparisons are possible; some Rufous/Allen's are nearly as small as some Calliopes. The relatively short bill and tail are better clues, creating a different overall shape. The tail, in particular, seems short and stubby even for the small size of the bird; when fully spread it can look quite rounded, but on the perched bird it looks short and squarish, and it does not reach the tips of the folded wings. Rufous in the tail is usually limited to small areas on the edges of the outer feathers, near the base, and it may not even be visible. The tips of the central tail feathers are vaguely spade-shaped, but this is very difficult to see in the field.

The sides and flanks are a very pale buff, and this color sometimes washes right across the center of the chest, not fading to white as on the larger *Selasphorus* hummers. The throat is lightly and evenly spotted, with the spots larger and more obvious on young males than on females. On adult females, and on many immatures, the white from the throat extends up over the base of the upper mandible, creating a face pattern not matched by other North American hummers.

Three views of Calliope Hummingbirds. Left: adult female in July. Note the whitish area coming up over the base of the bill. Center: juvenile, probably female, in August. Note the proportions, especially the short bill and tail and the broad, short wings. Right: juvenile male.

When hovering, the Calliope holds its tail very still and often angled up above horizontal. Its callnote, not heard very often, is a very thin musical *chip*, like that of Rufous/Allen's but noticeably softer and higher-pitched.

SEPARATING RUFOUS AND ALLEN'S HUMMINGBIRDS. Allen's Hummingbird poses one of the most challenging ID problems in North America and comes close to being unidentifiable in the field, at least away from its breeding grounds.

With Rufous and Allen's, identifying a bird to age and sex is not only easier than identifying it to species, it's a necessary first step. The diagnostic differences in shapes of tail feathers can't be used unless we first know the age and sex of the bird.

Adult males are distinctive, with solidly colored gorgets and no white in the tail. A bird that looks like an adult male Rufous Hummingbird, with a solidly rusty back, can be confidently identified. But a bird that looks like an adult male Allen's *might* also be a Rufous. Occasionally, a Rufous can develop the full adult gorget and tail while retaining an entirely green back, thus looking just like a classic Allen's. This variant of Rufous seems to be rare, so it is probably safe to identify adult male Allen's by sight in areas where they are known to be common (such as on the breeding grounds, or on the main migratory route). Anywhere else, it would be necessary to confirm the identity of a suspected adult male Allen's by confirming the shape of certain tail feathers. It may be possible to do this in the field if we can get excellent studies (for example, at a feeder). But individuals that are not adult males may be simply unidentifiable unless they can be examined in the hand.

adult male
Rufous

adult male
Allen's

Tail shapes of adult males. Rufous has a distinct notch on the inner web of r2, and all of its tail feathers are wider than those of Allen's. The same kinds of differences apply to other age and sex classes as well, although the notch on r2 is often obscure or lacking on young females.

During spring, Rufous/Allen's fall into two classes, adult males and adult females. As soon as fledged juveniles are independent (as early as late April for some Allen's, as early as late May for Rufous), there are three classes of "female-like" birds: adult females, juvenile males, and juvenile females. These differ most notably in throat pattern and in shapes of certain tail feathers, as illustrated on p. 337. Variation in Allen's very closely parallels that in Rufous, although in each age/sex class, the tail feathers of Allen's average slightly narrower. This kind of detail would not be visible in the field except, perhaps, for a few hummer specialists. There are no reliable field marks to separate the species, but within each of these three age/sex classes, Allen's tends to have more rufous color on the uppertail coverts.

Rufous Hummingbird is a regular stray to eastern North America, with dozens every winter at hummer feeders in the Southeast. Allen's is much less frequent in the East, but records have accumulated to prove that it can occur anywhere. Eastern records should be treated as Rufous/Allen's unless the birds are examined in the hand. Fortunately, some licensed hummingbird banders regularly make "house calls" to identify and band eastern vagrant hummers.

A nonmigratory race of Allen's Hummingbird, *S. sasin sedentarius,* deserves special mention. Originally limited to the Channel Islands off southern California, it has colonized the adjacent mainland since the 1960s and is now found year-round from coastal areas of Ventura County through much of Los Angeles and Orange counties. Distribution might be useful for ID in November and December, when most Rufous and nominate Allen's would be in Mexico. *S. s. sedentarius* is very similar to nominate Allen's but averages very slightly larger, and adult females tend to have more green mottling on their flanks.

24. LEARNING TO IDENTIFY WOODPECKERS

In North America, few bird families are as distinctive as the Picidae, the woodpecker family. Beginning birders may be momentarily confused by a flicker on the ground, but beyond that point, there's never a doubt as to whether a given bird is a woodpecker or not. Most of the species are distinctive as well, easily identified with a good view. But this family has some odd traits that can affect the identification process, and some odd species groups that challenge our abilities to understand what we're seeing in the field.

POINTS TO CONSIDER IN IDENTIFYING WOODPECKERS

Variations in red markings. North American woodpeckers are mostly patterned in black, white, or brown, but most have accents of red or yellow. The pattern of red on the head is often the major difference between the sexes, suggesting that it has an important signaling function for the birds themselves. The distribution of red and yellow is also important for separating the three closely related species that make up the Yellow-bellied Sapsucker complex and for separating the various forms of flickers. In looking at these birds, we need to remember that the carotenoid pigments that create the red and yellow colors in feathers are subject to some variations.

This becomes critical when we're trying to distinguish between the eastern Yellow-bellied and western Red-naped sapsuckers, since much of the difference involves the placement of red in their head patterns. A minority of Yellow-bellieds have red feathers in the white nape stripe, and in some, this red patch is obvious in the field. This occurs at times far to the east of any contact zone between these species, so it probably represents variation within Yellow-bellied, not a sign of past interbreeding. Some female Yellow-bellieds, apparently "pure" individuals otherwise, also have some red feathers on the throat. On the reverse side, some Red-naped Sapsuckers have very little red on the nape, occasionally none at all. Birds like this are most likely to be seen in summer, when the plumage is worn; the red is located at the tips of the nape feathers, and if there is only a little, it may wear off by summer. The amount of red on the throat of female Red-naped is also variable. An individual with very little red on the throat and nape could be hard to separate from either a Yellow-bellied or a hybrid.

Not an issue for ID, but reflecting the amount of variation possible in the pattern of red, some female Yellow-bellied Sapsuckers have the crown entirely black, lacking the usual red patch there.

Plumage areas of red and yellow are also important in separating the various forms of flickers, and these are also subject to variation. Occasional flickers have the "wrong" color on the flight feathers, either on just a few feathers or throughout the wings and tail, and this can result from aberrant effects on the carotenoid pigments at times. In a similar vein, an occasional Red-bellied Woodpecker has some of the red on its head replaced by yellow, inviting possible confusion with Golden-fronted Woodpecker.

Hybrid situations. Among North American woodpeckers there are several cases of closely related forms interbreeding where their ranges meet. The largest hybrid zone involves eastern "Yellow-shafted" and western "Red-shafted" flickers on the western Great Plains and much of southwestern Canada: interbreeding between these forms appears to be completely random, with essentially no "pure" individuals anywhere in the hybrid zones. The interbreeding appears to be just as random where Gilded Flicker meets "Red-shafted" Flicker, but because these areas of contact are limited, these are regarded as separate species for the moment. There are also situations involving more-or-less frequent interbreeding among the three species in the Yellow-bellied Sapsucker complex, between Ladder-backed and Nuttall's woodpeckers, and between Red-bellied and Golden-fronted woodpeckers. All of these happen in regions of contact that could be predicted by studying maps of breeding ranges. Birders should be aware of these possibilities to avoid being confused by such hybrids.

Juvenile patterns. Most juvenile woodpeckers are recognizably similar to adults of their species, although head patterns often differ. In some *Picoides* species in which adult males have red on the nape (Hairy, Downy, and Arizona, for example), juveniles (of both sexes) typically have red in the center of the crown instead. On Hairy Woodpecker this central crown spot is sometimes pink or yellow rather than red. Summer reports of American Three-toed Woodpeckers outside their normal range almost invariably refer to such juvenile Hairy Woodpeckers with yellow central crown spots.

25. LEARNING TO IDENTIFY TYRANT FLYCATCHERS

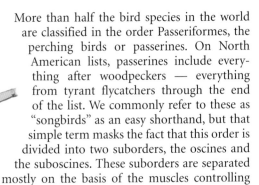

More than half the bird species in the world are classified in the order Passeriformes, the perching birds or passerines. On North American lists, passerines include everything after woodpeckers — everything from tyrant flycatchers through the end of the list. We commonly refer to these as "songbirds" as an easy shorthand, but that simple term masks the fact that this order is divided into two suborders, the oscines and the suboscines. These suborders are separated mostly on the basis of the muscles controlling the syrinx, or voice box. Almost all families of North American passerines are among the oscines, and our only suboscines are the Tyrannidae, the tyrant flycatchers. And as we might expect, flycatchers differ from the true songbirds in some fundamental ways.

To oversimplify, we could say that most oscines probably recognize their own kind by a combination of vocal and visual clues. The development of song in most oscines is thought to involve some learning, and it can go awry at times, so it might be important for species to look different as well as sound different, to avoid cases of mistaken identity. Among tyrant flycatchers, by contrast, the songs are thought to be hard-wired: innate and instinctive rather than learned. In theory, then, flycatchers could recognize their own kind entirely by sound, and it would not be essential for different species to look different.

There are some flycatchers with simple voices and ornate plumage, it's true, but there are also complexes of species of flycatchers that are separated mainly by their distinctive voices. In North America, classic examples include Eastern and Western wood-pewees, Couch's and Tropical kingbirds, Ash-throated and Nutting's flycatchers, and several of the *Empidonax* flycatchers (treated in detail in the next chapter). Therefore, in identifying flycatchers, we have to pay attention to voice, and we have to use visual clues with caution.

POINTS TO CONSIDER IN IDENTIFYING FLYCATCHERS

Putting birds in the right categories. A basic point, of course, is to make sure that a bird is a tyrant flycatcher in the first place. Experienced birders are not likely to have a problem with this, at least not in North America; confusion caused by poor looks at kinglets, vireos, etc., is likely to be brief. Flycatchers in the tropics are much more varied, and we may have to re-calibrate our expectations about the family when we travel. But in North America, a more typical challenge is placing a bird in the right group within the Tyrannidae.

Most field guides do a good job of separating out the major genera of flycatchers, showing how to tell the yellow-bellied kingbirds from the crested *Myiarchus* flycatchers, for example. A more intriguing problem involves those flycatchers that look "unique" in our local perspective, but that actually represent tropical groups. In any field guide for North America, Great Kiskadee looks unmistakable, a big flycatcher with black and white head stripes and a yellow belly. But in the tropics, at least ten flycatcher species look similar, and a few of those have the potential to wander northward. Likewise, the bold, streaky Sulphurbellied Flycatcher is unique among North America's usual avifauna, but at least three other tropical species could be confused with it, and all of them are likely candidates to wander to our area.

More potential for confusion, at least in the library, comes from unrelated families called "flycatchers" in the Eastern Hemisphere. Several Old World flycatchers (family Muscicapidae) occur in western Alaska as migrants or rare strays, several of them probably could occur farther south on this continent, and some of the plainest species might conceivably be confused with *Empidonax* or other tyrant flycatchers.

Learning the voices of flycatchers. Most flycatchers make a variety of different sounds. If we listen closely to one species, we may find that it has only a handful of basic notes — but that these can be combined in various ways, given at different pitches and different degrees of emphasis, so that they add up to quite a varied repertoire. For this reason, recognizing many flycatcher calls is partly a matter of learning their basic tone quality rather than memorizing particular patterns.

In contrast to the varied calls given at other times of day, many flycatchers have "dawn songs" that are very stereotyped. These songs often involve a series of short notes, given over and over in a very consistent pattern. They are heard just before sunrise, and sometimes at dusk as well, but seldom at other times of day. Sometimes these dawn songs are so different from other vocalizations that they can be mystifying for birders who think they know the species already: the rough, rasping dawn song of Cassin's Kingbird, heard in Arizona canyons at first light, is sometimes mistaken for the voice of Buff-collared Nightjar.

Studying birds of known identity. With flycatchers, even more than with most groups of birds, the best way to study identification is to focus on birds of known identity. Of course, our natural temptation is to focus on the unknowns: the silent *Empidonax,* the odd-looking *Myiarchus.* But when we're looking at such a bird, if we don't already have a lot of experience, all of our conclusions may be suspect. Is that bill wide or narrow, are those wing bars bright or dull? Well, compared to what? Comparative experience has to begin with solid identifications and build up from there.

To learn identification with confidence, we should focus on flycatchers that can be named with certainty: birds singing typical songs, birds on territory in typical habitat. Early summer, when birds are on nesting territory and their plumage is not yet too worn, is a good time to focus on learning flycatchers. At least a few species can be found breeding practically everywhere in North America; getting to know even a few of them really thoroughly is a very worthwhile project and an essential step for learning to recognize any of the others.

A silent wood-pewee seen in migration might pique our curiosity, but we'll learn more about ID by finding a bird of known identity, like this Eastern Wood-Pewee singing on territory, and studying it in detail.

Considering the condition of the plumage. Visual field marks for flycatchers often involve subtle differences in colors. We can't hope to apply such field marks unless we've already considered the condition of the plumage. If the bird has molted relatively recently, and the feathers are at least fairly fresh, the colors may mean a lot. If the plumage is worn, colors may not mean much: yellow may fade to whitish, olive may fade to gray. Wear also makes wing bars appear narrower and less contrasting and reduces the pale edgings on flight feathers of the wings and tail. A bird that is actively in molt may show odd patches of color, its wing bars may be uneven, its eye-ring may be broken, and its tail may be oddly shaped. Any time we are trying to identify a flycatcher by visual clues, we should try to determine the condition of its plumage so that we'll know how much faith to put in the bird's apparent color and markings.

26. THE *EMPIDONAX* FLYCATCHERS

Species treated in detail:

YELLOW-BELLIED FLYCATCHER *Empidonax flaviventris*
ACADIAN FLYCATCHER *Empidonax virescens*
ALDER FLYCATCHER *Empidonax alnorum*
WILLOW FLYCATCHER *Empidonax traillii*
LEAST FLYCATCHER *Empidonax minimus*
HAMMOND'S FLYCATCHER *Empidonax hammondii*
GRAY FLYCATCHER *Empidonax wrightii*
DUSKY FLYCATCHER *Empidonax oberholseri*
WESTERN FLYCATCHER COMPLEX:
   PACIFIC-SLOPE FLYCATCHER *Empidonax difficilis*
   CORDILLERAN FLYCATCHER *Empidonax occidentalis*
BUFF-BREASTED FLYCATCHER *Empidonax fulvifrons*

The problem. The small flycatchers of the genus *Empidonax* represent a classic challenge for birders. Like many other members of the tyrant flycatcher family (as described in the previous chapter), they seem to rely very heavily on voice for recognizing their own kind, so visible differences among species are often very subtle. All of the North American *Empidonax* are little gray birds (tinged with olive, brown, or yellow) with wing bars and eye-rings. Their specific characters are so subtle that there is often more variation *within* a species than there is between two species in the genus. Slight differences in color are often distinctive for birds in fresh plumage, but wear and fading quickly reduce the usefulness of these color differences, so a knowledge of the timing of molt becomes almost essential. Even museum specimens or birds in the hand may be difficult, or sometimes impossible, to name with certainty.

All of the species have distinctive songs on the breeding grounds, and many of their other vocalizations are helpful in identification as well. However, partly because of imprecise descriptions of voices, even the songs have been confused at times.

SEPARATING *EMPIDONAX* FROM OTHER FLYCATCHERS

A necessary first step is to be certain that a given bird is an *Empidonax* and not something else. Other small birds with wing bars and eye-rings, such as Ruby-crowned Kinglet and Hutton's Vireo, may be mistaken for flycatchers by beginners. But even experienced birders may confuse other flycatchers for Empids, at least temporarily.

Ruby-crowned
Kinglet

Eastern Wood-Pewee,
juvenile in fall

Eastern and Western wood-pewees show only a hint of eye-rings (just a narrow pale area behind the eye), and their wing bars are usually less distinct than those of most *Empidonax*. But the same could be said for many Willow Flycatchers, and there is potential for confusion there. Wood-pewees have longer wings, often appearing to extend more than a third of the way down the tail, and shorter legs, so that they often appear to be sitting on their feet. They have narrower bills than the Willow Flycatcher, and they are not so contrastingly white on the throat.

Sometimes mistaken for an *Empidonax* is the Northern Beardless-Tyrannulet of the Mexican border region. Superficially it is similar, but it has a narrow, stubby bill, suggesting a small version of a vireo's bill. It has a broken eye-ring and a narrow dark line through the eye, and its voice is different from that of any Empid.

Northern
Beardless-Tyrannulet

WHAT TO LOOK AT ON *EMPIDONAX*

Human nature being what it is, we birders tend to look most intently at those Empids that we have the lowest probability of actually identifying with certainty: silent birds, out of typical habitat, on migration. The best time for intense study of one of these birds, however, is when we already know what it is. If we find a singing bird, or one that is clearly identifiable by some combination of factors, we should study it to build up a solid basis for comparison with other individuals later.

In that situation, when we are studying an *Empidonax* flycatcher of known identity, here are points to consider.

Bill shape. The exact shape of the bill (as viewed from directly above or below) is not the easiest thing to see in the field, but it is among the most important. There are two basic groups, those in which the bill is relatively narrow and the sides are fairly straight, and those in which the base of the bill is broader and the sides appear slightly convex. (Least and Buff-breasted flycatchers are somewhat intermediate between these two groups.) Within these groups, species vary in the length and width of the bill relative to the size of the bird. With practice, bill shape can become one of the most helpful characters.

Pattern of lower mandible. When we achieve a good view of the bill shape from below, we should also focus on the color and pattern of the lower mandible. It may be entirely pale or it may have a dark tip, the dark tip may be limited or extensive, and it may be sharply defined or it may blend smoothly into the pale base.

Primary extension on
a Least Flycatcher

Wing and tail proportions. Often providing a useful clue is the primary projection — the extent of the primaries beyond the longest of the tertials on the folded wing. With experience, or with study of lots of good illustrations, it is possible to develop a sense for what constitutes a short, medium, and long primary projection for an Empid. Tail length is also an important clue for separating some species. However, primary projection can affect our impressions of tail length. For example, Hammond's Flycatcher is relatively short-tailed, but its long primary projection makes the tail seem even shorter than it is. While looking at the tail, it's also worthwhile to consider how wide it is and whether it appears notched at the tip.

Head shape and body shape. Difficult to quantify, but often helpful for experienced birders, are some aspects of head and body shape on Empids. These aspects include the bulk of the body (chunky or slim), the size of the head relative to the body, whether the forehead looks steep or flat, and whether the head looks smoothly rounded, slightly crested, or somewhere in between (although the effect of a crest can appear to change from minute to minute).

Condition of the plumage. Before we can make any use of characters involving the color or pattern of the plumage, we have to consider its condition, specifically the effects of molt and wear. Empids tend to look "cleanest" and most "colorful" when they are in very fresh plumage (just after completing a molt). As the plumage gradually becomes more worn during the following months, several changes occur. Areas of the upperparts that were greenish, brownish, or blue-gray in fresh plumage tend to fade toward a duller (and often slightly paler) gray. Yellow areas on the underparts tend to fade to whitish. The wings may become slightly paler, and wing bars that were buff or yellow in fresh plumage fade toward white. The wing bars and tertial edges also become narrower, as the edges of these feathers are worn away. As a general rule, most Empid species in worn plumage look even more similar to each other.

An Empid that is in the middle of an active molt may look odd in a variety of ways. Its plumage may look "patchy," with unexpected breaks in the wing bars or eye-ring. Its tail tip may look uneven. The length of the primary extension may become an unreliable character for a bird in molt if some primaries are missing or growing.

There are some differences among species in the timing of molt, so the fact that a given bird's plumage is fresh, worn, or molting can sometimes have a bearing on its identification. But the condition of the plumage will always affect the usefulness of all the color characters mentioned below. A birder who looks closely at Empids will get in the habit of always gauging the condition of the feathers before relying too much on their colors. But when a bird is in plumage that is at least moderately fresh, it is worth considering all the following points involving color and markings.

Throat color. The exact color of the throat (white, gray, pale yellow, grayish yellow) is often very important, and the degree to which the throat contrasts with the face is always worth noting.

Color of upperparts. This is potentially tricky, but it's important to study if you can get a good look at an Empid in good light (open shade is best — bright sunlight tends to wash out the colors). The general tone of the back can vary from gray to olive-brown to greenish, and it may or may not contrast noticeably with the color of the head. Color of the upperparts is most useful on fresh-plumaged birds.

BILL SHAPES, BILL PATTERNS, AND THROAT COLORS

Buff-breasted
Flycatcher

Least
Flycatcher

Yellow-bellied
Flycatcher

Alder
Flycatcher
(Willow Flycatcher
is very similar)

Acadian
Flycatcher

Pacific-slope
Flycatcher
(Cordilleran
Flycatcher
is very similar)

Hammond's
Flycatcher

Dusky
Flycatcher

Gray
Flycatcher

Eye-ring. Not all Empids have identical eye-rings. The eye-ring can be narrow, faint, or lacking on Willow, Alder, and sometimes Acadian flycatchers. The shape of the eye-ring can differ: typically it is not quite of even thickness all the way around, being slightly thinner across the top of the eye and slightly broader behind the eye. This effect is exaggerated in some species, including Pacific-slope and Cordilleran flycatchers, which often have the eye-ring lengthened to a point behind the eye. The degree of contrast between the eye-ring and the face is also worth noting.

Wing bar color and contrast. The color of the wing bars is always worth considering. They tend to be buff (especially on young birds) to pale olive or yellowish when the plumage is very fresh, but on adults of many species they soon fade to white. The degree of contrast in the wings is also worth noting. In some eastern species the ground color of the wings tends to be very blackish, so that the pale wing bars and tertial edgings show strong contrast; this is true of Least, Yellow-bellied, Acadian, and to some extent for Alder and eastern populations of Willow Flycatcher. In the western species, the ground color of the wings tends to be not quite as dark, so the contrast is less striking.

Voice. This is obviously a very important point, and not just the territorial songs of the males; callnotes are often of critical importance in identification. Five of the North American species have callnotes that sound like *whit,* very similar under field conditions, but the calls of the other six are quite different. Some of the species pairs that are most similar visually, such as Willow/Alder and Hammond's/Dusky, can be separated easily by callnotes. And in addition to songs and typical calls, most species have various other vocalizations. Not all of these will be distinctive or helpful in identification, but a birder would be wise to make note of any sound made by a mystery Empid.

WHAT NOT TO LOOK AT ON *EMPIDONAX*

That header is mostly in jest, of course, because there is nothing that we should avoid noticing when we're studying a bird. But the following points, while they may be eye-catching at times, should be considered of secondary importance in identification and used only as supporting characters.

Yellow belly. All Empids have yellow bellies when they are in fresh plumage. The brightness of the yellow varies with season and age more than it does according to species. It may be useful to note the intensity of the yellow on the belly as one clue to the freshness of the plumage.

Pale lores. All Empids have a pale area on the lores, between the eye and the bill. There is a slight tendency for this spot to be more obvious on some species than on others, but at best it is only a minor supporting mark.

Pale outer vanes. On most Empids, the outermost tail feather on each side has the outermost vane paler than the rest of the tail. The degree of contrast can be a useful character on museum specimens, or when studying birds in the hand, where lighting can be controlled and birds can be compared directly. In the field, however, the effects of lighting make this character unreliable.

Wing and tail action. All Empids flick the tail and wings at least occasionally while perched. Some tend to do this more often than others, and I mention these general tendencies in the species accounts below, but such vague trends cannot be used as field marks. At most, they are only minor supporting points. The one exception is the distinctive tail-dipping behavior of Gray Flycatcher.

VARIATION AND IDENTIFICATION

If we look only at books and other references, we may get the impression that identifying the Empids is easier than it really is. Illustrators of field guides (including this one) tend to show the most typical appearance of each species; in pictures, the birds all seem clearly separable. These sharp distinctions vanish once we get out in the field and start looking at the birds themselves. Seasonal and individual variations in the birds are enough to blur the lines between species, so that some look genuinely intermediate, or even suggest a different species from what they really are. This is why simply matching our impression of a bird to a published picture is not enough to identify Empids. To be on solid footing, we have to look consciously at a series of characteristics and analyze what we're seeing rather than relying on the bird's overall impression. And even then, the variability of each Empid means that we'll have to leave some individuals unidentified unless we can hear diagnostic vocalizations.

PROBABILITY, CERTAINTY, AND CAUTION IN SIGHT RECORDS

Before we talk about making positive identifications of Empids, we have to make allowance for two species pairs that are impossible to separate with complete certainty if they are silent: Willow and Alder flycatchers and Pacific-slope and Cordilleran flycatchers. During the breeding season, outside their areas of overlap, we can be virtually certain on the basis of range, and even in migration there are areas where one or the other member of each pair is very unlikely to occur. But over broad areas in migration, these birds can't be identified safely. It is perfectly acceptable (and accurate) to use the old group names for them: Willow and Alder were once lumped as "Traill's Flycatcher," and Pacific-slope and Cordilleran were lumped as "Western Flycatcher," and these names are still useful for birders.

If we treat each of these species pairs as a unit, then it's safe to say that we can learn to make confident identifications of most Empids that we see. In most cases, if we see an Empid in typical plumage, at an expected place and time, its identity will be straightforward. To name a Yellow-bellied or Buff-breasted or Gray flycatcher in typical habitat in late spring is no more challenging than naming, say, a Vesper Sparrow or a Pectoral Sandpiper.

In everyday birding, our identifications of Empids don't usually involve long, detailed studies of individuals. We are more likely to make quick assessments of the birds we see and to check these against our knowledge of which species are likely to be present. For example, if we glimpse an Empid in a southern swamp in summer and it looks about right for Acadian Flycatcher, we'll call it that, because Acadian is the only Empid likely to be there at that season. Only if the bird looks distinctly wrong for Acadian are we likely to pursue it further. Our identification may have been made casually, but it's probably correct, and this level of certainty is good enough for casual birding. Only if the species would represent a new local record do we need to document it more thoroughly.

In actual practice, my notes on Empids seen during a morning in late May in northwest Ohio might read like this:

Yellow-bellied Flycatcher 5
Least Flycatcher 4, + 2 probable
(Acadian Flycatcher 1 possible, silent and seen briefly)
Willow Flycatcher 8, + 3 probable
Alder Flycatcher 2 (calling)
Traill's (Willow/Alder) 4

In a similar vein, birding in an Arizona canyon in late April, my notes might include Hammond's Flycatcher 6, Dusky Flycatcher 2, Hammond's/Dusky 3.

In these cases, no birds were left simply as "*Empidonax,* sp." (although that would be a perfectly acceptable designation), but several were not identified firmly to species. (These identifications were from my perspective as someone who has looked closely at Empids for years. If I had less experience, and if I were honest enough to admit it, there might be more "possible" and "probable" birds on the list, fewer "definites," and a few "Empid sp.") Also in these cases, had I been willing to spend more time with each individual bird and follow each one until it called or sang, I might have moved most of them up to definite identifications. But a willingness to put birds down as "possible" or "probable" results in an honest account of what we encountered, without having our day hijacked by every Empid that crosses our path.

On rare occasions, though, we may find what appears to be an Empid outside its normal range. Such birds must be identified with much more care and documented thoroughly. A series of good photographs, showing the bird from all angles, may be enough to document some of the most distinctive species, but recordings of vocalizations may be necessary for most. A few of the most difficult species may not be possible to document without mist-netting and careful measurement and photography in the hand. The extra effort is worth it if we are to really understand the patterns of occurrence of these birds.

A NOTE ABOUT THE ILLUSTRATIONS

The illustrations in this chapter are meant to support the text, not to stand on their own. To reiterate a theme from this book's introduction, simple picture-matching is not enough for identifying subtle birds such as Empids. Unless you read the text and understand the variations in these birds, no set of illustrations, no matter how good, will be enough to enable you to name the birds accurately.

Although I show variability for each species here, you should assume that the real Empids actually vary a bit more than the illustrations. In choosing photographs, of course I used only those for which I could be certain of the identity of the birds. As a result, some images of birds that looked truly confusing or intermediate were not included here. The majority of individuals of each species should look like the examples illustrated in this guide, but there will be odd birds that exceed the variability shown here, and these birds won't be identifiable without careful analysis of the points described in the text of this chapter.

SPECIES ACCOUNTS

YELLOW-BELLIED FLYCATCHER is a small Empid breeding in humid coniferous forest. It is most common as a breeder in eastern Canada. It tends to be a late migrant in spring, with numbers still moving north through Texas in mid-May, and peak migration in the northeastern states in late May. In fall it is an early migrant, with many appearing south of the breeding range in the latter part of August.

Bill size, shape, and color. The bill is rather large for the size of the bird, looking broad at the base and with slightly convex outer edges. The lower mandible is entirely orange-yellow.

Size and shape. This small Empid often appears large-headed and short-tailed. Its crown usually looks smoothly rounded, only occasionally with a slight crested effect. Its wings show a moderate primary extension, which may emphasize the short-tailed look. Seen from the front or back, the tail looks narrow also.

Voice. Song, a rather hoarse *che-bunk,* without strong emphasis on either syllable; the second note seems to drop slightly in pitch. This is a softer vocalization than the snappy *che-beck* of Least Flycatcher, in which the second note is accented and higher-pitched. Yellow-bellied also gives a shorter, abrupt version of this song — *shlek* — sounding more one-syllabled. The most common call is a rising, whistled, two-syllabled *per-wee,* somewhat like one call of Eastern Wood-Pewee. This may be shortened to a rising *preee,* a *peer* on one pitch, or a sharper, decending *pyew.* Some of these may be similar to notes of Acadian Flycatcher, but most of the Yellow-bellied's calls have a more musical quality. Especially in migration and winter, Yellow-bellied often makes a note with a sharp, squeaky quality, *skweep!*

Plumage color. This species tends to look fairly uniform in its body plumage, not much paler below than above, although its wings show strong contrast. The upperparts are strongly washed green or olive. Despite the name (after all, most Empids have yellow bellies), the yellow *throat* is the most distinctive character among eastern Empids. This color is really a grayish yellow, or yellow washed over a pale gray background, and it does not contrast sharply with the sides of the head. The sides of the breast usually have a strong greenish olive wash. The eyering is usually conspicuous but narrow and of nearly even thickness all the way around. The wings are quite black, contrasting with the green back and setting off the wing bars and tertial edges in strong contrast.

Note the fairly long primary extension.

The four images above and right, all from June on the breeding grounds, show how much the apparent head shape can vary. Overall color can look dark and cold in shadow, washed out in sunlight. The yellow on the throat is often obscure.

(above and below) Two images of May migrants, showing compact shape, lack of contrast on face.

A closeup (hand-held) of a young bird in early September, with wing bars yellowish and buff, plumage fresh; adults at this season would be more worn and faded, as they molt after fall migration.

Variation in bill shape

Molt and seasonal variation. Adult Yellow-bellieds have a complete or incomplete prebasic molt in fall after arriving on the wintering grounds and a partial prealternate molt in early spring before they start north. They are in fresh plumage, with strongly contrasting wing bars and tertial edges, when they appear in North America as spring migrants, but by late summer (before they migrate south), adults can be so worn and faded that they look mostly gray and white, with narrow wing bars. Juveniles go through an incomplete preformative molt before they leave the nesting grounds, replacing the body plumage and some coverts; they look fresh in fall migration, with the wing bars appearing rich buff or a mix of yellowish white and buff.

Behavior. Yellow-bellied Flycatcher is usually found in the interior of dense woods, even in migration, so it is often difficult to observe. Generally it perches fairly low. It tends to be active, doing much flicking of the wings and tail.

Comparisons to other species. The most similar species are the members of the "Western Flycatcher" complex, which are usually separated from Yellow-bellied by range; see the discussion under that heading (p. 380). In the East, in late summer and fall, Yellow-bellied may be confused with Acadian Flycatcher (next), which is also very green-backed and can have a conspicuous yellow wash on the underparts, including the throat. Acadians with yellowish throats also might be seen in early spring (mostly before the arrival of Yellow-bellied, which is a late migrant). Acadian is a larger bird, with a larger bill (although Yellow-bellied also has a fairly large bill for its small size). The Acadian's primary extension is usually conspicuously longer, and Acadian also has a longer and broader tail. When Acadian does have yellow on the throat, it is usually a clear, pale yellow, subtly different from the grayish yellow tones of Yellow-bellied.

ACADIAN FLYCATCHER is the characteristic Empid of the southeastern U.S., barely extending north into extreme southeastern Canada (southern Ontario).

Bill size, shape, and color. The Acadian has the largest bill, on average, of any Empid: long and broad (especially broad at the base), with slightly convex outer edges. The lower mandible is almost always entirely pinkish yellow.

ACADIAN FLYCATCHER

Two figures from May showing typical head shape, contrasting wing bars, gray legs, very narrow eye-ring, overall pale color.

Only a few spring birds show as much yellow below and so much buff on the wing bars as the bird at left.

A May bird. In sunlight the green tones may be faint but the lack of contrast on the face remains obvious.

Looking up at this April bird, the bill shape and primary extension are noticeable.

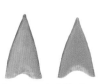

Variation in bill shape

A closeup (hand-held) of a bird in early June. The green tones are obvious here, as are the large bill with pale lower mandible and the very narrow eye-ring.

Size and shape. This is a large Empid with a large bill and long wings. Its primary projection averages longer than that of any other member of the genus, and its tail looks wide. The forehead and fore part of the crown look flat, often sloping up gradually to a point or corner at the rear edge of the crown, but the crown also can look low and smoothly rounded toward the rear.

Voice. Song, an explosive and loud *peet-sah!* or *peet-sup!,* variably accented on the first or second syllable or with equal emphasis on both. The most common call is a loud but flat *peek!,* usually reminiscent of the first note of the song, but sometimes given more quietly. Also frequently heard on the nesting grounds is a whistled *wheer* or *pr-prr-wheer,* with many variations, and a soft, long-running twittering. There is also a dawn song, given by males before sunrise, consisting of *peet-sah!* notes interspersed with sharp *seets* and other notes, all given very rapidly. A flight song, given in the evening, involves a rapid series of short notes delivered from a high perch and then in a brief flight.

Plumage color. Acadian could be characterized as very green above and very pale below. Uniformly greenish olive from the crown to the rump, it fades into a slightly paler and brighter green in the malar area of the face. Even though the throat is white, it does not contrast sharply with the face because of this pale green malar area, which is one of the most obvious visual marks for the species. The underparts show a faint olive breast band and a faint yellowish wash on the belly. The wings show strong contrast, with very blackish ground color setting off the buffy wing bars and tertial edges. The eye-ring is usually very narrow and rather sharply defined, but it can be faint on some individuals.

Molt and seasonal variation. The description above applies to spring Acadians. By midsummer, adults usually look very whitish below, and their wing bars usually have become whitish and very narrow. Unlike other eastern Empids, adult Acadians will go through a complete molt in late summer before they leave the breeding grounds; they will be in fresh plumage (with yellow wing bars and a yellow wash on the underparts) in fall migration, but they rapidly depart from North America as soon as their molt is completed.

Juveniles are very distinctive when they first fledge, rich greenish olive above with conspicuous buff tips to many feathers on the crown, nape, back, and wing coverts, forming a *scaled* effect. Their underparts may be lightly washed yellow, and they have rich buff wing bars. These birds go through a partial molt before they migrate, losing the buff-scaled look on the upperparts but not replacing most wing feathers; in fall migration they still have buff wing bars and their underparts may be strongly washed with yellow, often including the throat.

Leg and mouth lining color. Although these points are seldom apparent in the field, it's worth noting that Acadian Flycatcher has *gray* legs (not blackish like those of most Empids) and that its mouth lining is usually pale yellowish to pale pinkish yellow (brighter orange to orange-yellow in most Empids).

Behavior. Acadian usually gives an impression of lethargy, doing very little flicking of the wings and tail except when excited. It often perches with the wings drooped somewhat. Generally it stays inside forested areas, where it may perch low at times but often perches quite high, near the canopy of the trees.

Comparisons to other species. In the fall, when many Acadians are washed with yellow below, they may be confused with Yellow-bellied Flycatcher; see the discussion under that species (p. 358). Acadian is very similar in structure to Willow and Alder flycatchers. It can be especially close in appearance to the "classic" Alder, which has strong green tones above. However, Acadian usually has a longer primary extension. Its face is paler than that of Willow or Alder, and it usually contrasts much less with the white throat, partly because the lower part of its face (in the malar region) is washed with a pale green. The Acadian's call, a loud, flat *peek!,* is very different from the *whit* of Willow Flycatcher and recognizably different from the *kep* of Alder Flycatcher.

ALDER FLYCATCHER and Willow Flycatcher were regarded as constituting just one species, called "Traill's Flycatcher," until the 1970s. They are now known to be clearly distinct species, even though they are often difficult to distinguish. Their breeding ranges overlap in a narrow band of southern Canada and the northeastern U.S., but only the Alder extends north as a breeder into north-central Canada and Alaska. Virtually all of these northern breeders, even those from Alaska, apparently take a migratory route that passes through the eastern U.S., as Alder Flycatcher is very rare (or at least very rarely detected) south of Canada in the West.

Bill size, shape, and color. This is another species in which the bill is wide and may seem to have a slightly convex edge. The lower mandible usually is entirely yellowish pink but sometimes has a small dusky area at the tip.

Size and shape. Alder Flycatcher is a large Empid with a fairly heavy bill and a long primary extension. The tail is of only moderate length, but it often looks noticeably broad compared to the tails of smaller Empids. The head can look smoothly rounded or slightly peaked.

Voice. The songs of Alder and Willow flycatchers are similar enough that a casual or sloppy description could apply to either one, which is part of the reason why the distinction between the species was overlooked for so long. To really understand the differences, it would be worthwhile to read the descriptions in this book while listening to recordings (or to the birds themselves).

The song of Alder Flycatcher, harsh and burry, is often written as *fee-bee-oh,* but it seldom sounds clearly three-syllabled. It might be better written as *rrree-BEEP.* A faint third syllable, as in *rrree-BEEEo,* may be audible, especially at close range. The song is strongly accented on the *second* syllable, which sounds both louder and slightly higher-pitched than the first. At times the song is shortened to an ascending *rrreep!* The typical callnote is a flat *kep,* reminiscent of a distant Downy or Ladder-backed woodpecker, or the single note of a Western Kingbird. Another call, perhaps given mainly in alarm, is a thin *weeoo* with a wheezy quality. Occasionally a bird will give the *kep* note immediately followed by the *weeoo,* and this can sound superficially like the *FITZ-bew* song of Willow Flycatcher. For detailed comparison of the voices of Alder and Willow flycatchers, see pp. 364–366.

Plumage color. The most consistent plumage character of Alder (and Willow) is the white throat, contrasting noticeably with the face and usually contrasting somewhat with a faint breastband (but very few Alder/Willow flycatchers have the throat washed with pale yellow). The underparts are generally quite pale. In fresh plumage, Alder tends to be strongly washed with olive on the upperparts and has clear gray tones on the face. Its eye-ring varies from conspicuous (but narrow) to virtually absent. Although the wings are very dark, the contrast in the wing pattern may be lessened by the fact that the wing bars and tertial edgings are often somewhat dull, so the wings may not look as sharply contrasting as in some other "eastern" Empids.

Molt and seasonal variation. These birds are in fresh plumage during spring migration. By the time of fall migration, adult Alders (and Willows) are in worn plumage. Their wing bars, and their eye-rings if any, may be much reduced by wear, and the color of their upperparts will be very drab. Juveniles are somewhat fresher in fall, with buff wing bars, more yellow on the belly, and slightly more color on the upperparts,

These images of June adults convey the shape and overall color. The wing bars are off-white, showing only moderate contrast.

The very pale appearance of the underparts is typical.

As shown on this early June bird, the eye-ring is usually distinct but very narrow, so it may not be obvious at a distance.

On this late June bird, the wing bars are worn and whitish, and are already becoming quite narrow.

A closeup (hand-held) of a bird in late July. The wing bars have faded to white, so in an odd effect, they actually contrast somewhat more than in fresh plumage.

Variation in bill shape

363

but these colors are fading rapidly on these young birds. Both adults and juveniles molt after arriving on the wintering grounds. At least some of the birds may have their most extensive molt in late winter, just before spring migration.

Behavior. Alder (and Willow) Flycatchers tend to be relatively sedate, doing little flicking of the wings or tail except immediately after landing on a perch. Both species breed in habitats that are relatively open or of short stature, such as groves of alders or willows; in migration they tend to be found in similarly semi-open areas, not inside dense forest.

Comparisons to other species. Acadian Flycatcher can be quite similar, as discussed under that species. The most similar species by far is Willow Flycatcher, discussed in detail next.

WILLOW FLYCATCHER and Alder Flycatcher make up one of the most difficult species pairs among North American birds. With experience, they can be consistently separated by voice, but silent birds are almost impossible to name with confidence. Even in the hand, silent birds often have to be identified as "Traill's Flycatcher," the name applied to this complex before they were formally split in 1973.

Bill size, shape, and color. Essentially identical to that of Alder Flycatcher, the bill is wide and may seem to have a slightly convex edge. The lower mandible usually is entirely yellowish pink but sometimes has a small dusky area at the tip. Willow averages very slightly longer-billed than Alder, but there is much overlap and this is useless as a field mark.

Size and shape. Willow Flycatcher is essentially identical in shape to Alder Flycatcher, a large Empid with a large bill and a medium-length but broad-looking tail. Western subspecies of Willow show a slightly shorter primary projection.

Voice. The song is harsh and burry — a rough *FITZ-bew* or *FRITZ-beyew*. Like the song of Alder Flycatcher, this may sound vaguely three-syllabled. However, Willow Flycatcher puts the accent on the *first* syllable, and the second syllable seems to drop slightly in pitch; in Alder Flycatcher's song, as mentioned under that species, the second syllable is emphasized and seems to sound higher-pitched. Willow also gives a song in which the first note is not so strongly accented, which could be written *fizzz-bew;* in this variation, the first syllable still sounds stron-

These two figures are of eastern Willows in May. Visually they are extremely similar to Alder Flycatcher.

As with Alder, the wing bars are off-white and dull (but less so than on western races of Willow).

This is a juvenile of one of the western races of Willow in early September. The wing bars are deep buff. Those of adults would be faded to grayish white and very narrow or obscure at this season.

This juvenile western Willow in October is superficially similar to a wood-pewee.

An adult western Willow (probably *E. t. extimus*) in May.

Variation in bill shape

ger than the second, but not by much, and this could be confused with the normal song of Alder by birders who lack experience with the latter. At times the song of Willow is shortened to a strong *rrrip!*, dangerously similar to the *rreep!* of Alder. Willow also gives a softer *weeoo*. The typical callnote is a sharp, thick *whit!*, very different from Alder's call. It is easier to hear the difference than to describe it, but the *whit!* of Willow gives the impression of a rising pitch and the most sharply accented consonant on the end, whereas the *kep* of Alder is accented or emphasized at the beginning and may seem to drop slightly in pitch.

There is also a flight song, consisting of a rapid series of *wheet* notes and *fitz-bew* songs, usually given at dusk.

Comparing typical songs of Alder and Willow flycatchers

rrree - BEEEo

Alder Flycatcher: accent is on the higher-pitched second syllable; this note drops toward the end, creating the impression of a faint third syllable.

FITZ - beeyew

Willow Flycatcher: the first syllable is sharply accented, and the burry second note drops noticeably in pitch. The first syllable is sometimes replaced by a softer, more slurred note, however.

Plumage color. Eastern populations of Willow Flycatcher are extremely similar to Alder Flycatcher, so they are described here only by comparison to that species. Eastern Willows tend to be slightly browner (less greenish) in the tone of the back. The head tends to be slightly paler gray, and the lower part of the face is often paler, so that there is less direct contrast against the white throat. These eastern Willows also tend to have slightly duller wing bars at a given stage of wear and less obvious eye-rings than Alders. However, all of these points are variable among individuals, and even taken in combination, they are usually not enough to allow identification of silent birds.

Geographic variation in Willow Flycatcher. Unlike most Empids, Willow Flycatcher shows a substantial amount of regional variation. The birds breeding east of the Rockies (comprising one or two subspecies) are as described above, and very similar to Alder Flycatcher. The birds farther west, generally divided into three subspecies, differ from eastern Willows in several respects. They tend to be browner above, they are less likely to show obvious eye-rings, their wing bars are generally duller and contrast less with the ground color of the wings, and the edgings of the tertials and secondaries are duller and show less contrast. Within the western population, those nesting nearest the Pacific Coast, from southwestern British Columbia to southwestern California, tend to be darkest and brownest (subspecies *brewsteri*). Those of the Great Basin region, from southeastern British Columbia southward, east of the Sierras and west of the Rockies, tend to be somewhat more olive and paler (subspecies *adastus*). Those of the Southwest, nesting very locally along rivers from southeastern California to western New Mexico and north into southwestern Utah (and possibly farther north in the lowlands), are treated as an endangered subspecies ("Southwestern Willow Flycatcher," *E. t. extimus*). This form is paler than birds of the other western populations, especially on the head and chest, and the song is recognizably different from those of other Willow Flycatchers, with the last syllable (*beew*) more drawn out.

Comparisons to other species. The extreme similarity of eastern Willow Flycatchers to Alder Flycatchers cannot be stressed enough. Many individuals cannot be identified even in the hand, even by reference to formulae based on careful measurements, so obviously such birds could not be identified in the field if they were silent. The differences mentioned above under "plumage color" should be considered in that light. With enough experience, eastern birders may be able to call typical individuals "probable Alder" or "probable Willow" on the basis of appearance and upgrade the "probable" to "confirmed" if the bird gives any vocalization.

Western Willow Flycatchers are more distinct, and an experienced western birder can usually identify them by appearance, especially since Alder Flycatcher is rare south of Canada in the West. However, if a bird suggesting Alder is found in the West, identifying it with certainty would involve ruling out the possibility of a stray eastern Willow Flycatcher. Such a bird probably could not be documented without recording its voice or mist-netting it for careful measurement.

An additional challenge in identifying Willow Flycatcher, especially in the West, is the necessity of ruling out the wood-pewees. The latter have noticeably longer wingtips, and seen from below they have narrower bills. But the relatively dull wing bars and obscure eye-ring of Willow Flycatcher can make it superficially much like a wood-pewee, and birders must keep this in mind to avoid being thrown off.

LEAST FLYCATCHER is the most numerous migrant Empid through most of eastern North America and is found locally in the northwest as well. As a vagrant it may occur anywhere in the west.

Bill size, shape, and color. Least is intermediate in bill width between the "wide" and "narrow" types and is also short-billed, so it looks smaller-billed than other eastern species. Its lower mandible is mostly or entirely orange-yellow, sometimes with an ill-defined dusky tip.

Size and shape. As the name implies, this is a small and compact bird. Its head often looks rounded and proportionately large. The primary extension usually looks short. When viewed from the front or the back, the tail looks narrow.

Voice. Song: a sharp, snappy *che-beck,* the second syllable sounding a little higher-pitched and more emphatic. The song may be repeated many times at an interval of less than one second when the bird is excited. Both male and female are known to give this song. Call: a thin, dry *whit* or *pit.* In aggressive encounters, a series of thin *weep* notes. There is also a flight song that involves *weep* notes and *che-beck*s as well as other notes in rapid succession; usually performed in late evening, the flight song may last more than half a minute.

Plumage color. Least Flycatchers are a fairly uniform brownish gray on the upperparts, usually somewhat darker brown on the forehead and washed with olive on the back. The throat is whitish or off-white (not bright white), contrasting with the darker face and with the gray-brown wash crossing the chest. The white eye-ring is usually of fairly even thickness, well defined and conspicuous. Contrast on the wings is usually obvious, with blackish ground color setting off white wing bars and tertial edgings.

Molt and seasonal variation. Adult Least Flycatchers appear very worn by late summer, drab above and very pale below, with narrow wing bars. They may begin to molt a few feathers before they leave the nesting grounds, but their departure is quite early: most adults are gone from North America before September, and they complete most of their prebasic molt after arriving on the wintering grounds. Juveniles go through a limited preformative molt, mostly before leaving the nesting grounds; they don't replace wing feathers in this molt, so in fall migration they still have rich buff wing bars, brighter and much wider than the wing bars of adults in fall.

Least Flycatchers also have a spring (prealternate) molt that involves

Two images of adults in May to show typical colors of fairly fresh spring birds as well as features of shape.

Three images of birds in May. The wings always show strong contrast but the wing bars can be tinged tan or yellow on fresh plumage.

A November bird, judged to be young by the deep buff of the wing bars.

Variation in bill shape

much of the body plumage and a variable number of coverts, so the wing bars often look broad and fresh on spring migrants. This molt is mostly completed before the birds start northward, but some young birds in migration are still in the latter stages of molt; they may have a disheveled appearance about the head, perhaps with a less conspicuous eye-ring than usual.

Behavior. Least Flycatcher tends to be active, often changing perches. It tends to do a lot of flicking of the wings and tail, jerking the tail strongly upward and often flicking the wings at the same time. It will also flick the tail downward at times, in a quick down-up motion, faster than the exaggerated tail-dipping of Gray Flycatcher.

Comparisons to other species. For birders in the East, Least Flycatcher often will be the most common Empid, and it serves as a good point of comparison. Of the other eastern species, only Willow Flycatcher has a similar *whit* callnote. Compared to Willow, Alder, and Acadian, the typical Least may be recognized by its smaller size, smaller bill (both shorter and slightly narrower proportionately), shorter primary extension, and more prominent eye-ring.

Yellow-bellied Flycatcher (p. 356) is similar to Least in size and shape but usually differs in its much stronger green and yellow tones. On some worn adult Yellow-bellieds in late summer and fall, however, these colors may be much reduced; the birds may even look grayish white below. Such birds may still be separated from Leasts by their proportionately larger bills and by their calls, and they will usually show less contrast between the face and the grayish white throat.

HAMMOND'S FLYCATCHER is a western species that was often confused with Dusky Flycatcher in the past. Their breeding ranges overlap extensively, but Hammond's generally breeds in higher-elevation habitats, and it also extends much farther north in summer.

Bill size, shape, and color. The bill of Hammond's is narrow, straight-sided, and usually very short, the smallest bill (in proportion to overall size) of any Empid. The lower mandible is usually at least two-thirds dark, fading to dull dusky yellow or pinkish yellow at the base. Many Hammond's Flycatchers look entirely dark-billed in the field, and some (mainly young birds) can be mostly pale on the lower mandible, even to the extent of having the entire mandible pale orange. In both shape and color, the bill of Hammond's seems to be more variable than the bills of other Empids.

HAMMOND'S FLYCATCHER

The small bill contributes to the "punched in" look of the face.

This April bird still has a fair amount of color and distinct whitish wing bars.

Some adults in May can look very worn already.

A May adult. In shadow, the species looks very dingy and dark.

Another May bird showing much less wear.

Molting before fall migration, the bird looks very fresh in September.

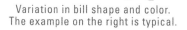

Variation in bill shape and color. The example on the right is typical.

Size and shape. Hammond's is a small Empid that tends to look compact overall, with a short tail, short neck, large head, and very short bill. Its head sometimes looks smoothly rounded, but more often it shows a squared-off "corner" at the back of the crown. Typically the primary extension is notably long for the size of the bird, and this contributes to the impression that the tail is short.

Voice. The song is variable but made up of three basic elements. First is a dry, rapid *chi-pit* or *tse-brrk,* sharply two-syllabled. When this element of the song is given by itself (which may happen often on the breeding grounds, especially late in the season), it can strongly suggest the *che-bek* of Least Flycatcher. The second element is a rough, low-pitched *brrrk.* The third element is similar but is vaguely two-syllabled and rises in pitch: *gurrrip!* When all three song elements are used, the usual sequence is *chi-pit . . . brrrk . . . gurrrip! . . .* with noticeable pauses between elements. More often, however, the bird gives only one or two of the elements, or it may repeat elements or give them in a different sequence.

The songs of Hammond's and Dusky flycatchers often have been confused, partly because of imprecise descriptions. Here are some differences to listen for. The first element of Hammond's is more sharply two-syllabled; the second element of Hammond's is lower-pitched and rougher than any song element of Dusky; the third part of Hammond's (the ascending note) is somewhat like the second element of Dusky's song, but sounds lower-pitched and shorter; and the song of Hammond's rarely or never includes a note like the high-pitched clear *pweet* in the song of Dusky (although Hammond's does give an isolated call-note that is clear and high-pitched).

Comparing typical songs of Hammond's and Dusky flycatchers

chi-pit . . . brrrk . . . gurrrip!

Hammond's Flycatcher: first element clearly two-syllabled, second one very low and rough. Most songs have only one or two of these elements, not all three.

chrip . . . ggrrreep . . . pweet

Dusky Flycatcher: first element slurred; last one high-pitched and clear. Sequence of elements in songs is quite variable. Both species have long pauses between notes.

The call heard most frequently at all seasons is a sharp *peep* or *peek,* similar to the call of a Pygmy Nuthatch or the single note of a Long-billed Dowitcher, and utterly unlike the common call of Dusky Flycatcher. Hammond's also gives a soft, descending whistled note and a soft, burry *fee-zhee;* both of these seem to be heard mainly on the breeding grounds.

Plumage color. Hammond's is relatively dark, and in fresh plumage it is relatively "colorful" for an Empid. The back is a fairly dark olive-gray, and although this color extends up onto the nape, the face is more gray and less olive, looking blue-gray in fresh plumage. The white eye-ring is usually conspicuous, well defined, and thicker behind the eye. No sharp contrast separates the face from the throat, which always looks gray. The breast is olive-gray or brownish gray, usually dark, especially toward the sides. The belly is pale to fairly bright lemon-yellow. Often the dark color of the breast extends down the sides and flanks, creating a "vested" look. The dusky gray wings have wing bars and tertial edges that look quite buffy in fresh plumage (fall and winter), fading toward dull white in spring and summer.

Molt and seasonal variation. Adults go through a complete molt in late summer, from late June or July to late August or September, before they leave the breeding grounds. Juveniles have a partial molt, replacing the body plumage, and this molt is also completed before their southward migration. Thus all Hammond's Flycatchers are in very fresh plumage during fall migration, with buffy wing bars, fairly bright yellow on the belly and dark olive-gray on the chest, and contrast between the gray head and olive back.

In late winter, before they start their spring migration, Hammond's Flycatchers go through a partial molt, involving mainly body plumage but also often including a variable number of coverts and tertials. This molt is more extensive in some individuals than others, so some spring Hammond's are in visibly fresher plumage than others.

Behavior. Hammond's tends to be active, flicking the tail frequently and often flicking the wings at the same time. This species has a very distinctive callnote; but, more than most Empids, it may remain frustratingly silent for long periods.

Comparisons to other species. The similarity between Hammond's and Dusky flycatchers is notorious. Only a few decades ago, it was a standing joke that no one had a sure-fire way to tell these two apart, even on the breeding grounds. We have come a long way since then, and many individuals can be separated quickly and confidently, but others remain extremely difficult to identify when they are silent.

Their songs are distinctive, but it requires careful concentration to hear the differences (see above, under "Voice"). Their common call-notes are also diagnostic, as the sharp *peep* of Hammond's is quite unlike the *whit* of Dusky.

Visually they are more challenging. There are structural clues that are helpful for typical birds. The Dusky's bill averages longer, with a less extensive dark area at the tip of the lower mandible. The Dusky has a slightly longer tail on average, emphasized by the fact that its primary extension averages much shorter than that of Hammond's.

Plumage color is very helpful for separating these two *in early fall,* because Hammond's molts before migrating south, so it is in very fresh plumage at that season. Dusky molts after migrating south, so in early fall Duskies look fairly pale and somewhat worn (juveniles) or very worn and drab (adults). By early winter, when a handful of these species can be found in the southwest, the Dusky is the fresher bird, but the distinction is less obvious. In spring and summer, Hammond's and Dusky are extremely similar in plumage color, although Hammond's may tend to be slightly darker on the face and chest.

Typical individuals may be separated by the combination of bill size and primary extension, and plumage color can be helpful for much of the year. However, this is true only for typical birds, and there is much variation in both species; many individuals will appear somewhat intermediate, and even a very experienced birder should not try to identify such birds without hearing their voices.

GRAY FLYCATCHER breeds mostly in the Great Basin region of the west and winters in the lowlands of the southwest. Although it seems very plain at first glance, its behavior, shape, and coloration make this one of the most distinctive members of the genus.

Bill size, shape, and color. Of the species with narrow, straight-sided bills, this one is on average the longest-billed (although some Grays overlap in bill shape with some Dusky Flycatchers). The lower mandible is mostly pale with a small well-defined dark area at the tip.

Size and shape. Gray Flycatcher is noticeably long-billed and long-tailed. The long bill often makes the head look proportionately small, and the crown usually looks smoothly rounded. The primary extension is fairly short for the size of the bird. Young birds in late summer can be visibly shorter-billed and shorter-tailed than adults.

Birds in November (left) and January (right), pale and gray even in fresh plumage.

Note the long-tailed and long-billed look.

Two images of adults in June on the breeding grounds. While most Empids become grayer in worn plumage, this species may tend to look more dusty brown, less purely gray, when worn. By late summer the wing bars can be essentially worn away.

This young bird in September shows wide buff wing bars, gray color overall.

Variation in bill shape

Voice. The song is a simple, uneven repetition of two elements. Given most frequently is an emphatic two-syllabled note with a low-pitched, almost chirping sound, *chuwip*. A higher-pitched, weaker *teeah* is tossed in at irregular intervals. The typical callnote is a dry *wit* or *pit*, perhaps thinner or with less of an initial "wh" sound than the calls of Least or Willow flycatchers. The female Gray's call is slightly lower than the male's, and this can be heard when members of a pair are both calling on territory. Additional calls include a soft *wheea* and a short rattling trill. The male is reported to have a flight song as well, consisting of a rapid series of notes, more complicated toward the end.

Plumage color. Gray Flycatcher generally looks paler than any other Empid (except the very different Buff-breasted). The upperparts and face are medium gray, with a faint olive wash on the back but not on the head. Although the white eye-ring is well defined, it may not contrast noticeably because the head is not very dark. The throat is very pale gray — sometimes nearly white — but there is no sharp separation in color between the throat and the sides of the head. The breast is pale to medium gray, usually with a slight olive tinge. The belly is a very pale yellow and may look white in the field. The dusky gray wings have dull whitish wing bars and tertial edges. The tail is very dark gray with a contrasting white outer vane to the outermost pair of tail feathers.

Molt and seasonal variation. Adults go through a complete molt in fall, after arriving on the wintering grounds. Juveniles have a partial molt, mostly involving body plumage, which may begin in late summer near breeding areas but is mostly completed after fall migration. Thus all Gray Flycatchers are in fresh plumage in early winter.

During the summer, as the plumage becomes more worn, adult Grays become slightly paler and plainer: the shades of yellow below and olive on the back and chest fade even further, but the clean gray areas of the plumage may take on a brownish tinge. The wing bars and tertial edges become narrow and inconspicuous.

Behavior. The tail-dipping behavior of Gray Flycatcher is the most distinctive behavioral trait of any Empid. This movement begins with a rapid, very slight upward twitch of the tail, followed by a slower, emphasized downward swing, after which the tail is raised to its original position, the whole action recalling a phoebe rather than any other Empidonax. Some other species, such as Least Flycatcher, sometimes flick the tail down-up instead of up-down, but these are still tail flicks almost too rapid for the eye to follow.

This species is relatively inactive, often dipping the tail but only infrequently flicking the wings. When foraging, the Gray tends to perch low and often flies down to take insects on or near the ground. (Many other Empids will do this at times, especially in cold weather when insects are relatively inactive.)

Comparisons to other species. The Gray Flycatcher is unlikely to be mistaken for others in the field, although Dusky Flycatcher (next) can be very similar in the hand.

DUSKY FLYCATCHER is a western species that is often identified mainly by elimination rather than by any distinctive feature of its own. Superficially it seems intermediate between Hammond's and Gray flycatchers in structure, plumage, and nesting habitat.

Bill size, shape, and color. The Dusky's bill is straight-sided, narrow, and of medium length (averaging between those of the short-billed Hammond's and the long-billed Gray). The lower mandible is usually extensively pale at the base, fading gradually toward the dark tip.

Size and shape. This is a medium-sized Empid with a medium-length narrow bill and a medium-long tail. The primary extension is short for the size of the bird, and this contributes to the impression that the bird is longer-tailed than Hammond's Flycatcher. Like all Empids, of course, it is variable in measurements, and some individuals can look as short-billed as the typical Hammond's or as long-billed as the typical Gray, so first impressions of shape can be deceiving. Its head can appear rounded, slightly bushy, or square-crested.

Voice. The song is variable in pattern but has three basic elements. The first is a short, medium-pitched *chrip*, rising slightly and sounding vaguely two-syllabled. Second is a rough note, *ggrrreep*, starting on a low pitch and slurring upward. Third is a clear, high-pitched *pweet*. The usual song sequence is *chrip . . . ggrrreep . . . pweet* or *chrip . . . ggrrreep . . . chrip . . . pweet*. Song elements may be left out or repeated out of sequence. See the detailed voice description under Hammond's Flycatcher (p. 372) for a comparison of the songs of these two.

The callnote is a dry *pit* or *whit*. The female's call is slightly lower than the male's, and the difference is apparent when both members of a pair are calling on the breeding grounds in summer. At that season, males also sometimes give a plaintive, *dew, dew-hic*, especially in the late morning and in the evening.

Plumage color. Dusky Flycatcher is drab for much of the year. The throat is pale gray but often looks whitish in bright light. The back is washed with olive but shows little apparent contrast against the gray head, and the wing bars usually do not contrast strongly. Although the eye-ring is white and well developed, it is not always conspicuous, because the head is not very dark. A pale area on the lores is often more pronounced on Dusky than on other Empids.

Molt and seasonal variation. Dusky Flycatcher molts in fall after arriving on the wintering grounds — a complete molt in adults, a partial one (mostly body plumage) in juveniles. During fall migration, adults are worn and drab, mostly gray above and whitish below, with narrow whitish wing bars. Juveniles at that season are slightly more colorful, with more buff on the wing bars, yellow on the belly, and olive on the back, but these colors are fading rapidly as late summer turns to fall.

In early winter (when few remain north of the Mexican border), the freshly molted Duskies are in their most "colorful" plumage of the year, with fairly bright pale yellow on the belly, olive on the back, olive-gray on the chest, and pale buff or yellowish wing bars. These colors are present but less pronounced on spring migrants. These birds will have undergone another partial molt in late winter, more extensive on some birds than others, so individuals will vary in the brightness of their plumage in spring. The colors fade during late spring and summer, so by late summer and fall, adults can look exceedingly worn.

Behavior. Dusky tends to be slightly less active than Hammond's. It occasionally flicks the tail while perched but does not seem to flick the wings at the same time quite as often as Hammond's or Least flycatchers. This tendency is too variable to be used as a field mark.

Choice of nest sites is a fairly consistent difference between Dusky and Hammond's flycatchers. Dusky usually builds its nest within about 12 feet of the ground, while Hammond's usually nests much higher. On the breeding grounds, Dusky also may be found singing and foraging in very open situations, while Hammond's spends more time surrounded by dense vegetation.

In summer, Hammond's, Dusky, and Gray flycatchers may all be found nesting in the same general regions, but they separate out by elevation and habitat. Hammond's is at the highest elevations, mostly in coniferous forest, although sometimes

adult Dusky Flycatcher
at the nest, in June

Two views of May birds, the one at left showing a moderate amount of color and distinct wing bars.

These July adults, worn and drab, might be separated from Hammond's only by structure and voice. By early fall, their wing bars may be essentially worn away and the plumage may look gray all over.

On this juvenile Dusky in September, the wing bars are buff and fairly distinct, and the plumage shows a moderate amount of color. But it is a much duller bird overall than Hammond's at the same season.

Variation in bill shape and pattern

it will be in pure aspen stands. Dusky is at slightly lower elevations in the mountains, in habitat with a mixture of tall trees and lower brush; coniferous forest with a brushy understory will meet its needs, and so will open chaparral with scattered taller trees. Gray Flycatcher favors still lower elevations, mostly arid sagebrush plains with scattered taller trees, also open woodlands of pinyon pine and juniper with scattered sagebrush.

Comparisons to other species. Hammond's Flycatcher is by far the most similar species, but the Dusky's lack of distinctive characters makes it subject to confusion with other Empids as well. Separation from Least Flycatcher can be a challenge if either species strays out of range, since both have similar *whit* notes and they can be fairly similar in plumage color. Least tends to have a slightly whiter throat, shorter tail, and more contrast in the wings. Its bill is proportionately wider, and it usually has an entirely pale lower mandible. Still, reports of Least Flycatcher in the West, or especially of Dusky Flycatcher in the East, must be documented carefully.

"WESTERN FLYCATCHER" complex:
PACIFIC-SLOPE FLYCATCHER
CORDILLERAN FLYCATCHER

In the late 1980s, the widespread Western Flycatcher was formally split into two species. The split created immediate problems for field observers, because the two resulting forms, Pacific-slope Flycatcher and Cordilleran Flycatcher, are frequently impossible to distinguish in the field. There are also lingering questions as to whether the split might have been premature. Regardless, I strongly recommend that birders continue to use the term "Western Flycatcher" for any bird in this complex that has not been identified with certainty.

The forms now classified as Pacific-slope Flycatcher nest from southeastern Alaska south through western British Columbia and the Pacific states to Baja. Cordilleran Flycatcher nests from Alberta, eastern Oregon, and northeastern California east to the Rockies and south to mainland Mexico. The studies that led to the formal split of these two were based on a limited area of northeastern California where the two come in contact. More recent studies, however, have shown that there is a broad hybrid zone between the two in southwestern Canada, occupying much of southern British Columbia and southwestern Alberta.

Away from these overlap zones, the two forms can be identified by range on the breeding grounds. During migration, however, Pacific-

Two views of adults in April. The crested look and the shape of the eye-ring are good marks for the "Western Flycatcher" complex.

A juvenile in September, with rich buff wing bars.

An adult in May. Drab birds like this one, with relatively little color, might be examples of the race *E. d. insulicola,* breeding on California's Channel Islands.

A juvenile in October, with the color of the wing bars beginning to fade.

Typical bill shapes of three populations

Cordilleran Flycatcher

Pacific-slope Flycatcher

Channel Islands race of Pacific-slope

381

slope Flycatcher spreads well to the east of its nesting range; in the low-lands of the southwest, it is actually a more common migrant than the Cordilleran Flycatcher that nests in the local mountains. Virtually all of the "Western Flycatchers" seen along the Pacific Coast are likely to be Pacific-slope Flycatchers, but stray Cordillerans there would probably go undetected most of the time.

Although I illustrate examples of both forms, this text will combine the two under the name Western Flycatcher, and I will mention the two component species only where they differ.

Bill size, shape, and color. The bill is wide and the lower mandible is entirely yellow-orange to pinkish. This color is usually fairly bright and conspicuous in the field. Cordilleran averages larger-billed than Pacific-slope. The population of Pacific-slope Flycatchers nesting on California's Channel Islands, *E. d. insulicola,* averages longer-billed than the populations on the coast.

Size and shape. Western Flycatcher is a fairly small Empid, with the Cordilleran averaging slightly larger than the Pacific-slope. Its primary extension is usually fairly short. It may appear slightly long-tailed for its size, and its head usually shows a slight peak or crest at the back of the crown.

Voice. The song is variable but always very high-pitched and thin, usually a repetition of three parts with pauses in between; for example: *tseweep . . . pttsik . . . tseep . . . tseweep . . . pttsik . . . tseep . . .* No other western *Empidonax* song is so high-pitched and squeaky. There are slight average differences between the songs of the Pacific-slope and Cordilleran, with the latter sounding slightly lower-pitched. In Cordilleran, the *pttsik* note seems to drop in pitch (or to have the second half slightly lower than the first half), while in the Pacific-slope, the second part of this note is slightly higher, but it takes very careful listening to be able to detect this.

The common callnote of males is the best distinction between Pacific-slope and Cordilleran flycatchers. Pacific-slope males give a single, slurred, sharply ascending note: *peweat!* or *pseeyeap!* Cordilleran males give this call at about the same range of pitch, but make it sharply two-syllabled, with the second note higher: *pit-peet!* Unfortunately, male Cordillerans also give some short rising notes that can sound extremely similar to the typical call of the male Pacific-slope Flycatcher. Birds from the overlap zone in the interior of the northwest may give two or three types of callnotes. Males of the Channel Islands form give a callnote similar to that of Pacific-slopes from the main-

A notably fresh spring adult in May.

An adult in early June. The pale lower mandible is often very obvious.

Two views of adults in early June. Overall color varies. As in Pacific-slope Flycatcher, the eye-ring is thickest behind the eye.

An adult in late June, showing classic shape and head pattern.

An August adult showing a lot of wear on the plumage. By late summer the yellow in the plumage can be obscure.

land, but lacking the initial slurred sound and emphasizing the final rising *weet!* I am not aware of cases of "pure" Pacific-slope Flycatchers giving the clearly two-parted *pit-peet* call of Cordilleran, so this may be a safe characteristic for identification, but Cordillerans can sound very much like Pacific-slopes, and birds from the hybrid zone can sound like either form.

The most common note of females (of both forms) is a very thin, high-pitched *tseet*.

Plumage color. This is the only western Empid with yellow (dull pale yellow or grayish yellow) on the throat, and it also has strong olive-green or olive-brown tones on the upperparts. The breast is washed with dull brownish olive. The eye-ring is conspicuous, white or yellowish white, and usually has a distinctive shape: narrowed or even broken across the top of the eye, broadened (often to a point) behind the eye, for a teardrop or almond-shaped effect. The wings are dusky and the wing bars usually look dull whitish, without strong contrast.

There is virtually no difference in color between Pacific-slope and Cordilleran flycatchers. However, the Pacific-slopes nesting on the Channel Islands average duller, both grayer above and paler below.

Molt and seasonal variation. Fresh-plumaged juveniles in midsummer have noticeably buff wing bars. Adults at that season are becoming worn, and by late summer they may be very pale below — some show essentially no yellow on the throat in early fall. Western Flycatchers have their prebasic molt after arriving on their wintering grounds (a complete molt in adults, a partial but variable one in juveniles). Their prealternate molt occurs in late winter just before the birds migrate north; it tends to be slightly more extensive in Cordilleran Flycatcher, with more of the coverts being replaced.

Comparisons to other species. Its strong green and yellow tones will usually separate the Western from the other Empids in its range. But in late summer and fall, some Westerns have no visible yellow on the throat. To recognize such individuals, it is important to note the wide bill with pale lower mandible, appearance of the eye-ring, callnotes, and other points.

In winter in the southwest, inexperienced birders sometimes mistake Hammond's or Dusky flycatchers for Westerns because those species have conspicuous yellow on the belly at that season. However, the lack of yellow on the *throat* on these fresh-plumaged winter birds should eliminate confusion.

Much more difficult is separation of Western and Yellow-bellied flycatchers. Their normal ranges barely overlap. The nesting range of the Yellow-bellied extends very far west in Canada (to northern British Columbia and the southern Yukon Territory, and even locally into eastern Alaska), but it is mostly north of the range of the Western Flycatcher. Yellow-bellieds from these far western populations apparently all migrate well east of the Rockies before they turn southward. On the western Great Plains, there is a gap where neither species is expected. But stray Westerns and Yellow-bellieds do turn up out of range, creating major challenges for birders.

Callnotes provide the best distinction. Overall colors differ slightly; Yellow-bellied has stronger green tones, while Western tends toward duller green above and more buffy or brownish yellow below. Yellow-bellied tends to have blacker wings, setting off the wing bars and tertial edges in sharper contrast. The eye-ring tends to be more teardrop-shaped in Western and of more even thickness in Yellow-bellied, but this is highly variable. Finally, Western tends to be slightly longer-tailed and to have more of a peak on the crown (Yellow-bellied may look more round-headed or bushy-headed). All of these points are variable, subtle, and hard to detect without direct comparison.

Separating vagrant Pacific-slope and Cordilleran flycatchers out of range may not be possible without capturing the birds and measuring them in the hand. There are a number of eastern records of Pacific-slope Flycatchers, but those that are based only on the typical male callnotes might be considered less than certain, given the known variation in these callnotes in Cordillerans and hybrids.

BUFF-BREASTED FLYCATCHER is our smallest and most distinctively colored *Empidonax*. A specialty of mountains near the Mexican border, it does not usually pose a challenge in identification.

Bill size, shape, and color. The bill is fairly short, and it is intermediate in shape between the wide-billed and narrow-billed categories. The lower mandible is entirely yellow or pinkish yellow.

Size and shape. This tiny bird has a rather short tail that may appear deeply notched at the tip. The primary extension is fairly long for the small size of the bird. Usually the crown looks smoothly rounded, often with a slight peak or corner at the rear edge of the crown, just above the nape.

Voice. The song is a rather musical *chee-bit*, with the second note lower than the first, often followed by a few soft notes or a short trill. Sometimes the second syllable is sharper and higher-pitched than the first: *chee-beet!* The typical call is a short, dry *pit* or *pt.*

Plumage color. Pale and dusty brownish overall. The head is pale enough that it does not contrast strongly with the eye-ring, which is whitish and often pointed at the rear edge; the only strong "pattern" on the face is the contrast of the dark eye. The throat is whitish, the breast is washed with pale buff, and the belly is buffy white to yellowish white. The wings are noticeably darker than the dusty brown of the back, but not blackish like those of some eastern Empids, and the whitish wing bars and tertial edgings are not sharply contrasted. The tail shows conspicuously white outer vanes to the outer tail feathers.

Molt and seasonal variation. Adult Buff-breasted Flycatchers are in fairly fresh plumage when they arrive in the southwest in early spring. They may become very worn and drab by midsummer, to the extent that the buff wash on the breast virtually disappears. They then undergo a complete molt on the breeding grounds in late summer. Patchy, molting birds might be seen in August, and very fresh-plumaged birds might be seen at the end of August or in early September, just before they leave the United States. By midsummer, fresh juveniles are being seen in the same areas as worn or molting adults, and these young birds will also undergo a partial molt before they migrate south.

Behavior. This is a fairly active bird of open pine woods, usually singing from high perches but foraging at all levels, including close to the ground. The Buff-breasted usually pumps its tail several times just after alighting, but otherwise it does not show much tail motion or wing flicking.

Comparisons to other species. Buff-breasted Flycatcher is unlikely to be confused with any other species. The only potential problem involves worn midsummer birds with little or no color on the breast, but these should be recognizable by their very small size and overall pale dusty or brownish look. Birds in the "Western Flycatcher" complex are occasionally misidentified as Buff-breasteds by birders who misinterpret their yellowish underparts as buffy, but these birds actually differ in many respects.

BUFF-BREASTED FLYCATCHER

These upper three figures show adults in April, just after arrival in Arizona and still in fairly fresh plumage. The overall pale dusty look is obvious.

An adult in late May, already showing the effects of some wear and fading. The eye-ring is barely visible against the pale face.

A juvenile in August, looking fresh, with buff wing bars.

This July adult is quite worn, with wing bars and tertial edgings obscure.

Variations in bill shape

27. LEARNING TO IDENTIFY SWALLOWS

As a general rule, swallows are not misidentified as much as they are simply left unidentified. Much of the time they are seen in distant, rapid flight, evading good views, and birders may despair of seeing them well enough to see standard field marks. When we find them perched, swallows are sometimes in such large flocks that it would take exceptional patience to look through them one by one. As a result of all this, only a small percentage of the swallows seen by most birders are actually named with confidence.

POINTS TO CONSIDER IN IDENTIFYING SWALLOWS

How to look at swallows. A big part of our problem with flying swallows may be our addiction to using binoculars. Finding and following a fast-moving swallow in binocs can be so challenging and distracting that we see less detail than we would with the unaided eye. Ultimately we'll identify more swallows with confidence if we practice recognizing them without the use of binoculars.

Practice is the key. Fortunately, we can orchestrate this for ourselves. The best time to practice is not with mystery swallows passing in migration, but with birds of known identity, such as near nesting sites. Improving our skill at swallow identification is a good project for early summer. We can position ourselves a discreet distance from swallow nesting sites — Tree Swallow nest boxes in open areas, Cliff or Barn swallows nesting at buildings or under bridges, etc. — and watch the birds in flight, memorizing every aspect of their appearance. Their shapes, wing action, and the way their markings appear at different distances all can be committed to memory. By just watching them, confirming their identity up close and then watching as they fly farther away, we can build up a mental library of what each swallow looks like. Even getting to know a few nesting species thoroughly will give us a basis for comparison with other swallows.

Variations in flight style. Since flight action is so important in swallow ID, we have to remember that it changes in some conditions. Strong or gusty winds can have a marked effect on a swallow's flight style. So can mating season: many swallows have courtship displays that involve a different flight action. If we're watching Barn Swallows, for example, and two birds go by in more rapid, twisting flight, they may not belong to a different species; they may be two more Barn Swallows engaged in an aerial courtship chase.

Timing of molt. The complete prebasic molt of swallows usually stretches over a period of months. In molting the primaries, generally they won't drop the next feather until the previous one is almost completely re-grown, so that there are never big gaps in the surface area of the wing. Many swallows begin their prebasic molt in summer, and some short-distance migrants complete the molt during late summer and early fall, on the breeding grounds or during migration. Long-distance migrant swallows are likely to complete most of the molt on the wintering grounds. In some cases this difference is useful in identification. Cliff Swallow (a long-distance migrant) molts the flight feathers on its wintering grounds, while adult Cave Swallows molt on the breeding grounds; a member of this species pair in active molt of wing feathers in summer is likely to be a Cave.

Seen in mid-September, this Tree Swallow is part-way through primary molt. Contrast between the fresh inner primaries and old outer ones is apparent, but there is no major gap in the flight feathers. Tail shape indicates that those feathers are molting also.

Long-distance vagrants. As we might expect of such strong fliers, swallows sometimes turn up far outside their normal ranges. Strays have been known to reach North America from Europe and Asia (Common House-Martin) and from South America (Brown-chested Martin), and other species are possible. As I write this, probably the most-overdue new bird for North America is the Blue-and-white Swallow *(Pygochelidon cyanoleuca)*. Widespread and migratory in the American tropics, it should be as likely to occur here as the Brown-chested Martin, which has been found several times, but the Blue-and-white Swallow would be much easier to overlook. (Even easier to overlook — and practically unidentifiable on current knowledge — would be some tropical relatives of Purple Martin. Gray-breasted, Southern, and Cuban martins are all known from old specimens from the southern U.S.) A truly odd-looking individual swallow should be identified with extreme care, not just ruling out other known North American species, but taking into account the possibility that it might be a visitor from elsewhere.

28. LEARNING TO IDENTIFY WARBLERS

No group of birds in North America separates birders from non-birders so sharply as the warblers. The average person may have never seen a warbler, even unknowingly, and may not know that such birds exist. Birders, on the other hand, may focus a major amount of their energy on warblers, especially in spring and fall. The arrival of warblers migrating north from the tropics is a highlight of spring for many birders, especially in the East. The challenge of identifying fall warblers is an absorbing puzzle for many observers, and the search for vagrant eastern warblers is a major preoccupation for many western birders, especially in fall.

Overview of the problem. Warblers offer tremendous variety, with well over 50 species north of the Mexican border and the chance to see up to 30 species in a day in some areas. There is variety within the species as well, with most warblers exhibiting several different plumages at different ages or different seasons. This diversity can add to the challenge of learning these birds. All North American warbler species are at least partly migratory, and most are long-distance migrants, with no overlap between their breeding and wintering ranges. This means that most birders' encounters with warblers are strongly seasonal, and with migrant species, we may have only a few chances every spring and fall to add to our level of experience with them.

Adult male Blackburnian Warbler. This tiny, active, treetop bird can be hard to see, but it is arguably worth the effort.

As hyperactive birds that spend much of their time among dense foliage, warblers may be heard more often than they are seen, and the attempt to identify them by voice offers its own challenges. The callnotes of some warblers are quite distinctive, but many have similar notes, even to the point of sounding identical. Most warbler species have at least two different songs, and some have many different song variations, making them harder to learn. Since many of the songs are high-pitched, their subtle distinctions can be difficult for the human ear to pick out. Warblers on migration may sing a lot as they approach or reach the breeding grounds, but farther away from breeding sites they are less vocal, so birders in southern regions have very limited opportunities to hear the songs of northern warblers. Many birders find that they must relearn the songs of warblers every year.

Of course, the same factors that make these birds challenging also make them rewarding, and warblers are perennial favorites with many birders.

HOW TO LOOK AT WARBLERS

It takes a particular mindset to look at warblers, utterly different from what we might apply to looking at gulls, for example. With gulls, we are likely to find them standing or swimming in the open, and studying them involves a leisurely perusal of fine points on a bird that may be stationary for minutes at a time. Warblers, by contrast, are almost always moving fast, even if they are in the open, and most of the time they are among foliage of some kind. If we simply wait for a clear view of an individual bird, most warblers will leave us mystified.

With warblers, the process of identification begins as soon as we catch a glimpse (or even as soon as we hear a bird calling from a hidden spot). Even if we are getting only fleeting looks at a bird that is moving inside the foliage, we can gain many clues by noting where the bird is in its habitat and how it is moving. (See the sections on habitat and foraging behavior, p. 398.) And when we do get partial views through the leaves, we can start to build up a mental list of plumage details. Even if we never see the whole bird at once, we

This is typical of the glimpses we get while we're waiting for a warbler to come out into view. A lot of field marks are visible here. We can see narrow black streaks on yellow flanks, a white lower belly, and a hint that yellow may extend up onto the rump. We can see some of the greater coverts on the wing, with dark centers and pale edges, but no obvious wing bar at the tip. In the field, of course, this view would last for only an instant, but we would have seen enough to get us thinking along the lines of Cape May Warbler.

can usually see enough fragments to add up to a complete mental picture and a solid identification.

Of course, warblers in migration often occur in mixed flocks, so it takes some concentration to stay on the same individual. If we lose the bird temporarily and then pick it up again, we have to consider the possibility that we're looking at a different individual — otherwise we may be trying to add up field marks from more than one species.

LEARNING THE GROUPS OF WARBLERS

Breaking the family down by genus is not as valuable for warblers as it is for some birds, but it is still useful for birders to be aware of the differences among the genus *Dendroica*, other genera that are similar to *Dendroica*, and miscellaneous smaller genera that are more distinctive. Many of the categories listed below are artificial groupings, meant to be useful for thinking about the field impressions of the birds more than their actual taxonomic relationships.

Group 1. Genus *Dendroica*

As currently classified, this large genus includes 21 or 22 species in North America, or over one-third of the warbler species north of the Mexican border. They live in a variety of habitats from open second growth to mature forest, and several species may coexist by foraging at different levels or in different parts of the trees. All species in North America are strongly migratory, many of them nesting in the far north and migrating to the tropics for the winter. Almost all have strongly contrasted white or yellow spots in the tail, and most species have wing bars. Most species show a noticeable degree of seasonal variation, with visibly different basic and alternate plumages, and the breeding males of most species are more strikingly patterned than the females. Their songs vary from clear and thin to relatively low-pitched and buzzy.

Magnolia Warbler. Strongly patterned, like most species in the genus *Dendroica*.

Dendroica in its current form might be broken up, or merged partly or entirely into *Parula*, but for the moment it is still useful to distinguish these birds from other warblers.

Group 2. Other genera that are similar to *Dendroica*

Genus *Vermivora*. This genus now includes only Blue-winged and Golden-winged warblers (plus Bachman's Warbler, probably extinct). Very suggestive of *Dendroica* in apearance, with dry buzzy songs.

Genus *Oreothlypis*. This genus includes six species formerly in *Vermivora* (Tennessee, Orange-crowned, Nashville, Virginia's, Colima, and Lucy's warblers). These are plain warblers, lacking strong pattern, and the sexes are similar. They mostly lack wing bars and tail spots. Most *Oreothlypis* have relatively simple songs. Although some will forage in the treetops, they often favor low growth, and most of them nest in low vegetation or even on the ground. Also in this genus is the rare Crescent-chested Warbler, formerly in *Parula*.

Orange-crowned Warbler of the Pacific Coast race
O. c. lutescens

Genus *Parula*. Northern Parula and Tropical Parula. These are very small warblers, usually foraging and nesting high in trees. Notable features include yellow on the lower mandible and buzzy songs.

Genus *Mniotilta*. Black-and-white Warbler. Noted for its foraging behavior, creeping along limbs and trunks of trees like a nuthatch. Aside from this behavior, it seems very similar to members of *Dendroica*.

Genus *Setophaga*. American Redstart. This warbler flits about actively with much fanning of wings and tail, often catching insects in midair. Well-developed rictal bristles are probably relevant to this flycatching behavior. Otherwise its behavior and voice mostly suggest *Dendroica*, and it may belong in the same genus. Males and females are very differently colored, and one-year-old males look similar to females.

Genus *Myioborus*. Painted Redstart and Slate-throated Redstart behave somewhat like American Redstart, with much fanning of the wings and tail, but are probably not closely related to it. They forage mostly at midlevels in trees and nest on the ground. Sexes are very similar. This genus is very widespread in the highlands of the American tropics, but it barely extends north of Mexico.

Genus *Wilsonia*. All three of these (Wilson's, Canada, Hooded) lack wing bars, and two of them lack white in the tail. All tend to forage fairly low in forest undergrowth or in thickets, but they forage very actively, often flitting about and catching insects in midair. Plumages are similar at all seasons, and sexes are similar, but males tend to have sharper or more extensive black patterning around the head.

male Wilson's Warbler of the eastern subspecies, in spring

adult Red-faced Warbler

Genus *Cardellina*. Red-faced Warbler. An active bird of southwestern mountain forests, often foraging high in trees, but nesting on the ground. Adult males are only slightly more colorful than females or young birds. Foraging behavior suggests members of the genus *Wilsonia,* but the song is more like that of a *Dendroica.*

Group 3. Chunky warblers of the understory

Genus *Geothlypis*. Yellowthroats are plain warblers lacking wing bars, tail spots, and streaked pattern. Only the Common Yellowthroat is widespread north of Mexico. It is a stout bird that skulks in marshes and other dense low growth, often acting more like a wren than a warbler, and it is often detected first by its fast repetitive song or sharp callnotes. The Gray-crowned Yellowthroat, rare in southern Texas, is more of a field bird with a very different voice, and it probably belongs in a different genus, *Chamaethlypis.*

adult male
Common Yellowthroat

Genus *Oporornis*. These four species (Mourning, MacGillvray's, Connecticut, and Kentucky) are also plain warblers lacking wing bars, tail spots, and streaks. All are plain olive above and rich yellow below. There are age and sex differences in head pattern, but little seasonal change in their plumage. All stay low in heavy cover, inside forest or dense second growth, and do most of their foraging on the ground. Generally they are hard to see and may be detected first by their rich, chanting songs or sharp callnotes.

adult male Mourning Warbler

Group 4. Brown ground warblers

Genus *Seiurus* (Ovenbird) **and genus *Parkesia*** (Northern and Louisiana waterthrushes). These are stout warblers that stay low, walking on the ground inside forest or along streams. Waterthrushes bob their tails, Ovenbird often holds its tail raised. All have plain brown or olive upperparts, strong head patterns, and streaked underparts. Sexes are similar and there are no significant seasonal changes in plumage. All have loud, emphatic songs and sharp callnotes.

Northern Waterthrush

Genus *Helmitheros*. Worm-eating Warbler. A stout warbler with a short tail and heavy, pointed bill. No wing bars or tail spots, plain overall except for strong head stripes. Both sexes and all ages look similar, and there is no seasonal change in appearance. This warbler mostly stays low inside forest, hopping on the ground, often foraging by probing into hanging clusters of dead leaves. The song is a dry trill.

Worm-eating Warbler

Genus *Limnothlypis*. Swainson's Warbler. A large stout warbler with a long pointed bill. It is very plain above and below except for a pale supercilium, and there is essentially no variation by sex, age, or season. Staying low inside the forest, it moves on the ground with an odd shuffling walk. Its song is loud and ringing, and it has sharp callnotes.

Group 5. Miscellaneous and non-warblers

Genus *Protonotaria*. Prothonotary Warbler. In pictures this bird might suggest a *Dendroica* but in life it gives a very different impression, with its bulky body, heavy bill, and short tail. The song is an emphatic repetition of clear notes. Breeding in southeastern swamps, it nests in tree cavities, unlike most warblers.

male Prothonotary Warbler

Genus *Basileuterus*. This is a widespread tropical genus of more than 20 species, of which only the Rufous-capped and Golden-crowned warblers stray north of Mexico. These warblers lack wing bars and tail spots but usually have some pattern on the head. Sexes are very similar. They tend to be found in pairs at all seasons and often forage low in dense thickets or forest understory.

Rufous-capped Warbler

Genus *Euthlypis*. Fan-tailed Warbler is a large, long-tailed tropical species that rarely strays north of the Mexican border. It skulks in dense low cover, often near water, and may be detected first by its loud, ringing song and sharp callnotes.

Genus *Icteria*. Yellow-breasted Chat. This species is included among the warblers in most books, but probably does not belong in this family. With its large size, thick bill, and raucous, mimidlike song, it is unlikely to be confused with any other warbler.

Genus *Peucedramus*. Olive Warbler. Superficially this looks like a member of the Parulidae, but its callnote is unique (a soft, descending *pheew*), and its rich, repetitive song is also unlike that of any other warbler. It is mostly a permanent resident in mountain pine forests of the southwest, foraging fairly high in the trees. Olive Warbler is now placed in its own family, Peucedramidae.

adult male Olive Warbler

The term "warbler" applied to other birds

The name "warbler" is applied to members of several bird families around the world that are unrelated to our American Warblers (family Parulidae). Prominent among these are the many species of Old World Warblers (family Sylviidae); one of these (Arctic Warbler) nests commonly in Alaska, and several others have occurred in Alaska and elsewhere in North America as strays from Eurasia. The Parulidae are sometimes identified with a modifier and called "wood-warblers," but one member of the Sylviidae is named Wood Warbler, adding to the potential for confusion. In the context of this chapter, the term "warbler" should be understood to apply to members of the New World family, the Parulidae.

WHAT TO LOOK FOR IN IDENTIFYING WARBLERS

Shapes of warblers. Subtle differences in the shapes of warblers are not the easiest points to notice when you are just learning the birds. But with enough experience, the shape of each species is a basic characteristic that will help to get you on the right track as soon as you glimpse a warbler, so it is worth paying a considerable amount of attention to this aspect of their appearance.

Most elements of shape are best understood in terms of comparisons to other birds, so the more time you have spent looking at warblers, the easier it will be to say when a given bird looks stout-bodied, or large-headed, or long-winged. Tail length is often a useful point, and it is fairly easy even for new birders to see that Yellow Warbler has a relatively short tail while that of Wilson's Warbler is relatively long for the bird's small size.

Bill shape is another point that may be noticed rather easily on some species, such as Prothonotary or Worm-eating warblers, which are very large-billed compared to most family members. With more experience, we can start to appreciate more subtle things such as the relatively short stout bill of Chestnut-sided Warbler, the slightly curved bill of Black-and-white Warbler, and the fine-pointed bill of Cape May Warbler.

The length of the undertail coverts, relative to the length of the tail, is noticeable on some birds. This is a minor supporting feature in separating Pine Warbler from Blackpoll and Bay-breasted warblers, as described in the next chapter. Swainson's Warbler has very long undertail coverts, and so do the species of *Oporornis* (Mourning, MacGillivray's, Kentucky, and especially Connecticut warblers), and this adds considerably to the impression that these are bulky birds.

Habitat. Every species of warbler has its own preferred habitat. The differences are most pronounced, and most reliable for identification, during the nesting season, when most species are quite particular in choice of surroundings. In early summer we are unlikely to find Prairie Warbler, for example, unless we visit an overgrown brushy field or a mangrove swamp, and we won't see Kirtland's Warbler unless we visit an open stand of young jack pines within a certain size range. During migration, warblers are more mixed and may show up in a much wider variety of habitats, but certain preferences still come into play.

Within any given habitat, there are subtle variations recognized by the birds, and an alert birder will try to notice these variations as well. Northern and Louisiana waterthrushes may both be found in the breeding season at the edge of water inside forest, but where their ranges overlap, the Louisiana tends to be along moving streams, while the Northern is more likely to be around still waters such as bogs or ponds. Cerulean Warbler and Hooded Warbler may summer in the same southern hardwood forests, but the Cerulean is likely to be high in the treetops while the Hooded usually forages in the undergrowth.

Even with warblers occupying the very same trees, there are microhabitat differences. In a classic study years ago, Robert MacArthur studied five species of *Dendroica* warblers nesting in spruce forest in Maine. He found that even when they foraged in the same trees, they specialized in different zones of the trees; for example, Cape May Warbler mostly foraged in the outer part of the top of the tree, while Bay-breasted Warbler focused more on midlevels and often was among the interior branches. This level of habitat partitioning breaks down during migration, but it is worth watching for whenever we're afield in the nesting season.

Foraging behavior. Most warblers have roughly similar diets (insects and other arthropods), but they differ in the ways in which they find their food. Along with their use of particular microhabitats, their foraging behavior contributes to the impression given by every warbler, and these points are very important in identification. Nashville Warbler and Connecticut Warbler both show a white eye-ring on a gray face, but the Nashville forages actively among twigs and stems at all levels, while the Connecticut walks deliberately on the ground under dense cover. Black-and-white Warbler creeps

Yellow-rumped Warbler: widespread and common, reflecting its adaptable foraging behavior.

about on trunks and branches, Canada Warbler flits actively in the undergrowth, American Redstart often flies out to catch insects in midair. Some warblers are quite specialized, but others are more general in their behavior. Yellow-rumped Warbler has a very wide array of foraging activities, sometimes flycatching from the tops of trees, sometimes foraging on tree trunks or in low thickets, and this adaptable behavior may be one reason why the species is so numerous.

When they are on the ground, most warblers hop, but a few walk instead: Ovenbird, the two waterthrushes, Connecticut. The slow shuffling gait of Swainson's Warbler, with occasional sideways shivering of its body, is practically enough to identify it even in a glimpse through dense undergrowth.

Wing pattern. One of the most useful points for identifying warblers at all seasons, and something that's often easy to see in a quick view, is the pattern of the wings. It's important, though, not to simply divide the warblers into categories of "wing bars" and "no wing bars." There are degrees of wing pattern beyond this simple dichotomy.

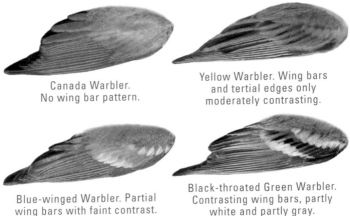

Canada Warbler.
No wing bar pattern.

Yellow Warbler. Wing bars
and tertial edges only
moderately contrasting.

Blue-winged Warbler. Partial
wing bars with faint contrast.

Black-throated Green Warbler.
Contrasting wing bars, partly
white and partly gray.

Bay-breasted Warbler.
White wing bars and tertial
edges contrasting strongly
against dark wing.

Blackburnian Warbler. Two
white wing bars, mostly
connected by white bases
to most greater coverts.

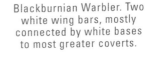

Of course, there are variations in wing pattern not shown on the preceding page, such as the white square on the folded wing of Black-throated Blue Warbler, formed by white bases of the outer primaries. The amount of contrast on tertials and on wing bars is often similar, but not always; Pine Warbler, for example, may have moderately bright wing bars and very dull tertial edges. It's also important to remember that width and brightness of the wing bars will vary with the degree of wear on the plumage; the wing bars may be striking on fall birds (which are all in fresh plumage), and much less obvious in midsummer (when all except juveniles will be in worn condition).

Face pattern. For one who knows the spring males of warblers such as Prairie, Magnolia, and Blackburnian, the drabness of some first-autumn females can be shocking. As

plain as these fall birds may be, however, their faces almost always show at least a subtle indication of the typical pattern. Look closely at the face of an unknown dull warbler, and you may find that you know it after all.

Young female Blackburnian Warbler in fall: drab, but with a recognizable face.

There are some difficulties that come up when we use the presence or absence of an eye-ring as a field mark, because this can vary within a species. In Mourning Warbler, adult males generally look plain-faced and adult females often do also, but other plumages often show a very thin, nearly complete eye-ring, leading to confusion with Connecticut or MacGillivray's warblers. Tropical Parula usually lacks an eye-ring, but some individuals have limited white above and below the eye, suggesting the broken eye-ring of Northern Parula. There are also some species in which the whole face is pale and plain, and these may have slightly lighter feathers around the eye, creating the appearance of an eye-ring; Yellow Warbler and Lucy's Warbler are good examples. For these reasons, simply noting that a warbler has or lacks an eye-ring is not as helpful as carefully describing the pattern around the eye.

Even subtle elements of face pattern can be helpful. On this one-year-old female Pine Warbler in spring, the dark lower edge of the ear-coverts, becoming more obvious toward the base of the bill, is a distinctive mark on an otherwise confusingly plain bird.

Tail pattern. Some warblers have the tail solidly colored, while others (including practically all the *Dendroica*) have spots of white (or rarely yellow or orange) within the outer tail feathers. When present, the white is in the outer tail feathers, so it shows up mainly from below, or when the tail is spread in flight. Of those that do have tail spots, there is great variation among species in the size and shape of the spots, and these often provide helpful ID clues. For example, the white is very extensive in the adult male Black-throated Green Warbler, which essentially appears to have white outer tail feathers in flight, while it is much more limited on Palm Warbler, which appears to have small white spots near the outer corners of the tail.

From left: Spread tails of adult female Yellow-rumped (Myrtle) Warbler and adult male Magnolia Warbler as seen from above; folded tail of adult female Magnolia Warbler as seen from below.

It's important to note that there is also much variation within species in the extent of the white tail spots. As a rule the white spots are smallest in young females, intermediate in young males and adult females, and most extensive in adult males, and the variation is noticeable in the field with close views.

Bill color and foot color. These are variable on most species. There is a general tendency for the bill to be darker (tending to blackish) on spring birds, especially adult males, and often slightly paler on autumn birds and on females and young. This seasonal variation is hardly noticeable on most birds, but on some species it is obvious. On Prothonotary Warbler, for example, spring males have black bills, but most individuals in fall have the bill fairly pale brownish pink.

The color of the legs and feet also varies on many warblers, but the variation is mostly slight and seems to be more individual than seasonal. Many warblers are darker on the legs and slightly paler on the toes, or on the soles of the toes (not easy to see in the field). Foot color can be significant in identifying some Blackpoll Warblers and similar birds, as discussed in the next chapter.

Timing of molts. Most warblers have similar molt patterns, making it relatively easy for us to understand the seasonal changes that we see in their plumages.

The most common molt pattern among warblers is the Complex Alternate Strategy (see Chapter 4), with basic and alternate plumages in each annual cycle and with an inserted formative plumage in the first cycle. Most warblers hold juvenile plumage for only a very brief period and may begin the preformative molt to formative (first-winter) plumage within a couple of weeks after leaving the nest. In some species, such as Magnolia and Black-throated Blue warblers, this molt may be well under way even before the young leave the nest. The preformative molt involves head and body feathers and usually greater and median coverts, occasionally some tertials, but not the flight feathers. Juveniles usually look quite different from older birds, often tinged brown, often heavily streaked, and often with buff wing bars even on species that are plain-winged as adults. Such birds could be extremely difficult to identify, but fortunately most are still tended by their parents when they are so young.

This streaky brown bird is a juvenile Yellow-rumped Warbler, but I know that only because the photographer saw the parents feeding it.

For adult warblers, the molt to basic plumage usually occurs in late summer on the nesting grounds and is generally completed before fall migration. As with most songbirds, the prebasic molt is complete.

For warblers with the Complex Alternate Strategy, the prealternate molt (to "breeding plumage") occurs mostly on the wintering grounds, although some may complete it during northward migration in spring. This is a partial molt, quite variable in its extent. Some species have only a very limited molt of some head feathers, others molt many head and body feathers, and some molt some of the coverts, tertials, or central tail feathers. In some species, there is a tendency for young males to replace more feathers in the prealternate molt than females or adult males. For species that have a strong seasonal change in appearance, like Blackpoll and Bay-breasted warblers, this seasonal change is brought about by the prealternate molt in late winter and early spring, producing the bright colors that we see on spring migrants.

For some warblers, the prealternate molt seems to take place gradually throughout the winter, but this is usually too gradual and subtle for observers in tropical areas to notice that the warblers become more colorful as the winter goes on.

Some warblers, especially among southern and tropical species, have a Complex Basic Strategy in molting, with just one (basic) plumage per annual cycle and with a formative (first-winter) plumage inserted in the first cycle. Examples include Pine, Hooded, Swainson's, and Red-faced warblers. As expected, these show no seasonal change in plumage other than the slight changes brought about by wear. There are also some species in which the prealternate molt may be either absent or very limited, such as Blue-winged and Wilson's warblers, and these also show no obvious seasonal changes.

Plumages of spring warblers. There are a few warbler species in which the sexes are very similar or identical in appearance (Palm, Swainson's, Worm-eating, Ovenbird, and a few others; aside from Palm Warbler, these tend to look about the same at all seasons as well). But in most warblers, males are more brightly patterned than females, at least in spring and summer. For most warblers it is possible to distinguish among adult male, first-cycle male, adult female, and first-cycle female individuals, at least in the hand, where the condition of certain feathers can be checked carefully. In the field, these plumages can't necessarily be separated, but their existence leads to substantial variation in the appearance of spring birds. In simplest terms, adults tend to be more cleanly patterned or more brightly colored than the one-year-old birds of the same sex. The most extreme difference among our

Cape May Warblers in spring. Above, one-year-old male; below, adult male. Superficially they look the same, but the adult is cleaner and brighter in several details.

North American warblers involves American Redstart, in which one-year-old males look superficially very much like adult females.

Breaking down the challenge of "confusing fall warblers." In an early edition of his field guide, Roger Tory Peterson included two plates of "confusing fall warblers." Some experts have since criticized that label, saying that fall warblers need not be confusing. That's true, but it's also a fact that new birders are often tripped up by these birds.

In a few warbler species, even adults have utterly different plumages in fall than in spring; Blackpoll and Bay-breasted warblers, detailed in the next chapter, are the best examples. In several others, the adults have a much less distinct pattern on the head and body plumage in fall than in spring; Yellow-rumped, Magnolia, and Chestnut-sided warblers are good examples, but these retain enough pattern that they are not especially challenging. Then there are some in which the adults look only slightly different in fall (Black-throated Green, Black-and-white, Blackburnian, Kentucky, and others), and a number of species in which the adults show no apparent seasonal change (Black-throated Blue, Yellow-throated, Worm-eating, and others). So in pursuing fall warblers, the observer is going to see some individuals that are easily identified.

Much of the challenge in fall comes from the presence of young birds in their first southward migration. The distinctness of these varies by species. For practically all of them, however, these first-autumn birds are quite similar in overall pattern to autumn adults. The differences are mostly matters of degree: the markings are present but less distinct, the colors may be less bright. Young males are often very similar to adult females in fall, while young females are the drabbest birds.

All of the points described above under "what to look for" apply equally well to the dullest fall warblers. Shape, habitat, foraging behavior, wing pattern, and face pattern will take us most of the way to an identification with every bird. Careful study of warblers in spring is one of the best ways to prepare for recognizing them in fall, as many of these factors will be the same (or at least very similar) at all seasons.

Warbler hybrids. Warblers, as a family, are not prone to interbreeding among species nearly as much as notorious groups such as ducks or hummingbirds. However, there are three well-known cases of species pairs in which hybridization is quite extensive, at least one other combination where interbreeding has been documented a number of times, and many other hybrid combinations that have been found at least once. Because there are so many species of warblers in North America, there are many possible hybrid combinations; and because birders are so interested in warblers, every new hybrid discovered draws a lot of attention.

Myrtle and Audubon's warblers are currently treated as subspecies groups and combined under the name Yellow-rumped Warbler. Recent studies suggest they are likely to be split again, but their interbreeding (mainly in southwestern Alberta and nearby areas) will continue to produce intermediate birds. Because Myrtle and Audubon's are both so widespread and abundant, the intermediates (hybrids or intergrades) make up only a very small percentage of the total population. First-generation hybrid males usually look obviously intermediate, but it may be impossible to tell some backcrosses from variants of the two parental forms.

In the other two cases, involving Blue-winged × Golden-winged and Townsend's × Hermit warblers, the interbreeding may be just as extensive as it is between Myrtle and Audubon's, but these other warblers are still classified as distinct species. Interactions of these species pairs both involve shifts in the hybrid zones, with Blue-winged Warblers expanding northward and swamping out Golden-winged genes, and Townsend's expanding southward, interbreeding with and swamping out the population of Hermit Warblers. In these species pairs, many birds that superficially look "pure" actually carry DNA from both parent species. For field purposes, however, if we examine these birds closely and see no obvious signs of hybrid ancestry, there is no reason why we shouldn't just call them what they look like.

Superficially this bird looks like a male Hermit Warbler. A second look shows that it has black extending forward onto the crown, a green wash on the back, a slight yellow tinge on the chest, and streaks on the sides, all suggesting mixed ancestry with Townsend's Warbler.

UNDERSTANDING WHAT YOU HEAR: WARBLER VOICES

Their hyperactive behavior and their liking for dense foliage often make warblers tough to see well, so their voices can be tremendously helpful in identifying them. Fortunately, most warblers are quite vocal, with frequent song from the males in spring and early summer and distinctive callnotes from most birds at all seasons. Learning to recognize the vocalizations of warblers is an absorbing and worthwhile project for birders.

Warbler songs. Even in areas of eastern North America where many species of warblers are common, it can be a challenge to learn their songs. This is partly because of the brief period of opportunity each year, especially for migrant species that are only passing through. (And males may do relatively little singing when they are still far from the breeding grounds, such as boreal forest nesting species that pause in spring along our Gulf Coast.) Many warbler songs are very high-pitched, making them hard for some human ears to hear, and making them hard to record and play back without very good quality audio equipment. There is also a lot of variation in the songs of most warbler species.

The variation in warbler songs is worthy of some extra discussion. Not much of it is geographic variation (although Northern Parulas have a different ending to their most common song type in the eastern and western parts of their range). In many species, individual males

A male Chestnut-sided Warbler may have a dozen different songs.

sing a variety of different songs. In a study of one population of Chestnut-sided Warblers, for example, individual males sang up to a dozen different songs, but the total number of different songs in the population as a whole was about 150. Is it any wonder that we human listeners get confused at times? Of course, most of these different songs are minor variations, with a consistent tone quality and shared elements of pattern that make them recognizable, but the existence of all these variations means that we have to be flexible in our interpretation of what we hear.

Two major song types. One fascinating aspect of warbler song is the fact that in many species, males have two distinct classes of song that they use in different contexts. The song types appear to have different functions, so often we will be more likely to hear one song type than the other. Knowing about this may make it easier to understand the variation that we hear.

Studies on these song types have used a confusing variety of different terms. The song that is called "Type A" by one researcher might be called "Unaccented Ending song" by another, or "Category II," or "Group B," or "serial mode," or "mixed mode," as different scientists have studied the phenomenon in different warblers. (The distinction of accented ending vs. unaccented ending has worked well for some species, but not at all for others.) A birder who tries to read up on these song types is likely to become confused by all the different terms used. For purposes of this chapter I will just use the terms "Type A" and "Type B," sorting out the songs by their apparent function, but be aware that published studies on most of these species have used other terms.

The two song types are easiest to learn in **Black-throated Green Warbler**, because it has relatively little song variation aside from the two very well defined types and because its song types are so distinct and easily described.

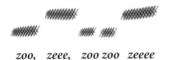

zoo, zeee, zoo zoo zeeee

Song Type A (or Unaccented Ending song) is usually of five buzzy notes, with the second and fifth higher-pitched. The first and second syllables are relatively long, the third and fourth are very short. The male often gives double chip notes between songs, and he usually delivers the song from a high perch. This song seems to function most importantly for communication with other males. On the breeding grounds it is heard a lot at dawn and dusk and when the birds are near their territorial boundaries, situations in which the males could be expected to be actively defending their territories against other males.

Song Type B (or Accented Ending song) is usually of five or six buzzy notes, with the first three or four all on the same pitch, the next one lower, and the last note higher and emphasized. The male rarely gives chip notes

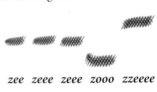

zee zeee zeee zooo zzeeee

between songs. He may deliver this song either from a high perch or while foraging. This song seems to be used mainly in communication with females, so it is given most frequently by unmated males or by the male in the presence of his mate. When a pair is isolated on a small island with no other males around, the male of the pair may continue to use mostly this song type.

Description of the two song types in some other species. Based on a wide variety of published sources and on a little of my own observation, I have listed a few other warblers that appear to exhibit the same division of song types. This list begins with some that seem to have a clear-cut difference, like that of the Black-throated Green, and ends with others in which the difference is more subtle or complicated. Note that the terms "Type A" and "Type B" have not been used by all researchers studying warbler songs. Also note that characterizing these songs in this way (as being used mainly for communication with either females or other males) is an *extreme oversimplification* of a complicated situation, and that every song may serve more than one function.

SONG TYPE A **Mainly for interactions with other males**	SONG TYPE B **Mainly for interactions with females**

Blackburnian Warbler

tp tp tp tzp tzp tzp tititi tzeeeee

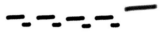

teesa teesa teesa teesa tszzeeee

Very high-pitched, especially last note. Often gives single or double chip note between songs.

Last note varies, may not always be included. First part of song suggests typical song of Black-and-white Warbler.

Golden-winged Warbler

*t-t-ss-ss-ss-ss-sz-sz-tsi-tsi-b*zzzzzzzzzz

bzzeeee, bee bee bee

A rapid lisping stutter followed by a lower buzzy note. Often given continuously at dawn. Songs may be interspersed with a few chip notes or interrupted by flight song.

Sung most by unmated males; after pair formation, use of this song declines, and song becomes more variable. Not interspersed with chip notes or flight songs.

Blue-winged Warbler

*t-t-t-t-t-t-t-t-t-t-t-b*zzzzzzzzzzz

*bzzeeee, bu*zzzzzzzzzzz

A rapid, thin trill followed by a buzz.

Two flat buzzes, the second one lower. Use of this song drops sharply after pair formation.

SONG TYPE A Male-male interactions	**SONG TYPE B** Male-female interactions

Magnolia Warbler

weeta weeta weesa weee

Thin sweet notes, with no strong accent. Given especially at dawn and dusk.

weeta weeta WEEtoh

Thin sweet notes, with strong accent on next-to-last note. The song most commonly heard during the day.

Northern Parula

zee pzee pzee pzee zzzzzzzeeee-up

Series of short buzzy notes, followed by a trill that rises slightly and a sharp final note.

zzzzzzzzzzzzzeeee-wup

A thin, rising buzz, snapping over sharply at the top. Those in the western part of the range have the last note higher-pitched.

Chestnut-sided Warbler

see see see swee syu syu swee see

Thin clear notes. There are many variations on this, and an individual male may use two to ten variations.

see sweswesee sisi WEET chew

This is the most common Type B song, but the species has about five such songs, with individual males using one to four of these.

Nashville Warbler

The songs used in all situations seem to be similar, but there is a tendency for the songs to be sung more rapidly in Type A situations (male-male communication), more slowly in Type B situations (male-female communication).

Yellow Warbler

In this species, across its very wide range, there is no consistent difference in Type A and Type B songs, but their delivery is different. In Type A situations (territorial defense, or communication with other males),

Like many other warblers, Yellow Warbler sings differently in different situations. But rather than having consistently distinct song types, it uses a different order and sequence of songs. Knowing this can help birders to understand what we are hearing.

a male Yellow Warbler will sing a variety of different songs, rapidly changing from one to another; an individual male may have 10 to 17 different songs, or even more. (This kind of singing is sometimes called "serial mode.") In Type B situations (attracting a female or communicating with a mate), the male will sing the same song over and over. (This kind of singing is sometimes called "repeat mode.") In some populations, songs of this latter type tend to have a strongly accented ending, but this does not apply everywhere, so the classification of "accented ending/unaccented ending" does not work well for this species.

American Redstart

As with Yellow Warbler, male American Redstarts address Type A situations (see above) by singing two to eight different songs in random order ("serial mode"). For Type B situations, they sing one song over and over. These "repeat mode" songs usually have an accented ending phrase, but not always. Redstarts have a wide variety of song patterns; some song patterns may be used as the "repeat mode" song by some males and as one of several "serial mode" songs by other males. Interestingly, many older books mentioned the alternation of different songs as a characteristic of this species; but this is true only in certain situations, and since Yellow Warbler does the same thing, this is not a good point for identification.

Warbler callnotes. Although warblers may make a variety of sounds in special situations, such as alarm calls, the begging calls of fledglings, and so on, the two basic kinds of most interest to birders are chip notes and flight notes.

Chip notes are the most commonly heard calls for most warblers, given in a variety of situations while perched, and also in flight (especially just after takeoff). They are sometimes called "contact calls" or "location calls." A birder with good aural acuity and with lots of time to spend with warblers in the field can learn to recognize the chip notes of most — if not to species, then at least to groups of closely similar species. As a general rule, warblers that live close to the ground in dense cover or near flowing water have the loudest, sharpest calls, but there are exceptions. Several warblers (such as Yellow, Blackpoll, Bay-breasted, and American Redstart) give a rather sweet, liquid *chip*. Others (such as Palm and Prairie) give a harder *tsip*, while still others (such as Hooded, Prothonotary, and Swainson's) give a loud, sharp *tchip*. A thin *tick, tsick,* or *tsit* is typical of Orange-crowned, Nashville, Lucy's, and others. Some give a dry, flat *tep* or *tek* (Black-throated Green, Hermit, Black-throated Gray, and others). Then there are some very distinctive warbler chips that are easily learned with enough practice, such as the low *chugk* of Common Yellowthroat, the hard *check* of Yellow-rumped Warbler, and the flat *chemp* of Wilson's Warbler.

One of the most distinctive of all warbler chip notes is the nasal *shlenk* of Magnolia Warbler.

Of course, descriptions like this may be meaningless until you have heard the sounds yourself. But any time you can see a calling warbler, it is worthwhile to pay close attention to the calls, try to commit them to memory, and try to compare them to the calls of other warblers you have heard.

Flight notes tend to be higher-pitched, thinner, and less distinctive than chip notes. Warblers occasionally give these calls while perched but more often in flight, including during their nocturnal migratory flights. Research has shown that many of these warbler night flight calls can be identified to species through spectrographic analysis and that some people can train their ears to hear the subtle differences. This is a promising area for birders who are looking for a challenge.

29. THE BLACKPOLL TRIO

Species treated in detail:

BLACKPOLL WARBLER *Dendroica striata*
BAY-BREASTED WARBLER *Dendroica castanea*
PINE WARBLER *Dendroica pinus*

The problem. Although the spring males of these three warbler species are utterly different, birds in fall plumage have caused many headaches for birders. Especially similar are the fall Blackpoll and Bay-breasted warblers, with their olive upperparts, yellowish to pale buff underparts, strong wing bars, and finely streaked backs. Their best-known field marks — pale legs and white undertail coverts in Blackpoll, dark legs and buff undertail coverts in Bay-breasted — can be unreliable in the field. Many fall Blackpolls actually have dark legs, and the difference between white and very pale buff on the undertail coverts of some birds can be very difficult to judge. Virtually all individuals can be named if seen well, but the identification must be based on a whole suite of characters, not just on one or two simple field marks.

Pine Warbler differs notably from the other two in having an unstreaked back. But this is not always enough for identification, because the back streaks on Blackpolls and Bay-breasteds are sometimes very faint. Some reports of Pine Warblers out of range in fall probably have been based on young female Blackpolls with dark legs and very faintly streaked backs.

PRELIMINARY POINTS

Fall plumages. The birds considered here, those to be seen during fall migration, belong to four plumage classes in each species:
1. young female in formative (first-winter) plumage;
2. young male in formative plumage;
3. adult female (more than one year old) in basic (winter) plumage;
4. adult male in basic plumage.

These species, like most other warblers, wear juvenile plumage only very briefly. Although the flight feathers of the wings and tail are retained for a full year, the juvenile head and body feathers start to be replaced by formative plumage not long after the young birds leave the nest. By the time they begin to migrate south, they are in fresh formative plumage. (Since the juvenile plumage is seen only on the breeding grounds, and often with easily identified adults in attendance, it is ignored in this chapter's discussions of field marks.) Adults go through a complete molt in late summer on the breeding grounds. By the time they begin to migrate south, they are in fresh basic plumage.

As a general rule, young females are the dullest or most indistinctly marked birds, adult males are the most distinctly marked, with young males and adult females somewhere in between. This trend shows up in a variety of characteristics. For example, Blackpoll and Bay-breasted warblers in fall have streaked backs, with the streaks created by dark centers to individual feathers; these dark centers tend to be small, indistinct, and grayish in young females; small but blackish in young males; similar or slightly larger in adult females; and large and black in adult males. In Bay-breasted Warbler in fall, the color of the flanks varies from dull pale buff in some young females to obviously chestnut in some adult males. In Pine Warblers in fall, the breast is dull buff with a faint yellow wash in young females, slightly more yellowish in young males, more obviously yellow in adult females, and bright yellow in adult males. Individual variation blurs the distinctions among these four plumage classes; many cannot be separated even in the hand, let alone in the field. But an awareness of the existence of these plumage classes will help us to understand the amount of variation that we see within each species.

What to look for first. With this group, as with many other groups of birds, an approach that begins with too much reliance on one field mark is likely to lead us astray some of the time. As mentioned in the previous chapter, when warblers are flitting actively among foliage it can be hard to see the whole bird at once, and we may not be able to choose which detail we see first. So a good strategy is to try to take in the overall impression of the bird, and to watch for these points:

1. Back streaks. If we don't see streaks at first it doesn't necessarily mean that the bird is a Pine Warbler, because the streaks are faint on some Blackpolls and Bay-breasteds. But if we do see streaks, we can rule out Pine immediately and concentrate on separating the other two.

2. Overall color. Despite a large amount of individual variation, the general color, especially the color and pattern of the underparts, will often suggest the correct identification.

3. Face pattern. Although this is a "soft" criterion and not to be relied upon by itself, the face patterns of the three species are usually somewhat different (and often easy to see).

4. Flank color. Most Bay-breasteds in fall have at least a trace of reddish brown on the flanks. On many the color is strong enough to be seen at first glance, immediately identifying the bird. Of course, an apparent lack of this color does not necessarily mean that the bird is *not* a Bay-breasted.

5. Leg color. If the legs are bright pale yellow or pinkish, the bird is almost certainly a Blackpoll. If the legs look dark, the bird could be any of the three species.

Some Bay-breasted Warblers have enough color on the flanks in fall to be identified at a glance. But many are more subtle than this.

FIELD MARKS — ALL THREE SPECIES IN FALL

Back pattern. The back and scapulars are streaked in Blackpoll and Bay-breasted, unstreaked in Pine Warbler. The streaks of the first two are usually apparent; but on some first-winter birds, especially females, they are very faint. On a few Blackpolls, the back may look essentially unstreaked even with a very good view. Determining that a bird's back is genuinely unstreaked is an important point for Pine Warbler, but it is never enough without the backup of other field marks. On well-streaked individuals of the Bay-breasted, the streaks tend to be more broken up into "chains" or series of short streaks, while in Blackpoll the streaks may tend to be more long and continu-ous, but this difference is rarely apparent.

Two examples of Blackpoll Warbler back pattern in fall. On the lower bird, probably a young female, the streaks almost cer-tainly would be invisible in the field.

Breast color and pattern. The fall Blackpoll tends to be a fairly bright pale greenish yellow on the breast, while the Bay-breasted tends toward dull pale buffy yellow. There is also a tendency for the breast to have streaks at the sides in Blackpoll, varying from vague and blurry to dark and distinct, and to be essentially unstreaked in Bay-breasted, but there is some overlap in this character. Both species often have a dusky olive wash at the side of the breast, near the bend of the wing. Some adult male Blackpolls in fall have some fine black spots on the throat, and some first-autumn birds of both species may show fine dark stippling elsewhere on the underparts.

Breast color in fall Pine Warblers varies from fairly bright yellow in adult males to pale brownish gray in young females. Fall adults usually show streaking at the sides of the breast, less apparent than in spring.

Bay-breasted

Blackpoll

Fall Blackpoll and Bay-breasted warblers, to show the typical difference in breast color and pattern. Both species are quite variable, so not all individuals will show such typical patterns.

Color of upperparts. Bay-breasted Warbler tends to be brighter above than Blackpoll Warbler. In particular, the relatively unmarked, pale lime-green nape and sides of the neck on Bay-breasted Warbler are often conspicuous. The upperparts of Pine Warbler vary from fairly bright olive-green to dull grayish or brownish, with the apparent brightness corresponding approximately to the brightness of the throat and breast color.

Face pattern. This is subtle and not really diagnostic, but often can be an excellent clue. Blackpoll usually has a well-defined dark eyestripe, setting off a conspicuous pale supercilium. Bay-breasted has a hint of the same pattern but usually with less contrast, so that the face tends to look relatively plain. It may have a wide pale area around the eye, but usually shows less of an extended supercilium than Blackpoll. Adding to the appearance of a stronger face pattern on Blackpoll, some fall birds (probably adult males) show a fairly distinct dark lateral throat-stripe, lacking on Bay-breasted. Pine Warbler usually has a distinctive pattern with a pale supercilium, dark lores, the beginnings of a dark moustachial stripe leading into the lower edge of a solid dark patch on the ear coverts, a pale crescent below the eye, and some pale area curving up from the throat onto the side of the neck. (This is easier to see than to describe; see the illustrations in this chapter.)

Flank color. Nearly all fall Bay-breasteds have at least a hint of reddish brown or chestnut on the flanks. On probably more than 70 percent of fall birds this color is sufficiently developed to be visible in the field. In its faintest form, however, this trace of color is hard to distinguish from the faint dusky streaks that often extend down onto the flanks of a Blackpoll. Note also that many fall Pine Warblers have a strong wash of dull dusky brown on the flanks.

Undertail coverts. As a generalization, these are pale buff in Bay-breasted, white in Blackpoll and Pine warblers. Actually, although this color is apparent on some individuals (with the area either bright white or strongly buff), on others it is a difficult field mark. The buff on Bay-breasted is often so pale as to appear white under field conditions; worse, the undertail coverts may rarely be washed with yellow on Blackpoll or with pale brown on Pine Warbler.

Pattern of lower underparts. On fall Blackpolls, generally the breast is yellowish, the undertail coverts are white, and the belly may be mostly white (on most males) or strongly washed yellow (on most females). Often there is a noticeable contrast between the white and yellow areas, and this may be easier to see than the exact shade of the undertail coverts. Bay-breasteds rarely show such a contrast, their belly and undertail coverts being all of about the same tone. Pine Warbler is variable in this character, with most yellow-breasted individuals showing some contrast.

Leg color. The legs are almost always dark (brown to black) in Bay-breasted and Pine warblers. It has been reported that Bay-breasted can have the legs dull pink on rare occasions, but this may be the case only with aberrant individuals. Most spring Blackpoll Warblers have legs varying from dull to bright yellow or pinkish, but most in fall have duller legs, varying from dull straw-yellow to blackish. So a bird with pale legs is almost certainly a Blackpoll, but one with dark legs could be any of the three species.

On almost all Blackpolls, including the darkest-legged individuals, the soles of the toes are yellow, and this can be seen in the field with a close view. Pine Warblers also sometimes have yellow soles, but in Bay-breasted they are apparently always dark.

Wing pattern. All three species show the same general pattern of whitish wing bars on dark wings, but there are some useful differences among the species. Pine Warbler typically shows less contrast in the wings than the other two species: the ground color of its wings often looks dark gray rather than blackish, and the wing bars may be off-white or pale grayish white rather than strikingly white. Lack of contrast on the *tertials* is even more apparent: while the other two species have sharply defined white edges on black tertials, these edges are gray on Pine Warbler, not contrasting with the rest of the wing.

Comparing Bay-breasted and Blackpoll, on fresh fall birds the wing bars tend to be a little wider and more obvious on Bay-breasted, adding to the impression that it is a brighter-looking bird overall. Both species have narrow pale tips to the outer primaries in fresh plumage, showing up as whitish crescents on the black wingtip when the wing is folded, and these tend to be more obvious on Blackpoll.

Tail shape and pattern. The three species are similar in tail length, with Blackpoll averaging very slightly shorter-tailed and Pine averaging very slightly longer-tailed. However, Pine Warbler usually looks noticeably longer-tailed than the other two, because its undertail coverts are shorter. Bay-breasted and especially Blackpoll warblers have notably long undertail coverts, so their tail extension looks relatively stubby. The white spots in the outer tail feathers, visible only from the underside when the tail is folded, are roughly the same in Blackpoll and Bay-breasted warblers, but longer in Pine Warbler, in all cases extending nearly to the edge of the undertail coverts.

Shape. Bay-breasted and Blackpoll warblers are very similar in shape, looking stocky and heavy-bodied for the genus *Dendroica,* but Bay-breasted tends to look a little bulkier and thicker-necked, with a slightly thicker bill. Pine Warbler is heavier overall than the other two, with a slightly larger bill and shorter wingtips. As noted above, it tends to look longer-tailed.

adult male Pine Warbler
in late winter

young female Pine Warbler
in formative (first-winter)
plumage

Pine Warblers past the juvenile stage have only one molt per year, a complete molt in fall, so they show less seasonal variation than the other species treated in this chapter.

COMPARING PINE WARBLER TO OTHER SPECIES

The combination of strong wing pattern and finely streaked olive up-perparts should separate Blackpoll and Bay-breasted from all other fall warblers. However, Pine Warbler may be confused with other species that show wing bars and plain backs.

Some Prairie Warblers, especially young females in fall, can be remarkably similar to some Pine Warblers. They can have virtually the same face pattern, and both species in fall can show wing bars that are well defined but not strongly contrasted against the rest of the wing. However, Prairie Warbler is a smaller, slimmer, more active bird, usually "wagging" its tail up and down in a noticeable action. It also tends to forage lower, although this is not a consistent difference. The yellow on the underparts is also usually smoother and more extensive in Prairie Warbler, reaching back nearly onto the undertail coverts.

Claimed sightings of dull-plumaged Pine Warblers in mountains near the Mexican border would have to rule out possible confusion with female or immature Olive Warblers, which also have unmarked gray backs, strong wing bars, large bills, and some dull yellow around the foreparts. Dull Olive Warblers should still show a different head pattern, with some yellowish on the side of the neck, a dark line behind the eye, and no trace of a dark moustachial stripe, and the edgings of their secondaries are yellow. The callnote of Olive Warbler, a soft *feew*, is unlike that of any true warbler in North America.

30. LEARNING TO IDENTIFY SPARROWS

The North American sparrows, as a group, present an inordinate amount of difficulty and consternation for the average birder. Technically, sparrows should not be that challenging. There are only a few species pairs that are genuinely hard to separate, and with one exception (noted in the next chapter), none of the resulting ID problems are as extreme as some of those presented by flycatchers, hummingbirds, gulls, or other classic tough groups. But for many birders, the challenge with sparrows starts at a more basic level — not trying to distinguish between two or three similar species, but trying to distinguish among all 30-plus species. Faced with an unknown sparrow, the birder is often simply at a loss as to its identity.

Based on my own experience as a beginner, I can describe a fairly typical encounter between a new birder and a sparrow. The sparrow sets off the encounter by flying up onto a fence wire. Fighting off a sense of panic, the birder tries to focus on field marks. Is the bird's breast plain or streaked? Okay, it looks streaked. Is there a pale central stripe on the crown? Can't see that from this angle. What about a central breast spot? And wing bars; do those pale lines qualify as wing bars? At that point the sparrow drops back into the grass. The observer has noted only one definite field mark: the streaked breast. That would rule out some species, except that even most plain-breasted sparrows have streaks in juvenile plumage.

On the other hand, an experienced birder often will know what a sparrow is after a split-second glimpse — narrowing down the choice at least to a group of two or three related forms. Can practiced eyes really tabulate field marks so fast? Not likely; the expert is probably using a different system entirely, one that begins not with field marks but with the characteristic shape and behavior of each group of sparrows.

Consider, for example, a comparison between the typical widespread forms of Savannah Sparrow and Song Sparrow. They are quite similar in plumage pattern, so much so that a very detailed plumage description of some individuals might not be enough to separate them. But they are so different in shape, flight action, social behavior, callnotes, and often even in their habitat preference, that an experienced birder is very unlikely to confuse them.

The key to identifying sparrows, then, is to make use of field marks in the right way: not as a starting point, but as the final thing to check. After we have quickly assessed everything else about the bird and arrived at a tentative idea as to which group of sparrows it fits, then we can look at the field marks to confirm or revise our identification.

PRELIMINARY POINTS IN SPARROW IDENTIFICATION

Ruling out other bird groups. Especially for new birders, a big issue in sparrow ID is just being certain that a given bird belongs in this group. Even House Sparrow is a source of confusion for one who is just starting out. Many small brownish birds can be separated from sparrows immediately by bill shape: pipits, for example, have very thin bills.

However, there are other streaky brown birds with somewhat sparrowlike bills, and these are worth considering. Pine Siskin and female House, Purple, and Cassin's finches are among the most frequent offenders. Surprisingly, the female Red-winged Blackbird is another. In all these cases, distinguishing them from sparrows is not just a matter of markings — their shapes and behaviors differ as well. The female Purple Finch may be streaked like a sparrow, but it is a chunky, long-winged, short-tailed bird that usu-

Female Purple Finch: unlike any sparrow in shape and behavior.

ally forages up in trees. The Pine Siskin may have a superficially sparrowlike pattern, but in shape, voice, and behavior it is clearly more like a goldfinch.

Additional problems are caused by other species that are relatively plain as adults but streaked as juveniles. Birds that are related to sparrows (such as towhees) or similar in shape (such as cowbirds) may take the birder by surprise when they show up in their streaky juvenile plumages. Again, characteristics of shape and behavior (and giveaway traits of juveniles, such as lax plumage and an expanded fleshy gape) should help to pinpoint what these birds really are.

Juvenile Canyon Towhee: easily mistaken for some streaky sparrow.

Field mark problems: streaked underparts. Some field guides in the past have made a broad separation of the sparrows into those with streaked underparts and those that are plain below. This dichotomy is potentially misleading. In almost all sparrows, the juveniles have finely streaked breasts, and some species (for example, Chipping Sparrow) may retain these streaks for some time after they are independent. Even adults of some plain-breasted species can show a vaguely streaked or mottled effect in this area; this can be fairly prominent in some species, such as White-throated Sparrow and Swamp Sparrow. Conversely, summer adults of some streaked-breasted sparrows can be in such worn plumage that they appear practically unstreaked. Of course the pattern of the underparts should be considered on any challenging sparrow, but it shouldn't be used as a basic point to divide the species.

Field mark problems: central breast spot. The central spot (or "stick-pin") on the breast is an often-quoted field mark for the Song Sparrow, American Tree Sparrow, and some others, but it is not an infallible mark. On any of the streaked-breasted sparrows, the streaks may or may not seem to coalesce into a central spot. Song Sparrow can lack such a central spot, while Savannah, Lincoln's, and other sparrows can have quite a noticeable spot in this area. On plain-breasted species, any ruffling of the feathers can expose their darker basal areas, briefly creating the impression of a dark spot.

Field mark problems: median crown stripe. In several cases among the sparrows, the presence or absence of a pale stripe down the center of the crown is a significant field mark. But there is a potential hazard here: some sparrows with crowns that are either solidly colored or evenly patterned with fine streaks may show a short, pale median stripe on the forehead, just above the base of the upper mandible. Viewed from some angles, this could be interpreted as a median crown stripe.

Field mark problems: white outer tail feathers. In most treatments of sparrow ID, only a few species are noted as having white on the outer tail feathers. This is often emphasized as the main field mark for Vesper Sparrow, for example. But this white can be hard to see when the bird is perched, and it may be reduced when the bird is in worn plumage. Conversely, some other sparrows, such as some populations of Savannah Sparrow, have the outer tail feathers quite pale. And almost any bird can appear to have the outer edge of the tail white when the bird is backlit, with light coming through the translucent outer vane of the outermost tail feather.

Visible effects of molt and wear. Sparrows in fresh plumage are beautiful birds, crisp and sharply patterned, with rich tones of browns and grays. Sparrows in worn plumage are not so inspiring and often more difficult to identify as well. The condition of their plumage has a strong impact on the usefulness of various field marks.

The molt of most North American sparrows fits Complex Alternate Strategy (see Chapter 4), with basic and alternate plumages in each annual cycle and with an inserted formative (first-winter) plumage in the first cycle. Most species go through the complete prebasic molt (adults) or the partial preformative molt (juveniles) in late summer, on the breeding grounds. Some, especially young birds, may start the molt later and complete it on the wintering grounds. Regardless, all sparrows should be in fresh plumage in early winter. Those that have a marked seasonal change in appearance may have the head pattern more muted in winter, but the rest of the plumage will be sharply marked.

Most sparrows have a limited prealternate molt in late winter, mainly replacing head and body feathers. Some (such as Swamp, Chipping, and Black-chinned) have major molt of head feathers, producing a brighter pattern in spring than in winter. Their wing and tail feathers will continue

to look steadily more worn in late spring and summer. Birds subject to abrasion against dense grass, such as Baird's, Grasshopper, and Cassin's sparrows, may look very worn by midsummer, even if they have replaced some feathers in spring.

Some sparrows molt on the Complex Basic Strategy, with only one plumage (basic) per annual cycle but with the inserted formative plumage in the first cycle. These birds also will be at their freshest in early winter and can be very worn by late summer; Vesper Sparrow and Song Sparrow are examples.

In looking at an unknown sparrow, it's always wise to try to gauge the condition of the plumage at the same time that we look for presence or absence of various field marks.

Two stages of plumage condition in Cassin's Sparrow. Above: in August, tuneful but very worn. Below: in December, freshly molted. Notice the major difference on the wings, scapulars, and uppertail coverts.

Subspecies of Song Sparrow. Upper left: *M. m. pusillula,* from California salt marshes. Upper right: *M. m. euphonia* from Ohio. Center: *M. m. fallax* from Arizona desert streams. Lower left: *M. m. kenaiensis* from south coastal Alaska. Lower right: *M. m. morphna* from coastal Washington.

Geographic variation. More than most groups of birds in North America, sparrows are subject to marked regional variation. Some sparrows vary so much from place to place that they have been in the past, or may be in the future, considered to constitute multiple species; examples include Savannah, Seaside, Sage, and Fox sparrows. Song Sparrow shows a remarkable amount of variation. Dozens of subspecies have been named, and close to forty of them are probably valid. Even experienced birders sometimes misidentify Song Sparrows when they travel away from their home areas, because they don't expect such a "familiar" bird to look so unfamiliar.

THE GENERIC APPROACH TO LOOKING AT A SPARROW

It is extremely helpful to think of each sparrow species in terms of the genus to which it belongs. On the following pages, I discuss all the genera of true sparrows in North America, as they are currently classified. Some of these generic placements may change in the near future, but these distinctions will continue to be useful. In fact, I encourage you to go through your favorite field guide and underline the name of the genus in the scientific name of each sparrow, perhaps with color-coding to help you remember the connections.

Genera *AIMOPHILA* and *PEUCAEA*

Rufous-crowned Sparrow
Rufous-winged Sparrow
Botteri's Sparrow
Cassin's Sparrow
Bachman's Sparrow

Overview. These are medium-sized to large sparrows, heavy-bodied and usually rather flat-crowned, with long tails that are rounded at the tip in most species. They inhabit dense vegetation near the ground, where they are often shy and difficult to observe. Some are found in pairs all year, and family groups may be seen during the breeding season, but they never form flocks. They flush reluctantly from cover and their flight is labored and usually low. The effects of wear on their feathers can have a major impact on their appearance at different times of year, but they do not have distinct seasonal plumages. The *Peucaea* species tend to be relatively quiet when not singing.

Identification notes. The long-standing genus *Aimophila* was broken up in 2010, with Rufous-winged, Botteri's, Cassin's, and Bachman's

Bachman's
Sparrow

placed in *Peucaea,* Rufous-crowned kept in *Aimophila,* and Five-striped Sparrow moved (back) to *Amphispiza.* The four *Peucaea* all have fairly musical songs and are extremely elusive when not singing. Rufous-winged is a little smaller and slimmer than the others in its group and not quite as hard to see, although it may forage quietly down in the grass.

Rufous-crowned Sparrow lives in pairs at all seasons and is more vocal than its former congeners; although it often hides in dense thickets, the varied callnotes used by members of a pair reveal their presence.

Rufous-crowned
Sparrow

Genus *SPIZELLA*

American Tree Sparrow
Chipping Sparrow
Clay-colored Sparrow
Brewer's Sparrow
Field Sparrow
Worthen's Sparrow (accidental)
Black-chinned Sparrow

Overview. These are small sparrows with rounded heads, small bills, and medium-long tails that are usually notched at the tip. Generally they are found in brushy areas or woodland edges, not open grassland or marshes. In migration and winter they are usually in flocks, ranging from a few birds to a few dozen. Typically they flock with their own species; strays may associate with other species of *Spizella*. They spend much of their time feeding on the ground, but they are also seen high in trees, and they often perch conspicuously in the open. Several of the species have distinct seasonal plumages, mainly involving changes in head pattern. Most of their callnotes are thin and lisping.

Identification notes. Over most of the U.S. and Canada, Chipping, Clay-colored, and/or Brewer's sparrows are common enough to serve as the generic *Spizella*, instantly recognized as such by their size, shape, and behavior. Separating these three can be a challenge, as detailed in the next chapter. The others are more distinctive. Tail length differs among species, and with experience, some can be distinguished by relative tail lengths, even as they fly away; Field Sparrow and Black-chinned Sparrow are close to the same body size as the others but conspicuously longer-tailed. American Tree Sparrow, the species

Field Sparrow

best adapted to cold climates, is visibly larger than the other species and has a fairly long tail. It has the most distinctive callnotes in the genus and is the only one with a sharply bicolored bill.

American Tree Sparrow

Genus *POOECETES* (Vesper Sparrow)

Overview. This is a fairly large bulky sparrow with a medium-long, squared or notched tail. It favors very open habitats, including grassland and farm fields, and may be in brushy areas but generally avoids dense cover. During migration and winter it is often seen in small loose flocks of a few individuals. Not especially secretive, it often perches up in the open.

Identification notes. The white outer vanes of outer tail feathers are often not visible until the bird flies. Rufous on the shoulder (lesser coverts) is often hidden by body feathers. On a perched bird, the darkly outlined ear coverts may furnish the best field mark. Geographic variation in color is overshadowed by effects of wear; worn adults in late summer can look darker and duller than fresh plumage of late fall. The common callnote is a loud *hsip.*

Vesper Sparrow

Genus *CHONDESTES* (Lark Sparrow)

Overview. A rather large sparrow; its tail is fairly long, with a broad, rounded tip and conspicuous white outer edges and corners. It inhabits brushy country near areas of bare ground and usually perches conspicuously in the open. In migration and winter it is usually seen in small loose flocks. Going from place to place it often flies high, giving a sharp, metallic callnote.

Identification notes. Of all North American sparrows, undoubtedly the easiest to identify. Juveniles are streaked below and have a muted face pattern at first, but have the distinctive tail pattern.

Genus *AMPHISPIZA*

Black-throated Sparrow
Sage Sparrow
Five-striped Sparrow

Overview. Medium-large sparrows with distinctive patterns, living on or near the ground in dry country. Often found in pairs or family groups at all seasons, but not seen in large flocks. Not secretive, regularly perching up in the open, and easily located by light, tinkling, or metallic calls.

Identification notes. The behavior described above applies to Black-throated and Sage sparrows. Five-striped is much more secretive and elusive, behaving like the classic sense of *Aimophila,* and it has been moved back and forth between these two genera. Sage Sparrow (which may be a complex of two species) is often most easily recognized by its behavior, bobbing its tail while perched, running on the ground with its tail raised.

Black-throated Sparrow

Genus *CALAMOSPIZA* (Lark Bunting)

Overview. Classified among the sparrows but quite different in shape and behavior. Bulky and thick-billed, with a fairly short wide tail and broad rounded wings. Easily identified on the breeding grounds. When not breeding, they wander in tightly packed flocks, feeding on the ground in open grassland, farm country, brush, perching up in the open when disturbed. Even the dullest winter birds look contrasty in flight, with pale patches on the coverts and conspicuous dark underwings.

adult male in winter

Genus *PASSERCULUS* (Savannah Sparrow)

Overview. This is a small, short-tailed sparrow, somewhat similar to *Ammodramus* (next), but not usually so chunky, large-headed, flat-crowned, or large-billed as some members of that genus. It nests in very open country, such as meadows and marshes, and in migration is often found in areas of sparse vegetation, such as farm fields or beaches with open ground and scattered clumps of grass. Not very secretive or elusive, it often perches up conspicuously in the open. During migration and winter it is typically in small loose flocks. It has thin, lisping callnotes, and it often calls when flushed. Compared to *Ammodramus,* most populations of Savannah Sparrow have longer and broader wings relative to their body size; this may not be apparent on perched birds, but in flight Savannahs look much more light and buoyant than other sparrows of open country.

Identification notes. Widespread, common, and variable, and perching in the open more than most similar sparrows, Savannah is often misidentified as other species. In fact, when viewing an unknown streaky sparrow, it's good to start by asking, "Why isn't this a Savannah?"

typical western interior Savannah

Geographic variation in Savannahs is considerable, with more than a dozen subspecies north of Mexico, and with three peripheral forms having been regarded as separate species in the past. The blackish "Belding's" of southern California salt marshes and the very pale "Ipswich" race wintering on Atlantic beaches are both readily recognizable, but the

"Belding's" Savannah Sparrow

"Large-billed" form that wanders north into California is not only different in shape but also pale and drab, lacking much of the pattern of other forms. Birders who are prepared for the appearance of these distinct forms are sometimes more confused by individuals that can lack all yellow on the supercilium.

Genus *AMMODRAMUS*

Grasshopper Sparrow
Baird's Sparrow
Henslow's Sparrow
Le Conte's Sparrow
Nelson's Sparrow
Saltmarsh Sparrow
Seaside Sparrow

Overview. These are chunky, short-tailed birds with flat foreheads; the first three species listed above look large-headed and large-billed, while the latter four have proportionately smaller heads and thinner bills. Most species require particular types of grasslands, meadows, or marshes; precise habitat is a strong clue in identification, because the birds themselves are usually hard to see, staying down out of sight when not singing. Generally they are hard to flush, and their flight looks labored as they fly away low and then dive into the vegetation again. Most of them are silent when flushed, although Le Conte's and Grasshopper will sometimes give a quiet chip note in flight. Outside the nesting season they are strictly solitary, not forming flocks even where they are common.

Identification notes. The biggest challenge in this genus (aside from just getting good looks at the birds) is distinguishing Nelson's and Saltmarsh sparrows, formerly treated as one species under the name Sharp-tailed Sparrow. These two hybridize to a limited extent where their breeding ranges overlap in southern Maine, so not all individuals will be identifiable to species. Juveniles of most members of the genus look noticeably different from adults, in a variety of ways. Range and precise habitat are good clues for these birds in summer; but Baird's, Grasshopper, and Le Conte's juveniles may migrate south while still partly or entirely in juvenile plumage, and such birds can be genuinely challenging to identify.

Henslow's
Sparrow

Seaside Sparrow, race
fisheri, in February

Genus *PASSERELLA* (Fox Sparrow)

Overview. A large chunky sparrow with a medium-length tail (populations of the western mountains are longer-tailed than others). Bill shape varies regionally; most look fairly large-billed, but some races in the West have the lower mandible oddly swollen. Usually on the ground in woods or dense brush, where it forages by scratching among the leaf-litter, making a little jump and kicking backwards with both feet at once. Generally seen only in small numbers. It often associates loosely with other sparrows in winter, but seldom forms flocks of its own kind.

Identification notes. Over most of the continent, this bird is seldom confused with any other species, although visitors may be misled by the very large dark Song Sparrows found in parts of Alaska. However, there is a good chance that Fox Sparrow will be split into three or four species in the future, and if that happens, distinguishing these species will present considerable challenges. Each of the four main populations — the eastern and northern "Red," northwestern "Sooty," interior western "Slate-colored," and "Thick-billed" of California and Oregon — is distinctive at the center of its range but intergrades with others where their ranges meet. Songs are basically similar, but "Red" sings clearest whistles, "Slate-colored" and "Thick-billed" have most variable songs. Three of these groups have the same common callnote, a hard *smak*, but the Thick-billed's call is a more metallic *tink*.

"Red" Fox Sparrow, race *P. i. zaboria,* in summer in Alaska

"Thick-billed" Fox Sparrow, race *P. i. stephensi,* in summer in California

Genus *MELOSPIZA*

Song Sparrow
Lincoln's Sparrow
Swamp Sparrow

Overview. These are all robust medium-large sparrows, and they have longish tails that are usually rounded or squared at the tip. Usually they are found low in dense vegetation, and they tend to be secretive (although Song Sparrow can become less so when it lives in yards and parks). They are never in flocks; generally they are solitary, or in pairs at times. All have loud and distinctive callnotes.

Identification notes. The main issue involving this genus is the extreme geographic variation in Song Sparrow, as mentioned on p. 423. Traveling birders sometimes misidentify unfamiliar local forms of Song Sparrow as Fox, Savannah, or Swamp sparrows. Despite the obvious visible variation, there is little regional variation in voice, and all Song Sparrows north of Mexico can be recognized quickly by their common callnote, a nasal *cheff.* Other points of ID interest in this genus include confusion between Song and Lincoln's sparrows. Juvenile Songs in summer are especially likely to be misidentified, because these juveniles often have a buff wash across the chest and narrower streaking below than the adults. If a purported Lincoln's is seen out of range in summer, it should

adult Lincoln's Sparrow
in late spring

be studied to see whether it has the rather worn plumage of an adult at that season or the fresh but somewhat loose plumage of a juvenile. Young Swamp Sparrows in their first winter can be confusing also, as they may lack all rufous on the crown, but the bright chestnut on the wings should give them away.

adult Swamp Sparrow

Genus *ZONOTRICHIA*

White-throated Sparrow
Harris's Sparrow
White-crowned Sparrow
Golden-crowned Sparrow

Overview. These are medium-large to large sparrows, with the tail fairly long and square-tipped, the crown slightly peaked, and the bill not disproportionately large. In winter they are found in brushy areas or woodland edges, almost always in flocks. They feed on the ground but often perch up conspicuously in the open when disturbed. Their callnotes are sharp and distinctive.

Identification notes. Identifying these sparrows to species is seldom a problem, although streaked juveniles in summer and some very dull Golden-crowned Sparrows in winter could be momentarily confusing. However, variation within the species offers a number of interesting situations to the field birder. Three or four well-marked forms of White-crowned Sparrows can be distinguished most of the time in the field, allowing observers to track the different timing of migration of these populations. Also in White-crowned Sparrow there are distinct regional song dialects, some quite localized, which have been the basis for important studies. Traveling birders are likely to notice these

adult White-crowned Sparrow
of eastern race *Z. l. leucophrys*

changes in song from place to place. More remarkable is the situation with color morphs of White-throated Sparrow. Tan-striped and white-striped birds are about equally common and can be of either sex, pairs are almost always one of each morph, and behavioral differences between the morphs have been documented.

White-throated Sparrow of the tan-striped morph

Genus *JUNCO* (Juncos)

Dark-eyed Junco
Yellow-eyed Junco

Overview. Distinctive sparrows with white outer tail feathers, mostly gray and brown, lacking streaks except in juvenile plumage. They breed mostly in cooler forests of the North and the mountains. Northern populations spread southward and to lowlands in winter, forming winter flocks that may number up to a few dozen birds. These flocks forage on the ground in open spots near taller cover, such as woodland clearings and edges; if disturbed, they fly up into trees and shrubs, making hard ticking callnotes. Almost all the juncos north of Mexico are currently classified as Dark-eyed Junco, and identifying them to species is rarely a problem, but separation of the many subspecies is an absorbing challenge for field birders.

Genera *CALCARIUS* and *RHYNCHOPHANES* (Longspurs)

Lapland Longspur
Chestnut-collared Longspur
Smith's Longspur
McCown's Longspur

Overview. They look similar to sparrows, but longspurs (and Snow and McKay's buntings) are now placed in a distinct family, Calcariidae. They breed on grassland or tundra, winter on short-grass prairies, barren flats, plowed fields. In migration and winter they occur in flocks, feeding on the ground; if disturbed, the flocks circle about in high flight. Summer males wear bright alternate plumages, but in basic plumage all are more cryptic; winter longspurs are most easily identified by distinctive callnotes, tail patterns seen when flushing or landing, differences in size and shape, and slight differences in preferred habitat.

Lapland Longspur, first-autumn female in September

31. THE *SPIZELLA* SPARROWS

Species treated in detail:

CHIPPING SPARROW *Spizella passerina*
CLAY-COLORED SPARROW *Spizella pallida*
BREWER'S SPARROW *Spizella breweri*
 (including "Timberline Sparrow," *S. b. taverneri*)

The problem. These common sparrows present a series of ID challenges that range from very easy to essentially impossible. This range of difficulty makes this trio a good focus for birders' attention. Identifying the birds requires us to remain flexible, adjusting our approach to the particular individuals in front of us.

Adult Chipping Sparrows in spring and summer can be identified at a glance, but some fall and winter birds, especially young birds, might be confused with Clay-colored or even Brewer's Sparrows. The latter two species are reasonably distinct from each other in spring and summer, but in fall and winter they are more variable and less distinctive. In fact, in all three of these *Spizella* species, most autumn immatures and many autumn adults converge on a generalized head pattern: their ear coverts have brown patches with moderately distinct dark outlines, and their crowns are finely streaked, with an ill-defined pale median stripe. The variation in Clay-colored and Brewer's sparrows is such that the dullest Clay-coloreds and most sharply marked Brewer's can be almost identical.

Adding to the challenge is the rather mysterious "Timberline Sparrow," currently classified as a subspecies of Brewer's Sparrow.

PRELIMINARY POINTS

Comparison to other sparrows. In order to identify these birds with confidence, we have to be sure that we've ruled out all other sparrows. That requires close attention to the characteristics of the *Spizella* sparrows (as described in the previous chapter on p. 425), with their small size, slim bodies, and small-headed, small-billed shape. There are some sparrows belonging to other genera that look superficially like these *Spizella* sparrows in pattern. Rufous-winged Sparrow, found locally in southern Arizona, can strongly suggest Chipping Sparrow, and it may take a second look before we notice that it is a larger, heavier bird with some pattern differences. Another southwestern bird, Cassin's Sparrow, has a pattern vaguely like that of Brewer's Sparrow, but Cassin's is a much more bulky, big-headed bird, solitary and elusive, generally hiding low in dense grass.

Geographic variation. Although it is not mentioned or illustrated in most field guides, there is regional variation in Chipping Sparrows. The widespread western race, *S. p. arizonae* (nesting from the Great Plains westward except for areas along the Pacific Coast), averages slightly larger and paler than the eastern population. If a western Chipping strayed to the Atlantic Seaboard in fall and was seen in the company of local birds, it might appear different enough to attract the attention of birders and cause some confusion. The "Timberline Sparrow," currently classified as a subspecies of Brewer's but sometimes proposed as a full species, is treated in a separate note at the end of this chapter.

Juvenile plumage. Brewer's and Clay-colored sparrows wear full juvenile plumage only briefly, beginning their molt into formative plumage before they leave the breeding grounds. They may not complete the molt until they reach the wintering grounds, but they seldom show much streaking on the underparts by the time they migrate. In Chipping Sparrow, however, preformative molt may begin later, especially in western populations; young birds may migrate a considerable distance in streak-breasted juvenile plumage and may be seen in this plumage as late as October. The juvenile Chipping is very different from the spring adult — its crown is finely streaked black on dull brown, its rump is brown instead of gray at first, and its breast is heavily marked with fine streaks — and birders may be mystified by it on first encounter. However, its shape and behavior should mark it as a *Spizella*.

Chipping

Brewer's

Juvenile Chipping and Brewer's sparrows. Face pattern and tail length are clues to their specific identity, as long as we have them in the right genus.

Tail length. These three species differ in average tail length, and occasionally this can be useful in the field — for example, in areas of the southwest where both Chipping and Brewer's sparrows may be common in winter, and tail length may be picked out easily on birds in flight. Of these three species, Brewer's has the longest tail on average, Chipping has the shortest, and Clay-colored is intermediate.

FIELD MARKS: CHIPPING SPARROW VS. THE OTHERS

Because Chipping Sparrow is the most distinctive of these three species, it is useful to discuss the points that isolate it first, before considering how to separate the other two.

Rump color. In Brewer's and Clay-colored sparrows, the rump is always dull brown, usually with vague streaks on Brewer's. In all Chipping Sparrows that are past juvenile plumage, the rump is unmarked gray. On juvenile Chippings the rump is brown and finely streaked, but this area of the plumage begins to change rather early in the preformative molt, and most individuals probably have completely grayish rumps by the time they lose the streaking on the breast.

Rump color is usually difficult to see on *Spizella* when they are foraging on the ground, but when perched upright they often hold the wings slightly drooped and their rump color can be easily discerned. On Chipping Sparrows, the contrast between the warm brown of the back and the gray rump may be conspicuous even in flight.

Chipping
Sparrow in
December

Lores. Most Chipping Sparrows have a distinct dark line from the eye to the bill — i.e., through the lores — and virtually all Chippings, even juveniles, have at least a vague line there. In Clay-colored and Brewer's sparrows the lores are usually pale, hardly contrasting with the tone of the supercilium, all the way down to where the moustachial stripe begins. In most cases this character will rapidly separate Chipping from the other two species, but some individuals have an intermediate appearance. In those cases in which we can't decide whether the lores are dark or pale, we should ignore this point and focus on other characteristics.

Two Chipping Sparrows from early fall to show elements of face pattern (including the line through the lores) and crown pattern.

Crown pattern. In Chipping Sparrow the crown is nearly solid rufous on spring and summer adults, but in fall and winter it is quite variable. Most young birds lack rufous on the crown until late fall; their crowns are medium brown with fine black streaks and usually with a poorly defined pale median crown stripe. This pattern is also seen on some fall and winter adults, but most have at least a small amount of visible rufous. There may be a tendency for eastern Chippings to show more rufous on the crown in fall, on average, than those in the West.

Brewer's and many Clay-coloreds in fall have much the same crown pattern as the dullest Chipping Sparrows. Some Clay-coloreds continue to have heavier black streaks toward the sides of the crown, and a more clearly defined pale median crown stripe, than any Chipping.

Outline of ear coverts. A contrasting brown patch on the ear coverts is a feature of Brewer's and Clay-colored sparrows all year and of immature and many adult Chipping Sparrows in fall and winter. In the first two, most of the edge of this patch is traced by a dark outline. This outline is darker on some individuals than others, but the moustachial stripe (which forms the forward part of the lower edge of the patch) is always as distinct as the eyestripe (which forms the upper border). In Chipping Sparrow, the very distinct eyestripe is always darker and more obvious than any part of the lower border of the ear coverts.

FIELD MARKS: BREWER'S VS. CLAY-COLORED SPARROWS

The pale median crown stripe of Clay-colored Sparrow, often suggested as the main field mark separating these two, is not diagnostic by itself, because many Brewer's have at least a suggestion of such a stripe. Clay-colored Sparrow tends to be more strongly patterned and more colorful than Brewer's Sparrow, but this generalization often is not enough for identification. Many dull Clay-coloreds and bright Brewer's approach each other very closely in appearance.

Crown pattern. There is not much variation in the crown pattern of Brewer's Sparrow, sandy brown with fine black streaks. Often there are fewer streaks down the center (especially toward the forehead), and sometimes the ground color is paler there also, creating a vague pale median stripe that is most noticeable from the front.

On adult Clay-colored Sparrows in spring and summer the sides of the crown are rich brown, and this color is heavily overlaid by wide black streaks. From a distance the effect is of very dark, broad lateral crown stripes, contrasting sharply with the pale supercilium and median crown stripe. Fall and winter birds typically have thinner black streaks on the brown lateral areas of the crown, but most still have stronger crown patterns than any Brewer's.

On some Clay-coloreds in fall and winter, however, the black streaks on the crown may be still thinner, and the pale median crown stripe may be less clearly defined. Although the color toward the sides of the crown on these birds is still a warmer brown than on the typical Brewer's Sparrow, some Clay-coloreds may look identical in crown pattern to some Brewer's under field conditions.

Supercilium. In Clay-colored Sparrow, the color of the pale stripe over the eye is variable. On summer adults it ranges from white (mostly males) through grayish white to brownish white (mostly females). On some fall birds, perhaps especially younger birds, the supercilium tends more to rich buff. The supercilium of Brewer's Sparrow is always some shade of pale brownish gray. It appears less "clean" — more invaded by very fine, subtle streaking or mottling — than the supercilium of Clay-colored, and usually contrasts less with the crown and ear coverts.

Malar region. In Clay-colored Sparrow the thin, dark lateral throat stripe is usually noticeable, and it helps to set off the pale submoustachial stripe just above it; this broad pale stripe often appears to be a slightly different color (more clearly whitish or buff) than the throat. In Brewer's Sparrow the dark lateral throat stripe tends to be less distinct, so that the dull pale stripe above it is rarely made more conspicuous.

Gray side of neck. All three species have a gray "collar" on the sides of the neck, extending up onto the nape. This is most noticeable on Clay-colored because it contrasts strongly with the brown and buff tones of adjacent areas. It is least noticeable on Brewer's, in which the collar is tinged dusty brown and usually crossed by vague darker streaks.

June

May

The apparent color differences of these two Clay-colored Sparrows are caused mostly by momentary light conditions.

Breast color. Clay-colored Sparrows in spring and summer usually have the breast grayish white, while fall and winter birds have a warm buffy wash across the breast, strongest toward the sides. Brewer's Sparrows are dingy grayish below, often washed with brown on the flanks and at the sides of the upper breast, but rarely with any warm buff.

Outline of ear coverts. Although many Brewer's Sparrows have the brown ear coverts just as distinctly outlined as the typical Clay-colored, a bird with a very indistinct outline to this patch is almost certain to be a Brewer's, not a Clay-colored.

March

July

Brewer's Sparrow shows little seasonal change in appearance, aside from the effects of wear as on the July bird at right.

NOTES ON THE "TIMBERLINE SPARROW"

The Timberline Sparrow was described as a new species *(Spizella tav-erneri)* in 1925, but the American Ornithologists' Union has always treated it as a subspecies of Brewer's Sparrow. While nominate Brewer's nests in sagebrush flats and other open desert of the interior of the West, the Timberline nests in scrubby habitat of high elevations of the northern Rockies, from east-central Alaska to southwestern Alberta. Recently it also has been found breeding at high elevations in north-western Montana; its southern limits are uncertain. The winter range and migratory route of Timberline Sparrow are very poorly known.

Birders who seek out this form in its breeding habitat may notice these differences from nominate Brewer's Sparrow. Timberline averages slightly darker-billed and perhaps shorter-tailed. Its face pattern tends to be a little more distinctly marked, with a more obvious dark outline around slightly darker ear coverts, a paler supercilium, and darker crown markings, although its pale eye-ring may be less obvious. The black streaks on its back may average heavier and more obvious, and streaking on the nape may be more apparent, but it also may show a more obvious gray collar. It may look darker gray across the breast, contrasting more with the white belly.

Timberline Sparrow, identified mainly by location: in the Yukon Territory in summer.

Differences in song may also be detected. Brewer's has both a short song of two or three buzzy trills and a longer song, lasting up to 15 seconds, consisting of buzzes, trills, bubbling notes, and high thin notes; both song types are quite variable. The Timberline Sparrow's song is also variable, but it tends to be made up of more musical trills, with less of a buzzy quality and without high thin notes.

Away from the breeding grounds, Timberline Sparrow is almost never identified with confidence. Essentially all of its visible differences from nominate Brewer's are differences of degree, so it's almost impossible to say whether a given individual is a Timberline or a strongly marked Brewer's. As mentioned in the previous section, a heavily marked Brewer's and a dull Clay-colored can look virtually identical, and the Timberline falls in this same zone, muddying the picture still further. Working out reliable field marks for Timberline Sparrow will be a valuable project for advanced birders of the future.

PHOTO CREDITS

Of the photos used to create the images in this guide, nearly half (over 300) were taken by Kenn and Kimberly Kaufman. Credits for the rest are listed below. Images are listed by page number (in bold), followed by a dash and the number of the image. Images on each page are numbered from left to right and from top to bottom, and line drawings are not counted.

G. Bailey/VIREO: 297-2

Glenn Bartley/VIREO: 82-1; 154-2; 156-1; 235-2

Thomas A. Benson: 310-8, 10

Rick and Nora Bowers/BowersPhoto.com: 75-1; 81-2, 3, 4; 83-1, 3, 4; 88-5; 109-1; 124-1; 144-2; 145-3; 146-2; 151-2; 152-1; 158-1; 160-1; 161-1; 162-7; 164-2; 178-2; 187-1; 198-1; 206-2, 4; 216-1; 217-2; 219-1, 2; 222-2; 230-2, 3, 5, 6; 235-1, 4; 236-3; 237-2; 252-2; 255-1; 257-1; 258-1; 261-1; 266-2; 267-1; 278-3; 282-1; 291-1; 292-1; 293-2, 3; 317-1; 322-1; 323-1; 325-1; 326-1, 2; 330-1; 332-1; 334-1; 335-1; 336-1; 338-1, 2, 3, 4; 340-1, 2, 3; 344-1; 348-3; 357-2, 4, 5; 363-1, 4, 5; 365-1; 369-3, 4, 5; 375-1; 379-7; 381-3, 5; 383-1, 2, 3, 4, 6; 387-4, 5; 388-1; 394-2, 3; 395-1; 396-2; 402-1; 420-2; 422-2; 423-3, 5; 424-2; 426-1; 427-2; 429-1; 433-1; 434-1; 436-1; 439-2, 3

Rick and Nora Bowers/VIREO: 414-1

Steve Byland (www.stevebyland.com): 199-1; 204-1; 206-1, 3, 5; 208-1, 2, 3, 4, 5, 6, 7

Rob Curtis/VIREO: 165-2, 3; 176-1

Ian Davies: 251-1; 294-2; 295-4; 298-1, 2, 3; 310-14, 15

John Dunning/VIREO: 415-2

Sam Fried/VIREO: 440-1

Martin Hale/VIREO: 241-1

Nic Hallam: 296-1

J. G. Holmes/VIREO: 239-1

M. Hyett/VIREO: 297-1

Jean Iron: 310-1, 2, 4

Jukka Jantunen/VIREO: 164-3

Greg Lavaty: 310-5, 6, 7

Tony Leukering: 96-1; 169-1; 172-1; 185-1, 2; 192-1; 193-1; 196-1; 234-1; 252-1; 260-3; 262-1; 266-3; 273-1; 300-1; 314-1; 389-1

Geoff Malosh/VIREO: 168-1

Avi Meir (www.flickr.com/photos/avi_meir_photography): 239-2, 3

Martin Meyers: 175-1; 177-1; 180-1, 2; 268-1; 295-1

Arthur Morris/VIREO: 297-3; 308-2

Kristin Munafo: 357-7; 400-1

Brian Patteson/VIREO: 310-12

Jeff Poklen/VIREO: 269-1, 2, 3; 307-1; 308-1

Steven Round (www.stevenroundbird-photography.com): 296-2, 3

Johann Schumacher/VIREO: 165-1

Mark C. Shieldcastle: 36-2; 40-1; 114-1; 116-1, 2; 126-1; 127-1, 2; 129-1; 401-2

Brian E. Small (www.briansmallphoto.com): 74-1; 82-2, 3; 84-1; 88-6; 91-1; 92-1; 110-1; 145-2; 146-1, 3; 149-1, 2; 162-1, 3, 4, 5, 6, 8; 163-1; 164-1; 167-1; 173-1, 2; 174-1, 2; 177-4; 178-1; 211-2, 3; 212-1; 227-1, 2; 230-4; 231-1; 236-1, 2; 237-1; 238-1; 251-2; 307-2, 3; 327-1; 329-1; 332-2; 335-2; 336-2; 357-1, 3; 359-1, 2, 3, 4; 363-2, 3; 365-2, 3, 4, 8; 369-1, 2, 9; 371-1, 2, 3, 4, 5, 9; 375-2, 3, 4, 7; 378-1; 379-1, 2, 3, 4; 381-1, 2, 4; 383-5; 387-1, 2, 3, 8; 396-1, 3; 405-1; 418-1; 422-1; 423-1, 4; 424-1; 428-1; 429-2; 430-1, 2; 435-1, 2; 437-1, 2; 439-1, 4

David Stemple: 363-8

Ruth Sullivan: 310-9

Glen Tepke/VIREO: 310-11

Ray Tipper/VIREO: 241-2

Jeremiah R. Trimble: 238-3; 310-13

Mats Wallin: 296-4

Doug Wechsler/VIREO: 155-1; 177-2; 292-2

J. Wedge/VIREO: 415-1

Christopher L. Wood: 238-2

Steve Young/VIREO: 310-3

INDEX OF BIRDS AND MAJOR SUBJECTS

This index includes every mention of a species name; page numbers in bold indicate an illustration. Other topics are indexed only where there is a substantial discussion. Scientific names are not indexed, except for names of genera that are specifically discussed as such.

Abnormal colors 125–129
Accipiters 191, 198–209
Accipitridae 188, 195
Aimophila 424
Albinism 125–126
Alderfer, Jonathan 135
Ammodramus 429
Amphispiza 427
Anhinga 85
Anous 279
Archilochus 326, 330, 331
Auklet, Cassin's 183
   Rhinoceros **185**
Avocet, American 217
Aythya 145

Basileuterus 396
Beardless-Tyrannulet, Northern 95, **348**
Beginners, our responsibility to 17
Bill deformities 40
Bill structure 64–65
Birding by detail 8–10
Birding by impression 7–10, 188
Bishop sp. **41**
Blackbird, Brewer's 99, 111
   Red-winged **19**, 99, 117, 140, 420
Black-Hawk, Common **188**
Brinkley, Ned 125
Bufflehead 146, 153
Bunting, Indigo 11, 39, **116**, 124
   Lark 32, **427**
   Lazuli 11, 91, 124
   McKay's 36
   Snow 36, 80, 89
   Varied 110
Burhinidae 216
Bushtit **111**

Calamospiza 427
Calcarius 433

Calidris 22, 23, 220
Calypte 327, 330, 331
Canvasback 90, 145, 157
Cape May, NJ 8
Cardellina 394
Cardinal, Northern **48**, 103, 106, 129
Catbird, Gray 100, **114**, 116
Cathartidae 188
Charadriidae 217
Charadrius 218
Chat, Yellow-breasted 116, 396
Chickadee, Black-capped 12
   Carolina 12
   foraging of 97
Chlidonias 279
Chondestes 426
Chuck-will's-widow 50
Contopus 22
Coot, American 143
Corben, Chris 76
Cowbird, Bronzed 99
   Brown-headed 99, 102
Crane, Sandhill 38
Creeper, Brown 97, 112
Crossbill, Red 12, 111
Crow, American 39, 106
   Fish **39**
Cuckoo, Black-billed **57**
Curlew, Long-billed **221**

Dendroica 392, 394, 398
Details, learning to see 27
Dickcissel 98
Dove, Inca 112
   Mourning **20**, 27, 109, **112**
   White-tipped **20**
Dowitcher, Long-billed 30, 108, **219**, 223, 224
   Short-billed **98**, 121, **219**, 223, **224**
Duck, American Black 111, 124, **151**, 154

Harlequin **145**, 148
Long-tailed **146**, 157
Masked 147, 157
Mottled **141**, **151**
Muscovy 159
Ring-necked **75**, **145**, 148, 151, 166, 167
Ruddy 100, **147**, 153, 157
Tufted **166**, 167
Wood 98, 106, **144**
Ducks, plumage designations for 155–158
Dunlin 8, 212, **214**, 215, 220, 228
Dunn, Jon 135
Dunne, Pete 8, 92

Eagle, as group name 190
   Bald **46**, **190**, 195
   Golden 100, 190
   White-tailed 190
"Eclipse" plumage 143, 155–157
Egret, Cattle 187
   Great **49**, 186, 187
   Little 186
   Reddish 122, 187
   Snowy 186, 187
Eider, Common 143
   King **145**
   sp. 145, 154, 157
   Steller's 145
Empidonax 22, 43, 345, 346, 347–387
Euplectes 41
Euthlypis 396

Falcon, Peregrine **6**, 108, 189, 192, 195
   Prairie 195
Falconidae 188
Fault bars 114
Feather structure 44–50
Feather tracts 50
Field exercises 138–140

Finch, Cassin's 103, 420
    House **62–63,** 88, 128,
        132, 420
    Purple 29, **66, 420**
Flicker, Gilded 343
    Northern 11, 124, 343
    "Red-shafted" 11, 124,
        343
    "Yellow-shafted" 11,
        47, 124, 343
Flight identification 99
Floyd, Ted 135
Flycatcher, Acadian **49,** 89,
        347–387, **351, 359**
    Alder 89, 347–387,
        351, 363
    Ash-throated 344
    Buff-breasted 347–387,
        351, 387
    Cordilleran 347–387,
        381, 383
    Dusky 89, 110, 347–
        387, **351, 378, 379**
    Dusky-capped **344**
    Gray 89, 110, 347–387,
        351, 375
    Hammond's 89, 347–
        387, **351, 371**
    Least, 347–387, **347,
        349, 351, 369**
    Nutting's 344
    Olive-sided 95
    Pacific-slope 347–387,
        351, 381
    Piratic **42**
    Scissor-tailed 32, 95,
        110
    Sulphur-bellied 42,
        345
    "Traill's" 354, 361
    Variegated 42
    Vermilion **139**
    "Western" 354, 380
    Willow 89, 347–387,
        365
    Yellow-bellied **39,** 95,
        347–387, **351, 357**
Fulmar, Northern 100

Gadwall 149, 152, **153**
Gannet, Northern 112, 185
Garganey, 150, 157
Gelochelidon 278

Geothlypis 394
Glareolidae 216
Gnatcatcher, Black-capped
        19
    Blue-gray 19
Godwit, Marbled **222**
Goldeneye, Barrow's **149,**
        150
    Common **146, 149**
Golden-Plover, American
        100, **212, 217,** 225
Goldfinch, American **83,**
        125
    Lawrence's 103
    Lesser 103
Goose, "Blue" 122
    Cackling **142**
    Canada 106, **142**
    Ross's 142
    Snow 122, 142
Goshawk, "Mexican" 191
    Northern 33, 191, 192,
        198–209, **202, 208**
Grackle, Common 97, 99
    Great-tailed 98
Grant, P. J. 6, 35
Grebe, Pied-billed 93
Grosbeak, Black-headed
        11, 91, 124
    Evening 132
    Rose-breasted 11, 124
Ground-Dove, Common
        67, 112
    Ruddy 67
Guillemot, Black **34**
Gull, American Herring
        244, **245,** 253, 255,
        256, **260,** 262, 264,
        267, 270, 271
    American Herring ×
        Glaucous-winged
        265, 267
    Belcher's 262
    Black-headed 251, 261,
        262, 264
    Black-tailed 262
    Bonaparte's **71, 85,**
        251, 255, 259, 261,
        262, **263**
    California 257, 302
    European Herring 267,
        270, 271
    Franklin's 28, **252,** 257

Glaucous 251, **254,**
        259, 265, 267, **268**
    Glaucous × Glaucous-
        winged 265
    Glaucous × Herring
        267, 268
    Glaucous-winged 12,
        123, 251, 259, 265,
        266, 267
    Glaucous-winged ×
        Slaty-backed 265
    Glaucous-winged ×
        Western 12, 41, 123,
        265, **266, 267**
    Great Black-backed
        251, **259,** 261, 264
    Great Black-backed ×
        Herring 268
    Heermann's **242,** 262,
        302, 315
    Herring **16,** 19, **68,**
        244, 251, **253,** 254,
        256, 257, 268, 270,
        271
    Herring × Lesser
        Black-backed 268
    Heuglin's 271
    Iceland 251, 256, 259,
        268, 269
    Ivory 32, 252, 254, 257
    Kelp 264
    Kumlien's Iceland 256,
        261, 268, 269, 270
    Laughing 28, 251, 257,
        264, 302
    Lesser Black-backed
        16, 19, 256, **260,** 263,
        264, 270
    Little 251, 259, 261, 264
    Mew 257, **258,** 260, 302
    "Nelson's" 268
    Ring-billed **25,** 244,
        246, **247–250,** 251,
        253, 255, 257, 260,
        302
    Ross's 261, 264
    Sabine's 182
    Slaty-backed **261,** 264,
        265, 271
    Thayer's 251, **252,** 257,
        259, 261, 267, 268,
        269, 270
    Vega Herring 267, 271

Gull (*cont.*)
Western 12, **76,** 244, 255, 265, **266**
Yellow-footed **255, 257**
Yellow-legged 270
Gyrfalcon 191, 196, 209

Habitat and ID 93–94
Haematopodidae 217
Harrier, Northern 100, 189, **191,** 196
Hawk, Broad-winged **26,** 90, 189, 192, 196
Cooper's 10, 31, 33, 90, 100, 108, 191, 198–209, **198, 202, 204, 208**
Ferruginous 192, 196
Gray 191
Harlan's Red-tailed **193**
Red-shouldered 10, 189, 191, 195
Red-tailed 32, **33, 36,** 75, 123, 189, 191, 193, 194, 195
Rough-legged **196**
Sharp-shinned 10, 31, 108, 191, **192,** 196, 198–209, **199, 202, 206**
Short-tailed 196
Swainson's 33, 90, 196
Hayman, Peter 6
Head pattern 51
Helmitheros 395
Heron, Great Blue **19,** 122, 123, 187
"Great White" 122
Little Blue 122, **186, 187**
Tricolored 187
House-Martin, Common 389
Howell, Steve N. G. 76, 79, 135
Hummingbird, Allen's 325, 328, 330, 336–341, **341**
Anna's 321, 323, 324, 327, 328, 330–336, **333, 335**
Berylline × Magnificent **329**

Black-chinned **321, 323,** 324, **326,** 327, 328, 330–336, **332, 333**
Broad-billed **318,** 322, 327
Broad-tailed 110, 325, 328, 330, 331, 336–341, **338**
Calliope 325, **330,** 336–341, **340**
Costa's 323, 324, 327, 328, 330–336, **336**
Lucifer **324,** 327
Magnificent 327
Ruby-throated 19, 320, 324, 326, 327, 328, 330–336, **333, 334**
Rufous **325,** 328, 330, 336–341, **337, 338, 341**
Violet-crowned **322**
White-eared 327
Humphrey, Philip 76
Humphrey-Parkes terminology 76
Hybridization 11–13, 40–41, 123–125
Hydrobatidae 183

Ibis, Glossy 139
White-faced **82,** 139
Icteria 396
Identification Guide to North American Birds 107, 121

Jacana, Northern **216**
Jacanidae 216
Jaeger, Long-tailed 123, 300–315, **303, 304, 307, 308, 310, 313**
Parasitic 31, 300–315, **303, 304, 307, 308, 310, 312, 313**
Pomarine 10, 31, 300–315, **300, 303, 304, 307, 310, 313, 314**
Jay, Blue 39, **47,** 100, 106
Brown 116
Green 77
Mexican 116
Steller's **48,** 100

Jonsson, Lars 135
Junco, Dark-eyed 120, 121, 433
"Oregon" 121
Yellow-eyed 433
Juvenal vs. juvenile 78
Juvenile plumage 112

Karlson, Kevin 8
Kestrel, American 140, 192
Killdeer 138, 139
Kingbird, Cassin's 345
Couch's 344
Eastern **110**
Tropical 344
Western **90**
Kingfisher, Belted **99**
Kinglet, Golden-crowned 104
Ruby-crowned 95, 97, **348**
Kiskadee, Great 345
Kite, as group name 190
Mississippi 190
Snail **190**
White-tailed 190
Kittiwake, Black-legged **260,** 302
Red-legged **262**
sp. 182, 257
Knot, Red 214, 220

Lark, Horned 117
Sky 10
Leucism 36, 125–126
Limnothlypis 395
Linnaeus, Carolus 117
Longspur, Chestnut-collared 433
Lapland **433**
McCown's **92,** 433
Smith's 433
Loon, Arctic 168–181, **176, 177**
Common 33, 34, 36, 168–181, **169, 177, 178, 179**
Pacific 168–181, **174, 175, 177**
Red-throated 168–181, **168, 172, 173**
Yellow-billed 33, 168–181, **179, 180**

MacArthur, Robert 398
Mallard 34, 36, 124, 144, 148, 151, **154, 156,** 159, 165
  × American Black Duck 40
  × Northern Pintail **158**
Martin, Brown-chested 389
  Cuban 389
  Gray-breasted 389
  Purple 184, 389
  Southern 389
Meadowlark, Eastern **31,** 139
  Western 140
Melospiza 431
Merganser, Common 149
  Hooded **147, 148,** 149, 153
  Red-breasted **150,** 152
Merlin 191, **192,** 195, 209
Mniotilta 393
Mockingbird, Northern 100, 103
Molt and migration 89–91
  limits 115
  of flight feathers 84–87
  strategies 74–84
  synchronous 85
Mullarney, Killian 135
Muscicapidae 345
Myiarchus 22, 345, 346
Myioborus 393

Nighthawk, Common 105
  Lesser 105
Night-Heron, Black-crowned 187
Nightjar, Buff-collared 345
Noddy, Black 279, 281
  Brown 100, 279, 281
Nuthatch, White-breasted 13, 97

O'Brien, Michael 8
Oddie, Bill 9
Onychoprion 279
Oporornis 394, 397
Oreothlypis 393
Oriole, Baltimore **11,** 29, 124

Baltimore × Bullock's 11, 41
Bullock's 11, 21, 29, 91, 124
Hooded 28, **103**
Northern 11
Orchard 28
Oscines vs. suboscines 101
Osprey **70,** 196
Ovenbird **29,** 134, 395, 399, 403
Owl, Barn **81,** 317
  Flammulated 317
  Great Horned **317**
  Long-eared 317
  Short-eared **316**
  Snowy 317
Oystercatcher, American × Black 217

Parkes, Ken 76
Parkesia 395
Parula 392, 393
Parula, Northern 393, 400, 406, 409
  Tropical 393, 400
Passerculus 428
Passerella 430
Penguin, Adelie **129**
Pete Dunne's Essential Field Guide Companion 92
Peterson, Roger Tory 14, 32, 403
Petrel, Cook's 183, **185**
  White-chinned **182**
Peucaea 424
Peucedramus 396
Phalarope, Red **222**
  Red-necked 222
  Wilson's 216, 222
Picture-matching, perils of 14–16
Pintail, Northern 38, 100, **148,** 151, 152, **153**
  × Green-winged Teal 41, 159
Pipit, American **8**
Pitfalls of identification 32–42
Plover, Black-bellied 214, 215, 217, **225**
  Common Ringed 54
  Mountain 218

Piping 28, 139
  Semipalmated 28, **54,** 139, 214, 218
Plumage condition 24–26
Plumage cycles 74–84
Pluvialis 217
Pochard, Common 150
  × Tufted Duck 167
Polymorphism 121–123
Pooecetes 426
"Portlandica" plumage 274
Pratincoles 216
Principles of identification 18–32, 42–43
Procellariidae 183
Procellariiformes 182
Protonotaria 396
Ptarmigan, Willow **84**
Pygmy-Owl, Ferruginous 316, 317
  Northern 317
Pyle, Peter 6, 76, 107, 121

Quail, Gambel's **44**

Raven, Common **21**
Recurvirostridae 217
Redhead 145, 147, 150, **153,** 154, 166
Redpoll, Common 12, 29
  Hoary 12
Redstart, American 393, 399, 403, 410, 411
  Painted **95,** 393
  Slate-throated 393
Rhynchophanes 433
Ridgway, Robert 14
Robin, American **78,** 106
Ruff 108, 221, 224

Sanderling **96, 211,** 214, **220,** 239
Sandpiper, Baird's 215, 220, 223, **227**
  Broad-billed 221
  Buff-breasted **221**
  Common 219
  Least 24, 30, **214,** 215, 220, 223, 224, 226–241, **230, 231, 234**
  Pectoral 9, 22, **23,** 108, 215, 220, 221, 223, 224, **227,** 354

Sandpiper (*cont.*)
Purple 215, 220
Rock 220
Semipalmated 226–241, **229, 233, 234, 235, 236**
Solitary 22, **23**, 100, 218, 219
Spoon-billed 221
Spotted 100, **219**
Stilt **210**, 215, **220**
Terek 219
Upland 222
Western 30, 223, 226–241, **226, 233, 234, 235, 236, 237**
White-rumped **69**, 215, 220, 227
Sapsucker, Red-naped 12, 342
Williamson's **109**
Yellow-bellied 12, 342
Scaup, Greater 149, 160–167, **161, 162, 163, 164, 165**
Lesser 149, 154, 160–167, **160, 162, 164, 165**
Scolopacidae 218
Scoter, Black 148, **152**
sp. 146, 154, 157
Surf **146**, 148, **157**
White-winged 148
Screech-Owl, Eastern **122**, 316, 317
Western 316
Scrub-Jay, Western **12**
Sea-Eagle, Steller's 190
Seiurus 395
Selasphorus 106, 329, 330, 336
Setophaga 393
Shearwater, Audubon's 183
Great 182
Little 183
Manx 183
Pink-footed 182
Short-tailed 183
Sooty 182, 183, 185
Shrike, Chinese Gray 131
Northern 26
Shoveler, Northern 148, 157, 159

Sketching as a learning technique 130–131
Sibley, David 120, 135
Siskin, Pine 13, 420
Size, perceptions of 34
Skua, Great 315
South Polar 315
Snipe, Wilson's 109, 222
Song types of warblers 406–410
Sparrow, American Tree 93, 421, **425**
Bachman's **424**
Baird's 422, 429
"Belding's" **428**
Black-chinned 41, 422, 425
Black-throated **427**
Botteri's 424
Brewer's 425, 434–440, **435, 439**
Cassin's **422**, 435
Chipping 39, 421, 422, 425, 434–440, **434, 435, 436, 437**
Clay-colored 425, 434–440, **439**
Field 11, 39, **425**
Five-striped 424, 427
Fox 106, 423, **430**
Golden-crowned **37**, 432
Grasshopper 11, 422, 429
Harris's 432
Henslow's 11, **429**
House 32, 36, 98, 420
"Ipswich" **428**
"Large-billed" 428
Le Conte's 429
Lincoln's 421, **431**
Nelson's 429
"Red" Fox **430**
Rufous-crowned **424**
Rufous-winged 424, 435
Sage 423, 427
Saltmarsh 429
Savannah 29, 419, 421, 423, **428**
Seaside 423, **429**
"Slate-colored" 430
Song 103, 106, 117, **419**, 421, 422, **423**, 431

"Sooty" 430
Swamp 421, 422, **431**
"Thick-billed" **430**
"Timberline" 434, 435, **440**
Vesper **88**, 140, 354, 421, 422, **426**
White-crowned **102**, **432**
White-throated **36**, 123, **128**, 133, 421, **432**
White-throated × Dark-eyed Junco 41
Worthen's 425
Spizella 424, 434–440
Spoonbill, Roseate **43**
Staffelmauser 86–87, 195
Starling, European 24, **27**, 80, 89, 97, 99, 103, 111
Stellula 330
Sterna 277
Sternula 278
Stilt, Black-necked **217**
Stint, Little 224, 226, 228, 229, **239**, 240
Long-toed 24, 226, 228, 238, 240, **241**
Red-necked 226, 228, 229, **238**, 239, 240
Temminck's 226, 228, **241**
Storm-Petrel, Ashy 183
Leach's 184
Wilson's 182, **184**
Subspecies, definition of 117–121
Surfbird 221
Surfbirds.com 136
Swallow, Bank 96
Barn 96
Blue-and-white 389
Cave **30**, 96, 389
Cliff 96, 389
Northern Rough-winged 96
Tree **389**
Violet-green **388**
Swan, Trumpeter **37**, **141**
Tundra 141
Sylviidae 397